CliffsStudySolver™
Spanish I

By Gail Stein

WILEY

Wiley Publishing, Inc.

Published by:
Wiley Publishing, Inc.
909 Third Avenue
New York, NY 10022
www.wiley.com

Copyright © 2003 Wiley Publishing, Inc. New York, New York

Published by Wiley Publishing, Inc., New York, NY
Published simultaneously in Canada

Library of Congress Cataloging in Publication Data available from publisher

ISBN: 0-7645-3765-2

Printed in the United States of America

10 9 8 7 6 5 4 3

1B/RR/QW/QT/IN

Study Guide Checklist

❑ 1. Take the Pretest, which will test your initial understanding of this workbook's subject matter.

❑ 2. Use the answer sections of the Pretest to guide you to the chapters and chapter sections you need to review.

❑ 3. Familiarize yourself with the content of the chapters you need to review.

❑ 4. Take the self tests provided in the chapters, including the Chapter Problems and Supplemental Chapter Problems tests located at the end of each chapter.

❑ 5. If, upon checking your answers to the Chapter Problems and Supplemental Chapter Problems self tests, you find you have some errors, go back to the specific section(s) of the chapter and review the section(s) again.

❑ 6. Take the Post Test, which tests your overall knowledge of the English grammar. The Post Test presents various levels of difficulty with directions on which questions to answer.

❑ 7. Review chapter sections as directed in the Customized Full-Length Test.

❑ 8. Explore the Glossary and Abbreviations appendix.

About the Author

Gail Stein, a French and Spanish teacher for 30 years, has written numerous textbooks.

Publisher's Acknowledgments

Editorial

Project Editor: Ben Nussbaum

Acquisitions Editor: Greg Tubach

Technical Editor: Elsa Pittman

Copy Editor: Suzanne R. Thompson

Composition

Project Coordinator: Regina Snyder

Indexer: Richard T. Evans

Proofreader: Dr. Enrica Ardemagni

Wiley Publishing, Inc. Composition Services

Table of Contents

Pretest

Use this pretest to get an idea of your strengths and weaknesses. The answer key includes suggestions for parts of the book that you may find particularly useful, depending on how you do on this pretest.

Problems 1–5

You are celebrating your birthday at the **Hotel Carlos V** on **Wednesday, March 31,** at **7:30 p.m.** Fill in the invitation below by translating the boldface information in the previous sentence into Spanish.

FIESTA

VAMOS A CELEBRAR: Mis quince años

LUGAR: Hotel Carlos _____ (problem 1)

FECHA: _____ (problems 2–4)

HORA: _____ (problem 5)

Problems 6–10

You are going food shopping. Express what you need by filling in the missing word.

   6. (the) _____ agua mineral

   7. (these) _____ legumbres

   8. (that) _____ pan

   9. (those) _____ limones

  10. (some) _____ manzanas

Problems 11–15

In each of the following Spanish dialogues, Person A states a fact that Person B doesn't hear very well. Write the first speaker's reply.

Example:

   A: Tengo un libro que le voy a prestar a Carlos.

   B: ¿Qué le vas a prestar a Carlos?

   A: <u>Mi libro.</u>

  11. A: María escucha muchos casetes todos los días.

   B: ¿Qué escucha todos los días?

   A: _____

12. A: Yo tengo unas fotografías de ti. Voy a enviártelas.

   B: ¿Qué vas a enviarme?

   A: _____

13. A: Necesito una camisa y no puedo encontrarla. Tengo que buscarla.

   B: ¿Qué vas a buscar?

   A: _____

14. A: José y Ricardo tienen un coche. Van a llevarlo al garaje.

   B: ¿Qué van a llevar al garaje?

   A: _____

15. A: Ana y yo tenemos una tarea muy difícil. Vamos a hacerla juntas.

   B: ¿Qué van a hacer juntas?

   A: _____

Problems 16–20

Express what the following people do at the beach by giving the correct present tense form of the verb in parentheses.

16. (nadar) Uds. _____ en el mar.

17. (escuchar) Yo _____ música.

18. (correr) Ellos _____ en la playa.

19. (beber) Tú _____ mucho.

20. (decidir) Luisa y yo _____ tomar el sol.

Problems 21–25

Complete each sentence by selecting the verb from the box that best indicates how each person spends a day off. Write the verb in the correct present tense form.

comenzar	dormir	preferir	seguir	traducir

21. Yo _____ la tarea de español a inglés.

22. Ella _____ a estudiar para sus exámenes.

23. Susana y yo _____ mirar la televisión.

24. Tú _____ un régimen de ejercicios.

25. Los muchachos _____ hasta el mediodía.

Problems 26–30

Express what the following subjects do to prepare themselves in the morning. Give the correct form of the reflexive verb in the present tense.

26. yo/levantarse temprano

    _____

27. ella/lavarse

    _____

28. nosotros/afeitarse

    _____

29. tú/despertarse a las seis

    _____

30. su esposa y él/despedirse

    _____

Problems 31–35

Express what each person does to prepare for a party by substituting a direct and/or an indirect object pronoun for the noun in bold.

31. Tomás y Ramón escogen **los discos** compactos.

    _____

32. Los muchachos preparan **la comida.**

    _____

33. Estela telefonea **a Ernesto.**

    _____

34. Bárbara va a pedir permiso **a sus padres para** ir a la fiesta.

    _____

35. María va a enviar **las invitaciones** a sus amigos.

    _____

Problems 36–40

Express what each person is doing at 8 p.m. by using the correct form of *estar* and the present participle to form the present progressive tense.

36. (trabajar) Yo _____.

37. (leer) Tú _____.

38. (dormir) El bebé _____.

39. (servir) Nosotros _____ la cena.

40. (desvestirse) Los niños _____.

Problems 41–45

Describe each person by giving the opposite of the adjective in bold.

41. La muchacha es **pequeña** pero el muchacho es _____.

42. El alumno está **contento** pero las alumnas están _____.

43. Carlos es **antipático** pero Julia es _____.

44. Mi hermano es **perezoso** pero mi hermana es _____.

45. Mi abuelo es **viejo** pero mis primos son _____.

Problems 46–50

Express how each person does things by changing the preposition and the noun to an adverb.

Example:

Él trabaja con cuidado. → Él trabaja cuidadosamente.

46. Ellos corren con rapidez.

   _____

47. Yo juego con energía.

   _____

48. Ud. va al centro con frecuencia.

   _____

49. Nosotros nos despedimos con tristeza.

   _____

50. Vosotros habláis con paciencia.

   _____

Problems 51–55

Compare the following people using adjectives and adverbs as necessary.

Example:

Margarita es perezosa. (+/Pablo)

Margarita es más perezosa que Pablo.

51. Rogelio es inteligente. (–/su hermano)

_____

52. Sonia y Rosalinda son bonitas. (=/Nilda y Luz)

_____

53. Felipe habla con fluidez. (+/ sus amigos)

_____

54. Mi hermano conduce bien. (=/yo)

_____

55. Yo cocino mal. (–/tú)

_____

Problems 56–60

Complete each sentence with the correct preposition, if necessary.

56. Marta y su novio van _____ centro.

57. Ella insiste _____ comprar un coche nuevo.

58. Ella quiere _____ un coche deportivo.

59. Su novio se alegra _____ comprar el coche para ella.

60. Al oír esto, Marta empieza _____ llorar de alegría.

Problems 61–65

Express what Julio did and didn't do because he was sick.

61. trabajar

_____

62. comer sopa

63. asistir a la escuela

_____

64. hacer sus tareas

_____

65. ir al consultorio del doctor

_____

Problems 66–70

Complete the story using the correct form of the preterit for the verbs in parentheses.

Anoche yo (empezar) _____ a escribir mis tareas a las siete. Un amigo me (pedir) _____ mi
                           66   67

ayuda. Él (llegar) _____ a mi casa a eso de las ocho. Él (oír) _____ decir que hay un examen
                        68   69

mañana. Yo le (explicar) _____ lo importante.
                               70

Problems 71–75

Complete the story using the correct form of the preterit or the imperfect.

_____ las ocho. Yo _____ de mi casa cuando el teléfono _____. Mis amigas Carmen y Gloria
   71   72   73

_____ saber si yo _____ conducirlas al centro.
   74   75

71. a. era   b. fue   c. fueron   d. eran

72. a. salgo   b. salía   c. salí   d. sale

73. a. sonó   b. sonaba   c. sono   d. suena

74. a. quiere   b. querías   c. querían   d. quisieron

75. a. puedo   b. podía   c. pude   d. puse

Problems 76–80

Complete the e-mail message by filling in the correct form of the present perfect.

Querido Pedro:

Yo (tratar) _____ de llamarte pero nadie me (responder) _____. Juan y yo (ver)
                 76   77

_____ a tus hermanos en la calle y ellos nos (decir) _____ que tú te (romper)
       78   79

_____ la pierna. ¡Qué lástima! Vamos a pasar por tu casa esta noche.
       80

Alfredo

Problems 81–85

Express what the following people will do by changing the sentences from the near future to the future tense.

81. Nosotros vamos a visitar a nuestros amigos.

_____

82. Tú vas a comer en el centro.

_____

83. Yo voy a hacer un viaje.

_____

84. Ellos van a venir a la fiesta.

_____

85. Ella va a salir.

_____

Problems 86–90

Use the conditional tense to express what the following people would do if they could do anything they wanted.

86. yo/aprender a esquiar

_____

87. él/comprar un coche nuevo

_____

88. nosotros/ir a España

_____

89. tú/tener una fiesta

_____

90. ellos/poder dormir hasta el mediodía

_____

Problems 91–95

Describe the unfortunate occurrence at the airport by completing each sentence with the correct form of the subjunctive or the present tense.

Es evidente que Ud. (tener) _____ un gran problema porque es probable que Ud. (perder)
91

_____ su cartera. Es necesario que yo te (ofrecer) _____ mi ayuda. Es importante que
92　　　　　　　　　　　　　　　　　　　93

nosotros (buscar) _____ su cartera por todas partes. ¿Piensa Ud. que alguien (ser) _____
94　　　　　　　　　　　　　　　　　　　　　　　　　　　　　　95

honrado?

Problems 96–100

Help a friend succeed by giving him the following advice. Use the imperative.

96. no mirar la televisión

_____

97. leer las reglas con cuidado

_____

98. no perder tiempo cuando estudies

_____

99. poner atención en clase

_____

100. hacer tus tareas

_____

Answer Key

1. Quinto

2. miércoles

3. el treinta y uno

4. de marzo

5. a las siete y media de la noche

If you missed problem 1, study Ordinal Numbers, p. 20.
If you missed problem 2, study Days of the Week, p. 24.
If you missed problem 3, study Cardinal Numbers, p. 15.
If you missed problem 4, study Months of the Year, p. 24.
If you missed problem 5, study Time, p. 29.

6. el

7. estas

8. ese

9. esos

10. unas

If you missed problem 6, study Definite Articles, p. 41.
If you missed problems 7–9, study Demonstrative Adjectives, p. 51.
If you missed problem 10, study Indefinite Articles, p. 47.

11. Sus casetes.

12. Tus fotografías.

13. Mi camisa.

14. Su coche.

15. Nuestra tarea.

If you missed any of the above problems, study Possessive Adjectives, p. 72.

16. nadan

17. escucho

18. corren

19. bebes

20. decidimos

If you missed any of the above problems, study Present Tense of Regular Verbs, p. 92.

21. traduzco

22. comienza

23. preferimos

24. sigues

25. duermen

If you missed any of the above problems, study Present Tense of Stem-Changing and
Spelling-Change Verbs, p. 95.

26. Yo me levanto temprano.

27. Ella se lava.

28. Nosotros nos afeitamos.

29. Tú te despiertas a las seis.

30. Su esposa y él se despiden.

If you missed any of the above problems, study Reflexive Verbs, p. 141.
If you missed problem 29 or 30, study Present Tense of Stem-Changing and Spelling-Change Verbs, p. 95.

31. Tomás y Ramón los escogen.

32. Los muchachos la preparan.

33. Estela le telefonea.

34. Bárbara va a pedirles permiso para ir a la fiesta. (Bárbara les va a pedir permiso para ir a la fiesta.)

35. María va a enviárselas. (María se las va a enviar.)

If you missed any of the above problems, study Object Pronouns, p. 155.

36. estoy trabajando

37. estás leyendo

38. está durmiendo

39. estamos sirviendo

40. están desvistiéndose (se están desvistiendo)

If you missed any of the above problems, study Present Progressive, p. 177.

41. grande

42. tristes

43. simpática

44. trabajadora

45. jóvenes

If you missed any of the above problems, study Adjectives, p. 185.

46. Ellos corren rápidamente.

47. Yo juego enérgicamente.

48. Ud. va al centro frecuentemente.

49. Nosotros nos despedimos tristemente.

50. Vosotros habláis pacientemente.

If you missed any of the above problems, study Adverbs, p. 201.

51. Rogelio es menos inteligente que su hermano.

52. Sonia y Rosalinda son tan bonitas como Nilda y Luz.

53. Felipe habla más fluidamente que sus amigos.

54. Mi hermano conduce tan bien como yo.

55. Yo cocino peor que tú.

If you missed problems 51 and 52, study Adjectives, p. 185.
If you missed problems 53–55, study Adverbs, p. 201.

56. al

57. en

58. no preposition necessary

59. de

60. a

If you missed any of the above problems, study Prepositions, p. 233.

61. Él no trabajó.

62. Él comió sopa.

63. Él no asistió a la escuela.

64. Él no hizo sus tareas.

65. Él fue al consultorio del doctor.

If you missed any of the above problems, study the Preterit of Regular and Irregular Verbs, p. 249.

66. empecé

67. pidió

68. llegó

69. oyó

70. expliqué

If you missed any of the above problems, study the Preterit of Spelling-Change and Stem-Changing Verbs, p. 253.

71. d

72. b

73. a

74. c

75. b

If you missed any of the above problems, study the Preterit of Regular and Irregular Verbs, p. 249, and the Imperfect, p. 269.

76. he tratado

77. ha respondido

78. hemos visto

79. han dicho

80. has roto

If you missed any of the above problems, study the Present Perfect, p. 283.

81. Nosotros visitaremos a nuestros amigos.

82. Tú comerás en el centro.

83. Yo haré un viaje.

84. Ellos vendrán a la fiesta.

85. Ella saldrá.

If you missed any of the above problems, study the Future, p. 295.

86. Yo aprendería a esquiar.

87. Él compraría un coche nuevo.

88. Nosotros iríamos a España.

89. Tú tendrías una fiesta.

90. Ellos podrían dormir hasta el mediodía.

If you missed any of the above problems, study the Conditional, p. 301.

91. tiene

92. pierda

93. ofrezca

94. busquemos

95. sea

If you missed any of the above problems, study the Subjunctive, p. 309.

96. No mires la televisión.

97. Lee las reglas con cuidado.

98. No pierdas tiempo cuando estudies.

99. Pon atención en clase.

100. Haz tus tareas.

If you missed any of the above problems, study the Imperative, p. 327.

Chapter 1
Daily Tools

Use this chapter to review two of the most basic elements of the Spanish language: numbers and dates.

Numbers

The Spanish-speaking world writes two numbers differently than the United States does: The number 1 has a little hook on top, which makes it look like a 7. So, to distinguish a 1 from a 7, a line is put through the 7, as shown in the following figure.

1   7

In numerals and decimals, Spanish uses commas where English uses periods, and vice versa:

English	Spanish
5,000	5.000
0.25	0,25
$18.95	$18,95

Cardinal Numbers

Cardinal numbers are the numbers used for counting: 1, 2, 3, 4, and so on. They are listed below in Spanish:

Number	Spanish
0	cero
1	uno
2	dos
3	tres
4	cuatro
5	cinco
6	seis
7	siete
8	ocho
9	nueve
10	diez

Number	Spanish
11	once
12	doce
13	trece
14	catorce
15	quince
16	dieciséis (diez y seis)
17	diecisiete (diez y siete)
18	dieciocho (diez y ocho)
19	diecinueve (diez y nueve)
20	veinte
21	veintiuno (veinte y uno)
22	veintidós (veinte y dos)
23	veintitrés (veinte y tres)
24	veinticuatro (veinte y cuatro)
25	veinticinco (veinte y cinco)
26	veintiséis (veinte y seis)
27	veintisiete (veinte y siete)
28	veintiocho (veinte y ocho)
29	veintinueve (veinte y nueve)
30	treinta
40	cuarenta
50	cincuenta
60	sesenta
70	setenta
80	ochenta
90	noventa
100	cien (ciento)
101	ciento uno
200	doscientos
500	quinientos
1000	mil
2000	dos mil
100.000	cien mil
1.000.000	un millón
2.000.000	dos millones
1.000.000.000	mil millones
2.000.000.000	dos mil millones

Note the following about Spanish numbers:

❑ *Uno*, used only when counting, becomes *un* before a masculine singular noun and *una* before a feminine singular noun:

uno, dos, tres . . . (one, two, three . . .)

un hombre y una mujer (a man and a woman)

cuarenta y un libros (41 books)

veintiuna páginas (21 pages)

❑ The conjunction *y* (and) is used only for numbers between 16 and 99. It is not used directly after hundreds:

94: noventa y cuatro

194: ciento noventa y cuatro

❑ The numbers 16–19 and 21–29 are generally written as one word. The numbers 16, 22, 23, and 26 have accents on the last syllable:

16: dieciséis   23: veintitrés

22: veintidós   26: veintiséis

❑ When used before a masculine noun, *veintiún* has an accent on the last syllable:

veintiún muchachos (21 boys)

BUT

veintiuna muchachas (21 girls)

❑ *Ciento* becomes *cien* before nouns of either gender and before the numbers *mil* and *millones*. Before all other numbers, *ciento* is used:

cien dólares (100 dollars)

cien casas (100 houses)

cien mil personas (100,000 people)

cien millones de habitantes (100 million inhabitants)

ciento diez estudiantes (110 students)

❑ In compounds of *ciento (doscientos, trescientos)*, there must be agreement with a feminine noun:

doscientos pesos (200 pesos)

trescientas pesetas (300 pesetas)

❑ *Un*, which is not used before *cien(to)* or *mil*, is used before *millón*. When a noun follows *millón*, put *de* between *millón* and the noun:

cien hombres (100 men)

ciento cuarenta páginas (140 pages)

mil pesos (1,000 pesos)

un millón de personas (one million people)

❑ The following words are used to express common arithmetic functions:

y or *más*	plus (+)
menos	minus (–)
por	times (×)
dividido por	divided by (÷)
son	equals (=)

Example Problems

1. Imagine that you are doing a report on Spain and have to give its population. How would you write "39 million people"?

   Answer: treinta y nueve millones de personas

   1. Select *treinta y nueve* as the first number. Note that the numbers are written separately and are joined by *y* (and).

   2. The word *millón* must be made plural by adding *-es*. Because *millón* ends in a consonant, the accent is dropped from *millón* to maintain the proper stress in the plural.

   3. It is necessary to add the preposition *de* (of) when *millón* is followed by a noun.

2. You are working in a store and a Spanish-speaking person asks you for the price of an item. How would you express "$116.95"?

   Answer: ciento dieciséis dólares (con) noventa y cinco (centavos)

   1. Use *ciento* to express 100 before another number.

   2. Select *dieciséis* and remember that this compound number is the only one of the numbers in the teens that requires an accent on its last syllable. If this poses a problem, use *diez y seis*.

   3. Add the word for "dollars," noting that because *dólar* ends in a consonant, it is made plural by adding *-es*. *Dólar* retains its accent in the plural.

   4. The preposition *con* (with) may or may not be included in the price when spoken.

   5. Add the number of cents by using *noventa y cinco* (95).

   6. The word *centavos* (cents) may or may not be included in the price.

3. You are tutoring a Spanish-speaking person in math. How would you help your student do the following problem: 41 × 18 = 738?

   Answer: cuarenta y uno por dieciocho son setecientos treinta y ocho

   1. Use *cuarenta y uno* (41). Note that *uno* (rather than *un*) is used when the number stands alone.

   2. To multiply, use the word *por*.

   3. Select the correct number for 18: *dieciocho*.

   4. Use *son* (are) to express "equals."

   5. The word for 700 is irregular and must be memorized: *setecientos*.

   6. Follow *setecientos* immediately with *treinta y ocho* (38).

Work Problems

Use these problems to give yourself additional practice.

1. You are in a bank in a Spanish-speaking country and would like to change your dollars into pesos. Express that you want to change $450: *Quisiera cambiar _____ en pesos.*

2. You are looking for a room in an office building in a Spanish-speaking country. Ask for Room 1273: *¿Dónde está la sala _____, por favor?*

3. You meet a Spanish-speaking woman at a club and she asks you for your phone number. How would you express (917) 555-1434? *Mi número de teléfono es _____.*

4. You are trying to do a math problem in Spanish. Express the following equation: 5,621 + 9,437 = 15,058.

5. A Spanish-speaking person asks you for the population of the U.S. Give the approximate answer: "281,450,000 inhabitants."

Worked Solutions

1. **cuatrocientos cincuenta dólares**

    1. Select *cuatrocientos* to express 400, remembering to add *-s* to show that 400 is plural.

    2. Immediately follow *cuatrocientos* with *cincuenta* (50).

    3. Use the word *dólar* in the plural. Remember to retain the accent and add *-es* to the consonant ending of *dólar* to arrive at the plural: *dólares*.

2. **mil doscientos setenta y tres**

    1. Select *mil*, keeping in mind that it is unnecessary to use any word for "one."

    2. Add the word *doscientos* to express 200. Remember that the two numbers, *dos* and *cientos*, are joined.

    3. The word for 70 is *setenta*, to which you must add *tres* (three). The two numbers are joined by *y*.

3. **novecientos diecisiete, quinientos cincuenta y cinco, mil cuatrocientos treinta y cuatro**

    1. Remember that the word for 900 is irregular in Spanish and must be memorized: *novecientos*. Add the compound number *diecisiete*.

    2. Remember that the word for 500 is irregular in Spanish and must be memorized: *quinientos*. Add *cincuenta* (50), then add *y*, then add *cinco* (five).

    3. Add *mil* to express 1,000, keeping in mind that it is unnecessary to use any word for "one." Add *cuatrocientos* to express 400, remembering to leave *cuatro* in the singular but making *ciento* plural by adding *-s*. Add the words *treinta y cuatro* to express 34.

4. **cinco mil seiscientos veintiuno y (más) nueve mil cuatrocientos treinta y siete son quince mil cincuenta y ocho**

   1. "Five thousand" is expressed by using *cinco* and adding *mil*, without making the latter plural. Use *seis* and join *cientos* to it to form the word for 600: *seiscientos*. To express 21, use *veintiuno*. Remember that *uno* is used with *veinte* when counting and when not followed by a noun.

   2. To add, use the word *y* (or *mas*).

   3. "Nine thousand" is expressed by using *nueve* and adding *mil*, without making the latter plural. Use *cuatro* and join *cientos* to it to form the word for 400: *cuatrocientos*. "Thirty-seven" is expressed by joining *treinta* and *siete* with *y*: *treinta y siete*.

   4. To express "equals," use *son*.

   5. "Fifteen thousand" is expressed by using *quince* and adding *mil*, without making the latter plural. "Fifty-eight" is expressed by joining *cincuenta* and *ocho* with *y*: *cincuenta y ocho*.

5. **doscientos ochenta y un millones, cuatrocientos cincuenta mil personas**

   1. "Two hundred" is expressed by combining *dos* and *cientos*: *doscientos*. "Eighty-one" is a combination of *ochenta* and *uno* joined by *y*: *ochenta y un*. Note that *un* (not *uno*) must be used before the word *millón or millones*.

   2. Add the word for "million" in the plural. Note that *-es* is added to the singular *millón* because it ends with a consonant and that the accent is dropped.

   3. "Four hundred" is expressed by joining *cuatro* and *cientos*: *cuatrocientos*. Use *cincuenta* to express "fifty." Add the word *mil*, which is only used in the singular, for "thousand."

   4. Do not add the preposition *de* because *mil* does not require it.

   5. The word for people is *personas*.

Ordinal Numbers

Ordinal numbers allow you to express numbers in a series:

Ordinal	Spanish
1st	primero
2nd	segundo
3rd	tercero
4th	cuarto
5th	quinto
6th	sexto
7th	séptimo
8th	octavo
9th	noveno
10th	décimo

Note the following about ordinal numbers:

❑ In Spanish, ordinal numbers are seldom used after "10th." After that, cardinal numbers are usually used in the spoken language:

el séptimo día (the seventh day)

el siglo veinte (the 20th century)

❑ Ordinal numbers must agree in gender with the nouns they modify. Ordinal numbers are made feminine by changing the final -o of the masculine form to -a:

el noveno mes (the ninth month)

la novena semana (the ninth week)

❑ *Primero* and *tercero* drop the final -o before a masculine singular noun:

el primer edificio (the first building)

el tercer piso (the third floor)

BUT

el siglo tercero (the third century)

❑ The Spanish ordinal numbers are abbreviated as follows (the superscript ° is used for masculine nouns while superscript ª is used for feminine nouns):

primero: $1^{o(a)}$ primer: 1er

segundo: $2^{o(a)}$

tercero: $3^{o(a)}$ tercer: 3er

cuarto: $4^{o(a)}$

❑ A cardinal number that replaces an ordinal number is always masculine because *número*, a masculine word, is understood:

la avenida (número) veintiuno (21st Avenue)

❑ In dates, *primero* is the only ordinal number used. All other dates use the cardinal number:

el primero de enero (January 1st)

el once de julio (July 11th)

❑ In Spanish, cardinal numbers precede ordinal numbers:

los dos primeros capítulos (the first two chapters)

❑ In the first part of an address, use cardinal numbers:

setenta y siete Calle Cruz (77 Cruz Street)

Example Problems

1. Someone asks you in Spanish for the location of an office. Explain that it is on the fifth floor.

    Answer: Está en el quinto piso.

    1. The word *piso* is masculine and singular.

    2. Select the word for "fifth" that will agree with *piso: quinto.*

2. While traveling, you engage in a conversation with a Spanish-speaking person. Express that this is the eighth time you are going to Spain.

Answer: Es la octava vez que voy a España.

1. The word *vez* (time) is feminine and singular.

2. Select the word for "eighth" that will agree with *vez: octava*.

3. You are in your Spanish class and your teacher asks you on what page certain information is given. Express that it is on the 35th page.

Answer: Está en la página (número) treinta y cinco.

1. Any number in a series above 10 is generally expressed by a cardinal number.

2. Select the correct cardinal number for 35: *treinta y cinco*.

3. Put the cardinal number after the noun it modifies.

Work Problems

Use these problems to give yourself additional practice.

1. You are having a conversation with the maitre d' in a Cuban restaurant. He asks how many times you've eaten at his restaurant. Express that it's the third time.

2. A Spanish-speaking friend is admiring your new car. Express that it is your first car.

3. A Spanish-speaking person asks you which anniversary your company is celebrating. Express that it is the 18th anniversary.

4. You are having a problem with a question on your Spanish test. The teacher asks you which question it is. Express that it is the 10th question.

5. You ordered something from a Spanish company by phone. Give your address: 239 57th Avenue.

Worked Solutions

1. **Es la tercera vez.**

1. The word for "time" is *vez*, which is feminine and singular.

2. Put an *-a* at the end of the masculine singular form (*tercer*) to get the feminine singular form (*tercera*).

3. The ordinal number is placed before the noun it modifies.

2. **Es mi primer coche (carro, automóvil).**

   1. The word for car is *coche, carro,* or *automóvil.* All these words are masculine singular.

   2. The masculine singular word for "first" is *primer.* (Remember that the final *-o* is dropped from *primero* and *tercero* before a masculine singular noun.)

   3. The ordinal number is placed before the noun it modifies.

3. **Es el aniversario número dieciocho.**

   1. The word for "anniversary" is masculine singular: *aniversario.*

   2. The word for 18th must be a cardinal number. Use the word for 18: *dieciocho.*

   3. The cardinal number follows the noun.

4. **Es la décima pregunta.**

   1. The word for "question" is feminine singular: *pregunta.*

   2. Replace the *-o* at the end of the masculine singular form (*décimo*) to get the feminine singular form (*décima*).

   3. Remember to put the accent on the *e* of *décima.*

   4. The ordinal number is placed before the noun it modifies.

5. **Mi dirección es doscientos treinta y nueve avenida cincuenta y siete.**

   1. The first part of the address must use cardinal numbers.

   2. Use *doscientos* to express 200, remembering to add the *-s.*

   3. The words *treinta* and *nueve* are joined by *y.*

   4. Because 57 is a number higher than 10, the cardinal number can also be used.

   5. The words *cincuenta* and *siete* are joined by *y.*

   6. The word for "avenue" is feminine: *avenida.*

Days, Months, and Dates

To express the date in Spanish, it is necessary to know the names of the days and months.

Use the following when asking or telling someone what day of the week it is:

¿Qué día es hoy?	What day is today?
Hoy es . . .	Today is . . .

Days

Unlike the English calendar, the Spanish calendar starts with Monday:

English	Spanish
Monday	lunes
Tuesday	martes
Wednesday	miércoles
Thursday	jueves
Friday	viernes
Saturday	sábado
Sunday	domingo

Note the following about the Spanish days:

❑ Days of the week aren't capitalized in Spanish.

❑ Spanish uses the definite article *el* to express a happening *on* a certain day. *Los* is used to express something that takes place habitually. Note that, with the exception of *sábados* and *domingos*, the plural forms of the days of the week are the same as the singular forms:

Yo no voy a trabajar el lunes. (I'm not going to work on Monday.)

Yo no trabajo los lunes. (I don't work on Mondays.)

Months

Many of the months in Spanish have names similar to their English counterparts:

English	Spanish
January	enero
February	febrero
March	marzo
April	abril
May	mayo
June	junio
July	julio
August	agosto
September	septiembre (setiembre may also be used)
October	octubre
November	noviembre
December	diciembre

Note the following about the months:

❑ The months of the year are not capitalized in Spanish.

❑ Use the preposition *en* to express "in" with months:

Llueve mucho en abril. (It rains a lot in April.)

Dates

Use the following when asking or telling someone what date it is:

¿Cuál es la fecha de hoy?	What is today's date?
Hoy es (el) . . .	Today is . . .

Dates in Spanish are expressed as follows:

day + *(el)* + cardinal number (except for *primero*) + *de* + month + *de* + year

Friday, May 3, 2003 = viernes (el) tres de mayo de dos mil tres

Note the following when expressing a date:

❑ To express "it is," use *es* or *estamos a* before the date.

❑ The first of each month is expressed by *primero*. Cardinal numbers are used for all other days:

el primero de enero (January 1st)

el treinta y uno de enero (January 31st)

el dos de julio (July 2nd)

❑ Years are expressed in thousands and hundreds, not in only hundreds as in English:

mil novecientos ochenta y cuatro (1984)

❑ In Spanish, dates follow the sequence day/month/year:

el veintidós de abril de dos mil cuatro = 22/4/04

❑ To express *on* with Spanish days of the week or dates, use *el:*

Te veo el lunes. (I'll see you on Monday.)

Viene el nueve de junio. (He's coming on June 9th.)

Here is a list of date-related vocabulary:

English	Spanish
a day	un día
a week	una semana
a month	un mes
a year	un año
in	en
ago	hace
per	por
during	durante
next	próximo(a)
last	pasado(a)
last (in a series)	último(a)
eve	la víspera
day before yesterday	anteayer
yesterday	ayer
today	hoy

English	Spanish
tomorrow	mañana
tomorrow morning	mañana por la mañana
tomorrow afternoon	mañana por la tarde
tomorrow night	mañana por la noche
day after tomorrow	pasado mañana
from	desde
a week from today	de hoy en una semana
two weeks from tomorrow	de mañana en dos semanas

Example Problems

1. You are going to visit your Spanish-speaking pen pal. Express that you will arrive on Wednesday, August 1.

    Answer: Llego el miércoles primero de agosto.

    1. Use the verb *llegar* (to arrive). Drop the *-ar* ending and add *-o* for the *yo* (I) form of the verb. See Chapter 4.

    2. Express "on Wednesday" by using *el miércoles*.

    3. Use the ordinal number *primero* to indicate the 1st of the month.

    4. The ordinal number is followed by *de* (of).

    5. Write the name of the month, remembering to lowercase the first letter.

2. A Spanish-speaking friend asks you what year you were born. How would you express "1974"?

    Answer: (Yo) Nací en mil novecientos setenta y cuatro.

    1. Use the *yo* form of the preterit (past tense) of the verb *nacer* (to be born). See Chapter 13.

    2. The preposition *en* expresses the English word "in."

    3. Begin the date with *mil* because dates cannot be given in hundreds alone.

    4. The word for 900 is irregular and must be memorized: *novecientos*.

    5. Join *setenta* (70) and *cuatro* (four) with the word *y*.

3. You are writing a report in Spanish. Express the date that Columbus first sighted the New World: Saturday, October 12, 1492.

    Answer: Fue el sábado doce de octubre de mil cuatrocientos noventa y dos.

    1. Use the preterit (past tense) of the verb *ser* (to be) to express "it was." See Chapter 13.

    2. Write the day of the week, remembering to lowercase the first letter.

3. Use the definite article *el* before the day.

4. Use the cardinal number to express the date.

5. Use the preposition *de* to express "of."

6. Write the name of the month, remembering to lowercase the first letter.

7. Use *de* before the number of the year.

8. Because hundreds may not be used to express the date, start with *mil*.

9. Combine *cuatro* and *cientos* to express 400.

10. Join *noventa* (90) and *dos* (2) with *y*.

Work Problems

Use these problems to give yourself additional practice.

1. A Spanish-speaking friend asks you what days you work. Say that you work on Mondays, Wednesdays, Fridays, and Saturdays. *Trabajo_____.*

2. A new Spanish-speaking friend does not know when Valentine's Day is. Say that it's on February 14th. *Celebramos el día de San Valentín _____.*

3. A Spanish-speaking friend wants to meet you for lunch. Say that you are free on Tuesday, March 26. *Estoy libre _____.*

4. Somebody in your Spanish class asks for today's date. Say that it is Friday, October 18, 2002. *Es _____.*

5. You are writing a report in Spanish about your family. Express that your grandparents arrived in the United States on Thursday, August 7, 1969. *Mis abuelos llegaron a los Estados Unidos _____.*

Worked Solutions

1. **Trabajo los lunes, los miércoles, los viernes y los sábados.**

   1. Use the definite article *los* to express "on" when something is habitual.

   2. Repeat *los* before each day of the week to express "on."

   3. Begin each day of the week with a lowercase letter.

2. **Celebramos el día de San Valentín el catorce de febrero.**

   1. Use the definite article *el* before the number.

   2. Use the cardinal number *catorce* to express "the 14th" of the month.

3. Use *de* to express "of" after the number.

4. Begin the month with a lowercase letter.

3. **Estoy libre el martes (el) veintiséis de marzo.**

1. Begin the word for Tuesday, "martes," with a lowercase letter.

2. Use the definite article *el* before the name of the day "martes."

3. *Veinte* may be joined to *seis* by adding *y*, or the two words may be combined, in which case an accent must be added: *veintiséis*.

4. Use *de* to express "of."

5. Begin the month with a lowercase letter.

4. **Es viernes (el) dieciocho de octubre de dos mil dos.**

1. The name of the day must begin with a lowercase letter.

2. Use the definite article *el* before the number. This article is optional.

3. Combine *diez* and *ocho* into *dieciocho*.

4. Use *de* to express "of."

5. Begin the month with a lowercase letter.

6. Use *de* before the year.

7. Because hundreds may not be used to express the date, start with *dos mil*.

8. Add *dos* (two).

5. **Mis abuelos llegaron a los Estados Unidos el jueves (el) siete de agosto de mil novecientos sesenta y nueve.**

1. Begin the day of the week with a lowercase letter.

2. Use the definite article *el* before the name of the day of the week "jueves."

3. Use the cardinal number to express the date. You may or may not choose to use the definite article before the number in the date.

4. Use the preposition *de* to express "of."

5. Begin the month with a lowercase letter.

6. Use *de* before the number of the year.

7. Because hundreds may not be used to express the date, start with *mil*.

8. Remember that *nueve* and *cientos* combine to create the irregular form: *novecientos*.

9. Join *sesenta* (60) and *nueve* (nine) with *y*.

Time

To ask or give the time, use the following:

| ¿Qué hora es? | What time is it? |
| Es (Son) . . . la (las) . . . | It is . . . |

To ask or explain "at" what time something will occur, use the following:

| ¿A qué hora . . .? | At what time . . .? |
| A la (las) . . . | At . . . |

Here are some examples of how to tell time in Spanish:

Although most Spanish speakers use military time, since most American speakers are unaccustomed to its use, military time has not been included in the table below.

Time	Spanish
1:00	la una
2:05	las dos y cinco
3:10	las tres y diez
4:15	las cuatro y cuarto *or* las cuatro y quince
5:20	las cinco y veinte
6:25	las seis y veinticinco
7:30	las siete y media *or* las siete y treinta
7:35	las ocho menos veinticinco *or* las siete y treinta y cinco
8:40	las nueve menos veinte *or* las ocho y cuarenta
9:45	las diez menos cuarto *or* las nueve y cuarenta y cinco
10:50	las once menos diez *or* las diez y cincuenta
11:55	las doce menos cinco *or* las once y cincuenta y cinco
noon	el mediodía
midnight	la medianoche

Here are some more specifics on how to express time:

❏ Use *es* for "it is" when it is one o'clock. The other numbers are plural and require *son:*

Es la una. (It's one o'clock.)

Son las cinco y media. (It's 5:30.)

❏ Use *a la* to express "at" one o'clock and *a las* to express "at" for every other hour:

Salgo a la una. (I'm going out at one o'clock.)

Comemos a las siete. (We eat at seven o'clock.)

❏ To express the time after the hour (but before half past the hour) use *y* and the number of minutes:

Son las ocho y diez. (It's 8:10.)

❏ Use *menos* + the number of the following hour to express the time before the next hour (after half past the hour):

Son las dos menos cinco. (It's 1:55.)

❑ Time before the hour may also be expressed by *faltar* + minutes + *para* + the next hour:

Faltan veinticinco minutos para las tres. (It's 2:35.)

❑ Time may also be expressed numerically:

Son las nueve y cuarenta. (It's 9:40.)

❑ *Media* (half) is used as an adjective, and it agrees with *hora* (hour). *Cuarto* (quarter) is used as a noun and shows no agreement:

Son las tres y media. (It's 3:30.)

Son las tres y cuarto. (It's 3:15.)

Here is some time-related vocabulary:

English	Spanish
a second	un segundo
a minute	un minuto
a quarter of an hour	un cuarto de hora
an hour	una hora
a half hour	una media hora
in the morning (a.m.)	por la mañana
in the afternoon (p.m.)	por la tarde
in the evening (p.m.)	por la noche
at what time?	¿a qué hora?
at exactly eight o'clock	a las ocho en punto
at about three o'clock	a eso de las tres
in an hour	en una hora
in a while	dentro de un rato
until one o'clock	hasta la una
before six o'clock	antes de las seis
after eleven o'clock	después de las once
since what time?	¿desde qué hora?
since four o'clock	desde las cuatro
two hours ago	hace dos horas
per hour	por hora
early	temprano
late	tarde
late (in arriving)	de retraso

Example Problems

1. You are going to meet a Spanish-speaking friend at a restaurant. Tell the person that you will meet at 7:30.

   Answer: Te veo a las siete y media.

   1. Use the verb *ver* (to see). Drop the final *-r* and add *-o* for the irregular *yo* (I) form of the verb. See Chapter 4.

2. Express "you" by using the direct object pronoun *te*. See Chapter 7.

3. Express "on" by using *a*.

4. Use *las siete* for "seven o'clock."

5. Use *media* (half) to express "half past the hour."

6. Combine the hour and half past with *y* (and).

2. A Spanish-speaking friend asks you when you will be ready to leave. Express that you will be ready in 15 minutes.

   Answer: Estaré listo en quince minutos (en un cuarto de hora).

   1. Use the verb *estar* to express "to be" because the condition is temporary. See Chapter 4.

   2. Use the *yo* form of the future of the verb *estar* (to be). See Chapter 16.

   3. Use *listo* to express the masculine singular form of "ready." (If you are a woman, the feminine form is *lista*.) See Chapter 9.

   4. The preposition *en* expresses "in."

   5. "A quarter of an hour" may be expressed in one of two ways: *quince minutos* or *un cuarto de hora*.

3. A Spanish-speaking person stops you on the street and asks for the time. Express that it is 9:40 a.m.

   Answer:

   There are three possible solutions:

   A: Son las diez menos veinte (de la mañana).

   B: Son las nueve y cuarenta (de la mañana).

   C: Faltan veinte minutos para las diez.

   A:

   1. Use *son* to express "it is."

   2. Use the definite article *las* before the number.

   3. Although the time is nine o'clock, use *diez* (10) because you will be subtracting minutes from the next hour.

   4. Express "less" or "minus" by using *menos*.

   5. Use *veinte* (20) because it is 20 minutes before the next hour.

B:

1. Use *son* to express "it is."

2. Use the definite article *las* before the number.

3. Use *nueve* (nine).

4. Use *cuarenta* (40) to express the number of minutes after the hour.

5. Join *nueve* (nine) and *cuarenta* (40) with *y*.

C:

1. Use the third person plural form of the verb *faltar* to express that it is more than one minute before the hour.

2. Use *veinte minutos* to express that it is 20 minutes before the hour.

3. Use the definite article *las* before the number of the hour.

4. Use *diez* (10) because it is 20 minutes before 10 o'clock.

5. Use the preposition *para* to join the number of minutes before the hour to the hour.

Work Problems

Use these problems to give yourself additional practice.

1. A Spanish-speaking friend asks you what time the concert you are going to see starts. Express that it starts at 8 p.m. sharp. *Empieza* _____.

2. You are riding in a bus and a Spanish-speaking passenger asks you for the time. You consult your digital watch. Say that it is 11:14 a.m. *Son las* _____.

3. A Spanish-speaking friend wants to meet you for a cup of coffee. Say that you are free at 2:45 p.m. *Estoy libre* _____.

4. You are waiting to take a flight to Guatemala, and your flight is late. Express to the Spanish-speaking person sitting next to you that the flight is 3 hours and 15 minutes late. *El vuelo tiene* _____.

5. A Spanish-speaking acquaintance asks you for your work hours. Say that you work from 10:15 in the morning until 6:55 at night. *Trabajo* _____.

Worked Solutions

1. **Empieza a las ocho en punto de la noche.**

   1. Use the preposition *a* to express "at."

   2. Use *las ocho* to express "eight o'clock."

3. Because you are referring to a time in the evening, use the expression *de la noche.*

4. Use *en punto* to express that the event will occur "on the dot."

2. **Son las once y catorce de la mañana.**

1. Use the plural form of the verb *ser (son)* to express that it is later than one o'clock.

2. Use the cardinal number *once* to express "11 o'clock."

3. Use *catorce* to express that it is 14 minutes past the hour.

4. Use *y* to join the hour and the number of minutes.

5. Because you are referring to a morning time, use the expression *de la mañana.*

3. **Estoy libre a las tres menos cuarto (quince) de la tarde.**

1. Use the preposition *a* to express "at."

2. Although the time is two o'clock, use *tres* (three) because you will be subtracting minutes from the next hour.

3. Express "less" or "minus" by using *menos.*

4. Use *cuarto* (a quarter of an hour) or *quince* to express that it is 15 minutes before the hour.

5. Alternatively, you may use *son* to express "it is."

6. Use the definite article *las* before the number.

7. Use *dos* (two).

8. Use *cuarenta y cinco* (45) to express the number of minutes after the hour.

9. Join *cinco* (five) and *cuarenta* (40) with *y.*

10. Because you are referring to afternoon time, use the expression *de la tarde.*

4. **El vuelo tiene tres horas y cuarto (quince) de retraso.**

1. Use *tres horas* (three hours) to express the number of hours the flight is late.

2. Use *y* to join the number of hours to *cuarto* (a quarter of an hour). Alternatively, *quince* (15) can be substituted for *cuarto.*

3. *De retraso* expresses that the flight is late in arriving at its destination.

5. **Trabajo desde las diez y cuarto (quince) de la mañana hasta las siete menos cinco (las seis y cincuenta y cinco) de la noche.**

1. Use the preposition *desde* to express "from" a certain time.

2. Use the definite article *las* before *diez* (10) to indicate the hour.

3. Use the preposition *y* followed by the number of minutes after the hour.

4. Use either *cuarto* (a quarter) or *quince* (15) to express the number of minutes after the hour.

5. Because you are referring to a morning time, use the expression *de la mañana.*

6. Use the preposition *hasta* to express "until."

7. Use *las siete* (seven o'clock) for the next hour.

8. Use *menos* to express "minus."

9. Use *cinco* to show that you are subtracting 5 minutes from the next hour.

10. Alternatively, you may use *las seis* (six o'clock) and add the number of minutes.

11. Use *cincuenta* to express 50 and *cinco* to express five. Join the two numbers with *y.*

Chapter Problems and Solutions

Problems

Using the information given in the sentence below, provide the dates for the following days.

Hoy es el lunes treinta de diciembre.

1. mañana

2. ayer

3. pasado mañana

4. de hoy en una semana

5. de hoy en un mes

In problems 6–10, you have decided to go see a Spanish movie. Express at what times the film is showing.

CINE CARLOS V presenta

ABRE LOS OJOS: 11:15 a.m., 2:30 p.m., 4:45 p.m., 7:55 p.m., 10:25 p.m.

In problems 11–15, you have planned a trip to San Juan, Puerto Rico. Replace the information in bold on your airline ticket with Spanish words.

	TIME	DATE	FLIGHT	SEAT NO.
LV NEW YORK JFK	**1012AM**	**16AUG03**	**1639**	**21C**
AR SAN JUAN PR	**253PM**			

In problems 16–20, look at Tomás's schedule. The names of his classes have been provided for you in Spanish but you're responsible for expressing the days and times for each. Tell from what time until what time he has certain classes. For example, for his first class:

Tiene arte los lunes desde las siete y cinco hasta las ocho menos cuarto.

	HORA	DÍA	CLASE
	7:05–7:45	(Mon.)	arte
16.	7:49–8:29	(Mon.)	historia
17.	8:33–9:15	(Tues.)	español
18.	9:20–10:00	(Wed.)	inglés
19.	10:04–10:44	(Thurs.)	matemáticas
20.	10:48–11:28	(Fri.)	biología

In problems 21–25, express when the following famous Spanish writers were born *(nació en)* and died *(murió en)*.

21. Miguel de Cervantes Saavedra (1547–1616)

22. Pedro Calderón de la Barca (1600–1681)

23. Miguel de Unamuno (1864–1936)

24. José Ortega y Gasset (1883–1955)

25. Federico García Lorca (1898–1936)

Answers and Solutions

1. **Answer: martes (el) treinta y uno de diciembre.** *Mañana* means "tomorrow." The day after *lunes* (Monday) is *martes* (Tuesday). The number after *treinta* (30) is *treinta y uno* (31). The definite article *el* may be used before the number. The two cardinal numbers are joined with *y.* Use the preposition *de* before the name of the month, which remains the same.

2. **Answer: domingo (el) veintinueve de diciembre.** *Ayer* means "yesterday." The day before *lunes* (Monday) is *domingo* (Sunday). The number before *treinta* (30) is *veintinueve* (29). The definite article *el* may be used before the number. The two cardinal numbers are joined with *y.* Use the preposition *de* before the name of the month, which remains the same.

3. **Answer: miércoles (el) primero de enero.** *Pasado mañana* means "the day after tomorrow." Because tomorrow is *martes* (Tuesday), the following day is *miércoles* (Wednesday). The ordinal number *primero* must be used to express the 1st of the month. The month changes from *diciembre* (December) to *enero* (January).

4. **Answer: lunes (el) seis de enero.** *De hoy en una semana* means "a week from today." The day of the week remains the same. Seven days later would be January 6th. The definite article *el* may be used before the number. Use the preposition *de* before the name of the month, which changes to *enero.*

5.　**Answer: (el) treinta de enero.** *De hoy en un mes* means "a month from today." A month later would be January 30th. The definite article *el* may be used before the number. Use the preposition *de* before the name of the month, which changes to *enero*.

6.　**Answer: a las once y cuarto (quince) de la mañana.** Use the preposition *a* to express "at." Use *las once* to express "11 o'clock." Use *y* to join the hour and the number of minutes. Because you are referring to a morning time, use the expression *de la mañana*.

7.　**Answer: a las dos y media de la tarde.** Use the preposition *a* to express "at." Use *las dos* to express "two o'clock" and use *media* to express "half past the hour." Join the two with *y*. Because you are referring to an afternoon time, use the expression *de la tarde*.

8.　**Answer: a las cinco menos cuarto (quince) de la tarde.** Use the preposition *a* to express "at." Although the time is four o'clock, use *a las cinco* (at five o'clock) because you will be subtracting minutes from the next hour. Express "less" or "minus" by using *menos*. Use *cuarto* to express that it is a quarter to the hour or use *quince* to express that it is 15 minutes before the hour. Alternatively, you may use *a las cuatro* (at four o'clock), followed by *cuarenta y cinco* (45) to express the number of minutes after the hour, joining the hour and the number of minutes with *y*. Because you are referring to an afternoon time, use the expression *de la tarde: a las cuatro y cuarenta y cinco de la tarde*.

9.　**Answer: a las ocho menos cinco de la noche.** Use the preposition *a* to express "at." Although the time is seven o'clock, use *a las ocho* (at eight o'clock), because you will be subtracting minutes from the next hour. Express "less" or "minus" by using *menos*. Use *cinco* to show that you are subtracting five minutes from the next hour. Because you are referring to an evening time, use the expression *de la noche*. Alternatively, you may use *a las siete* (at seven o'clock), followed by *cincuenta y cinco* (55) to express the number of minutes after the hour, joining the hour and the number of minutes with *y*. Because you are referring to an evening time, use the expression *de la noche: a las siete y cincuenta y cinco de la noche*.

10.　**Answer: a las diez y veinticinco de la noche.** Use the preposition *a* to express "at." Use *a las diez* to express "at 10 o'clock." Use *y* to join the hour and *veinticinco* (25), the number of minutes. Because you are referring to an evening time, use the expression *de la noche*.

11.　**Answer: a las diez y doce de la mañana (1012AM).** Use the preposition *a* to express "at." Use *a las diez* to express "at 10 o'clock." Use *y* to join the hour and *doce* (12), the number of minutes. Because you are referring to a morning time, use the expression *de la mañana*.

12.　**Answer: a las tres menos siete de la tarde (253PM).** Use the preposition *a* to express "at." Although the time is two o'clock, use the definite article *las* and *tres* (three) because you will be subtracting minutes from the next hour. Express "less" or "minus" by using *menos*. Use *siete* because it is seven minutes before the hour. Alternatively, you may use *a las dos* (at two o'clock), followed by *cincuenta y tres* (53) to express the number of minutes after the hour, joining the hour and the number of minutes with *y*. Because you are referring to an afternoon time, use the expression *de la tarde: a las dos y cincuenta y tres de la tarde*.

13.　**Answer: el dieciséis de agosto de dos mil tres (16AUG03).** Use the definite article *el* before the number of the day. Use the cardinal number for "sixteen": *dieciséis*. Use the preposition *de* to express "of." Select the word for August: *agosto*. Use *de* to express "of" before the year. Use *dos* before *mil* to express 2,000. Follow *dos mil* with the number of the year, *tres* (three), without using *y* to join them.

14. **Answer: mil seiscientos treinta y nueve (1639).** Use *mil* to express 1,000. Combine *seis* with *cientos* to form the word for 600: *seiscientos*. Add *treinta* (30) and *nueve* (9); join the two words with *y*.

15. **Answer: veintiuno C (21C).** Drop the final *e* from *veinte*, add an *i*, then add *uno* to form *veintiuno*.

For problems 16–20: Use the definite article *los* before the day to express that Tomás has these classes repeatedly throughout the semester. Select the correct day of the week. Use *desde* (from) and *hasta* (until) to express the time frame of the classes. Both *desde* and *hasta* are followed by the definite article *las* and the time.

16. **Answer: Tiene historia los lunes desde las ocho menos once hasta las ocho y veintinueve.** For the first time, use *las ocho* (eight o'clock) with *menos* (minus or less) and *once* (11). Alternatively, use *las siete* (seven o'clock) and add *cuarenta* (40) and *nueve* (9), joining them with *y*: *las siete y cuarenta y nueve*. For the second time, use *las ocho,* followed by *y* (and) and the number of minutes: *las ocho y veintinueve.*

17. **Answer: Tiene español los martes desde las nueve menos veintisiete hasta las nueve y cuarto.** For the first time, use *las nueve* (nine o'clock) with *meno* (minus or less) and *veintisiete* (27). Alternatively, use *las ocho* (eight o'clock) and add *treinta* (30) and *tres* (three), joining them with *y*: *las ocho y treinta y tres.* For the second time, use *las nueve,* followed by *y* (and) and the number of minutes (*cuarto* for "a quarter past" or *quince* for "15 minutes past"): *las nueve y quince.*

18. **Answer: Tiene inglés los miércoles desde las nueve y veinte hasta las diez.** For the first time, use *las nueve* (nine o'clock) and add the number of minutes: *veinte* (20). Join the two with *y*. For the second time, simply use *las diez* (10 o'clock).

19. **Answer: Tiene matemáticas los jueves desde las diez y cuatro hasta las once menos dieciséis.** For the first time, use *las diez* (10 o'clock) and add the number of minutes: *cuatro* (four). Join the two with *y*. For the second time, use *las once* (11 o'clock) with *menos* (minus or less) and *dieciséis* (16). Alternatively, use *las diez,* followed by *y* (and) and the number of minutes (*cuarenta* for 40 and *cuatro* for "four"), also joined by *y: las diez y cuarenta y cuatro.*

20. **Answer: Tiene biología los viernes desde las once menos doce hasta las once y veintiocho.** For the first time, use *las once* (11 o'clock) with *menos* (minus or less) and *doce* (12). Alternatively, use *las diez,* followed by *y* (and) and the number of minutes (*cuarenta* for 40 and *ocho* for "eight"), also joined by *y: las diez y cuarenta y ocho.* For the second time, use *las once,* followed by *y* (and) and the number of minutes: *veintiocho* (28).

For problems 21–25: Use *mil* to express 1,000 in dates. Remember that hundreds may not be used alone.

21. **Answer: Cervantes nació en mil quinientos cuarenta y siete y murió en mil seiscientos dieciséis.** The word for 500 *(quinientos)* is irregular and must be memorized. Select *cuarenta* (40) and *siete* (seven) and join them with *y*. The word for 600 is one word that combines *seis* (six) and *cientos* (the plural form of 100). Add *dieciséis* (16).

22. **Answer: Calderón de la Barca nació en mil seiscientos y murió en mil seiscientos ochenta y uno.** The word for 600 is one word that combines *seis* (six) and *cientos* (the plural form of 100). For the second year, use *seiscientos* and add *ochenta* (80) and *uno* (one), joined with *y*.

23. **Answer: Unamuno nació en mil ochocientos sesenta y cuatro y murió en mil novecientos treinta y seis.** The word for 800 is one word that combines *ocho* (eight) and *cientos* (the plural form of 100). Select *sesenta* (60) and *cuatro* (four) and join them with *y*. The word for 900 *(novecientos)* is irregular and must be memorized. Select *treinta* (30) and *seis* (six) and join them with *y*.

24. **Answer: Ortega y Gasset nació en mil ochocientos ochenta y tres y murió en mil novecientos cincuenta y cinco.** The word for 800 is one word that combines *ocho* (eight) and *cientos* (the plural form of 100). Select *ochenta* (80) and *tres* (three) and join them with *y*. The word for 900 *(novecientos)* is irregular and must be memorized. Select *cincuenta* (50) and *cinco* (five) and join them with *y*.

25. **Answer: García Lorca nació en mil ochocientos noventa y ocho y murió en mil novecientos treinta y seis.** The word for 800 is one word that combines *ocho* (eight) and *cientos* (the plural form of 100). Select *noventa* (90) and *ocho* (eight) and join them with *y*. The word for 900 *(novecientos)* is irregular and must be memorized. Select *treinta* (30) and *seis* (six) and join them with *y*.

Supplemental Chapter Problems

Problems

In problems 1–5, solve the mathematical problems below.

1. $50 \times 30 = 1.500$

2. $1.000 - 300 = 700$

3. $10.000 \div 2 = 5.000$

4. $1.000.000 + 2.000.000 = 3.000.000$

5. $362 + 553 = 915$

In problems 6–10, give the dates of the following Hispanic national holidays.

6. September 18, 1810 (Chile's Independence Day)

7. July 9, 1816 (Argentina's Independence Day)

8. February 27, 1844 (the Dominican Republic's Independence Day)

9. November 3, 1903 (Panama's Independence Day)

10. January 1, 1959 (Cuba's Liberation Day)

In problems 11–16, look at Rogelio's personal calendar. Tell on what days and at what times he has to do certain things. For example:

> ir de compras
>
> *El lunes a las nueve y media de la mañana tiene que ir de compras.*

lunes	martes	miércoles	jueves	viernes	sábado	domingo
9:30 a.m.	1:45 p.m.	7:50 p.m.	8:35 a.m.	6:50 p.m.	10:40 p.m.	10:55 a.m.
ir de compras	lavar la ropa	estudiar español	ir al doctor	preparar la cena	cuidar a los niños	cocinar

11. estudiar español

12. cuidar a los niños

13. ir al doctor

14. preparar la cena

15. cocinar

16. lavar la ropa

In problems 17–21, look at your return ticket from Puerto Rico. Replace the information in bold on your airline ticket with Spanish words.

	TIME	DATE	FLIGHT	SEAT NO.
LV SAN JUAN PR	**455PM**	**7SEP03**	**2799**	**14A**
AR NEW YORK JFK	**937PM**			

In problems 22–25, the following information about Spain is based on figures from 2002. Spell out the numerical information in bold.

Rey: Juan Carlos **I**

Área: **504.782** kilómetros cuadrados

Población de España: **40.077.100** habitantes

Población de Madrid: **5.050.000** habitantes

Answers

1. Cincuenta por treinta son mil quinientos. (arithmetic, p. 17)

2. Mil menos trescientos son setecientos. (arithmetic, p. 17)

3. Diez mil dividido por dos son cinco mil. (arithmetic, p. 17)

4. Un millón y (más) dos millones son tres millones. (arithmetic, p. 17)

5. Trescientos sesenta y dos y (más) quinientos cincuenta y tres son novecientos quince. (arithmetic, p. 17)

6. el dieciocho de septiembre de mil ochocientos diez (dates, p. 25)

7. el nueve de julio de mil ochocientos dieciséis. (dates, p. 25)

8. el veintisiete de febrero de mil ochocientos cuarenta y cuatro (dates, p. 25)

9. el tres de noviembre de mil novecientos tres (dates, p. 25)

10. el primero de enero de mil novecientos cincuenta y nueve (dates, p. 25)

11. El miércoles a las ocho menos diez (a las siete y cincuenta) de la noche tiene que estudiar español. (days of the week, p. 24; time, p. 29)

12. El sábado a las once menos veinte (a las diez y cuarenta) de la mañana tiene que cuidar a los niños. (days of the week, p. 24; time, p. 29)

13. El jueves a las nueve menos veinticinco (ocho y treinta y cinco) de la mañana tiene que ir al doctor. (days of the week, p. 24; time, p. 29)

14. El viernes a las siete menos diez (a las seis y cincuenta) de la noche tiene que preparar la cena. (days of the week, p. 24; time, p. 29)

15. El domingo a las once menos cinco (a las diez y cincuenta y cinco) de la mañana tiene que cocinar. (days of the week, p. 24; time, p. 29)

16. El martes a las dos menos cuarto (quince) (a la una y cuarenta y cinco) de la tarde tiene que lavar la ropa. (days of the week, p. 24; time, p. 29)

17. (455PM) a las cinco menos cinco (a las cuatro y cincuenta y cinco) de la tarde (time, p. 29)

18. (937PM) a las diez menos veintitrés (a las nueve y treinta y siete) de la noche (time, p. 29)

19. (7SEP03) el siete de septiembre de dos mil tres (dates, p. 25)

20. (2799) dos mil setecientos noventa y nueve (cardinal numbers, p. 15)

21. (14A) catorce A (cardinal numbers, p. 15)

22. Primero (ordinal numbers, p. 20)

23. quinientos cuatro mil, setecientos ochenta y dos (cardinal numbers, p. 15)

24. cuarenta millones, setenta y siete mil, cien (cardinal numbers, p. 15)

25. cinco millones, cincuenta mil (cardinal numbers, p. 15)

Chapter 2
Articles and Nouns

Use this chapter to find out the basics on articles and nouns. You will have plenty of chances to do problems that will let you test your knowledge. Articles are discussed in the first half of the chapter; nouns are discussed in the second half.

Markers

Markers are small words that are generally classified as definite or indefinite articles or demonstrative adjectives and indicate that a noun will follow. Spanish articles and demonstrative adjectives are masculine or feminine and singular or plural depending on the noun that follows.

The three most commonly used markers in Spanish are:

❑ Definite articles, which express "the."

❑ Indefinite articles, which express "a" or "an."

❑ Demonstrative adjectives, which express "this," "that," "these," and "those."

The following table shows you the masculine and feminine and the singular and plural forms of the most common Spanish articles.

	SINGULAR			PLURAL		
ARTICLE	*Meaning*	*Masculine*	*Feminine*	*Meaning*	*Masculine*	*Feminine*
Definite	the	el	la	the	los	las
Indefinite	a, an	un	una	some	unos	unas
Demonstrative	this	este	esta	these	estos	estas
	that (near)	ese	esa	those	esos	esas
	that (far)	aquel	aquella	those	aquellos	aquellas

Definite Articles

The definite article, which expresses the English word "the," indicates a specific person or thing: "**the** man" or "**the** car," for example. The definite article precedes the noun it modifies and agrees with that noun in gender and number. In Spanish, the gender of a noun is generally, but not always, easily identifiable by its ending: Masculine nouns usually end in *-o*, while feminine nouns usually end in *-a*. Plural nouns end in *-s* or *-es*:

el niño (the [little] boy) **la** niña (the [little] girl)
los niños (the [little] boys) **las** niñas (the [little] girls)

Uses of the Definite Articles

The definite article is used:

- With nouns that have a general or abstract sense:

    La buena salud es importante. Good health is important.

- With the names of languages, except directly after *hablar, en,* and *de*:

    El español es fácil. Spanish is easy.

    Hablo español. I speak Spanish.

    Está escrito en español. It's written in Spanish.

    Es profesor de español. He's a Spanish teacher.

    Note: The definite article is generally omitted after *estudiar* (to study), *enseñar* (to teach), *aprender* (to learn), *saber* (to know), *escribir* (to write), and *leer* (to read):

    Ella enseña (el) español. She teaches Spanish.

- With parts of the body or apparel when the possessor is clear:

    Abra **los** ojos. Open your eyes.

    Me pongo **el** abrigo. I put on my coat.

    BUT:

    ¿Te gusta **mi** camisa? Do you like my shirt?

- With titles of rank or profession, except when addressing the person:

    El doctor ha llegado. The doctor has arrived.

    Adiós, doctor Rivera. Goodbye, Dr. Rivera.

- With days of the week in a singular or plural sense, except after the verb *ser* (to be) when expressing the day of the week:

    No voy a la escuela **el** lunes. I'm not going to school on Monday.

    No voy a la escuela **los** sábados. I don't go to school on Saturdays.

    Hoy es martes. Today is Tuesday.

- With seasons, except that the article may be omitted after *en:*

    No me gusta **el** invierno. I don't like winter.

    Voy a esquiar en (**el**)* invierno. I go skiing in the winter.

    Parentheses are used to show the word is optional.

- With dates:

    Es **el** diez de junio. It's June 10th.

- With time:

    Es **la** una. It's one o'clock.

    Son **las** dos y media. It's 2:30.

- With geographical names of rivers, mountains, and oceans; with geographical names that are modified (described by an adjective); and with some names of countries, states, and cities. There is no rule for when these names should be preceded by a definite article. Here are some examples (current usage often allows for the omission of the definite article before the name of some countries):

la América Central	Central America
la América del Norte	North America
la América del Sur	South America
la Argentina	Argentina
el Brasil	Brazil
el Canadá	Canada
el Cairo	Cairo
la China	China
el Ecuador	Ecuador
los Estados Unidos	the United States
la Florida	Florida
la Habana	Havana
el Japón	Japan
el Paraguay	Paraguay
el Perú	Peru
la República Dominicana	the Dominican Republic
el Uruguay	Uruguay

For example:

El Orinoco es un río. The Orinoco is a river.

La América del Norte es grande. North America is big.

Vivimos en **(los)** Estados Unidos. We live in the United States.

❏ With weights and measures to express "a," "an," and "per":

Los huevos cuestan dos dólares **la** docena. Eggs cost two dollars per [each] dozen.

❏ With the infinitive of a verb that is serving as a noun (note, however, that the article is optional when the infinitive serves as the subject of the sentence):

(El) mentir es peligroso. Lying is dangerous.

❏ With common expressions of time:

Me levanto temprano por **la** mañana. I wake up early in the morning.

La semana próxima voy a Europa. Next week I'm going to Europe.

Omission of the Definite Article

Omit the definite article:

❏ Before nouns that are in *apposition* — meaning the two terms explain each other and are next to each other, as in the example below:

San Juan, capital de Puerto Rico, es una ciudad interesante. (San Juan, the capital of Puerto Rico, is an interesting city.)

Note: If the apposition expresses a family or business relationship the article is needed:

Carlos Rivera, el padre de María, es abogado. Carlos Rivera, María's father, is a lawyer.

❑ Before numerals expressing the numerical order of rulers:

Carlos Cuarto　Charles the Fourth

Contractions with the Definite Article

The definite article *el* contracts with the preposition *a* to become *al* and with the preposition *de* to become *del:*

Voy **al** supermercado.	I go to the supermarket.
Busco **al** empleado.	I'm looking for the employee.
Es el supermercado más grande **del** pueblo.	It's the biggest supermarket in the town.

The Neuter Lo

The neuter definite article *lo* is used:

❑ Before an adjective that is used as a noun to express an abstract idea or a quality:

¿Piensas **lo** mismo que yo? Do you think the same as I do?

Lo viejo no es siempre peor que lo nuevo. Old is not always worse than new.

❑ To express "how" as follows: *Lo* + adjective (or adverb) + *que:*

Ya ven **lo** importante que es. They see how important it is.

¿Ves **lo** rápidamente que trabaja? Do you see how fast he works?

Example Problems

When writing a paragraph, you will often have to decide when to use the definite article. Complete the paragraph about Ramón using definite articles when necessary.

Es ___ nueve de junio. Son ___ seis de la mañana. ___ radio-despertador está roto y no
　　　1　　　　　　　　　　　　2　　　　　　　　　3

suena. Ramón Blanca, ___ director de ___ escuela Molina, continúa durmiendo. ___
　　　　　　　　　　　　4　　　　　　5　　　　　　　　　　　　　　　　　　6

señora Blanca, ___ esposa de Ramón, entra en ___ cuarto y le dice, "Ramón, abre ___
　　　　　　　7　　　　　　　　　　　　　　8　　　　　　　　　　　　　　　9

ojos. Tienes que ir a ___ escuela." Ramón mira ___ calendario y responde a su esposa,
　　　　　　　　　　10　　　　　　　　　　11

"Ay, hoy es ___ domingo. No hay clases ___ domingos. No voy a levantarme antes de
　　　　　12　　　　　　　　　　　13

___ una." Su esposa le dice, "Ay, Ramón, ___ dormir es tan importante."
14　　　　　　　　　　　　　　　　15

Solution to Problems:

1. **el**   Use the definite article with dates. Put *el* before the number of the day.

2. **las**   Use the definite article with time. Put *las* before the number of the hour of the day, *seis* (six o'clock).

3. **el**   Use the definite article *el* before a masculine singular noun that is used in a general sense. You can determine that the noun *radio-despertador* is masculine by looking at the adjective *roto* (broken), which has the masculine *-o* ending.

4. **none**   No definite article is used before a noun in apposition.

5. **la**   Use the definite article *la* before the feminine noun *escuela*, which is used in a general sense.

6. **La**   The definite article is used before *señora*.

7. **la**   Use the definite article *la* before the feminine noun *esposa*. If the apposition expresses a family or business relationship, the article is needed.

8. **el**   Use the definite article *el* before a noun to express "the."

9. **los**   Use the definite article with parts of the body *(ojos)* when the possessor (Ramón) is clear.

10. **la**   Use the definite article *la* before the feminine noun *escuela*, which is used in a general sense.

11. **el**   Use the definite article *el* before the masculine noun *calendario*, which is used in a general sense.

12. **none**   No definite article is used with the name of a day of the week after the verb *ser* (to be).

13. **los**   Use the masculine plural definite article, *los*, before the name of a day to express "on."

14. **la**   Use the feminine singular definite article, *la*, with the singular number of the hour of the day, *una* (one o'clock). Use *las* for all other hours.

15. **(el)**   Using the masculine singular definite article with an infinitive serving as a noun is optional.

Work Problems

Complete the paragraph describing this person's day by using the correct form of the definite article when needed.

No voy a ___ oficina hoy. Estoy de vacaciones. Tengo una habitación en ___ hotel lujoso,
             1   2

Carlos ___ Tercero en Madrid. Me levanto temprano por ___ mañana, a ___ siete. Yo
         3   4   5

tomo ___ desayuno en mi cuarto. Estamos en ___ otoño y hace fresco. Me pongo ___
       6   7   8

abrigo y ___ bufanda y tomo ___ autobús de ___ ocho. Tengo ganas de pasar toda ___
          9   10   11   12

mañana visitando ___ Prado, ___ museo famoso donde se pueden ver colecciones de
                  13   14

___ obras de ___ fabulosos pintores españoles. Mi profesor de español dice que es ___
15   16   17

museo más famoso de España. Yo pienso ___ mismo que él. Me gusta mucho visitar esta
                                        18

ciudad. Madrid, ___ capital de ___ España, es una ciudad maravillosa.
                 19   20

Worked Solutions

1. **la**   Use the feminine singular definite article before the noun *oficina*, which is used in a
    general sense.

2. **un**   Use the masculine singular indefinite article before the noun *hotel*, which is used in a
    general sense. The adjective *lujoso*, which ends in *-o*, indicates that *hotel* is masculine.

3. **none**   The definite article is omitted before numerals expressing the numerical order of
    rulers.

4. **la**   Use the feminine singular definite article before the time of day to express "in."

5. **las**   Use the feminine plural definite article before a number indicating a time.

6. **el**   Use the masculine singular definite article before the noun *desayuno*, which is used in
    a general sense.

7. **(el)**   The masculine singular definite article is optional before the season, *otoño*, to
    express "in."

8. **el**   Use the masculine singular definite article before the noun *abrigo* when the possessor
    is clear.

9. **la**   Use the feminine singular definite article before the noun *bufanda* when the possessor
    is clear.

10. **el**   Use the masculine singular definite article before the noun, *autobús*.

11. **las**   Use the feminine plural definite article before a number indicating a time.

12. **la**   Use the feminine singular definite article before the time of day to express "in."

13. **el**   Use the masculine singular definite article before the noun *Prado*, which is used in a
    general sense to express "the Prado Museum."

14. **el**   Use the masculine singular definite article before the noun *museo*, which is used in a
    general sense.

15. **las**   Use the feminine plural definite article before the noun *obras*, which is used in a general sense.

16. **los**   Use the masculine plural definite article before the noun *pintores* to express "the." The adjective *famosos*, which ends in *-os*, indicates that *pintores* is masculine and plural.

17. **el**   Use the masculine singular definite article before the noun *museo* to express "the."

18. **lo**   Use the neuter definite article before an adjective that is being used as a noun to express an abstract idea.

19. **none**   Omit the definite article when there is a noun in apposition.

20. **none**   The definite article may be used with the names of some countries, but it is generally not used with *España*.

Indefinite Articles

Indefinite articles refer to persons and objects that are not specifically identified—a boy, an orange, some trees—as opposed to Juan, that orange on the table, or the maple in Grandma's yard. The indefinite article precedes the noun it modifies and agrees with that noun in gender and number.

un niño (a [little] boy)   **una** niña (a [little] girl)

unos niños (some [little] boys)   **unas** niñas (some [little] girls)

Omission of the Indefinite Article

Omit the indefinite article:

❑ Before nouns in apposition, except when modified by an adjective:

Salvador Dalí, artista español, pertenecía a la escuela surrealista.
Salvador Dalí, a Spanish artist, belonged to the surrealist school.

Salvador Dalí, un gran artista español, pertenecía a la escuela surrealista.
Salvador Dalí, a great Spanish artist, belonged to the surrealist school.

❑ Before **unmodified** nouns showing a class or group (occupation, nationality, religion, and so on):

Quiere hacerse abogada. She wants to become a lawyer.

Es **una** abogada famosa. She's a famous lawyer.

The second example requires the use of the indefinite article because the adjective *famosa* modifies *abogada*.

❑ Before or after certain words that usually use the indefinite article in English:

otro problema	**an**other problem
cierto año	**a** certain year
tal cosa	such **(a)** thing
¡Qué casa tan bonita!	What **a** lovely house!
cien muchachos	**(a hundred boys)** one hundred boys
mil personas	**(a thousand people)** one thousand people

For the last two examples, you would use the article in English if you were talking about "a $100 bill" or "a 1,000-seat arena" but you would never do so in Spanish.

Example Problems

Problem 1: Complete the definitions by using the correct form of the definite article and indefinite article as needed.

1. ___ pera es ___ fruta.

2. ___ italiano es ___ lengua.

3. ___ cena es ___ comida.

4. ___ matemáticas es ___ materia.

5. ___ Pacífico es ___ océano.

Answer to Problem 1:

1. La; una

2. El; una

3. La; una

4. Las; una

5. El; un

Solution to Problem 1:

1. Use *la* because definite articles are used before nouns used in a general sense. The *-a* ending indicates that *pera* is feminine. Select *una* to express "a" before the feminine singular noun *fruta*.

2. Use *el* because the definite article is used with the names of languages. The *-o* ending indicates that *italiano* is masculine. Select *una* to express "a" before the feminine singular noun *lengua*.

3. Use *la* because the definite article is used before nouns that are used in a general sense. The *-a* ending indicates that *cena* is feminine. Select *una* to express "a" before the feminine singular noun *comida*.

4. Use *las* because the definite article is used before nouns that are used in a general sense. The *-as* ending indicates that *matemáticas* is feminine and plural. Select *una* to express "a" before the feminine singular noun *materia*.

5. Use *el* because the definite article is used with geographical names. The *-o* ending indicates that *Pacífico* is masculine.

Problem 2: Complete the sentences expressing what someone sees from his or her window. Use the indefinite article if necessary.

1. ___ niñas juegan al fútbol.

2. ___ mil personas caminan.

3. ___ perros corren.

4. ___ muchacha salta a la cuerda.

5. ___ doctor famoso visita al señor Pidal.

6. El señor Diego, ___ vecino del señor Valles, lo ayuda.

7. Hay ___ otro accidente.

8. ___ personas regresan del trabajo.

Answer to Problem 2:

1. Unas

2. none

3. Unos

4. Una

5. Un

6. none

7. none

8. Unas

Solution to Problem 2:

1. Use the indefinite article to refer to persons who are not specifically identified. *Unas* must agree with the feminine plural noun *niñas*.

2. The indefinite article is not used before the number *mil*.

3. Use the indefinite article to refer to persons who are not specifically identified. *Unos* must agree with the masculine plural noun *perros*.

4. Use the indefinite article to refer to persons who are not specifically identified. *Una* must agree with the feminine singular noun *muchacha*.

5. Use the indefinite article to refer to persons who are not specifically identified. *Un* must agree with the masculine singular noun *doctor*.

6. The indefinite article is not used with nouns in apposition.

7. The indefinite article is not used with *otro*.

8. Use the indefinite article to refer to persons who are not specifically identified. *Unas* must agree with the feminine plural noun *personas*.

Work Problems

Use these problems to give yourself additional practice.

Problem 1: Complete the definitions with the definite and indefinite articles, as needed.

1. ___ oro es ___ piedra preciosa.

2. ___ miedo es ___ sentimiento.

3. ___ biología es ___ ciencia.

4. ___ almuerzo es ___ comida.

5. ___ florería es ___ tienda.

Problem 2: Complete the sentences expressing what someone sees in a small city. Some of the sentences may be correct as is. If an article is needed, use the indefinite article.

1. Hay ___ iglesias grandes.

2. Hay ___ mil personas.

3. Hay ___ centro comercial.

4. Hay ___ ciertos estadios famosos.

5. Hay ___ cien bodegas españolas.

6. Hay ___ bibliotecas.

Worked Solutions

Problem 1:

1. **el, una**   Use the masculine singular definite article before the noun *oro*, which is used in a general sense. Use the feminine singular indefinite article before the noun *piedra* to express "a."

2. **el, un**   Use the masculine singular definite article before the noun *miedo*, which is used in a general sense. Use the feminine singular indefinite article before the noun *sentimiento* to express "a."

3. **la, una**   Use the feminine singular definite article before the noun *biología*, which is used in a general sense. Use the feminine singular indefinite article before the noun *ciencia* to express "a."

4. **el, una**   Use the masculine singular definite article before the noun *almuerzo*, which is used in a general sense. Use the feminine singular indefinite article before the noun *comida* to express "a."

5. **la, una**   Use the feminine singular definite article before the noun *florería*, which is used in a general sense. Use the feminine singular indefinite article before the noun *tienda* to express "a."

Problem 2:

1. **unas**   Use the feminine plural indefinite article before *iglesias* to express "some."

2. **none**   The indefinite article is omitted before the number *mil*.

3. **un**   Use the masculine singular indefinite article before *centro* to express "a."

4. **none**   The indefinite article is omitted before the word *ciertos*.

5. **none**   The indefinite article is omitted before the number *cien*.

6. **unas**   Use the feminine plural indefinite article before *bibliotecas* to express "some."

Demonstrative Adjectives

Demonstrative adjectives indicate or point out the person, place, or thing that is being referred to. In Spanish, demonstrative adjectives precede and agree in number and gender with the nouns they modify.

In Spanish, the demonstrative adjective is selected according to the distance of the noun from the speaker:

❑ *Este (esta)* expresses "this" and *estos (estas)* expresses "these" when the nouns are close to and directly concern the speaker:

este niño	this (little) boy	estos niños	these (little) boys
esta niña	this (little) girl	estas niñas	these (little) girls

❑ *Ese (esa)* expresses "that" and *esos (esas)* expresses "those" when the nouns are not particularly near to or don't directly concern the speaker:

ese niño	that (little) boy	esos niños	those (little) boys
esa niña	that (little) girl	esas niñas	those (little) girls

❑ *Aquel (aquella)* expresses "that" and *aquellos (aquellas)* expresses "those" when the nouns are quite far from and don't directly concern the speaker at all:

aquel niño	that (little) boy	aquellos niños	those (little) boys
aquella niña	that (little) girl	aquellas niñas	those (little) girls

Remember to repeat the demonstrative adjective before each noun:

este hombre y **esa** mujer   **this** man and **that** woman

For clarity, the following adverbs may be used for reinforcement:

with *este, esta, estos, estas*	use *aquí*	here
with *ese, esa, esos, esas*	use *ahí*	there (but not too far)
with *aquel, aquella, aquellos, aquellas*	use *allá*	over there (rather far)

For example:

esta casa aquí	this house here
esa casa ahí	that house there
aquella casa allá	that house over there

Example Problems

Problem 1: Describe the people by selecting the correct demonstrative adjective.

1. _____ abogado es egoísta.

   A. Ese **B.** Esa **C.** Esos **D.** Esas

2. _____ médicos son serios.

   A. Esta **B.** Estas **C.** Estos **D.** Este

3. _____ profesora es simpática.

   A. Aquel **B.** Aquella **C.** Aquellos **D.** Aquellas

4. _____ bomberos son valientes.

   A. Esa **B.** Esas **C.** Ese **D.** Estos

Answer to Problem 1:

1. A

2. C

3. B

4. D

Solution to Problem 1:

1. Use *ese* because *abogado* is a masculine singular noun.

2. Use *estos* because *médicos* is a masculine plural noun.

3. Use *aquella* because *profesora* is a feminine singular noun.

4. Use *estos* because *bomberos* is a masculine plural noun.

Problem 2: Express what you buy by giving the correct form of "this" ("these") or "that" ("those"). Follow the example:

Compro **este** libro y **esa** revista en **aquella** librería.

1. Compro _____ huevos y _____ crema en _____ tienda.

2. Compro _____ frutas y _____ queso en _____ mercados.

3. Compro _____ torta y _____ panecillos en _____ panaderías.

4. Compro _____ pollo y _____ papas en _____ supermercado.

Answer to Problem 2:

1. estos, esa, aquella

2. estas, ese, aquellos

3. esta, esos, aquellas

4. este, esas, aquel

Solution to Problem 2:

All the masculine singular nouns end in *-o*, and all the feminine singular nouns end in *-a*. All the masculine plural nouns end in *-os*, and all of the feminine plural nouns end in *-as*.

1. Use the masculine plural demonstrative adjective for "these" before *huevos*. Use the feminine singular demonstrative adjective for "that" before *crema*. Use the feminine singular demonstrative adjective for "that" before *tienda*.

2. Use the feminine plural demonstrative adjective for "these" before *frutas*. Use the masculine singular demonstrative adjective for "that" before *queso*. Use the masculine plural demonstrative adjective for "those" before *mercados*.

3. Use the feminine singular demonstrative adjective for "this" before *torta*. Use the masculine plural demonstrative adjective for "those" before *panecillos*. Use the feminine plural demonstrative adjective for "that" before *panaderías*.

4. Use the masculine singular demonstrative adjective for "this" before *pollo*. Use the feminine plural demonstrative adjective for "those" before *papas*. Use the masculine singular demonstrative adjective for "that" before *supermercado*.

Work Problems

Use these problems to give yourself additional practice.

Problem 1: Select the demonstrative adjective that best describes the places.

1. ___ monumento es grande.

    A. Esta **B.** Aquellas **C.** Esa **D.** Aquel

2. ___ plazas son famosas.

    A. Aquellas **B.** Esos **C.** Esta **D.** Aquellos

3. ___ iglesia es impresionante.

    A. Estos **B.** Esta **C.** Aquel **D.** Ese

4. ___ estadios son pequeños.

    A. Aquel **B.** Ese **C.** Esos **D.** Estas

Problem 2: Express what the members of the Reyes family say about the furniture and appliances they see in a store. Use the clues *aquí*, *ahí*, and *allá* to select the correct demonstrative adjective.

1. ___ cama ahí es confortable.

2. ___ lavadoras aquí son caras.

3. ___ lámparas allá son grandes.

4. ___ burós aquí son bonitos.

5. ___ piano allá es feo.

6. ___ horno aquí es pequeño.

7. ___ espejos ahí son magníficos.

8. ___ cuadro allá es perfecto.

Worked Solutions

Problem 1:

1. **D**   Use the masculine singular demonstrative adjective before the noun *monumento* to express "that."

2. **A**   Use the feminine plural demonstrative adjective before the noun *plazas* to express "those."

3. **B**   Use the feminine singular demonstrative adjective before the noun *iglesia* to express "this."

4. **C**   Use the masculine plural demonstrative adjective before the noun *estadios* to express "those."

Problems 2:

1. **Esa**   Use the feminine singular demonstrative adjective indicated by the adverb *ahí*.

2. **Estas**   Use the feminine plural demonstrative adjective indicated by the adverb *aquí*.

3. **Aquellas**   Use the feminine plural demonstrative adjective indicated by the adverb *allá*.

4. **Estos**   Use the masculine plural demonstrative adjective indicated by the adverb *aquí*.

5. **Aquel**   Use the masculine singular demonstrative adjective indicated by the adverb *allá*.

6. **Este**   Use the masculine singular demonstrative adjective indicated by the adverb *aquí*.

7. **Esos**   Use the masculine plural demonstrative adjective indicated by the adverb *ahí*.

8. **Aquel**   Use the masculine singular demonstrative adjective indicated by the adverb *allá*.

Nouns

A noun is a word used to name a person, place, thing, idea, or quality. All Spanish nouns have a number (singular or plural) and a gender (masculine or feminine) that can usually be determined by the noun's ending: *-o* for masculine and *-a* for feminine. A few nouns do not follow this rule, and their gender must be memorized.

Gender-Obvious Nouns

Nouns that refer to males are always masculine, and nouns that refer to females are always feminine, no matter what their ending:

el muchacho	the boy	la muchacha	the girl
el padre	the father	la madre	the mother
el rey	the king	la reina	the queen

Nouns in Reverse

Some nouns that end in *-o* are feminine:

la mano	the hand
la radio	the radio

Some nouns that end in *-a* are masculine:

el clima	the climate
el día	the day
el drama	the drama
el idioma	the language
el mapa	the map
el planeta	the planet
el problema	the problem
el programa	the program
el tema	the theme

Nouns That Change Gender

Some nouns can be either masculine or feminine regardless of their ending, depending on to whom you are referring:

el artista	the male artist	la artista	the female artist
el joven	the male youth	la joven	the female youth
el estudiante	the male student	la estudiante	the female student

Nouns That Never Change Gender

Some nouns are always masculine or feminine regardless of the gender of the person to whom you are referring, and will be so indicated in a dictionary:

una persona	a person (male or female)
una víctima	a victim (male or female)

Nouns That Give You a Hint

In some cases, you can determine that a noun is feminine by its special ending. Nouns that have the following endings are feminine:

-dad	la verdad	the truth
-tad	la mitad	half
-tud	la juventud	youth
-umbre	la muchedumbre	the crowd
-ie	la serie	the series
-ión	la lección	the lesson

Two exceptions are *el avión* (the airplane) and *el camión* (the truck).

Nouns ending in *-d* and *-z* tend to be feminine: *la pared* (the wall), *la nariz* (the nose), *la luz* (the light), and *la vez* (the time). Exceptions include *el pez* (the fish) and *el lápiz* (the pencil).

Nouns ending in *-e, -l, -ma, -n, -r,* and *-s* tend to be masculine: *el valle* (the valley), *el papel* (the paper), *el problema* (the problem), *el tren* (the train), *el color* (the color), and *el mes* (the month). Exceptions include *la calle* (the street), *la clase* (the class), *la llave* (the key), *la noche* (the night), *la suerte* (luck), and *la tarde* (the afternoon).

Nouns Whose Meaning Changes

Some nouns have different meanings depending on whether they are used in a masculine or feminine sense:

el capital	the capital (money)	la capital	the capital (city)
el cura	the priest	la cura	the cure
el guía	the guide (male)	la guía	the guidebook, the guide (female)
el policía	the policeman	la policía	the police force, the policewoman

Special Cases

Masculine nouns that refer to people and end in *-or, -és,* or *-n* require the addition of a final *-a* to get the female equivalent. For example:

el profesor	the (male) teacher	la profesora	the (female) teacher
el inglés	the Englishman	la inglesa	the Englishwoman
el alemán	the (male) German	la alemana	the (female) German

Two exceptions are:

| el actor | the actor | la actriz | the actress |
| el emperador | the emperor | la emperatriz | the empress |

Example Problems

Problem 1: Fill in the missing male or female counterpart.

Male	Female
1. _____	la muchacha
2. el padre	_____
3. el hombre	_____
4. el inglés	_____
5. _____	la dentista

Answer to Problem 1:

1. el muchacho

2. la madre

3. la mujer

4. la inglesa

5. el dentista

Solution to Problem 1:

1. Use the definite article *el* to show that you are speaking about one male. The word for "boy," *muchacho,* must end in an *-o.*

2. Use the definite article *la* to show that you are speaking about one female. The word for "mother," like the word for "father," ends in an *-e.*

3. Use the definite article *la* to show that you are speaking about one female. The word for "woman" is irregular and must be memorized: *mujer.*

4. Use the definite article *la* to show that you are speaking about one female. The word for an Englishwoman needs a final *-a,* so the accent is dropped from the *-e* to maintain the proper stress.

5. Use the definite article *el* to show that you are speaking about one male. The masculine word for dentist is irregular and uncharacteristically ends in an *-a.*

Problem 2: Complete the sentences by selecting the correct word and supplying it, along with the appropriate definite or indefinite article.

rey	mano	llave	artista
color	capital	país	maestra

1. Un sinónimo de una profesora es _____.

2. El esposo de la reina es _____.

3. Madrid es _____ de España.

4. Yo toco las cosas con _____.

5. El rojo es _____.

6. Picasso es _____ famoso.

Answer to Problem 2:

1. una maestra

2. el rey

3. la capital

4. la mano

5. un color

6. un artista

Solution to Problem 2:

1. Because you need a synonym of a feminine word, and because the indefinite article is used before the noun in the example, use the feminine singular indefinite article *una.* The word *maestra* means teacher.

2. Because you need the masculine counterpart (*el esposo,* or the husband) of "the queen," and because the feminine singular definite article *la* is used for *reina,* use the masculine singular definite article *el* before the Spanish word for king: *rey.*

3. Madrid is "the" (not "a") capital of Spain. Although nouns ending in -*l* are generally masculine, this word is an exception. Use the feminine singular definite article *la* before *capital.*

4. Because the possessor is clear, use the singular definite article for *mano.* Although nouns ending in -*o* are generally masculine, this word is an exception, and the feminine *la* must be used.

5. Red is "a" (not "the") color. Nouns ending in -*r* are generally masculine. Use the masculine singular indefinite article *un.*

6. The indefinite article is used before a profession that is modified by an adjective. *Artista* is both the masculine and feminine form of the word. Use the indefinite article *un* because Picasso was a man.

Work Problems

Use these problems to give yourself additional practice.

Problem 1: Fill in the missing male or female counterpart.

Male	Female
1. _____	la estudiante
2. el rey	_____
3. _____	la persona
4. _____	la francesa
5. _____	la actriz
6. _____	la alemana
7. el emperador	_____

Problem 2: Supply the best word to complete the sentence. Use an appropriate definite or indefinite article.

1. Junio es _____.

2. Martes es _____.

3. La Tierra es _____.

4. El español es _____.

5. El 50% es _____.

6. Un hombre de la iglesia es _____.

Worked Solutions

Problem 1:

1. **el estudiante**   The word *estudiante* can be either masculine or feminine. Use the definite article for the masculine singular, *el.*

2. **la reina**   Use the definite article for the feminine singular, *la.* The word for queen is *reina.*

3. **la persona**   Whether the person is masculine or feminine, the word for "person" is always *la persona.*

4. **el francés**   Use the definite article for the masculine singular, *el*. The word *francesa* drops the *-a* and an accent is needed on the *-e* to maintain the proper stress.

5. **el actor**   Use the definite article for the masculine singular, *el*. *Actriz* is irregular. The masculine form of the noun is *actor*.

6. **el alemán**   Use the definite article for the masculine singular, *el*. The word *alemana* drops the final *-a* and an accent is needed on the second *-a* to maintain the proper stress.

7. **la persona**   Whether the person is masculine or feminine, the word for "person" is always *la persona*.

8. **la emperatriz**   Although an *-a* is generally added to form the feminine of nouns that end in *-or*, this word is irregular. Use the definite article for the feminine singular, *la*.

Problem 2:

1. **un mes**   *Junio* is a month. The word *mes* ends in *-s*, which generally indicates a masculine word. Use the indefinite article *un* to express "a."

2. **un día**   *Martes* is a day. The word *día* ends in an *-a*, which generally indicates a feminine word. *Día*, however, is an exception. Use the indefinite article *un* to express "a."

3. **un planeta**   *La Tierra* is a planet *(planeta)*. Nouns ending in *-a* are generally feminine, but this is an exception. Use the indefinite article *un* to express "a."

4. **un idioma (una lengua)**   *El español* is a language. The word *idioma* ends in an *-a*, which generally indicates a feminine word. *Idioma*, however, is an exception. Use the indefinite article *un* to express "a." *Lengua* is a feminine singular noun that also means "language." Use the indefinite article *una* to express "a."

5. **una mitad**   "50%" represents half *(mitad)*. Nouns ending in *-tad* tend to be feminine. Use the indefinite article *una* to express "a."

6. **un cura**   A man of the church is a priest *(cura)*. The word *cura* ends in an *-a*, which generally indicates a feminine word. *Cura*, however, is an exception because it refers to a man. Use the indefinite article *un* to express "a."

Noun Plurals

Just as in English, when a Spanish noun refers to more than one person, place, thing, idea, or quality, it must be made plural. When you change the noun to the plural form, you must also change its respective article.

Nouns Ending in a Vowel

Add an *-s* to form the plural of Spanish nouns that end in a vowel:

el niño	los niños	la niña	las niñas
un niño	unos niños	una niña	unas niñas
este niño	estos niños	esta niña	estas niñas
ese niño	esos niños	esa niña	esas niñas
aquel niño	aquellos niños	aquella niña	aquellas niñas

Nouns Ending in a Consonant

Add -es to form the plural of Spanish nouns that end in a consonant:

el rey	los rey**es**	la ley	las ley**es**
el actor	los actor**es**	la mujer	las mujer**es**

Nouns with Plural Changes

For nouns that end in -z, change -z to -ce before adding -s:

el lápi**z**	the pencil	los lápi**ces**	the pencils
la actri**z**	the actress	las actri**ces**	the actresses

For some nouns ending in -n or -s, you must add or delete an accent mark to maintain the original stress:

el joven	the youth	los jóvenes	the youths
el examen	the test	los exámenes	the tests
la canción	the song	las canciones	the songs
el francés	the Frenchman	los franceses	the Frenchmen

Exception: el país → los países (the countries)

Nouns ending in an unstressed -s undergo no change in the plural, while those ending in a stressed -s must add -es to form the plural:

el martes	Wednesday	los martes	Wednesdays
el paraguas	the umbrella	los paraguas	the umbrellas
la dosis	the dose	las dosis	the doses
el mes	the month	los meses	the months

Mixed Genders

When there is a group of people from both genders, the masculine plural prevails:

el niño y la niña	=	los niños (the children)
el abuelo y la abuela	=	los abuelos (the grandparents)

Nouns That Are Always Plural

Some nouns are only used in the plural form. For example:

las gafas/los espejuelos	eyeglasses
las matemáticas	mathematics
las vacaciones	the vacation

Collective Nouns

Collective nouns refer to a group of people. The collective noun is considered a single unit and requires the third person singular of the verb:

el público	the audience
la pareja	the couple
la muchedumbre	the crowd
todo el mundo	everybody
la familia	the family
el grupo	the group
la orquesta	the orchestra
la nación	the nation
el par	the pair
la gente	the people
el equipo	the team

For example:

El equipo gana el campeonato.	The team wins the championship.

Example Problems

Problem 1: Ask someone to show you more than one thing in a city.

Example: esta plaza → Muéstreme estas plazas.

1. el teatro

2. esa catedral

3. aquella bodega

4. este jardín

5. la estación

6. un almacén

Answer to Problem 1:

1. Muéstreme los teatros.

2. Muéstreme esas catedrales.

3. Muéstreme aquellas bodegas.

4. Muéstreme estos jardines.

5. Muéstreme las estaciones.

6. Muéstreme unos almacenes.

Solution to Problem 1:

1. Use the masculine plural definite article *los* to show that you are speaking about more than one masculine place. Because *teatro* ends in a vowel, add *-s* to get the plural.

2. Use the feminine plural demonstrative adjective *esas* to show that you are speaking about more than one feminine place. Because *catedral* ends in a consonant, add *-es* to get the plural.

3. Use the feminine plural demonstrative adjective *aquellas* to show that you are speaking about more than one feminine place. Because *bodega* ends in a vowel, add *-s* to get the plural.

4. Use the masculine plural demonstrative adjective *estos* to show that you are speaking about more than one masculine place. Add *-es* to *jardín* to get the plural because it ends in a consonant. Because *jardín* ends in an *-n*, drop the accent from the *i* from the singular form to maintain the original stress.

5. Use the feminine plural definite article *las* to show that you are speaking about more than one feminine place. Add *-es* to *estación* to get the plural because it ends in a consonant. Because *estación* ends in an *-n*, drop the accent from the *ó* in the singular form to maintain the original stress.

6. Use the masculine plural indefinite article *unos* to show that you are speaking about more than one masculine place. Add *-es* to *almacén* to get the plural because it ends in a consonant. Because *almacén* ends in an *-n*, drop the accent from the *é* in the singular form to maintain the original stress.

Work Problem

Express the plural of what you see in the classroom.

Example: Veo el bolígrafo. → Veo los bolígrafos.

1. Veo el ejercicio.

2. Veo ese mapa.

3. Veo esta palabra.

4. Veo a aquel portugués.

5. Veo la oración.

6. Veo a un profesor.

Worked Solutions

1. **Veo los ejercicios.**   Use the masculine plural definite article *los* to show that you are speaking about more than one masculine thing. Because *ejercicio* ends in a vowel, add *-s* to get the plural.

2. **Veo esos mapas.**   Use the masculine plural demonstrative adjective *esos* to show that you are speaking about more than one masculine thing. Although *mapa* ends in an *-a*, it is a masculine word. Because *mapa* ends in a vowel, add *-s* to get the plural.

3. **Veo estas palabras.**   Use the feminine plural demonstrative adjective *estas* to show that you are speaking about more than one feminine thing. Add *-s* to *palabra* to get the plural because it ends in a vowel.

4. **Veo a aquellos portugueses.**   Use the masculine plural demonstrative adjective *aquellos* to show that you are speaking about more than one masculine person. Add *-es* to *portugués* to get the plural because it ends in a consonant. *Portugués* has an é in the singular that is replaced with e in the plural to maintain the original stress.

5. **Veo las oraciones.**   Use the feminine plural definite article *las* to show that you are speaking about more than one feminine thing. Because *oración* ends in a consonant, add *-es* to get the plural. Because *oración* ends in an *-n,* drop the accent from the ó in the singular form to maintain the original stress.

6. **Veo a unos profesores.**   Use the masculine plural indefinite article *unos* to show that you are speaking about more than one masculine person. Add *-es* to *profesor* to get the plural because it ends in a consonant.

Chapter Problems and Solutions

Problems

In problems 1–10, express what is important by giving the correct definite article for each noun.

1. ___ orgullo es una emoción importante.

2. ___ virtud de ser honorable es importante.

3. ___ costumbres son importantes.

4. ___ felicidad es importante.

5. ___ respeto de sus amigos es importante.

6. ___ paz es importante.

7. ___ leyes son importantes.

8. ___ buena salud es importante.

9. ___ alegría en el hogar es importante.

10. ___ honor es importante.

In problems 11–15, combine the two people in each pair to get the plural. Use the definite article before each noun and in your final answer.

    Example: el tío + la tía = los tíos

11. ___ hija + ___ hijo = _____

12. ___ abuelo + ___ abuela = _____

13. ___ madre + ___ padre = _____

14. ___ joven + ___ joven = _____

15. ___ francesa + ___ francés = _____

In problems 16–18, complete the sentences by filling in the correct demonstrative adjectives that refer to the clothing these people buy.

16. Yo compro ____ camisa, ____ chaleco, ____ calcetines y ____ blusas ahí.

17. Ella prefiere ____ guantes, ____ camisetas, ____ falda y ____ cinturón aquí.

18. Él escoge ____ impermeable, ____ suéteres, ____ chaquetas y ____ corbata allá.

Answers and Solutions

1. **Answer: El.** Use the masculine singular definite article. Words that end in -o are generally masculine.

2. **Answer: La.** Use the feminine singular definite article. Words that end in -tud are generally feminine.

3. **Answer: Las.** Use the feminine plural definite article. Words that end in -umbre are generally feminine and words that end in -s are generally plural.

4. **Answer: La.** Use the feminine singular definite article. Words that end in -dad are generally feminine.

5. **Answer: El.** Use the masculine singular definite article. Words that end in -o are generally masculine.

6. **Answer: La.** Use the feminine singular definite article. Words that end in -z are generally feminine.

7. **Answer: Las.** Use the feminine plural definite article because ley is feminine and the -es ending indicates that the word is plural.

8. **Answer: La.** Use the feminine singular definite article. Words that end in -ud are generally feminine.

9. **Answer: La.** Use the feminine singular definite article. Words that end in -a are generally feminine.

10. **Answer: El.** Use the masculine singular definite article. Words that end in -r are generally masculine.

11. **Answer: la hija + el hijo = los hijos.** Use the feminine singular definite article before the noun ending in -a and the masculine singular definite article before the noun ending in -o. The masculine plural definite article must be used to modify a noun that refers to a group that includes both genders. The masculine singular noun is made plural by adding an -s because the noun ends in a vowel.

12. **Answer: el abuelo + la abuela = los abuelos.** Use the masculine singular definite article before the noun ending in -o and the feminine singular definite article before the noun ending in -a. The masculine plural definite article must be used to modify a noun that refers to a group that includes both genders. The masculine singular noun is made plural by adding an -s because the noun ends in a vowel.

13. **Answer: la madre + el padre = los padres**. Use the feminine singular definite article before the noun ending in -e and the masculine singular definite article before the noun ending in -o. The masculine plural definite article must be used to modify a noun that refers to a group that includes both genders. The masculine singular noun is made plural by adding an -s because the noun ends in a vowel.

14. **Answer: el joven + la joven = los jóvenes**. Use the masculine or feminine definite article before either noun because *joven* can refer to a male or a female. The masculine plural definite article must be used to modify a noun that refers to a group that includes both genders. The masculine singular noun is made plural by adding an -es because it ends in a consonant. The unaccented singular o is changed to ó in the plural to maintain the proper stress.

15. **Answer: la francesa + el francés = los franceses**. Use the feminine singular definite article before the noun ending in -a and the masculine singular definite article before the noun ending in -es. The masculine plural definite article must be used to modify a noun that refers to a group that includes both genders. The masculine singular noun is made plural by adding an -es because it ends in a consonant. The accented é is replaced by e in the plural to maintain the proper stress.

16. **Answer: esa, ese, esos, esas**. Use forms of the demonstrative adjective *ese* because of the clue word, *ahí*. Use *esa* before the feminine singular *camisa* and *ese* before the masculine singular *chaleco* because they end appropriately. Use *esos* before the masculine plural *calcetines* (nouns ending in -n tend to be masculine). Use *esas* before the feminine plural *blusas*.

17. **Answer: estos, estas, esta, este**. Use forms of the demonstrative adjective *este* because of the clue word, *aquí*. Use *estos* before the masculine plural *guantes* (nouns ending in -e tend to be masculine). Use the feminine plural *estas* before the feminine plural *camisetas* and the feminine singular *esta* before the feminine singular *falda* because they end appropriately. Use *este* before the masculine singular *cinturón* (nouns ending in -n tend to be masculine).

18. **Answer: aquel, aquellos, aquellas, aquella**. Use forms of the demonstrative adjective *aquel* because of the clue word, *allá*. Use *aquel* before the masculine singular *impermeable* (nouns ending in -e tend to be masculine). Use the masculine plural *aquellos* before the masculine plural *suéteres* (nouns ending in -r tend to be masculine). Use the feminine plural *aquellas* before the feminine plural *chaquetas* and the feminine singular *aquella* before the feminine singular *corbata* because they end appropriately.

Supplemental Chapter Problems

Problems

In problems 1–10, express what is important by giving the correct definite article for each noun.

Lo esencial es . . .

1. ____ familia es importante.

2. ____ lealtad es una virtud importante.

3. ___ gustos son importantes.

4. ___ cortesía es importante.

5. ___ piedad es importante.

6. ___ amor es un sentimiento importante.

7. ___ pasiones son importantes.

8. ___ verdad es una virtud importante.

9. ___ valores son cosas importantes.

10. ___ generosidad es una virtud importante.

In problems 11–15, combine the two people in each pair to get the plural. Use the definite article before each noun and in your final answer.

Example: el niño + la niña = los niños

11. ___ dentista + ___ dentista = _____

12. ___ actor + ___ actriz = _____

13. ___ alemana + ___ alemán = _____

14 ___ portugués + ___ portuguesa = _____

15. ___ escultor + ___ escultora = _____

In problems 16–20, express what each person is reading by filling in the correct indefinite article.

16. Yo leo___ cuento.

17. Ella lee___ novela.

18. Nosotros leemos___ periódico.

19. Tú lees___ revistas.

20. Uds. leen___ poemas.

In problems 21–23, complete the sentences by filling in the correct demonstrative adjectives that refer to the furniture and appliances these people buy.

21. Yo compro ____ espejo, ____ almohadas, ____ estufa y ____ televisores allá.

22. Ella prefiere ____ lámpara, ____ horno, ____ sillones y ____ mesas ahí.

23. Él escoge ____ cuadros, ____ congelador, ____ pintura y ____ cortinas aquí.

Answers

1. La (gender of nouns, p. 55)

2. La (gender of nouns, p. 55)

3. Los (gender of nouns, p. 55; plural of nouns, p. 60)

4. La (gender of nouns, p. 55)

5. La (gender of nouns, p. 55)

6. El (gender of nouns, p. 55)

7. Las (gender of nouns, p. 55; plural of nouns, p. 60)

8. La (gender of nouns, p. 55)

9. Los (gender of nouns, p. 55; plural of nouns, p. 60)

10. La (gender of nouns, p. 55)

11. el dentista + la dentista = los dentistas (definite articles, p. 41, gender of nouns, p. 55; plural of nouns, p. 60)

12. el actor + la actriz = los actores (definite articles, p. 41, gender of nouns, p. 55; plural of nouns, p. 60)

13. la alemana + el alemán = los alemanes (definite articles, p. 41, gender of nouns, p. 55; plural of nouns, p. 60)

14. el portugués + la portuguesa = los portugueses (definite articles, p. 41, gender of nouns, p. 55; plural of nouns, p. 60)

15. el escultor + la escultora = los escultores (definite articles, p. 41, gender of nouns, p. 55; plural of nouns, p. 60)

16. un (indefinite articles, p. 47)

17. una (indefinite articles, p. 47)

18. un (indefinite articles, p. 47)

19. unas (indefinite articles, p. 47)

20. unos (indefinite articles, p. 47)

21. aquel, aquellas, aquella, aquellos (demonstrative adjectives, p. 51)

22. esa, ese, esos, esas (demonstrative adjectives, p. 51)

23. estos, este, esta, estas (demonstrative adjectives, p. 51)

Chapter 3
Possession

Possession shows that something or someone belongs to another person. In English, possession is often shown in writing by 's or s'. This option does not exist in Spanish because apostrophes are not used in the language.

Possession Using *De*

The preposition *de* (of) is used to express relationship and possession. If the sentence contains more than one noun, it is unnecessary to repeat *de* before each noun, although *de* + the definite article is used before each noun. The Spanish construction to demonstrate possession is the reverse of the standard English construction:

English	Reverse Order	Spanish
He's Esteban's father.	He's the father of Esteban.	Es el padre de Esteban.
He's Esteban and Roberto's father.	He's the father of Esteban and Roberto.	Es el padre de Esteban y Roberto.
They're Mr. Molina and Mrs. Ruiz's cars.	They are the cars of Mr. Molina and Mrs. Ruiz.	Son los coches del señor Molina y de la señora Ruiz.

If the possessor is referred to by a masculine singular noun, *de* contracts with the definite article *el* to form *del* (of the):

Es el padre del muchacho.   He's the boy's father.

To avoid repetition in a sentence, the noun being possessed may be replaced by its definite article + *de:*

Mi coche es más cómodo que el de mi esposo.	My car is more comfortable than my husband's.
Su casa y la de sus hermanas son grandes.	Her house and her sisters' are big.

¿De quién es? and *¿de quiénes son?* express "whose?" when referring to one or more than one person, respectively. Note that the verb agrees with the item possessed:

¿De quién es este paraguas?	Whose umbrella is this?
¿De quiénes son esos libros?	Whose books are those?
¿De quién son esos zapatos?	Whose shoes are those?
¿De quiénes es esa casa?	Whose house is that?

Example Problems

1. You found a wallet. Ask to whom it belongs.

    Answer: ¿De quién es esta cartera?

    1. Select *¿de quién?* to express "whose" because the wallet belongs to one person.

    2. Use the third person singular form of the verb *ser* (to be) to express "is."

    3. The word for "wallet" is *cartera*. Because the word ends in *-a*, it is feminine and singular.

    4. Choose the feminine singular demonstrative adjective that expresses "this" *(esta)* and place it before the noun.

2. Express that it belongs to Jose's mother.

    Answer: Es de la madre de José.

    1. Use the third person singular form of the verb *ser* (to be) to express "it is."

    2. Because there is no *'s* to express possession in Spanish, you must say that the wallet is "of the mother of José," despite the fact that this sounds quite awkward in English.

    3. Use the preposition *de* to express "of."

    4. Use the definite article *la* to express "the" before the feminine singular noun, *madre*.

    5. Use the preposition *de* to express "of" before *José*.

3. You see some cars parked in front of your house. Ask to whom they belong.

    Answer: ¿De quiénes son esos carros?

    1. Select *¿de quiénes?* to express "whose" because the cars belong to more than one person.

    2. Use the third person plural form of the verb *ser* (to be) to express "are."

    3. The word for "cars" is *carros*. Because the word ends in *-os*, it is masculine and plural.

    4. Choose the masculine plural demonstrative adjective that expresses "those" *(esos)* and place it before the noun.

Work Problems

1. You found two tickets in the airport. Ask to whom they belong.

2. No one answers you, so you give the tickets to an airline employee. Express how he would say that they are the passports of Miss Rueda and Mr. Padilla.

3. You found some money. Ask to whom it belongs.

4. Express that the money belongs to Ricardo.

5. Express that the money belongs to Ana's brother and sister.

6. You have found some important documents in a restaurant. Ask to whom they belong.

Worked Solutions

1. **¿De quiénes son estos boletos?**

   1. Select *¿de quiénes?* to express "whose" because the tickets belong to more than one person.

   2. Use the third person plural form of the verb *ser* (to be) to express "are."

   3. The word for "tickets" is *boletos*. Because the word ends in *-os*, it is masculine and plural.

   4. Choose the masculine plural demonstrative adjective that expresses "these" *(estos)* and place it before the noun.

2. **Son los boletos de la señorita Rueda y del señor Padilla.**

   1. Use the third person plural form of the verb *ser* (to be) to express "they are."

   2. Because there is no 's to express possession in Spanish, you must say that they are the tickets "of Miss Rueda and of Mr. Padilla," despite the fact that this sounds quite awkward in English.

   3. Use the preposition *de* to express "of."

   4. Use the definite article *la* to express "the" before the feminine singular noun, *señorita*. There is no contraction with the preposition *de* and the definite article *la*. Use *de la* to express "of" before the feminine singular title and name, *señorita Rueda*.

   5. Normally, you would use the definite article *el* to express "the" before the masculine singular noun, *señor*. In this case, however, the preposition *de* contracts with the masculine singular definite article to become *del*. Use the contraction *del* to express "of" before the title and name, *señor Padilla*.

   6. Use *y* to express "and" between the two names.

3. **¿De quién es este dinero?**

   1. Select *¿de quién?* to express "whose" because the money belongs to one person.

   2. Use the third person singular form of the verb *ser* (to be) to express "is."

   3. The word for "money" is *dinero*. Because the word ends in *-o*, it is masculine and singular.

   4. Choose the masculine singular demonstrative adjective that expresses "this" *(este)* and place it before the noun.

4. **Es de Ricardo.**

   1. Use the third person singular form of the verb *ser* (to be) to express "it is."

   2. Because there is no '*s* to express possession in Spanish, you must say that the money is "of Ricardo," despite the fact that this sounds quite awkward in English.

   3. Use the preposition *de* to express "of" before Ricardo.

5. **Es del hermano y de la hermana de Ana.**

   1. Use the third person singular form of the verb *ser* (to be) to express "it is."

   2. Since there is no '*s* to express possession in Spanish, you must say that the money is "of the brother and of the sister of Ana," despite the fact that this sounds quite awkward in English.

   3. Use the preposition *de* to express "of."

   4. Normally, you would use the definite article *el* to express "the" before the masculine singular noun, *hermano*. In this case, however, the preposition *de* contracts with the masculine singular definite article to become *del*. Use the contraction *del* to express "of the" before the noun, *hermano*.

   5. Use *y* to express "and" between the words for "brother" and "sister."

   6. Use the definite article *la* to express "the" before the feminine singular noun, *hermana*. There is no contraction with the preposition *de* and the definite article *la*. Use *de la* to express "of the" before the feminine singular noun, *hermana*.

   7. Use the preposition *de* to express "of" before *Ana*.

6. **¿De quién son estos documentos?**

   1. Select *¿de quién?* to express "whose" because the documents probably belong to one person.

   2. Use the third person plural form of the verb *ser* (to be) to express "are" because "documents" is plural.

   3. The word for "documents" is *documentos*. Because the word ends in *-os*, it is masculine and plural.

   4. Choose the masculine plural demonstrative adjective that expresses "these" *(estos)* and place it before the noun.

Possessive Adjectives

Possessive adjectives, like other Spanish adjectives, agree in number and gender with the nouns they modify (the item that is possessed) and not with the subject (the possessor).

Short Forms

The short forms of Spanish possessive adjectives are used only before the nouns they modify and must be used before each noun:

English	Before Masc. Nouns		Before Feminine Nouns	
	Singular	Plural	Singular	Plural
my	mi	mis	mi	mis
your (informal)	tu	tus	tu	tus
his, her, your (formal), its	su	sus	su	sus
our	nuestro	nuestros	nuestra	nuestras
your (informal)	vuestro	vuestros	vuestra	vuestras
their, your (formal)	su	sus	su	sus

Here are some examples in sentences:

Él está esperando a su madre.   He is waiting for his mother.

Él está esperando a su madre y a su hermano.   He is waiting for his mother and his brother.

Nuestro tío y nuestras primas vienen pronto.   Our uncle and our cousins are coming soon.

In addition, keep the following in mind about possessive adjectives:

❑ To avoid ambiguity with *su* (which can mean "his," "her," or "their"), you can replace the possessive adjective with the corresponding definite article and insert *de* + *Ud.* (or *Uds., él, ellos, ella, ellas*) after the noun:

She needs their advice. Necesita sus consejos.

OR (to avoid ambiguity)

Necesita los consejos de ellos (ellas).

❑ With parts of the body or clothing, when the possessor is clear, the possessive adjective is replaced with the definite article:

Él se lava la cara. (He washes his face.)

Abrí el abrigo. (I opened my coat.)

Example Problems

Problem 1: Express what different people take on vacation by filling in the possessive adjective that agrees with the subject.

Example: Él lleva <u>su</u> maleta.

1.   Yo llevo ____ vestidos nuevos.

2.   Tú llevas ____ despertador.

3.   Ellos llevan ____ diccionario.

4.   Nosotros llevamos ____ medicamentos.

5. Ella lleva ____ tarjetas de crédito.

6. Vosotros lleváis ____ cámaras.

Answer to Problem 1:

1. mis

2. tu

3. su

4. nuestros

5. sus

6. vuestras

Solution to Problem 1:

1. Although the subject is singular *(yo)*, the item possessed ends in *-os*, and is, therefore, masculine plural. Use the plural possessive adjective, *mis*.

2. The item possessed ends in *-or*; nouns with this ending tend to be masculine. This noun is also singular because it doesn't end in *-s*. Use the singular possessive adjective, *tu*.

3. Although the subject is plural *(ellos)*, the item possessed ends in *-o*, and is, therefore, masculine singular. Use the singular possessive adjective *su*, which can mean "his," "her," or "your."

4. The item possessed ends in *-os*, and is, therefore, masculine plural. Use the masculine plural possessive form, *nuestros*.

5. Although the subject is singular *(ella)*, the item possessed ends in *-as*, and is, therefore, feminine plural. Use the plural possessive adjective *sus*, which can mean "their" or "your."

6. The item possessed ends in *-as*, and is, therefore, feminine plural. Use the feminine plural possessive adjective *vuestras*.

Problem 2: You are in an office and hear someone asking people for personal information. Complete each sentence with the correct form of the possessive adjective:

Él necesita . . .

1. (their [formal]) ____ fecha de nacimiento.

2. (her) ____ números de teléfono.

3. (his) ____ dirección.

4. (your [informal plural]) ____ edades.

5. (our) ____ nacionalidad.

6. (your [formal singular]) ____ nombre.

Answer to Problem 2:

1. su

2. sus

3. su

4. vuestras

5. nuestra

6. su

Solution to Problem 2:

1. Although the item belongs to more than one person, the item possessed is singular. Use the possessive adjective *su* before the noun to express "their."

2. Although the item belongs to one person, the item possessed is plural. Use the possessive adjective *sus* before the noun to express "her."

3. The item possessed is singular. Use the possessive adjective *su* before the noun to express "his."

4. Nouns ending in *-dad* tend to be feminine. This noun, ending in *-es*, is also plural. The familiar plural possessive adjective *vuestras* is required.

5. Nouns ending in *-dad* tend to be feminine. The singular possessive adjective *nuestra* is required to express "our."

6. The item possessed is singular. The singular possessive adjective *su* is required to express "your."

Work Problems

Problem 1: Express what each person or group talks about by completing each sentence with the possessive adjective that agrees with the subject.

Example: Ud. habla de <u>su</u> familia.

1. Nosotros hablamos de _____ problemas.

2. Uds. hablan de _____ sueños.

3. Yo hablo con _____ hermanas.

4. Vosotras habláis de _____ ideas.

5. Tú hablas de _____ miedos.

6. Él habla de _____ discusiones.

Problem 2: The teacher is going to read aloud the work of some students. Express what he is going to read by supplying the correct form of the possessive adjective.

Él va a leer . . .

1. (your [informal plural]) _____ poemas.

2. (your [formal singular]) _____ resumen.

3. (our) _____ párrafos.

4. (her) _____ cuentos.

5. (their) _____ diario.

6. (his) _____ tareas.

Problem 3: It is cold outside. Tell your mother that you are putting on certain articles of clothing.

Me pongo . . .

1. _____ guantes.

2. _____ sombrero.

3. _____ bufanda.

4. _____ botas.

5. _____ chaleco.

Worked Solutions

Problem 1

1. **nuestros**   Although *problema* ends in an -*a*, some words with an -*a* ending (including this one) are masculine. Because the noun also ends in -*s*, it is plural. The item possessed is masculine and plural.

2. **sus**   The item possessed is plural. Use the formal plural possessive adjective to express "your."

3. **mis**   The item possessed is plural. Use the plural possessive adjective to express "my."

4. **vuestras**   The -*as* ending on the item possessed indicates that it is feminine plural. Use the informal feminine plural form to express "your."

5. **tus**   The item possessed is plural. Use the informal plural possessive adjective to express "your."

6. **sus**   The item possessed is plural. Use the plural possessive adjective to express "his."

Problem 2

1. **vuestros**   Nouns ending in -a tend to be feminine, but *poema* is a noun that doesn't follow this rule and, thus, is masculine. This noun, ending in -*as,* is also plural. The familiar plural possessive adjective is required.

2. **su**   Although "your" may be singular or plural, the item possessed is singular. The singular possessive adjective is required to express "your."

3. **nuestros**   Nouns ending in -*os* are masculine plural. Use the masculine plural possessive adjective to express "our."

4. **sus**   Although the item belongs to one person, the item possessed is plural. Use the possessive adjective *sus* before the noun to express "her."

5. **su**   Although the item belongs to more than one person, the item possessed is singular. Use the singular possessive adjective before the noun to express "their."

6. **sus**   Although the item belongs to one person, the item possessed is plural. Use the plural possessive adjective before the noun to express "his."

Problem 3

For each question, because the possessor is clear, use the definite article rather than the possessive article, which would be redundant.

1. **los**   Nouns ending in -*e* tend to be masculine. This noun also ends in -*s* and, thus, is plural. The masculine plural definite article is required.

2. **el**   The noun is masculine singular. The masculine singular definite article is required.

3. **la**   The noun is feminine singular. The feminine singular definite article is required.

4. **las**   The -*as* ending indicates that the noun is feminine plural. The feminine plural definite article is required.

5. **el**   The noun is masculine singular. The masculine singular definite article is required.

Long Forms

The long forms of Spanish possessive adjectives are used only after the nouns they modify:

	Used After Masculine Nouns		Used After Feminine Nouns	
English	**Singular**	**Plural**	**Singular**	**Plural**
my	mío	míos	mía	mías
your (informal)	tuyo	tuyos	tuya	tuyas
his, her, your (formal), its	suyo	suyos	suya	suyas
our	nuestro	nuestros	nuestra	nuestras
your (informal)	vuestro	vuestros	vuestra	vuestras
their, your (formal)	suyo	suyos	suya	suyas

Here are some examples in sentences:

El hermano mío se llama Jorge.	My brother's name is Jorge.
El tío y la tía suyos son españoles.	His (Her, Their, Your [formal]) aunt and uncle are Spanish.
Unas amigas tuyas llamaron.	Some of your friends called.

When using these adjectives, keep in mind that, to avoid ambiguity, you may replace the possessive adjective with the corresponding definite article and insert *de + Ud.* (or *Uds., él, ellos, ella, ellas*) after the noun:

Her father is a doctor.	El padre suyo es médico.
	OR (to avoid ambiguity)
	El padre de ella es médico.

Example Problems

Problem 1: Express that each classroom item belongs to the person in another way.

> Example: Ella tiene su bolígrafo.
>
> Ella tiene el bolígrafo suyo.

1. Yo tengo mi calculadora.

2. Él tiene sus reglas.

3. Nosotros tenemos nuestro diccionario.

4. Uds. tienen sus libros.

5. Vosotros tenéis vuestras gomas.

6. Tú tienes tus lápices.

Answer to Problem 1:

1. Yo tengo la calculadora mía.

2. Él tiene las reglas suyas.

3. Nosotros tenemos el diccionario nuestro.

4. Uds. tienen los libros suyos.

5. Vosotros tenéis las gomas vuestras.

6. Tú tienes los lápices tuyos.

Solution to Problem 1:

1. The item possessed is feminine singular. Use the feminine singular long form of the possessive adjective after the noun possessed to express "my": *mía*.

2. The item possessed is feminine plural. Use the feminine plural long form of the possessive adjective after the noun possessed to express "his": *suyas*.

3. The item possessed is masculine singular. Use the masculine singular long form of the possessive adjective after the noun possessed to express "our": *nuestro*.

4. The item possessed is masculine plural. Use the masculine plural long form of the possessive adjective after the noun possessed to express "your": *suyos*.

5. The item possessed is feminine plural. Use the familiar feminine plural long form of the possessive adjective after the noun possessed to express "your": *vuestras*.

6. Although nouns ending in *-z* tend to be feminine, *lápiz* is an exception. The *-es* ending indicates that the noun is plural. Use the masculine plural long form of the possessive adjective after the noun possessed to express "your": *tuyos*.

Problem 2: Express the opinions of these people in another way.

Example: Su coche es muy deportivo.
El coche suyo es muy deportivo.

1. Mi profesor es simpático.

2. Su casa es bonita.

3. Nuestras tareas son difíciles.

Answer to Problem 2:

1. El profesor mío es simpático.

2. La casa suya es bonita.

3. Las tareas nuestras son difíciles.

Solution to Problem 2:

The long form of the possessive adjective is used after each noun.

1. Because the noun is masculine singular, use the masculine singular long form after the noun. To do so, delete the short form and replace it with the masculine singular definite article. Place the possessive adjective that corresponds to "my" after the noun. Then complete the sentence.

2. Because the noun is feminine singular, use the feminine singular long form after the noun. To do so, delete the short form and replace it with the feminine singular definite article. Place the possessive adjective that corresponds to "her," "his," or "your" (singular form) after the noun. Then complete the sentence.

3. Because the noun is feminine plural, use the feminine plural long form after the noun. To do so, delete the short form and replace it with the feminine plural definite article. Place the possessive adjective that corresponds to "our" after the noun. Then complete the sentence.

Work Problems

Problem 1: Express that each person or group prefers the item that he/she/it possesses.

> Example: Ella prefiere su broche.
>   Ella prefiere el broche suyo.

1. Yo prefiero mis pulseras.

2. Vosotras preferís vuestra cadena.

3. Tú prefieres tu reloj.

4. Ella prefiere su anillo.

Problem 2: Express the opinions of these people in another way.

> Example: Sus ojos son bonitos.
>   Los ojos suyos son bonitos.

1. Mi pelo es corto.

2. Sus manos son finas.

3. Vuestras narices son grandes.

4. Tus labios son rojos.

Worked Solutions

Problem 1

1. **Yo prefiero las pulseras mías.**   The item possessed is feminine plural. Use the feminine plural long form of the possessive adjective after the noun possessed to express "my."

2. **Vosotras preferís la cadena vuestra.**   The item possessed is feminine singular. Use the feminine singular long form of the possessive adjective after the noun possessed to express "your."

3. **Tú prefieres el reloj tuyo.**   The item possessed is masculine singular. (*Reloj* is a noun that must be memorized.) Use the masculine singular long form of the possessive adjective after the noun possessed to express "your."

4. **Ella prefiere el anillo suyo.**   The item possessed is masculine singular. Use the masculine singular long form of the possessive adjective after the noun possessed to express "her."

Problem 2

1. **El pelo mío es corto.**   Because the noun is masculine singular, use the masculine singular long form after the noun. To do so, delete the short form and replace it with the masculine singular definite article. Place the possessive adjective that corresponds to "my" after the noun. Then complete the sentence.

2. **Las manos suyas son finas.**   Although nouns ending in-*o* tend to be masculine, *mano* is an exception. Because the noun is feminine plural, use the feminine plural long form after the noun. To do so, delete the short form and replace it with the feminine plural definite article. Place the possessive adjective that corresponds to "her," "his," or "your" after the noun. Then complete the sentence.

3. **Las narices vuestras son grandes.**   Because the noun is feminine plural, use the feminine plural long form after the noun. To do so, delete the short form and replace it with the feminine plural definite article. Place the possessive adjective that corresponds to "your" after the noun. Then complete the sentence.

4. **Los labios tuyos son rojos.**   Because the noun is masculine plural, use the masculine plural long form after the noun. To do so, delete the short form and replace it with the masculine plural definite article. Place the possessive adjective that corresponds to "your" after the noun. Then complete the sentence.

Possessive Pronouns

A possessive pronoun replaces a possessive adjective and the noun it modifies. It must agree in number and gender with the noun being possessed, not with the possessor. A possessive pronoun is formed by selecting the definite article corresponding to the number and gender of the noun being possessed, then adding the long form of the corresponding possessive adjective.

	Replaces Masculine Nouns		Replaces Feminine Nouns	
English	*Singular*	*Plural*	*Singular*	*Plural*
mine	el mío	los míos	la mía	las mías
yours (informal)	el tuyo	los tuyos	la tuya	las tuyas
his/hers/yours (formal)	el suyo	los suyos	la suya	las suyas
ours	el nuestro	los nuestros	la nuestra	las nuestras
yours (informal)	el vuestro	los vuestros	la vuestra	las vuestras
theirs/yours (formal)	el suyo	los suyos	la suya	las suyas

Here is an example:

Mi libro está en casa.   My book is at home.

¿Dónde está el tuyo?   Where is yours?

Keep the following in mind about possessive pronouns:

❑ After the verb *ser* (to be), the definite article is generally omitted:

Esta casa es mía. (This house is mine.)

❑ To avoid ambiguity, you may replace *el suyo* (or *la suya, los suyos, las suyas*) with the corresponding definite article and insert *de* + *usted* (or *ustedes, él, ellos, ella, ellas*) after the noun:

I need your address and hers.   Necesito su dirección y la suya.

                                          OR (to avoid ambiguity)

                                          Necesito su dirección y la de ella.

Example Problems

Problem 1: People have some lost things. Ask where they are.

     Examples: (él/libros) ¿Dónde están los suyos?

                  (él/llave)   ¿Dónde está la suya?

1. (ella/gafas de sol)

2. (tú/teléfono celular)

3. (yo/tarjeta de crédito)

4. (nosotros/abrigos)

Answer to Problem 1:

1. ¿Dónde están las suyas?

2. ¿Dónde está el tuyo?

3. ¿Dónde está la mía?

4. ¿Dónde están los nuestros?

Solution to Problem 1:

1. The item possessed is feminine plural. Be sure to use the plural verb form *están*. Use the feminine plural definite article *las*. Use the feminine plural long form of the possessive adjective after the noun possessed to express "her": *suyas*.

2. The item possessed is masculine singular. Be sure to use the singular verb form *está*. Use the masculine singular definite article *el*. Use the masculine singular long form of the possessive adjective after the noun possessed to express "your": *tuyo*.

3. The item possessed is feminine singular. Be sure to use the singular verb form *está*. Use the feminine singular definite article *la*. Use the feminine singular long form of the possessive adjective after the noun possessed to express "mine": *mía*.

4. The item possessed is masculine plural. Be sure to use the plural verb form *están*. Use the masculine plural definite article *los*. Use the masculine plural long form of the possessive adjective after the noun possessed to express "our": *nuestros*.

Problem 2: Say that the things belong to the people.

Example: (Ud./casa) Esta casa es suya.

1. (ella/coche)

2. (tú/joyería)

3. (nosotros/cosas)

4. (yo/vestidos)

Answer to Problem 2:

1. Este coche es suyo.

2. Esta joyería es tuya.

3. Estas cosas son nuestras.

4. Estos vestidos son míos.

Solution to Problem 2:

After the verb *ser*, no definite article is needed.

1. Nouns that end in *-e* tend to be masculine. Although *ella* is feminine, the item "she" possesses is masculine singular. Use the masculine singular demonstrative adjective before the noun, use the third person singular of the verb *ser*, and use the masculine singular possessive pronoun after the verb.

2. The gender of *tú* is indeterminate, but this is insignificant because the item possessed is feminine singular. Use the feminine singular demonstrative adjective before the noun, use the third person singular of the verb *ser*, and use the feminine singular possessive pronoun after the verb.

3. Although *nosotros* indicates a masculine plural subject, the item possessed is feminine plural. Use the feminine plural demonstrative adjective before the noun, use the third person plural of the verb *ser*, and use the feminine plural possessive pronoun after the verb.

4. The gender of *yo* is indeterminate, but this is insignificant because the item possessed is masculine plural. Use the masculine plural demonstrative adjective before the noun, use the third person plural of the verb *ser*, and use the masculine plural possessive pronoun after the verb.

Work Problems

Problem 1: You are sleeping at someone else's house. Ask if you can have things that belong to you or to other people.

Example: (ella/espejo) ¿Puedes darme el suyo?

1. (él/aspirinas)

2. (yo/peine)

3. (nosotros/pasta dentrifica)

4. (tú/pinzas)

Problem 2: Say that these pets belong to the person indicated.

   Example: (Ud./hámster) Este hámster es suyo.

1. (ella/gato)

2. (vosotros/serpientes)

3. (yo/perro)

4. (tú/caballos)

Worked Solutions
Problem 1

1. **¿Puedes darme las suyas?**   The item possessed is feminine plural. Use the feminine plural definite article *las*. Use the feminine plural long form of the possessive adjective after the noun possessed to express "his."

2. **¿Puedes darme el mío?**   The item possessed is masculine singular. Use the masculine singular definite article *el*. Use the masculine singular long form of the possessive adjective after the noun possessed to express "my."

3. **¿Puedes darme la nuestra?**   The item possessed is feminine singular. Use the feminine singular definite article *la*. Use the feminine singular long form of the possessive adjective after the noun possessed to express "our."

4. **¿Puedes darme las tuyas?**   The item possessed is feminine plural. Use the feminine plural definite article *las*. Use the feminine plural long form of the possessive adjective after the noun possessed to express "your."

Problem 2

After the verb *ser*, no definite article is needed.

1. **Este gato es suyo.**   Although *ella* is feminine, the item "she" possesses is masculine singular. Use the masculine singular demonstrative adjective before the noun, use the third person singular form of the verb *ser*, and use the masculine singular possessive pronoun after the verb.

2. **Estas serpientes son vuestras.**   Although nouns that end in -*e* tend to be masculine, *serpiente* is an exception. And although *vosotros* is masculine plural, the item possessed is feminine plural. Use the feminine plural demonstrative adjective before the noun, use the third person plural form of the verb *ser*, and use the feminine familiar plural possessive pronoun after the verb.

3. **Este perro es mío.**   The gender of *yo* is indeterminate, but that is insignificant because the item possessed is masculine singular. Use the masculine singular demonstrative adjective before the noun, use the third person singular form of the verb *ser,* and use the masculine singular possessive pronoun after the verb.

4. **Estos caballos son tuyos.**   The gender of *tú* is indeterminate, but that is insignificant because the item possessed is masculine plural. Use the masculine plural demonstrative adjective before the noun, use the third person plural form of the verb *ser,* and use the masculine familiar plural possessive pronoun after the verb.

Chapter Problems and Solutions

Problems

In problems 1–6, express what each person does by filling in the correct form of the possessive adjective.

1. Yo llevo ___ traje nuevo.

2. Ellas les dan ___ recuerdos.

3. Él vende ___ casa.

4. Nosotros leemos ___ poemas.

5. Tú comes ___ helado.

6. Vosotros compráis ___ vestidos.

In problems 7–11, answer each question in two ways.

Example: Él tiene un apartamento grande. Va a pintarlo. ¿Qué va a pintar?
su apartamento/el apartamento suyo

7. Sarita tiene discos compactos. Ella va a escucharlos. ¿Qué va a escuchar?

8. Esteban y Paco tienen una computadora. Van a utilizarla. ¿Qué van a utilizar?

9. Nosotros tenemos composiciones por escribir. Vamos a escribirlas juntas. ¿Qué vamos a escribir?

10. Yo tengo un amigo. Voy a darle mi número de teléfono. ¿Qué voy a darle?

11. Tú tienes muchas tareas. Tú tienes que hacerlas. ¿Qué tienes que hacer?

Answers and Solutions

1. **Answer: mi.** *Traje* is masculine singular. Use the singular possessive adjective to express "my."

2. **Answer: sus.** *Recuerdos* is masculine plural. Use the plural possessive adjective to express "their."

3. **Answer: su.** *Casa* is feminine singular. Use the singular possessive adjective to express "his."

4. **Answer: nuestros.** Although *poemas* ends in *-as*, it is masculine. Use the masculine plural possessive adjective to express "our."

5. **Answer: tu.** *Helado* is masculine singular. Use the singular possessive adjective to express "your."

6. **Answer: vuestros.** *Vestidos* is masculine plural. Use the masculine familiar plural possessive adjective to express "your."

7. **Answer: sus discos compactos/los discos compactos suyos.** *Discos* is a masculine plural noun. Use the masculine plural possessive adjective before the noun or use the masculine plural definite article before the noun with the masculine plural possessive pronoun after the noun to express "her."

8. **Answer: su computadora/la computadora suya.** *Computadora* is a feminine singular noun. Use the feminine singular possessive adjective before the noun or use the feminine singular definite article before the noun with the feminine singular possessive pronoun after the noun to express "their."

9. **Answer: nuestras composiciones/las composiciones nuestras.** Nouns that end in *-ión* tend to be feminine. *Composiciones* is a feminine plural noun. Use the feminine plural possessive adjective before the noun or use the feminine plural definite article before the noun with the feminine plural possessive pronoun after the noun to express "our."

10. **Answer: mi número de teléfono/el número de teléfono mío.** *Número* is a masculine singular noun. Use the masculine singular possessive adjective before the noun or use the masculine singular definite article before the noun with the masculine singular possessive pronoun after the noun to express "my."

11. **Answer: tus tareas/las tareas tuyas.** *Tareas* is a feminine plural noun. Use the feminine plural possessive adjective before the noun or use the feminine plural definite article before the noun with the feminine plural possessive pronoun after the noun to express "your."

Supplemental Chapter Problems

Problems

In problems 1–6, express what each person does by filling in the correct form of the possessive adjective.

1. Ellos estudian _____ lecciones.

2. Yo preparo ___ comida.

3. Tú escribes ___ tareas.

4. Nosotros escuchamos a _____ profesoras.

5. Ud. conduce ___ carro.

6. Vosotros perdéis _____ libros.

In problems 7–11, answer each question in two ways.

> Example: Ella tiene una bicicleta. Ella va a venderla. ¿Qué va a vender?
>
>   su bicicleta/la bicicleta suya

7. Pedro tiene una casa grande. Tiene que limpiarla. ¿Qué tiene que limpiar?

8. Yo tengo un libro interesante. Voy a leerlo. ¿Qué voy a leer?

9. Anita y Nina tienen muchos vestidos sucios. Tienen que lavarlos. ¿Qué tienen que lavar?

10. Tú tienes pulseras elegantes. Tú tienes que ponértelas. ¿Qué tienes que ponerte?

11. Nosotros tenemos pasteles deliciosos. Vamos a comerlos. ¿Qué vamos a comer?

In problems 12–16, use the subject pronouns as clues to fill in the missing words showing possession.

> Example: (él) ____ hermano tiene pelo rubio. (Julia) ____ tiene pelo negro. (nosotros) ____ tiene pelo moreno.
>
>   <u>Su</u> hermano tiene pelo rubio. <u>El de Julia</u> tiene pelo negro. <u>El nuestro</u> tiene pelo castaño.

12. (tú) ____ clase favorita es el español. (tus primos) ____ es la historia. (él) ____ es el arte.

13. (yo) ____ ojos son pardos. (Ramón) ____ son verdes. (vosotros) ____ son negros.

14. (nosotros) ____ plato favorito es la carne. (Blanca y Josefa) ____ es el pollo. (Uds.) ____ es el pescado.

15. (ella) ____ hermanos son guapos. (esos muchachos) ____ son curiosos. (tú) ____ son cómicos.

16. (Ud.) ____ familia es española. (Clara y Enrique) ____ es italiana. (yo) ____ es francesa.

Answers

1. sus (possessive adjectives, p. 72)

2. mi (possessive adjectives, p. 72)

3. tus (possessive adjectives, p. 72)

4. nuestras (possessive adjectives, p. 72)

5. su (possessive adjectives, p. 72)

6. vuestros (possessive adjectives, p. 72)

7. su casa/la casa suya (possessive adjectives, p. 72)

8. mi libro/el libro mío (possessive adjectives, p. 72)

9. sus vestidos/los vestidos suyos (possessive adjectives, p. 72)

10. tus pulseras/las pulseras tuyas (possessive adjectives, p. 72)

11. nuestros pasteles/los pasteles nuestros (possessive adjectives, p. 72)

12. Tu; La de tus primos; La suya (possessive adjectives, p. 72)

13. Mis; Los de Ramón; Los vuestros (possessive adjectives, p. 72)

14. Nuestro; El de Blanca y Josefa; El suyo (possessive adjectives, p. 72)

15. Sus; Los de esos muchachos; Los tuyos (possessive adjectives, p. 72)

16. Su; La de Clara y Enrique; La mía (possessive adjectives, p. 72)

Chapter 4

Subject Pronouns, the Present Tense, and Verbal Distinctions

The function of subject pronouns is to express clarity, emphasis, and politeness. Understanding which subject pronoun is needed, whether or not you choose to use it, enables you to correctly conjugate a verb in any of the different Spanish tenses because the verb must agree with the subject.

Subject Pronouns

A subject pronoun replaces a subject noun (the noun performing the action of the verb). In Spanish, subject pronouns may be omitted (*Ud.* and *Uds.* are generally not omitted) because the verb ending indicates who the subject is. Just as in English, Spanish subject pronouns are given a person and a number (singular or plural), as the following table shows:

	Singular		*Plural*	
1st person	yo	I	nosotros	we
2nd person	tú	you	vosotros	you
3rd person	Ud.	you	Uds.	you
	él	he	ellos	they
	ella	she	ellas	they

Unlike the English pronoun "I," *yo* is capitalized only when it begins a sentence. This is also true for all other Spanish subject pronouns.

Here are some example sentences that use subject pronouns:

Yo estudio español.	I study Spanish.
José y yo estudiamos juntos.	José and I study together.
Yo sé que él viene.	I know that he is coming.

Tú and *Ud.*

Tú is used to address one friend, relative, child, or pet and is the informal singular form of "you."

Ud. is used to show respect to an older person or when speaking to a stranger or someone you do not know well. *Ud.* is the formal singular form of "you."

¿Dónde vives tú?	Where do you live?
¿Dónde vive Ud.?	Where do you live?

Vosotros (Vosotras) and *Uds.*

Vosotros and *vosotras* are used primarily in Spain to address more than one friend, relative, child, or pet and are the informal plural forms of "you." *Vosotros* is used when speaking to a group of males or to a combined group of males and females. *Vosotras* is only used when speaking to a group of females.

Uds. is used throughout the Spanish-speaking world to show respect to more than one older person or when speaking to strangers or people you do not know well. *Uds.* is the formal plural form of "you" and replaces *vosotros (vosotras)* in Latin America.

¿Dónde vivís vosotros?	Where do you live?
¿Dónde viven Uds.?	Where do you live?

Él and *Ella*

Él (he, it) and *ella* (she, it) may refer to a person or to a thing.

El hombre llega.	The man arrives.	El paquete llega.	The package arrives.
Él llega.	He arrives.	Él llega.	It arrives.
La mujer viene.	The woman is coming.	La carta viene.	The letter is coming.
Ella viene.	She is coming.	Ella viene.	It is coming.

Ellos and *Ellas*

Ellos refers to more than one male or to a combined group of males and females, despite the number of each gender present. *Ellas* refers only to a group of females.

Paco y Julio salen.	Paco and Julio go out.
Ellos salen.	They go out.
Ana y María salen.	Ann and Maria go out.
Ellas salen.	They go out.
Paco y Ana salen.	Paco and Ana go out.
Ellos salen.	They go out.

Nosotros and *Nosotras*

Nosotros refers to more than one male or a combined group of males and females, despite the number of each gender present. *Nosotras* refers only to a group of females.

Nosotros hablamos español.   We speak Spanish.

Nosotras hablamos español.   We speak Spanish.

Example Problem

Indicate what pronouns you would use to speak about the following people.

1. yourself

2. Pepe and yourself

3. two friends (one male and one female)

4. you (a person you don't know)

5. Lucinda

Answers:

1. yo

2. nosotros

3. ellos

4. Ud.

5. ella

Solutions:

1. Use the pronoun *yo* to express "I."

2. Whenever you are speaking about yourself and another person, you must use the pronoun *nosotros* to express "we."

3. Whenever you are speaking about a group of people and at least one person in the group is a male, you must use the masculine plural pronoun *ellos* to express "they."

4. Use the pronoun *Ud.* to express "you" when speaking about a person you don't know well and to whom you must be polite.

5. Use the pronoun *ella* to express "she."

Work Problems

Indicate the pronoun you would use to answer questions about the following people.

1. Ud.

2. Nilda y tú

3. María

4. los muchachos

5. Jorge y yo

6. yo

7. vosotras

8. Tomás y Carolina

Worked Solutions

1. **yo**   If a question asks about *Ud.* (you), you must answer about yourself.

2. **nosotros**   If a question asks about someone else and includes you, you must answer about yourselves to express "we."

3. **ella**   If a question asks about one single female, you must answer about her.

4. **ellos**   If a question asks about more than one male, you must answer about them.

5. **Uds.**   If a question asks about someone else and includes the speaker, you must answer about them by expressing "you."

6. **tú** or **Ud.**   If a question asks about the speaker, you must answer about that person by using *tú* to be familiar or by using *Ud.* to be polite.

7. **nosotras**   If a question asks about the feminine plural *vosotras* (you), you must answer using the feminine plural to express "we."

8. **ellos**   If a question asks about a male and a female, the male pronoun dominates when you must answer about them.

The Present Tense

The Present Tense of Regular Verbs

In Spanish, regular verbs are grouped into three main families (*-ar, -er,* and *-ir*), because these are their endings in the infinitive form. Each regular verb within its respective family follows the same rules of conjugation. Memorize the pattern for one family, and you will know the pattern for all the verbs within that family. A list of regular verbs can be found at the back of the book. To form the present tense of *-ar, -er,* and *-ir* verbs, drop the infinitive ending and add the endings for the subject pronouns, as indicated:

Subject	-ar Verbs	-er Verbs	-ir Verbs
	hablar (to speak)	comer (to eat)	vivir (to live)
Yo	-o (hablo)	-o (como)	-o (vivo)
Tú	-as (hablas)	-es (comes)	-es (vives)
Él	-a (habla)	-e (come)	-e (vive)
Ella	-a (habla)	-e (come)	-e (vive)
Ud.	-a (habla)	-e (come)	-e (vive)
Nosotros	-amos (hablamos)	-emos (comemos)	-imos (vivimos)
Vosotros	-áis (habláis)	-éis (coméis)	-ís (vivís)
Ellos	-an (hablan)	-en (comen)	-en (viven)
Ellas	-an (hablan)	-en (comen)	-en (viven)
Uds.	-an (hablan)	-en (comen)	-en (viven)

Example Problems

Using the present tense, express what each person does in his or her spare time.

Example: (cantar) Nosotros <u>cantamos</u>.

1 (leer)

Ellas _____ libros, nosotras _____ periódicos, Ud. _____ revistas, yo _____ obras de teatro, vosotros _____ novelas y tú _____ libros de comics.

Answer: leen, leemos, lee, leo, leéis, lees

To conjugate regular -er verbs, drop the -er ending, and do the following:

1. For *ellas,* add -en as the ending.

2. For *nosotras* add -emos as the ending.

3. For *Ud.,* add -e as the ending.

4. For *yo,* add -o as the ending.

5. For *vosotros,* add -éis as the ending.

6. For *tú,* add -es the ending.

2. (escribir)

Wigberto _____ cartas, vosotras _____ tarjetas postales, yo _____ poemas, Uds. _____ cuentos, tú _____ misterios y nosotros _____ artículos científicos.

Answer: escribe, escribís, escribo, escriben, escribes, escribimos

To conjugate regular -ir verbs, drop the -ir ending, and do the following:

1. For the masculine name Wigberto (él), add -e as the ending.

2. For vosotras, add -ís as the ending.

3. For yo, add -o as the ending.

4. For ellas, add -en as the ending.

5. For tú, add -es as the ending.

6. For nosotras, add -imos as the ending.

Work Problems

Complete the sentences with the correct form of the verb to express what each person does to succeed.

1. (trabajar) Yo _____ mucho.

2. (responder) Tú _____ en clase.

3. (insistir) Vosotros _____ en tener éxito.

4. (aprender) Ella _____ los modismos.

5. (estudiar) Ellos _____ todas las noches.

6. (recibir) Nosotros _____ buenas notas.

7. (comer) Yo _____ en restaurantes españoles.

8. (decidir) Vosotros _____ practicar.

9. (escuchar) Tú _____ los programas españoles.

10. (ayudar) Nosotros _____ a nuestros amigos.

11. (aprender) Él _____ la gramática.

12. (asistir) Uds. _____ a todas sus clases.

Worked Solutions

1. **trabajo**   To conjugate regular -ar verbs, drop the -ar ending, and add -o as the ending.

2. **respondes**   To conjugate regular -er verbs, drop the -er ending, and add -es as the ending.

3. **insistís**   To conjugate regular -ir verbs, drop the -ir ending, and add -ís as the ending.

4. **aprende**   To conjugate regular -er verbs, drop the -er ending, and add -e as the ending.

5. **estudian**   To conjugate regular *-ar* verbs, drop the *-ar* ending, and add *-an* as the ending.

6. **recibimos**   To conjugate regular *-ir* verbs, drop the *-ir* ending, and add *-imos* as the ending.

7. **como**   To conjugate regular *-er* verbs, drop the *-er* ending, and add *-o* as the ending.

8. **decidís**   To conjugate regular *-ir* verbs, drop the *-ir* ending, and add *-ís* as the ending.

9. **escuchas**   To conjugate regular *-ar* verbs, drop the *-ar* ending, and add *-as* as the ending.

10. **ayudamos**   To conjugate regular *-ar* verbs, drop the *-ar* ending, and add *-amos* as the ending.

11. **aprende**   To conjugate regular *-er* verbs, drop the *-er* ending, and add *-e* as the ending.

12. **asisten**   To conjugate regular *-ir* verbs, drop the *-ir* ending, and add *-en* as the ending.

The Present Tense of Spelling-Change Verbs

Some Spanish verbs undergo spelling changes in order to preserve the original sound of the verb once a new ending is added. In the present tense, the following verbs, the complete conjugations of which can be found in the Appendix, undergo the spelling changes listed:

Ending	Change	When
vowel + *cer/-cir*	$c \rightarrow zc$	before *o* or *a*
consonant + *cer/-cir*	$c \rightarrow z$	before *o* or *a*
-ger/-gir	$g \rightarrow j$	before *o* or *a*
-guir	$gu \rightarrow g$	before *o* or *a*

In the present tense, verbs that fit into this category will change only in the *yo* form; all other forms will be followed by an ending starting with *e* or *i*:

conco**cer** (to know)	yo cono**zc**o
condu**cir** (to drive)	yo condu**zc**o
conven**cer** (to convince)	yo conven**z**o
espar**cir** (to spread out)	yo espar**z**o
esco**ger** (to choose)	yo esco**j**o
diri**gir** (to direct)	yo diri**j**o
distin**guir** (to distinguish)	yo distin**g**o

Example Problems

Express what each subject does.

>   Example: (coger) Él siempre <u>coge</u> el periódico.

1. (conducir)

    Ellos _____ bien, yo _____ mal y nosotros _____ rápidamente.

    Answer: conducen, conduzco, conducimos

To conjugate -cir verbs, drop the -ir ending and do the following: For *ellos*, add -en as the ending; for *yo*, change the c to zc and then add -o as the ending; for *nosotros*, add -imos as the ending.

2. (ejercer)

Tú _____ la profesión de entrenador personal, vosotros _____ la profesión de programador y yo _____ la profesión de investigador.

Answer: ejerces, ejercéis, ejerzo

To conjugate -cer verbs, drop the -er ending, and do the following: For *tú*, add -es as the ending; for *vosotros*, add -éis as the ending; for *yo*, change the c to z and add -o as the ending.

3. (dirgir)

Yo _____ una orquesta, ella _____ una compañía de actores y Uds. _____ una tragedia teatral.

Answer: dirijo, dirige, dirigen

To conjugate -gir verbs, drop the -ir ending, and do the following: For *yo*, change the g to j and add -o as the ending; for *ella*, add -e as the ending; for *Uds.* add -en as the ending.

Work Problems

You are bragging about what you can do and your brother can't. Fill in the correct form of the verbs.

1. (merecer) Yo _____ el trofeo y él no lo _____.

2. (escoger) Yo _____ la respuesta correcta y él no la _____.

3. (vencer) Yo _____ a todos mis enemigos y él no _____ a los suyos.

4. (dirigir) Yo _____ las obras de teatro y él no las _____.

5. (distinguir) Yo _____ los sabores y él no los _____.

6. (conocer) Yo _____ a todo el mundo y él no _____ a nadie.

Worked Solutions

1. **merezco, merece**   To conjugate -cer verbs, drop the -er ending. For *yo*, change the c to zc (because -cer is preceded by a vowel) and add -o as the ending; for *él*, add -e as the ending.

2. **escojo, escoge**   To conjugate -ger verbs, drop the -er ending. For *yo*, change the g to j and add -o as the ending; for *él*, add -e as the ending.

3. **venzo, vence**   To conjugate *-cer* verbs, drop the *-er* ending. For *yo*, change the *c* to *z* (because *-cer* is preceded by a consonant) and add *-o* as the ending; for *él*, add *-e* as the ending.

4. **dirijo, dirige**   To conjugate *-gir* verbs, drop the *-ir* ending. For *yo*, change the *g* to *j* and add *-o* as the ending; for *él* add *-e* as the ending.

5. **distingo, distingue**   To conjugate *-guir* verbs, drop the *-ir* ending. For *yo*, change the *gu* to *g* and add *-o* as the ending; for *él*, add *-e* as the ending.

6. **conozco, conoce**   To conjugate *-cer* verbs, drop the *-er* ending. For *yo*, change the *c* to *zc* (because *-cer* is preceded by a vowel) and add *-o* as the ending; for *él*, add *-e* as the ending.

The Present Tense of Stem-Changing Verbs

In the present tense, all changes occur in the *yo, tú, él (ella, Ud.)*, and *ellos (ellas, Uds.)* forms. The *nosotros* and *vosotros* forms are conjugated regularly. Some present tense verbs require both a spelling change and a stem change.

In the present tense, the following changes occur:

Infinitive Endings	Stem Vowel Change	When
-ar/-er	*e → ie*	all forms except nosotros and vosotros
	o → ue	
-ir	*e → ie*	all forms except nosotros and vosotros
	o → ue	
	e → i	
some *-iar* verbs	*i → í*	all forms except nosotros and vosotros
-uar verbs	*u → ú*	all forms except nosotros and vosotros
-uir (but not *-guir*)	add *y* after *u*	all forms except nosotros and vosotros

For example:

pensar (to think)	yo pienso	nosotros pensamos
querer (to want)	yo quiero	nosotros queremos
almorzar (to eat lunch)	yo almuerzo	nosotros almorzamos
volver (to return)	yo vuelvo	nosotros volvemos
preferir (to prefer)	yo prefiero	nosotros preferimos
dormir (to sleep)	yo duermo	nosotros dormimos
pedir (to ask)	yo pido	nosotros pedimos
enviar (to send)	yo envío	nosotros enviamos
continuar (to continue)	yo continúo	nosotros continuamos
concluir (to conclude)	yo concluyo	nosotros concluimos

Example Problems

Select the word that best completes each sentence and give its proper form.

actuar	almorzar	comenzar	confiar	destruir
dormir	perder	preferir	recomendar	volver

1. Cuando él tiene sueño, él _____.

2. Cuando ella tiene hambre a las once, ella _____.

3. Cuando yo estoy muy triste yo _____ a llorar.

4. Cuando la profesora repasa las reglas cinco veces ella _____ la paciencia.

5. Cuando las clases terminan los alumnos _____ a casa.

6. Cuando tú estás en ese restaurante, el mozo siempre _____ pollo.

Answer:

1. duerme

2. almuerza

3. comienzo

4. pierde

5. vuelven

6. recomienda

Solution:

1. *Dormir* is conjugated like a regular *-ir* verb. The *o* of *dormir,* however, changes to *ue* in all forms except *nosotros* and *vosotros*.

2. *Almorzar* is conjugated like a regular *-ar* verb. The *o* of *almorzar,* however, changes to *ue* in all forms except *nosotros* and *vosotros*.

3. *Comenzar* is conjugated like a regular *-ar* verb. The *e* of *comenzar,* however, changes to *ie* in all forms except *nosotros* and *vosotros*.

4. *Perder* is conjugated like a regular *-er* verb. The *e* of *perder,* however, changes to *ie* in all forms except *nosotros* and *vosotros*.

5. *Volver* is conjugated like a regular *-er* verb. The *o* of *volver,* however, changes to *ue* in all forms except *nosotros* and *vosotros*.

6. *Recomendar* is conjugated like a regular *-ar* verb. The *e* of *recomendar,* however, changes to *ie* in all forms except *nosotros* and *vosotros.*

Work Problems

Express the intentions of the following people regarding a party by giving the correct form of the verb indicated.

1. (querer) Ud. _____ tocar la guitarra, pero nosotros_____ tocar el piano.

2. (contar) Ud. _____ en bailar pero, nosotros _____ en cantar.

3. (pensar) Ud. _____ preparar flan, pero nosotros _____ preparar tortas.

4. (poder) Ud. _____ ayudar a Ana, pero nosotros no _____ ayudarla.

5. (preferir) Ud. _____ decorar la sala, pero nosotros _____ no decorarla.

6. (servir) Ud. _____ sándwiches, pero nosotros _____ paella.

7. (morir) Ud. se _____ de alegría, pero nosostros nos _____ de felicidad.

8. (continuar) Ud. _____ trabajando, pero nosotros _____ descansando.

9. (enviar) Ud. _____ invitaciones a los muchachos, pero nosotros _____ invitaciones a las muchachas.

10. (incluir) Ud. _____ a todo el mundo, pero nosotros _____ solamente a nuestros mejores amigos.

Worked Solutions

1. **quiere, queremos**   *Querer* is conjugated like a regular *-er* verb. The *e* of *querer,* however, changes to *ie* in all forms except *nosotros* and *vosotros.*

2. **cuenta, contamos**   *Contar* is conjugated like a regular *-ar* verb. The *o* of *contar,* however, changes to *ue* in all forms except *nosotros* and *vosotros.*

3. **piensa, pensamos**   *Pensar* is conjugated like a regular *-ar* verb. The *e* of *pensar,* however, changes to *ie* in all forms except *nosotros* and *vosotros.*

4. **puede, podemos**   *Poder* is conjugated like a regular *-er* verb. The *o* of *poder,* however, changes to *ue* in all forms except *nosotros* and *vosotros.*

5. **prefiere, preferimos**   *Preferir* is conjugated like a regular *-ir* verb. The second *e* of *preferir,* however, changes to *ie* in all forms except *nosotros* and *vosotros.*

6. **sirve, servimos**   *Servir* is conjugated like a regular *-ir* verb. The *e* of *servir,* however, changes to *i* in all forms except *nosotros* and *vosotros.*

7. **muere, morimos**   *Morir* is conjugated like a regular *-ir* verb. The *o* of *morir*, however, changes to *ue* in all forms except *nosotros* and *vosotros*.

8. **continúa, continuamos**   *Continuar* is conjugated like a regular *-ar* verb. The *u* of *continuar*, however, changes to *ú* in all forms except *nosotros* and *vosotros*.

9. **envía, enviamos**   *Enviar* is conjugated like a regular *-ar* verb. The *i* of *enviar*, however, changes to *í* in all forms except *nosotros* and *vosotros*.

10. **incluye, incluimos**   *Incluir* is conjugated like a regular *-ir* verb. A *y* is added after the *u* before the ending in all forms except *nosotros* and *vosotros*.

The Present Tense of Irregular Verbs

Irregular Yo Forms

In the present tense, some verbs are irregular only in the first person singular *(yo)* form. The verb forms have the regular *-ar*, *-er*, or *-ir* verb endings that correspond to the subject pronoun:

caber	to fit	quepo
caer	to fall	caigo
dar	to give	doy
hacer	to make, to do	hago
poner	to put	pongo
saber	to know a fact, to know how to	sé
salir	to go out	salgo
traer	to bring	traigo
valer	to be worth	valgo
ver	to see	veo

Irregular Yo, Tú, Él (Ella, Ud.), and Ellos (Ellas, Uds.) Forms

In the present tense, some verbs are irregular in all forms except *nosotros* and *vosotros*:

Verb	Meaning	Yo	Tú	Él	Nosotros	Vosotros	Ellos
decir	to say, to tell	**digo**	**dices**	**dice**	decimos	decís	**dicen**
estar	to be	**estoy**	**estás**	**está**	estamos	estáis	**están**
oler	to smell	**huelo**	**hueles**	**huele**	olemos	oléis	**huelen**
tener	to have*	**tengo**	**tienes**	**tiene**	tenemos	tenéis	**tienen**
venir	to come	**vengo**	**vienes**	**viene**	venimos	venís	**vienen**

*Note: Tener followed by que means "to have to" and shows obligation.

Completely Irregular Verbs

Some verbs are irregular in all or most of their forms and must be memorized:

Verb	Meaning	Yo	Tú	Él	Nosotros	Vosotros	Ellos
haber	to have*	he	has	ha	hemos	habéis	han
ir	to go	voy	vas	va	vamos	vais	van
oír	to hear	oigo	oyes	oye	oímos	oís	oyen
reír	to laugh	río	ríes	ríe	reímos	reís	rien
ser	to be	soy	eres	es	somos	sois	son

As an auxiliary verb to form the perfect tenses.

Example Problems

Complete the sentences by selecting the phrase that best expresses what you do or feel in the following situations.

estar contento   hacer mi maleta   ir al centro comercial   oler la gasolina

reír   tener que estudiar   traer un regalo   oír el pronóstico del día

1. Cuando hay una película muy cómica en la televisión yo me _____.

2. Cuando tengo que comprar vestidos nuevos yo _____.

3. Cuando te veo durante las Navidades yo te _____.

4. Cuando recibo una buena nota en mi examen de español yo _____.

5. Cuando viajo yo _____.

6. Cuando quiero ir a la playa pero hay nubes yo _____.

7. Cuando hay un examen en mi clase de biología yo _____.

8. Cuando trabajo en una estación de servicio yo _____.

Answer:

1. río

2. voy al centro comercial

3. traigo un regalo

4. estoy contento

5. hago mi maleta

6. oigo el pronóstico del día

7. tengo que estudiar

8. huelo la gasolina

Solution:

1. The verb *reír* (to laugh) drops the *e* from the stem in all forms except *nosotros* and *vosotros*. The *i* is accented in all forms: *í*. The ending for *yo* is *-o*.

2. The verb *ir* (to go) is irregular in all forms and must be memorized. The *yo* form, like that of a few irregular verbs, ends in *-oy*. All forms start with a *v*.

3. The verb *traer* (to bring) is irregular in the *yo* form only and has a *-go* ending: *traigo*. All other forms use the *e* from the infinitive ending.

4. The verb *estar* (to be) is irregular in all forms except *nosotros* and *vosotros*. The *yo* form, like that of a few irregular verbs, ends in *-oy*.

5. The verb *hacer* (to make, to do) is irregular in the *yo* form only and has a *-go* ending: *hago*. All other forms use the *e* from the infinitive ending.

6. The verb *oír* (to hear) is irregular in all forms and must be memorized. The *yo* form has a *-go* ending: *oigo* (with an unaccented *i*).

7. The verb *tener* (to have) is irregular in the *yo* form and has a *-go* ending: *tengo*. The *tú*, *él*, and *ellos* forms use the *e* from the infinitive ending but have an internal change of *e* to *ie*. The *nosotros* and *vosotros* forms are regular.

8. The verb *oler* (to smell) is irregular in all forms except *nosotros* and *vosotros*. The irregular forms begin with an *h* and the *o* in the stem converts to *ue*. The *nosotros* and *vosotros* forms are regular. The ending for *yo* is *-o*.

Work Problems

Complete the conversations by conjugating the verb in bold.

1. ¿**Sabes** jugar al tenis?

   Sí, nosotros _____ jugar al tenis.

   Yo solamente _____ jugar al golf.

2. ¿**Eres** estudiante?

   Sí, yo _____ estudiante.

   Carlos y yo _____ estudiantes también.

3. ¿Siempre **dice** Ud. la verdad?

    Yo siempre _____ la verdad.

    No, algunas veces tú _____ mentiras.

4. ¿Cuándo **vienen** Uds. al concierto?

    Yo _____ a las siete.

    Nosotros _____ a las siete y media.

5. ¿A qué hora **sale** Ud.?

    Yo _____ a las nueve.

    Nosotros no _____.

6. ¿Qué **ve** Ud. en la foto?

    Yo _____ montañas grandes.

    Ellos _____ un cielo azul.

Worked Solutions

1. **sabemos, sé**   The verb *saber* (to know) is irregular in the *yo* form only. All other forms use the *e* from the infinitive ending.

2. **soy, somos**   *Eres* is the *tú* form of the verb *ser* (to be), which is irregular in all forms. The *yo* form, like that of a few irregular verbs, ends in *-oy*. Use the *nosotros* form of the verb when the subject contains someone else and yourself.

3. **digo, dices**   The verb *decir* (to say, to tell) is irregular in the *yo* form and has a *-go* ending: *digo*. The *tú, él,* and *ellos* forms use the *e* from the infinitive ending but have an internal change of *e* to *i*. The *nosotros* and *vosotros* forms are regular.

4. **vengo, venimos**   The verb *venir* (to come) is irregular in the *yo* form and has a *-go* ending: *vengo*. The *tú, él,* and *ellos* forms use the *e* from the infinitive ending but have an internal change of *e* to *ie*. The *nosotros* and *vosotros* forms are regular.

5. **salgo, salimos**   The verb *salir* (to go out) is irregular in the *yo* form only and has a *-go* ending: *salgo*. All other forms follow the regular rules of conjugation.

6. **veo, ven**   The verb *ver* (to see) is irregular in the *yo* form only. All other forms use the *e* from the infinitive ending.

Using the Present Tense

Use the present tense:

❑ To describe or introduce people or events:

    Le presento a Julia.   Let me introduce you to Julia.

    Vive en California.   She lives in California.

❑ To give information about events taking place:

Yo trabajo esta noche.　　　　I'm working tonight.

❑ To express habitual actions:

Generalmente, come mucho.　　　Generally, he eats a lot.

❑ To ask for instructions or to discuss an action that will take place in the immediate future:

¿Empiezo a hablar?　　　　Shall I begin to speak?

Te veo pronto.　　　　I'll see you soon.

❑ To express an event or action that began in the past and is continuing in the present by using *hace . . . que* or *desde hace*:

　¿Cuánto tiempo hace que lees?

　¿Desde cuándo lees?　　　How long have you been reading?

　Hace una hora (que leo).

　Leo desde hace una hora.　　I've been reading for an hour.

Example Problems

1. Say that you generally sleep late.

   Answer: Generalmente, duermo tarde.

   1. Use the adverb *generalmente* to express "generally."

   2. Use the *yo* form of the verb *dormir* (to sleep) by dropping the *-ir* ending and adding *-o*. *Dormir* is a spelling-change verb. The internal *o* changes to *ue* in all forms except *nosotros* and *vosotros*.

   3. Use the adverb *tarde* to express "late."

2. Say that you are studying tonight.

   Answer: Estudio esta noche.

   1. Use the *yo* form of the verb *estudiar* (to study) by dropping the *-ir* ending and adding *-o*.

   2. Use the noun *noche* to express "night."

   3. Although nouns that end in *-e* tend to be masculine, *noche* is an exception (see Chapter 2). Use the feminine singular demonstrative adjective to express "this."

3. Say that your cousin is a doctor.

   Answer: Mi primo es doctor.

   1. Use the word *primo* to express "cousin."

   2. Use the singular possessive adjective *mi* to express "my."

   3. Use the verb *ser* (to be) to express a person's occupation. Use the third person singular form of the verb *(es)* to express "is."

4. No indefinite article is required before the name of an unmodified occupation.

5. Use the word *doctor* to express "doctor."

Work Problems

1. Say that you generally drive well.

2. Say that today you are going to the mall.

3. Tell someone that your mother is a dentist.

4. Ask a friend in two ways how long she has had her car.

5. Say in two ways that you have been coming to Francisco's restaurant for three months.

Worked Solutions

1. **Generalmente, conduzco bien.**

   1. Use the adverb *generalmente* to express "generally."

   2. Use the *yo* form of the verb *conducir* (to drive) by dropping the *-ir* ending and adding *-o*. *Conducir* is a spelling-change verb. The *c* is preceded by a vowel; therefore, the *c* changes to *zc* in the *yo* form only to keep the soft sound of *c*.

   3. Use the adverb *bien* to express "well."

2. **Voy al centro comercial hoy.**

   1. Use the irregular *yo* form of the verb *ir* (to go).

   2. *Centro* is a masculine singular noun. The preposition *a* (to) contracts with the masculine singular definite article *el* to become *al* (to the).

   3. Use *centro comercial* to express "mall."

   4. Use the adverb *hoy* to express "today."

3. **Mi madre es dentista.**

   1. Use the word *madre* to express "mother."

   2. Use the singular possessive adjective *mi* to express "my."

   3. Use the verb *ser* (to be) to express a person's occupation. Use the third person singular form of the verb *(es)* to express "is."

   4. No indefinite article is required before the name of an unmodified occupation.

   5. Use the word *dentista* to express "dentist."

4. **¿Cuánto tiempo hace que tienes tu carro?**

¿Desde cuándo tienes tu carro?

1. Use either *¿Cuánto tiempo hace que . . . ?* or *¿Desde cuándo . . . ?* to ask how long a person has had something.

2. Because you are speaking to a friend, use the informal singular "you" form of the verb *tener* (to have).

3. Drop the *-er* ending from *tener* and add the ending for *tú: -es.*

4. *Tener* is an irregular verb. The *e* in the stem changes to *ie* in the *tú, él,* and *ellos* forms.

5. Use the singular possessive adjective *tu* to express "your."

6. Use *carro* to express "car."

5. **Hace tres meses que vengo al restaurante de Francisco.**

Vengo al restaurante de Francisco desde hace tres meses.

1. Use *hace* before the period of time to express that the action or event began in the past and is continuing in the present.

2. Use *tres* to express "three."

3. Use *mes* to express "month" and, because it ends in a consonant, add *-es* to make it plural.

4. Either begin or end your sentence with *hace tres meses.*

5. If you begin with *hace tres meses,* add the conjunction *que* (that).

6. If you end with *hace tres meses,* put the preposition *desde* before *hace.*

7. Use the verb *venir* to express that you come to the restaurant.

8. Use the irregular *yo* form of the verb *venir: vengo.*

9. Nouns ending in *-e* tend to be masculine. Use the word *restaurante,* which is masculine singular, to express "restaurant."

10. The preposition *a* (to) contracts with the masculine singular definite article *el* to become *al* (to the) before the noun *restaurante.*

11. Because Spanish does not use an apostrophe and an *s* to show possession, use the preposition *de* to express "of" before the name *Francisco.*

Verbal Distinctions

In Spanish, it may be necessary to use different verbs when English connotations differ. It is important to use these verbs correctly to get across the proper meaning.

Conocer and Saber

Conocer means "to know" in the sense of being acquainted with a person, place, or thing. If you can substitute the words "acquainted with" for the word "know," use *conocer:*

Yo conozco al señor López.	I know (I am acquainted with) Mr. López.
Nosotros conocemos bien esa ciudad.	We know (are acquainted with) that city well.
Él conoce el poema.	He knows the poem. (He's heard of it, but doesn't know the words.)

Saber means "to know a fact" or, when followed by an infinitive, "to know how to do something":

Yo sé su dirección.	I know your address.
Nosotros sabemos dibujar.	We know how to draw.

Note the difference in connotation between *conocer* and *saber* in the following sentences:

Yo conozco la canción. I know the song.	(I am acquainted with it.)
Yo me sé la canción. I know the song.	(I have memorized it and can sing it.)

Deber and Tener Que

Deber generally expresses a moral obligation, while *tener que* is used to express something that the subject has to do:

Debo telefonear a mis padres.	I must call my parents.
Tengo que telefonearlos porque tengo un problema.	I have to call them because I have a problem.

Dejar and Salir

Dejar means "to leave something or someone behind," while *salir* means "to go away," "to go out," or "to leave a place":

Yo dejé mi dinero en casa.	I left my money at home.
Yo salí rápidamente.	I left quickly.

Estar and Ser

Both verbs mean "to be" and often create confusion. The rules governing the use of each of these verbs follow.

Use *estar* to express:

❑ Health

¿Cómo estás?	How are you?
Estoy bien.	I'm well.

❑ Location, position, or situation:

Madrid está en España.	Madrid is in Spain.
¿Dónde está mi libro?	Where is my book?
Su casa está ahí.	Her house is there.

❏ A temporary state or condition of the subject (person, place, or thing):

| Él está optimista. | He is optimistic. |
| La puerta está abierta. | The door is open. |

❏ A progressive tense:

| Estamos estudiando. | We're studying. |

Use *ser:*

❏ To express a quality or characteristic inherent to the subject:

| Ramón es alto. | Ramón is tall. |
| La casa es blanca. | The house is white. |

❏ To describe or identify the subject:

| Susana es inteligente. | Susana is smart. |
| Mi madre es profesora. | My mother is a teacher. |

❏ To give the time, date, and place of an event:

Son las tres.	It's three o'clock.
Es lunes.	It's Monday.
¿Dónde es la fiesta?	Where is the party?

❏ In impersonal expressions:

| Es fácil hablar español. | It's easy to speak Spanish. |

❏ In passive constructions:

| La ventana fue cerrada por Jorge. | The window was closed by Jorge. |

Gastar and Pasar

Use *gastar* when you speak of spending money and *pasar* when you speak of spending time:

| Gasta mucho dinero durante el fin de semana. | He spends a lot of money during the weekend. |
| Paso mucho tiempo cocinando. | I spend a lot of time cooking. |

Jugar and Tocar

Use *jugar + a* to express that the subject is playing a sport or game and *tocar* when the subject is playing a musical instrument:

| Juego al fútbol. | I play soccer. |
| ¿Juega al ajedrez? | Do you play chess? |

Note: In colloquial speech, the *a* + definite article is omitted:

| Juego fútbol. | I play soccer. |
| Tocamos piano. | We play the piano. |

Llevar and Tomar

Llevar and *tomar* mean "to take." *Llevar* is used to express the idea of taking a person somewhere, of carrying or transporting a thing, or of leading someone to a place. *Tomar* is used when something is picked up or carried in your hands:

Yo tomo la taza de café y la llevo a la mesa.　　I take the cup of coffee and carry it to the table.

Pedir and Preguntar

Pedir and *preguntar* mean "to ask." *Pedir* means to request or ask for something, and *preguntar* means to ask a question or to inquire about something or someone:

Voy a pedir la cuenta.　　I'm going to ask for the bill.

Voy a preguntarle si puede venir.　　I'm going to ask him if he can come.

Poder and Saber

Poder and *saber* express "can." *Poder* shows that the subject possess the ability to perform an action, and *saber* shows that the subject actually knows how to perform the action:

No puedo nadar.　　I can't swim.

No sé hacerlo.　　I can't do it. (I don't know how to do it.)

Volver and Devolver

Volver means "to return" or "to come back." *Devolver* means "to return" or "to give something back to its owner or a place":

¿Vas a volver a las cinco?　　Are you going to return at five o'clock?

Yo voy a devolver el dinero mañana.　　I'm going to return the money tomorrow.

Example Problems

Complete each sentence using the correct verb according to its connotation.

1. (gastar/pasar)

   Cuando yo _____ mucho tiempo en el centro comercial yo _____ mucho dinero.

2. (conocer/saber)

   Yo _____ que ellas _____ a mi hermana.

3. (jugar/tocar)

   Roberto _____ al fútbol y su hermano _____ el piano.

4. (poder/saber)

   Yo no _____ cocinar pero yo _____ aprender a hacerlo.

5. (estar/ser)

Yo _____ seguro que él _____ rubio.

Answer:

1. paso, gasto

2. sé, conocen

3. juega, toca

4. sé, puedo

5. estoy, es

Solution:

1. *Pasar* means "to spend time," while *gastar* means "to spend money." Both are regular *-ar* verbs. Drop the *-ar* ending and add the *-o* ending for *yo*.

2. *Saber* means "to know a fact," while *conocer* means "to be acquainted with." The *yo* form of *saber* verbs is irregular and must be memorized. To form the third person plural of *conocer*, drop the *-er* ending and add *-en*.

3. *Jugar* means "to play a game or sport," while *tocar* means "to play an instrument." The *yo*, *tú, él,* and *ellos* forms of *jugar* have a stem change. The internal *u* changes to *ue* in the third person singular. Drop the *-ar* ending and add the third person singular ending: *-a*.

4. *Saber* expresses what the subject knows or doesn't know how to do. The *yo* form of *saber* is irregular and must be memorized. *Poder* expresses what the subject is able to (can) do. The internal *o* of *poder* changes to *ue* in the first person singular.

5. *Estar* expresses a temporary state or condition, while *ser* expresses an inherent characteristic. The *yo* form of *estar* is irregular and must be memorized. The third person singular of *ser* is also irregular and must be memorized.

Work Problems

Complete each sentence using the correct verb according to its connotation.

1. (llevar/tomar) Yo _____ el sándwich y lo _____ a mi cuarto.

2. (pedir/preguntar) Yo le _____ el precio de la casa. Él dice que él _____ un millón por ella.

3. (estar/ser) Cuando _____ las ocho, yo _____ en la cama.

4. (dejar/salir) Cuando yo _____ rápido, yo _____ mis llaves en casa.

5. (conocer/saber) Yo _____ hablar español, pero yo no _____ estas palabras.

6. (deber/tener que) Yo _____ contribuir a esta institución benéfica porque yo _____ reducir los impuestos míos.

Worked Solutions

1. **tomo, llevo**   *Tomar* is used when something is picked up and held, while *llevar* is used when the item can be carried. Both are regular *-ar* verbs. Drop the *-ar* ending and add the *-o* ending for *yo*.

2. **pregunto, pide**   *Preguntar* means "to inquire about something," while *pedir* means "to request something." *Preguntar* is a regular *-ar* verb. Drop the *-ar* ending and add the *-o* ending for *yo*. *Pedir* changes the internal *e* to *i* in all forms except *nosotros* and *vosotros*. Add *-e* for the third person singular ending.

3. **son, estoy**   *Ser* is used to express time, while *estar* expresses a temporary state or condition. The third person singular of *ser* is irregular and must be memorized. The *yo* form of *estar* is also irregular and must be memorized.

4. **salgo, dejo**   *Salir* means "to leave a place," while *dejar* means "to leave something behind." The *yo* form of *salir* is irregular and must be memorized. *Dejar* is a regular *-ar* verb. Drop the *-ar* ending and add the *-o* ending for *yo*.

5. **sé, conozco**   *Saber* means "to know a fact," while *conocer* means "to be acquainted with." The *yo* form of *saber* verbs is irregular and must be memorized. Because *conocer* ends in a vowel + *cer*, the *yo* form requires that the final *c* be changed to *zc* before adding *-o*.

6. **debo, tengo que**   *Deber* expresses a moral obligation, while *tener que* expresses what the subject must do. *Deber* is a regular *-er* verb. Drop the *-er* ending and add the *-o* ending for *yo*. Tener is irregular and must be memorized.

Chapter Problems

Fill in the correct form of the missing verbs:

(ser) _____ sábado por la noche. (hacer) _____ fresco. Mis amigos y yo (querer) _____
            1   2   3

ir a acampar. Mis padres (ir) _____ a permitirlo porque yo (ser) _____ un muchacho
                              4   5

responsable. Yo (convencer) _____ a mis amigos de acompañarme porque yo (tener)
                              6

_____ muchas ganas de ir. Ellos finalmente (decir) _____ que sí. Yo (estar) _____
    7   8   9

contento. Yo (escoger) _____ el lugar que yo (preferir) _____ para acampar. Mis
                          10   11

amigos (venir) _____ a mi casa a las ocho. Afortunadamente, todos nosotros (caber)
                  12

_____ en el coche. Yo (conducir) _____ bien, pero yo no (saber) _____ la ruta
    13   14   15

exacta. Además, yo no (distinguir) _____ bien los caminos. Yo (diriger) _____
                                      16   17

el coche a una estación de servicio. Yo (tener) _____ que preguntarle al propietario
                                                  18

cuál es la ruta correcta. Él (conocer) _____ bien el campo y él me (mostrar) _____
                                          19   20

la ruta. Yo (continuar) _____ y finalmente nosotros (llegar) _____ al campamento.
                          21   22

Inmediatamente, yo (salir) _____ de mi coche y (oír) _____ el zumbido de los
                                    23   24

insectos. Yo (oler) _____ los olores del campo y yo me (sonreír) _____. Esta noche,
                          25   26

yo (esparcir) _____ mi saco de dormir y yo (dormir) _____ al aire libre. Yo (pensar)
                    27   28

_____, ¡Qué felicidad! y mis amigos (concluir) _____ lo mismo.
      29   30

Answer:

1.	Es	11.	prefiero	21.	continúo
2.	Hace	12.	vienen	22.	llegamos
3.	queremos	13.	cabemos	23.	salgo
4.	van	14.	conduzco	24.	oigo
5.	soy	15.	sé	25.	huelo
6.	convenzo	16.	distingo	26.	sonrío
7.	tengo	17.	dirijo	27.	esparzo
8.	dicen	18.	Tengo	28.	duermo
9.	estoy	19.	conoce	29.	pienso
10.	escojo	20.	muestra	30.	concluyen

Solutions

1. To express "it is," use the third person singular of the verb *ser*. All forms of the verb *ser* are irregular and must be memorized.

2. To express "it is" with weather, use the third person singular of the verb *hacer*. Drop the *-er* ending and add *-e*.

3. *Querer* is regular in the *nosotros* form. Drop the *-er* ending and add *-emos*.

4. *Ir* is irregular and must be memorized.

5. *Ser* is irregular in all forms and must be memorized. Like several other irregular verbs, the *yo* form ends in *-oy*.

6. *Convencer* is a consonant + *cer* verb. The *c* changes to *z* in the *yo* form before adding *-o*.

7. *Tener* is irregular in all forms except *nosotros* and *vosotros*. The *yo* form retains the *-e* from the stem and ends in *-go*.

8. *Decir* is irregular in all forms except *nosotros* and *vosotros*. Drop the *-ir* ending and add *-en* for the third person plural.

9. *Estar* is irregular in all forms and must be memorized. Like several other irregular verbs, the *yo* form ends in *-oy*.

10. *Escoger* is a *-ger* verb. The *g* changes to *j* in the *yo* form before adding *-o*.

11. *Preferir* has an internal stem change: The *e* changes to *ie* in all forms except *nosotros* and *vosotros*. Drop the *-ir* ending and add *-o* for the *yo* form.

12. *Venir* is an irregular verb and has an internal stem change: The *e* changes to *ie* in all forms except *yo*, *nosotros*, and *vosotros*. Drop the *-ir* ending and add *-en* for the third person plural.

13. *Caber* is regular in the *nosotros* form. Drop the *-er* ending and add *-emos*.

14. *Conducir* is a vowel + *cir* verb. The *c* changes to *zc* in the *yo* form before adding *-o*.

15. *Saber* has an irregular *yo* form that must be memorized.

16. *Distinguir* is a *-guir* verb. The *gu* changes to *g* in the *yo* form before adding *-o*.

17. *Dirigir* is a *-gir* verb. The *g* changes to *j* in the *yo* form before adding *-o*.

18. *Tener* is irregular in all forms except *nosotros* and *vosotros*. The *yo* form retains the *-e* from the stem and ends in *-go*.

19. *Conocer* is regular in the third person singular. Drop the *-er* ending and add *-e*.

20. *Mostrar* has an internal stem change of *o* to *ue* in all forms except *nosotros* and *vosotros*. Drop the *-ar* ending and add *-a* for the third person singular.

21. *Continuar* is a *-uar* verb. The *u* before the infinitive ending is accented in all forms except *nosotros* and *vosotros*. Drop the *-ar* ending and add *-o* for the *yo* form.

22. *Llegar* is a regular *-ar* verb. Drop the *-ar* ending and add *-amos* for the *nosotros* form.

23. *Salir* has an irregular *yo* form: Drop the *-ir* ending and add *-go*.

24. *Oír* is an irregular verb. The *yo* form drops the *-r* from the infinitive ending, changes *í* to *i*, and ends in *-go*.

25. *Oler* is irregular in all forms except *nosotros* and *vosotros*. An *h* is added to the beginning of all other forms and the *o* changes to *ue*. The *yo* form ends in *-o*.

26. *Sonreír* drops the *e* from the stem in all forms except *nosotros* and *vosotros*. The *i* is accented in all forms: *í*. The ending for *yo* is *-o*.

27. *Esparcir* is a consonant + *cir* verb. The *c* changes to *z* in the *yo* form before adding *-o*.

28. *Dormir* has an internal stem change of *o* to *ue* in all forms except *nosotros* and *vosotros*. Drop the *-ir* ending and add *-o* for *yo* form.

29. *Pensar* has an internal stem change. The *e* changes to *ie* in all forms except *nosotros* and *vosotros*. Drop the *-ar* ending and add *-o* for the *yo* form.

30. *Concluir* is conjugated like a regular *-ir* verb. A *y* is added after the *u* before the ending in all forms except *nosotros* and *vosotros*. Drop the *-ir* ending and add *-en* for the third person plural.

Supplemental Problems

Fill in the correct form of the missing verbs:

(ser) _____ las diez de la noche. Yo (tener) _____ mucha hambre. Yo me (morir) _____
      1   2   3

por comer una hamburguesa con queso. Yo le (pedir) _____ dinero a mi padre. Yo le
                                                  4

(convencer) _____ de que yo (estar) _____ sin fondos. Mi padre me (decir) _____,
           5   6   7

"Yo te (dar) _____ veinte dólares. ¿No (ser) _____ suficiente?" Yo le (decir) _____,
           8   9   10

"(pensar) _____ que sí. Muchas gracias, Papi." Yo (saber) _____ que con esa
           11   12

cantidad de dinero yo (poder) _____ comprar no solamente una hamburguesa con
                                     13

queso sino también un postre. Yo (preferir) _____ el flan. Yo no (perder) _____
                                             14   15

mucho tiempo. Yo (conducir) _____ el carro a mi restaurante favorito donde yo
                                       16

(conocer) _____ al cocinero. Yo me (sentar) _____ y (escoger) _____ mi plato
         17   18   19

favorito. El camerero me (explicar) _____ que esta noche ellos no (servir) _____
                                     20   21

hamburguesas. Yo no lo (poder) _____ creer. (ser) _____ imposible. Yo (ir) _____
                               22   23   24

a la oficina del proprietario. Él no (querer) _____ ayudarme. Yo (hacer) _____
                                     25   26

mucho ruido. Él finalmente (entender) _____ y enojado me (decir) _____,
                                   27   28

"Ya lo (oír) _____, señor. Pero yo no (poder) _____ servirle su hamburguesa. Yo lo
              29   30

(sentir) _____ mucho. Yo (ver) _____ que Ud. se (poner) _____ furioso. Yo le
        31   32   33

(traer) _____ la especialidad de la casa, el estofado." Yo le (responder) _____ que
        34   35

yo (contar) _____ con su consejo y él (sonreír) _____. Cinco minutos después, el
            36   37

camarero (venir) _____ a mi mesa. El estofado (oler) _____ bien y (estar) _____
                               38   39   40

muy delicioso. ¡Qué comida tan rica!

Solutions

1. Son (irregular verbs, p. 100)

2. tengo (irregular verbs, p. 100)

3. muero (stem-changing verbs, p. 97)

4. pido (stem-changing verbs, p. 97)

5. convenzo (spelling-change verbs, p. 95)

6. estoy (irregular verbs, p. 100)

7. dice (irregular verbs, p. 100)

8. doy (spelling-change verbs, p. 95)

9. es (irregular verbs, p. 100)

10. digo (irregular verbs, p. 100)

11. Pienso (stem-changing verbs, p. 97)

12. sé (irregular verbs, p. 100)

13. puedo (irregular verbs, p. 100)

14. prefiero (stem-changing verbs, p. 97)

15. pierdo (stem-changing verbs, p. 97)

16. conduzco (spelling-change verbs, p. 95)

17. conozco (spelling-change verbs, p. 95)

18. siento (stem-changing verbs, p. 97)

19. escojo (spelling-change verbs, p. 95)

20. explica (spelling-change verbs, p. 95)

21. sirven (stem-changing verbs, p. 97)

22. puedo (stem-changing verbs, p. 97)

23. Es (irregular verbs, p. 100)

24. voy (irregular verbs, p. 100)

25. quiere (irregular verbs, p. 100)

26. hago (irregular verbs, p. 100)

27. entiende (stem-changing verbs, p. 97)

28. dice (irregular verbs, p. 100)

29. oigo (irregular verbs, p. 100)

30. puedo (stem-changing verbs, p. 97)

31. siento (stem-changing verbs, p. 97)

32. veo (irregular verbs, p. 100)

33. pone (irregular verbs, p. 100)

34. traigo (irregular verbs, p. 100)

35. respondo (regular verbs, p. 92)

36. cuento (stem-changing verbs, p. 97)

37. sonríe (stem-changing verbs, p. 97)

38. viene (irregular verbs, p. 100)

39. huele (irregular verbs, p. 100)

40. está (irregular verbs, p. 100)

Chapter 5
Asking and Answering Questions

There are two types of questions: those that ask for a yes or no answer and those that ask for information. Each type of question can be asked in several ways: Some are more colloquial than others and are used when speaking; others are used more formally and when writing.

Asking Yes/No Questions

Questions that demand a simple yes or no answer are the easiest to form. There are four ways to do this:

- ❑ Use intonation
- ❑ Use the tag *¿(No es) verdad?*
- ❑ Use the tag *¿Está bien?*
- ❑ Use inversion

Using Intonation

You can ask a question by raising your voice at the end of a statement and by adding an imaginary question mark at the end of your thought. When you make a statement of fact, your voice rises and then lowers by the end of the sentence. When you ask a question, your voice starts out lower and gradually keeps rising until the end of the sentence. In writing, Spanish requires the insertion of an inverted question mark at the beginning of the sentence in addition to a regular question mark at the end of the sentence:

¿Ud. quiere comer algo?   Do you want to eat something?

To form a negative question, simply put *no* before the conjugated verb:

¿Ud. no quiere comer algo?   Don't you want to eat something?

Using the Tags *¿No Es Verdad?* and *¿Está Bien?*

¿No es verdad? and *¿Está bien?* are tags that can have a variety of meanings, including:

Isn't that so?

Right?

Isn't (doesn't) he/she?

Aren't (don't) they?

Aren't (don't) we?

Aren't (don't) you?

¿No es verdad? and *¿Está bien?* are generally placed at the end of a statement, especially when the expected answer is "yes":

Ella quiere comer, ¿no es verdad?	She wants to eat, doesn't she?
Ella quiere comer. ¿Está bien?	She wants to eat. Is that all right?

Using Inversion

Inversion requires that you reverse the word order of the subject (noun or pronoun) and conjugated verb. Any pronouns tied to the verb remain before the verb:

Ud. tiene hambre. (You are hungry.)	¿Tiene Ud. hambre? (Are you hungry?)
Gloria es de Nueva York. (Gloria is from New York.)	¿Es Gloria de Nueva York? (Is Gloria from New York?)
Ella se acuesta tarde. (She goes to bed late.)	¿Se acuesta ella tarde? (Does she go to bed late?)

In most instances, however, the subject pronoun is omitted:

Quieres ir al centro. (You want to go to the city.)	¿Quieres ir al centro? (Do you want to go to the city?)

When there are two verbs, the subject noun or pronoun generally goes after the phrase containing the second verb:

Uds. deben estudiar.	¿Deben estudiar Uds.?
María quiere salir ahora.	¿Quiere salir ahora María?

To negate an inverted question, put *no* before the inverted verb and noun or pronoun. For reflexive verbs (see Chapter 6), or for verbs preceded by an object pronoun (see Chapter 7), the pronoun remains before the conjugated verb:

¿No habla español su amigo?	Doesn't your friend speak Spanish?
¿No se acostó temprano Alberto?	Didn't Alberto go to bed early?
¿No te habla ella?	Doesn't she speak to you?

Example Problems

1. Use *¿No es verdad?* to ask a friend if he can translate this sentence.

    Answer: (Tú) Puedes traducir esta oración, ¿no es verdad?

    1. Select *poder* to express "to be able to." Because you are speaking to a friend, use the informal "you" *(tú)* form.

    2. *Poder* is a stem-changing verb. Change the internal *o* to *ue*, then drop the *-er* ending and add the ending for *tú (-es)*.

    3. The verb *traducir* expresses "to translate." Because there is only one subject but are two verbs, the second verb remains in the infinitive.

    4. Words ending in *-ción* tend to be feminine, and *oración* is no exception. Use the feminine singular demonstrative adjective *esta* before the noun to express "that."

    5. Add the tag *¿no es verdad?* to the end of the phrase.

2. Use *¿Está bien?* to tell a group of friends you want to go to the park and ask if that is all right.

    Answer: Quiero ir al parque. ¿Está bien?

    1. Select *querer* to express "to want." Because you're speaking about yourself, use the *yo* form.

    2. *Querer* is a stem-changing verb. Change the internal *e* to *ie*, then drop the *-er* ending and add the ending for *yo (-o)*.

    3. The verb *ir* expresses "to go." Because there is only one subject but are two verbs, the second verb remains in the infinitive.

    4. The preposition *a* expresses "to."

    5. Use the word *parque* to express "park." Words ending in *-e* tend to be masculine. The masculine singular definite article *el* contracts with *a* to become *al* and expresses "to the."

    6. Add the tag *¿Está bien?* to the end of the phrase.

3. Use inversion to ask me if I have children.

    Answer: ¿Tiene Ud. hijos?

    1. Select *tener* to express "to have."

    2. Because you are speaking to someone you don't know, use the formal "you" *(Ud.)* form.

    3. *Tener* is a stem-changing verb. Change the internal *e* to *ie*, then drop the *-er* ending and add the ending for *Ud. (-e)*.

    4. Invert the verb *tener* and the subject *Ud*.

    5. Use the word *hijos* to express "children."

Work Problems

Use these problems to give yourself additional practice.

1. Use intonation to ask a friend if she can go to the mall this afternoon.

2. Use *¿No es verdad?* to ask a group of friends if they prefer to eat fish.

3. Use *¿Está bien?* to tell your parents that you're going to go to the movies tonight and ask if that is all right.

4. Use inversion to ask me if I know how to play the piano.

Worked Solutions

1. **¿(Tú) Puedes ir al centro comercial esta tarde?**

    1. Select *poder* to express "to be able to." Because you are speaking to a friend, use the familiar "you" *(tú)* form.

    2. *Poder* is a stem-changing verb. Change the internal *o* to *ue,* then drop the *-er* ending and add the ending for *tú (-es).*

    3. The verb *ir* expresses "to go." Because there is only one subject but are two verbs, the second verb remains in the infinitive.

    4. The preposition *a* expresses "to."

    5. Use the word *centro comercial* to express "mall." Words ending in *-o* tend to be masculine. The masculine singular definite article *el* contracts with *a* to become *al* and expresses "to the."

    6. Although words ending in *-e* tend to be masculine, *tarde* is feminine.

    7. Use the feminine singular demonstrative adjective *esta* before the noun to express "this."

2. **(Uds.) Prefieren comer pescado, ¿no es verdad?**

    1. Select *preferir* to express "to prefer." Because you are speaking to a group of friends, use a plural "you" *(Uds.* or *vosotros)* form.

    2. *Preferir* is a stem-changing verb. Change the internal *e* to *ie,* then drop the *-er* ending and add the ending for *Uds. (-en)* or *vosotros (-ís).*

    3. The verb *comer* expresses "to eat." Because there is only one subject but two verbs, the second verb remains in the infinitive.

    4. The noun *pescado* refers to fish that is prepared to eat, as opposed to *pez,* which is a fish that is still alive and swimming.

    5. Add the tag *¿no es verdad?* to the end of the phrase.

3.   Quiero ir al cine esta noche. ¿Está bien?

1. Select *querer* to express "to want." Because you are speaking about yourself, use the *yo* form.

2. *Querer* is a stem-changing verb. Change the internal *e* to *ie,* then drop the *-er* ending and add the ending for *yo (-o).*

3. The verb *ir* expresses "to go." Because there is only one subject but are two verbs, the second verb remains in the infinitive.

4. The preposition *a* expresses "to."

5. Use *el cine* to express "the movies." Words ending in *-e* tend to be masculine. The masculine singular definite article *el* contracts with *a* to become *al* and expresses "to the."

6. Although words ending in *-e* tend to be masculine, *noche* is feminine. Use the feminine singular demonstrative adjective *esta* before the noun to express "this."

7. Add the tag *¿Está bien?* to the end of the phrase.

4.   ¿Sabe Ud. tocar el piano?

1. Select *saber* to express "to know how to do something." Because you are speaking to someone you don't know, use the formal "you" *(Ud)* form.

2. Drop the *-er* ending and add the ending for *Ud (-e).*

3. Invert the verb *saber* and the subject *Ud.*

4. Use the word *tocar* to express "to play a musical instrument."

5. Use *el piano to* express "the piano."

Asking Information Questions

When you need more than a simple yes or no answer, it is imperative that you know how to ask for information. Interrogative adjectives, adverbs, and pronouns allow you to accomplish this task.

Using Interrogative Adjectives

The interrogative adjective *¿cuánto?* is used before a noun and its modifiers when the noun may be counted or measured. *¿Cuánto?* must agree in number and gender with the noun it modifies. The interrogative adjective *¿qué?* is invariable and refers to a noun that is not being counted, and it is equivalent to the English interrogative adjectives "what?" or "which?" In spoken Spanish, you may hear the interrogative adjective placed after the verb, but only for emphasis or to imply surprise, amazement, or incredulity.

	Masculine	**Feminine**
Singular	¿cuánto?	¿cuánta?
Plural	¿cuántos?	¿cuántas?

¿Qué casete estás escuchando? ¿Estás escuchando qué casete?	What cassette are you listening to?
¿Cuánto dinero necesitan? ¿Necesitan cuánto dinero?	How much money do they need?
¿Cuántos muchachos vienen? ¿Vienen cuántos muchachos?	How many boys are coming?
¿Cuánta leche te queda? ¿Te queda cuánta leche?	How much milk do you have left?
¿Cuántas camisas vas a comprar? ¿Vas a comprar cuántas camisas?	How many shirts are you going to buy?

Interrogative adjectives may be preceded by a preposition:

¿A qué hora salen?	What time are they going out?
¿De cuántos muchachos hablas?	How many boys are you speaking about?
¿Con cuánta rapidez funcionan?	With how much speed (how quickly) do they work?

Example Problems

Reynaldo is working on a job. Complete each question he is asked by selecting the correct interrogative adjective from the box.

¿cuánto?	¿cuántos?	¿cuánta?	¿cuántas?	¿qué?

1. ¿ _____ información puedes encontrar?

   Answer: Cuánta

   Words that end in -ción tend to be feminine. *Información,* which means "information," is singular. Select the feminine singular interrogative adjective that expresses an amount or quantity.

2. ¿ _____ tiempo necesitas?

   Answer: Cuánto

   Words that end in -o tend to be masculine. *Tiempo,* which means "time," is singular. Select the masculine singular interrogative adjective that expresses an amount or quantity.

3. ¿ _____ trabajo prefieres?

   Answer: Qué

   Because the amount or quantity of work isn't being measured, use the invariable *¿qué?* to express "which?" or "what?"

4. ¿ _____ errores hay?

   Answer: Cuántos

   Words that end in -r tend to be masculine. *Errores*, which has the plural -es ending, means "errors." Select the masculine plural interrogative adjective that expresses an amount or quantity.

5. ¿ _____ horas más necesitas?

   Answer: Cuántas

   Words that end in -a tend to be feminine. *Horas*, which has the plural -s ending, means "hours." Select the feminine plural interrogative adjective that expresses an amount or quantity.

Work Problems

Some friends are discussing a party they are planning. Complete each question by selecting the correct interrogative adjective from the box.

¿cuánto?	¿cuántos?	¿cuánta?	¿cuántas?	¿qué?

1. ¿ Con _____ dinero puedes comprar todo lo necesario?

2. ¿ _____ refrescos tenemos que comprar?

3. ¿ _____ personas vienen?

4. ¿ _____ carne vas a preparar para la fiesta?

5. ¿ _____ agua vas a necesitar?

Worked Solutions

1. **cuánto**   Words that end in -o tend to be masculine. *Dinero*, which means "money," is singular. Select the masculine singular interrogative adjective that expresses an amount or quantity.

2. **Cuántos**   Words that end in -o tend to be masculine. *Refrescos*, which has the plural -s ending, means "soft drinks." Select the masculine plural interrogative adjective that expresses an amount or quantity.

3. **Cuántas**   Words that end in -a tend to be feminine. *Personas*, which has the plural -s ending, means "people." Select the feminine plural interrogative adjective that expresses an amount or quantity.

4. **Qué**   Because the amount or quantity of meat isn't being measured, use the invariable *¿qué?* to express "which?" or "what?"

5. **Cuánta**   Words that end in -a tend to be feminine. *Agua*, which means "water," is singular. Select the feminine singular interrogative adjective that expresses an amount or quantity.

Using Interrogative Adverbs

Interrogative adverbs are most often used with inversion to form questions:

Adverb	Spanish
how?	¿cómo?
when?	¿cuándo?
where?	¿dónde?
why? (for what reason)	¿por qué?
why? (for what purpose)	¿para qué?

Here are some examples in sentences:

¿Cómo te llamas (tú)?	What's your name?
¿Cuándo van a llegar sus amigos?	When are your friends going to arrive?

Where logical, interrogative adverbs can be preceded by prepositions:

¿Para cuándo necesitan (ellos) el coche?	When do they need the car by?
¿A dónde (Adónde) vas (tú)?	Where are you going?

Using ¿Para Qué? and ¿Por Qué?

¿Para qué? asks about a purpose and requires an answer with *para* (for, to). *¿Por qué?* asks about a reason and requires an answer with *porque* (because). Here are some examples:

¿Para qué usa (Ud.) ese cuchillo?	Why (For what purpose) do you use that knife?
Uso ese cuchillo para cortar el pan.	I use that knife to cut bread.
¿Por qué van al centro?	Why (For what reason) are they going downtown?
Van al centro porque quieren ir de compras.	They go downtown because they want to go shopping.

Example Problems

You meet a neighbor you don't know too well in the street. Ask him for the following information.

1. where he works

   Answer: ¿Dónde trabaja (Ud.)?

   1. Use the interrogative adverb *¿Dónde?* to express "where?"

   2. Because you are speaking to someone you don't know well, use the formal singular *(Ud.)* form to express "you."

   3. Use the verb *trabajar* to express "to work."

   4. Drop the *-ar* ending and add the ending for *Ud. (-a).*

   5. Invert the pronoun and verb after the interrogative adverb.

2. how he is

   Answer: ¿Cómo está (Ud.)?

   1. Use the interrogative adverb *¿Cómo?* to express "how?"

   2. Because you are speaking to someone you don't know well, use the formal singular *(Ud.)* form to express "you."

   3. Use the verb *estar* to express "to be" because you are referring to a temporary state.

   4. *Estar* is an irregular verb. Use the form for *Ud. (está).*

   5. Invert the pronoun and verb after the interrogative adverb.

Work Problems

You are being nosey. Use interrogative adverbs to ask your friend the following questions.

1. how she is going to the party on Saturday

2. why she is studying Spanish

3. where she is going tonight

4. for what purpose she uses a computer

5. when she needs your help by

Worked Solutions

1. **¿Cómo vas (tú) a la fiesta el sábado?**

   1. Use the interrogative adverb *¿Cómo?* to express "how?"

   2. Because you are speaking to someone you know well, use the informal singular *(tú)* form to express "you."

   3. Use the irregular verb *ir* to express "to go." The irregular *tú* form is *vas.*

   4. Invert the pronoun and verb after the interrogative adverb.

   5. Use *a la* to express "to the" before the feminine singular word for "party" *(fiesta).*

   6. Use the definite article *el* to express "on" before the word for "Saturday" *(sábado).*

2. **¿Por qué estudias (tú) español?**

   1. Use the interrogative adverb *¿Por qué?* to express "why?"

   2. Because you are speaking to someone you know well, use the informal singular *(tú)* form to express "you."

3. *Estudiar* is a regular verb. Drop the *-ar* ending and add *-as* for the subject *(tú)*.

4. Invert the pronoun and verb after the interrogative adverb.

5. Use the masculine singular definite article before the name of the language *(español)*.

3. **¿Adónde vas (tú) esta noche?**

1. Use the interrogative adverb *¿Adónde?* to express "to where?"

2. Because you are speaking to someone you know well, use the informal singular *(tú)* form to express "you."

3. Use the irregular verb *ir* to express "to go." The *tú* form is *vas*.

4. Invert the pronoun and verb after the interrogative adverb.

5. Words that end in *-e* tend to be masculine; however, *noche* (night) is an exception.

6. Use the feminine singular demonstrative adjective *esta* to express "this" before *noche*.

4. **¿Para qué utilizas (tú) una computadora?**

1. Use the interrogative adverb *¿qué?* to express "what?"

2. Use the preposition *para* to express "for." *Para* is generally used to express purpose.

3. Because you are speaking to someone you know well, use the informal singular *(tú)* form to express "you."

4. *Utilizar* is a regular verb. Drop the *-ar* ending and add *-as* for the subject *(tú)*.

5. Invert the pronoun and verb after the interrogative adverb.

6. Words that end in *-a* tend to be feminine. Use the feminine singular indefinite article *una* to express "a" before the word for "computer" *(computadora)*.

5. **¿Para cuándo necesitas (tú) mi ayuda?**

1. Use the interrogative adverb *¿cuándo?* to express "when?"

2. Use the preposition *para* to express "for." *Para* is generally used to express time.

3. Because you are speaking to someone you know well, use the informal singular *(tú)* form to express "you."

4. *Necesitar* is a regular verb. Drop the *-ar* ending and add *-a* for the subject *(tú)*.

5. Invert the pronoun and verb after the interrogative adverb.

6. Use the singular possessive adjective *mi* to express "my."

7. The word for "help" is *ayuda*.

Using Interrogative Pronouns

The interrogative pronouns *¿quién(es)?* and *¿cuál(es)?* agree in number only with the nouns they replace, while *¿cuánto?* agrees in both number and gender with the noun it replaces. *¿Qué?* and *¿cuánto?* remain invariable.

Pronoun	Spanish
who?	¿quién(es)?
what?	¿qué?
what? (which one[s]?)	¿cuál(es)?
how much?	¿cuánto?
how many?	¿cuántos(as)?

Here are some examples in sentences:

¿Quién habla?	Who is speaking? (The answer requires the name of one person.)
¿Quiénes hablan?	Who is speaking? (The answer requires at least two names.)
¿Qué es esto?	What is this?
¿Cuál de estos periódicos lee?	Which (one) of these newspapers do you read? (The answer requires the name of one newspaper.)
¿Cuáles de estos periódicos lee?	Which (ones) of these newspapers do you read? (The answer requires at least two names.)
¿Cuánto vale este anillo?	How much is this ring worth?
¿Cuántos vienen a la fiesta?	How many are coming to the party?

A preposition + *quién* refers to people. A preposition + *que* refers to things.

¿De quién hablan?	About whom are they speaking?
¿De qué hablan?	About what are they speaking?
¿A quiénes te refieres?	To whom are you referring?
¿A qué te refieres?	To what are you referring?

¿Qué? and ¿Cuál?

When *¿qué?* precedes a verb, it means "what?" and asks about a definition, description, or an explanation. When *¿qué?* precedes a noun, it expresses "which?":

¿Qué haces en esa situación?	What do you do in that situation?
¿Qué libro compras para la clase?	Which book are you buying for the class?

¿Cuál? means "what?" or "which (one[s])?" and asks about a choice or a selection:

¿Cuál es su dirección?	What is your address?
¿Cuál de los dos prefieres?	Which (one) of the two do you prefer?
¿Cuáles son los meses del año?	What are the months of the year?

Hay

Hay ("there is [are]" or "is [are] there?") is a form of the verb *haber* and is used impersonally to ask and answer questions.

Hay can be used by itself using intonation or it can be used with a preceding question word:

¿(No) Hay un cine por aquí?   Is(n't) there a movie theater nearby?
¿Dónde hay un cine por aquí?   Where is a nearby movie theater?

When *hay* is used in the question, use *hay* to answer the question:

(No) Hay un cine por aquí.

Example Problems

The Rivera family wants to buy a new car. Write the questions that were probably asked to get the information provided.

Example: El señor Rivera le habla <u>a su esposa</u>.
         ¿A quién le habla el señor Rivera?

1. <u>Los Rivera</u> van a comprar un coche.

   Answer: ¿Quiénes van a comprar un coche?

   1. The answer to the question refers to more than one person: *Los Rivera*.

   2. The question must ask "who?"

   3. Use the plural interrogative pronoun *¿quiénes?*

   4. Put the interrogative pronoun before the verb.

2. Este coche cuesta <u>treinta mil dólares</u>.

   Answer: ¿Cuánto cuesta este coche?

   1. The answer to the question refers to a number: *treinta mil dólares*.

   2. The question must ask "how much?"

   3. Use the singular interrogative pronoun *¿cuánto?*

   4. Put the interrogative pronoun before the verb.

3. Ellos no prefieren el coche rojo. Prefieren <u>el azul</u>.

   Answer: ¿Cuál de los coches prefieren (ellos)?

   1. The answer to the question refers to a choice: *el rojo* or *el azul*.

   2. The question must ask "which one?"

   3. Use the singular interrogative pronoun *¿cuál?*

4. Use the preposition *de* to express "of."

5. Follow *de* with *los coches* (the cars).

6. Put the entire question before the verb.

7. For clarification, the pronoun may be added after the verb.

Work Problems

María is looking for a job. Write the questions that were probably asked to get the information provided.

> Example: María lee <u>el periódico</u>.
>
> ¿Qué lee María?

1. María busca <u>un puesto</u>.

2. Ella habla <u>con sus padres</u>.

3. No quiere el puesto de dependienta. Prefiere el puesto <u>de programadora o de secretaria</u>.

4. Su educación vale <u>mucho</u>.

Worked Solutions

1. **¿Qué busca María?**

   1. The answer to the question refers to a thing: *un puesto*.

   2. The question must ask "what?" *(¿qué?)*.

   3. Invert the verb *busca* with the subject *María*.

2. **¿Con quiénes habla (ella)?**

   1. The answer to the question refers to more than one person: *sus padres*.

   2. The question must ask "who?"

   3. Use the preposition *con* to express "with" before the plural interrogative pronoun *¿quiénes?*

   4. Invert the verb *habla* with the pronoun *ella*.

3. **¿Cuáles de los puestos prefiere (ella)?**

   1. The answer to the question refers to two options: *el puesto <u>de programadora o de secretaria</u>*.

   2. The question must ask "which ones?"

   3. Use the plural interrogative pronoun *¿cuáles?*

4. Use the preposition *de* to express "of."

5. Follow *de* with *los puestos* (the jobs).

6. Put the entire question before the verb.

7. For clarification, the pronoun may be added after the verb.

4. **¿Cuánto vale su educación?**

1. The answer to the question refers to an amount: *mucho*.

2. The question must ask "how much?"

3. Use the singular interrogative pronoun *¿cuánto?*

4. Invert the verb *vale* with the noun phrase *su educación*.

Answering Yes/No Questions

Answering "Yes"

Use *sí* to answer "yes" to a question:

¿Quiere jugar al tenis?	Do you want to play tennis?
Sí, con mucho gusto.	Yes, I'd be delighted.

Answering "No"

Most frequently, *no* (no, not) is used for a negative response. Other common negatives, which may or may not be used in conjunction with *no,* include:

ni . . . ni	neither . . . nor
tampoco	neither, not either
jamás, nunca	never, not ever
nadie	no one, nobody
ninguno(a)	no, none, not any
nada	nothing

To answer negatively, put *no* before the conjugated verb. If the conjugated verb is preceded by a pronoun, put *no* before the pronoun (see Chapter 6). *No* may be repeated for emphasis:

¿Cocinas bien?	No cocino bien.	No, no cocino bien.
Do you cook well?	I don't cook well.	No, I don't cook well.
¿Quiere trabajar?	No quiero trabajar.	No, no quiero trabajar.
Do you want to work?	I don't want to work.	No, I don't want to work.
¿Te levantas temprano?	No me levanto temprano.	No, no me levanto temprano.
Do you get up early?	I don't get up early.	No, I don't get up early.

Note the following about Spanish negatives:

❑ It is perfectly acceptable for a Spanish sentence to contain a double negative. If *no* is one of the negatives, it precedes the conjugated verb. When *no* is omitted, another negative precedes the verb:

No bailo nunca *or* Nunca bailo. (I never dance.)

No sale nadie *or* Nadie sale. (No one is going out.)

No le cree a nadie nunca *or* Nunca le cree a nadie. (He never believes anyone.)

No lo quiero tampoco *or* Tampoco lo quiero. (I don't want it either.)

No tomo ni café ni té *or* Ni café ni té tomo. (I don't drink either coffee or tea.)

❑ Each part of the *ni . . . ni* construction precedes the word or words stressed:

No me gustan ni el golf ni el tenis. (I don't like either golf or tennis.)

La película no es ni buena ni mala. (The film is neither good nor bad.)

No quiero ni nadar ni pescar. (I don't want either to swim or to fish.)

❑ An infinitive may be negated:

Es preferible no hacer nada. (It's preferable not to do anything.)

❑ The negatives *nadie, nada, nunca,* and *jamás* are used after comparisons and in phrases beginning with *sin,* which means "without," or *antes* (*de* or *que*), which means "before":

Baila mejor que nadie. (She dances better than anyone.)

Comprendemos la lección más que nunca. (We understand the lesson better than ever.)

Prefiero viajar más que nada. (I prefer traveling more than anything.)

Sale sin decir nada. (He leaves without saying anything.)

Voy a llegar antes que nadie. (I am going to arrive before anyone else.)

No puedo hacer nada, sin antes llamarle. (I cannot do anything, without calling him.)

❑ Negatives may be used alone (without *no*):

¿Qué quieres? Nada. (What do you want? Nothing.)

¿Cuándo mientes? Jamás. (When do you lie? Never.)

❑ When there are two verbs, place *no* before the conjugated verb and another negative word after the second verb:

No quiere comer nada. (He doesn't want to eat anything.)

No le creo a nadie. (I don't believe anyone.)

❑ Before a masculine singular noun, *ninguno* (not any) drops the final *-o* and adds an accent to the *u* (*ningún*). The feminine singular form is *ninguna*. No plural forms exist. When used as an adjective, *ninguno* may be replaced by *alguno* (a more emphatic negative), which follows the noun:

No tiene ninguna. (He doesn't have any.)

No tiene ninguna enfermedad. (He doesn't have any illness.)

No tiene enfermedad alguna. (He doesn't have an illness.)

❑ A negative preceded by a preposition retains that preposition when placed before the verb:

A nadie escribe. (He doesn't write to anyone.)

❑ Some words, when used in questions, require a negative in the response:

If the question contains:	The answer contains:
alguien (someone, anyone)	nadie (no one, nobody)
siempre (always)	jamás *or* nunca (never)
algo (something)	nada (nothing)
también (also)	tampoco (neither)
alguno(a) (some, any)	ninguno(a) (none, [not] any)

Here are some examples in sentences:

¿Buscas a alguien? No busco a nadie. (Are you looking for someone? I'm not looking for anyone.)

Example Problems

You are at work and a friend asks you some questions. Answer them all negatively.

1.   ¿Siempre trabajas los sábados?

   Answer: Nunca trabajo los sábados.

   1. If *no* is not used in the sentences, the negative precedes the conjugated verb.

   2. *Nunca* (never) answers the question *siempre* (always).

   3. Answer the question about yourself using the *yo* form of the verb *trabajar*. Drop the *-ar* ending and add *-o*.

2.   ¿Haces algo en especial?

   Answer: No hago nada en especial.

   1. Put *no* before the conjugated verb.

   2. *Nada* (nothing) answers the question *algo* (something). The negative word *nada* comes after the conjugated verb.

   3. Answer the question about yourself using the *yo* form of the verb *hacer,* which is irregular *(hago).*

   4. Complete the rest of the sentence.

Work Problems

The chores in the Padilla house are not getting done. Complete each sentence by putting the Spanish negative word in its proper place in the sentence.

1.   (nobody) Cocina.

2.   (never) Julio lava los platos.

3.   (either) Rosa lava los platos.

4.   (not) Gustavo saca la basura.

5.   (never . . . anyone) Beatriz ayuda.

6.   (not) El señor Padilla lava el coche.

Worked Solutions

1.   **Nadie cocina. (No cocina nadie.)**   Put *nadie* before the verb to express "nobody." Alternatively, put *no* before the conjugated verb and *nadie* after the conjugated verb.

2.   **Julio nunca lava los platos. (Julio no lava nunca los platos.)**   If *no* is not used in the sentences, the negative precedes the conjugated verb. Put *nunca* before the verb to express "never." Alternatively, put *no* before the conjugated verb and *nunca* directly after the conjugated verb.

3.   **Rosa tampoco lava los platos. (Rosa no lava los platos tampoco.)**   If *no* is not used in the sentences, the negative precedes the conjugated verb. Put *tampoco* before the verb to express "neither." Alternatively, put *no* before the conjugated verb and *tampoco* after the phrase following the conjugated verb.

4.   **Gustavo no saca la basura.**   The word *no* expresses "not." Put *no* before the conjugated verb. Note that "does" is part of the conjugated verb and isn't translated into Spanish.

5.   **Beatriz nunca ayuda a nadie. (Beatriz no ayuda nunca a nadie.)**   If *no* is not used in the sentences, the negative precedes the conjugated verb. Put *nunca* before the verb to express "never." The personal *a* (see Chapter 7) is required after the phrase following the conjugated verb to show that a person is the direct object. *Nadie* (no one) comes after the preposition. Alternatively, put *no* before the conjugated verb for emphasis and put *nunca* directly after the conjugated verb, which is then followed by *a nadie*.

6.   **El señor Padilla no lava el coche.**   The word *no* expresses "not." Put *no* before the conjugated verb. Note that "does" is part of the conjugated verb and isn't translated into Spanish.

Answering Information Questions

Certain key words and phrases will help you identify what information is being requested and how to respond correctly.

Answering Questions That Contain *¿Qué?* and *¿Cuál?*

In order to answer questions that contain the interrogative adjective *¿qué?* (what? which?) or the interrogative pronoun *¿cuál(es)?* (which one[s]?) you must keep in mind the number and gender of the nouns to which they refer. *¿Cuál?* implies a choice, while *¿qué?* asks for a definition, a description, or an explanation. To express "the . . . one(s)," use a definite article + an appropriate adjective (which serves as a noun) that agrees in number and gender with the noun to which the interrogative refers. This generally applies to adjectives showing color (*el rojo,* or "the red one"), size (*las pequeñas,* or "the small ones"), and nationality (*el español,* or "the Spanish one").

You could answer these questions:

¿Cuáles camisetas quiere Ud.?   Which (ones of the) T-shirts do you want?

¿Qué camisetas quiere Ud.?   Which T-shirts do you want?

Like this:

Las rojas.	The red ones.
Las pequeñas.	The small ones.
Las españolas.	The Spanish ones.

When a preposition appears in the question, it must also appear in the answer:

¿De qué programa hablas? (Which program are you speaking about?)

Del programa español. (*de* + name of program)

¿A quiénes de sus amigos les da regalos? (To which of your friends do you give gifts?)

A Rogelio y a Marco. (*a* + names of friends)

Answering Questions with Interrogative Adverbs

To answer questions containing interrogative adverbs, note the following:

❑ *¿Cómo?* (how?) may be answered with a noun, a preposition (*por, en,* or *a*) + noun, or an explanation:

What's your name? My name is Juan. (¿Cómo se llama Ud.? Me llamo Juan.)

How are they traveling to Madrid? By plane. (¿Cómo viajan a Madrid? En avión.)

How are you? I'm fine. (¿Cómo está Ud.? Estoy bien.)

❑ *¿Cuánto(a)(s)* (how much? how many?) must be answered with a number or a quantity:

How much does this coat cost? A hundred dollars. (¿Cuánto cuesta este abrigo? Cien dólares.)

How many shirts do you have? A dozen. (¿Cuántas camisas tienes? Una docena.)

❑ A question with *¿cuándo?* (when?) is answered by giving a time or an expression of time:

When are you going away? (¿Cuándo te vas?)

In 20 minutes. (En veinte minutos.)

At 4:30. (A las cuatro y media.)

Immediately. (En seguida.)

❑ Name a place and use the preposition *en* to answer a question with *¿dónde?*:

Where do you work? I work at the factory (¿Dónde trabaja Ud.? Trabajo en la fábrica.)

❑ Use the preposition *a (al, a los, a las)* (see Chapter 12) + a place to answer the question *¿(a dónde) adónde?*:

Where are you going? I'm going downtown. (¿Adónde vas? Voy al centro.)

❑ Use the preposition *de (del, de la, de los)* + a place to answer the question *¿de dónde?*:

Where are you from? I'm from Chicago. (¿De dónde es? Soy de Chicago.)

❑ Use *porque* + a reason to answer the question *¿por qué?* (why):

Why arn't you coming? Because I'm tired. (¿Por qué no viene? Porque estoy cansado.)

❑ Name a person to answer a question with *¿quién?* (who? whom?), whether it is used as a subject, a direct object, or after a preposition:

Who is going to the restaurant? Clara. (¿Quién va al restaurante? Clara.)

Whom are you calling? My sister. (¿A quién estás llamando? A mi hermana.)

With whom do you travel? With my family. (¿Con quién viajas? Con mi familia.)

❑ Answer *¿qué?* with a noun:

What do you need? My glasses. (¿Qué necesitas? Mis gafas.)

When a preposition is used in a question, the same preposition must also be used in the answer:

¿Para quién trabajas?	Para mi tío.
For whom do you work?	For my uncle.
¿De qué está hablando?	De mi coche.
About what are you speaking?	About my car.

Example Problems

Match the questions about school with their appropriate answers.

1. ¿Qué habla?   A. todo el tiempo

2. ¿Cuándo habla?   B. de sus problemas

3. ¿Por qué habla?   C. español

4. ¿Quién habla?   D. en su clase

5. ¿De qué habla?   E. porque tiene que practicar

6. ¿Dónde habla?   F. el profesor

Answer:

1. C

2. A

3. E

4. F

5. B

6. D

Solution:

1. *¿Qué?* asks "what?" and requires the name of a thing as the answer.

2. *¿Cuándo?* asks "when?" and requires an answer with a time period.

3. *¿Por qué?* asks "why?" and requires an explanation, usually preceded by *porque* (because).

4. *¿Quién?* asks "who?" and requires the name of or a reference to a person.

5. *¿De qué?* asks "about what?" and requires an answer with the preposition *de,* explaining "about."

6. *¿Dónde?* asks "where?" and requires an answer that names a place.

Work Problems

Match the questions about eating with their appropriate answers.

1.	¿Cómo quiere comer?	A. las papas y los guisantes
2.	¿Cuándo quiere comer?	B. en un restaurante
3.	¿Quién quiere comer?	C. en silencio
4.	¿Cuáles legumbres quiere comer?	D. cinco
5.	¿Qué comida quiere comer?	E. porque tiene hambre
6.	¿Por qué quiere comer?	F. a las dos y media
7.	¿Dónde quiere comer?	G. la cena
8.	¿Cuántas galletas quiere comer?	H. Sofía

Worked Solutions

1. **C** *¿Cómo?* asks "how?" and requires an answer that expresses "in what manner."

2. **F** *¿Cuándo?* asks "when?" and requires an answer with a time period.

3. **H** *¿Quién?* asks "who?" and requires the name of or a reference to a person.

4. **A** *¿Cuáles?* asks "which ones?" and requires a reference to more than one thing.

5. **G** *¿Qué?* asks "what?" and requires the name of a thing as the answer.

6. **E** *¿Por qué?* asks "why?" and requires an explanation, usually preceded by *porque* (because).

7. **B** *¿Dónde?* asks "where?" and requires and answer that names a place.

8. **D** *¿Cuántas?* asks "how many?" and requires an answer with a number.

Chapter Problems

Problems

You are sitting next to a stranger on a plane and you strike up a conversation. Write the questions and answers that you exchange.

1. What's your name? (John Q. Public.)

2. What's your nationality? (American.)

3. Where are you from? (California.)

4. Where do you live? (San Francisco.)

5. How many children do you have? (Three.)

6. What is your profession? (I'm a lawyer.)

7. Why do you travel? (To visit my family.)

8. With whom do you travel? (I travel with my wife.)

9. How much time are you (plural) going to spend in Puerto Rico? (We're spending two months in Puerto Rico.)

10. Do you smoke? (Never.)

Answers and Solutions

1. **Answer: ¿Cómo se llama (Ud.)? (¿Cuál es su nombre?) Me llamo (Mi nombre es) John Q. Public.**

   Question: *¿Cómo?* asks "how?" Use the reflexive verb *llamarse* (see Chapter 6). Drop the *-ar* ending from the infinitive and add the ending for *Ud.* *(-a)*. Put the reflexive pronoun *se* in front of the conjugated verb. Invert the subject pronoun and the conjugated verb form. Alternatively, use *¿cuál?* to express "how?" Use the third person singular of *ser* to express "is" *(es)*. Use the possessive adjective *su* to express "your" when speaking politely. Use the masculine singular noun *nombre* to express "name."

   Answer: Use the reflexive pronoun *me* to speak about yourself. Drop the *-ar* ending from the infinitive and add the ending for *yo* *(-o)*. Alternatively, use the possessive adjective *mi* to express "my." Add the word *nombre* and follow it with the name.

2. **Answer: ¿Cuál es su nacionalidad? Soy americano.**

   Question: Use *¿cuál?* to express "what?" because a choice is implied. Use the third person singular of *ser* to express "is" *(es)*. Use the possessive adjective *su* before the feminine singular noun *nacionalidad* to express "your" when speaking politely.

   Answer: Use the *yo* form of the irregular verb *ser* *(soy)*. An *-o* is the ending for *americano* because a male is being described (see Chapter 9).

3. **Answer: ¿De dónde es (Ud.)? Soy de California.**

   Question: *¿Dónde?* asks "where?" Use the preposition *de* before *¿dónde?* to ask "from where?" Use the third person singular of *ser* to express "is" *(es)*. Invert the subject pronoun and the conjugated verb form.

   Answer: Use the *yo* form of the irregular verb *ser (soy)*. Use the preposition *de* to express "from."

4. **Answer: ¿Dónde vive (Ud.)? Vivo en San Francisco.**

   Question: *¿Dónde?* asks "where?" The verb *vivir* expresses "to live." Drop the *-ir* ending from the infinitive and add the ending for *Ud. (-e)*. Invert the subject pronoun and the conjugated verb form.

   Answer: Use the *yo* form of the regular verb *vivir (vivo)*. Use the preposition *en* to express "in."

5. **Answer: ¿Cuántos hijos tiene (Ud.)? Tengo tres hijos.**

   Question: *¿Cuántos?* asks "how many?" before the masculine plural noun *hijos* (children). The verb *tener* is irregular and has an internal change of *e* to *ie* in all forms except *yo*, *nosotros,* and *vosotros.* Drop the *-er* ending from the infinitive and add the ending for *Ud. (-e)*. Invert the subject pronoun and the conjugated verb form.

   Answer: Use the irregular *yo* form of the verb *tener (tengo)*. Use the word for three *(tres)* before the word *hijos.*

6. **Answer: ¿Cuál es su profesión? Soy abogado.**

   Question: Use *¿cuál?* to express "what?" because a choice is implied. Use the third person singular form of *ser* to express "is" *(es)*. Use the possessive adjective *su* before the feminine singular noun *profesión* to express "your" when speaking politely.

   Answer: Use the *yo* form of the irregular verb *ser (soy)*. Use *abogado* because a male is answering.

7. **Answer: ¿Por qué viaja (Ud.)? Para visitar a mi familia.**

   Question: *¿Por qué?* asks "why?" Use the verb *viajar* (to travel). Drop the *-ar* ending from the infinitive and add the ending for *Ud. (-a)*. Invert the subject pronoun and the conjugated verb form.

   Answer: The preposition *para* may be used instead of *porque* (because) to show intention or purpose. *Para* is followed by the infinitive of the verb. Use the personal *a* to show that the direct object refers to people (see Chapter 7). Use the possessive adjective *mi* before the feminine singular noun *familia* to express "my."

8. **Answer: ¿Con quién viaja (Ud.)? Viajo con mi esposa.**

   Question: *¿Quién?* asks "who?" or "whom?" Use the preposition *con* before *¿quién?* to ask "with whom?" Use the verb *viajar* (to travel). Drop the *-ar* ending from the infinitive and add the ending for *Ud. (-a)*. Invert the subject pronoun and the conjugated verb form.

   Answer: Drop the *-ar* ending from the infinitive and add the ending for *yo (-o)*. Use the possessive adjective *mi* before the feminine singular noun *esposa* (wife) to express "my."

9. **Answer: ¿Cuánto tiempo van (Uds.) a pasar en Puerto Rico? Vamos a pasar dos meses en Puerto Rico.**

    Question: *¿Cuánto?* asks "how much?" and is used before the masculine singular noun *tiempo.* Use the third person plural form of the irregular verb *ir* to express "go" *(van).* Use the formal plural form of you *(Uds.).* Invert the subject pronoun and the conjugated verb form. *Ir* is followed by the preposition *a* when it expresses what the subject is going to do. *Ir a* is followed by the infinitive of the verb *pasar,* which connotes "to spend time." Use the preposition *en* to express "in" before the name of the country: *Puerto Rico.*

    Answer: Use the first person plural form of the irregular verb *ir* to express "to go" when the subject includes someone in addition to yourself. Use the *nosotros* form of *ir (vamos).* *Ir* is followed by the preposition *a* when it expresses what the subject is going to do. *Ir a* is followed by the infinitive of the verb *pasar,* which connotes "to spend time." Give the amount of time *(dos meses).* The word for month *(mes)* is made plural by adding *-es.* Use the preposition *en* to express "in" before the name of the country: *Puerto Rico.*

10. **Answer: ¿Fuma (Ud.)? Nunca fumo. (No fumo nunca.)**

    Question: Drop the *-ar* ending from the infinitive and add the ending for *Ud.* *(-a).* Invert the subject pronoun and the conjugated verb form.

    Answer: Drop the *-ar* ending from the infinitive and add the ending for *yo (-o).* Put *nunca* (never) before the conjugated verb form. Alternatively, put *no* before the conjugated verb form and *nunca* after it.

Supplemental Chapter Problems

Problems

In problems 1–12, you are speaking to a friend about her wedding. Write the questions and answers that you exchange.

1. What is the date of the wedding? (It's August 7th.)

2. Who is coming? (My family and friends are coming.)

3. How many people are you going to invite? (I'm going to invite 200 people.)

4. What color is your wedding gown? (It's white.)

5. Where is the church? (It's in Puerto Vallarta.)

6. At what time is the wedding? (It's at 7 p.m.)

7. How much does the wedding cost? (It costs $25,000.)

8. Why do you (plural) want to go on a honeymoon? (Because it is very fun.)

9. Don't you (plural) want a gift? (We don't want anything.)

10. Are you (plural) serving chicken or fish? (We're serving chicken.)

Solutions

1. ¿Cuál es la fecha de la boda? Es el siete de agosto. (interrogative pronouns, p. 127; dates, p. 25)

2. ¿Quiénes vienen? Mi familia y mis amigos vienen. (interrogative pronouns, p. 127; possessive adjectives, p. 72)

3. ¿Cuántas personas vas a invitar? Voy a invitar doscientas personas. (interrogative pronouns, p. 127; regular *-ar* verbs, p. 92; numbers, p. 15)

4. ¿De qué color es tu traje de novia? Es blanco. (interrogative pronouns, p. 127)

5. ¿Dónde está la iglesia? Está en Puerto Vallarta. (interrogative adverbs, p. 124)

6. ¿A qué hora es la boda? A las siete de la noche. (interrogative adjectives, p. 121; time, p. 29)

7. ¿Cuánto cuesta la boda? Cuesta veinticinco mil dólares. (interrogative adjectives, p. 121; numbers, p. 15)

8. ¿Por qué quieren irse de luna de miel? Porque es muy divertido. (interrogative adverbs, p. 124)

9. ¿No quieren Uds. un regalo? No queremos nada. (asking yes/no questions, p. 117; answering yes/no questions, p. 130)

10. ¿Sirven Uds. pollo o pescado? Servimos pollo. (asking information questions, p. 133; stem-changing verbs, p. 97)

Chapter 6
Reflexive Verbs

A reflexive verb in Spanish can be identified by the *-se* ending that is attached to the verb infinitive (the form ending in *-ar, -er,* or *-ir*). A reflexive verb is one where the action is performed by the subject on itself. A reflexive verb has a reflexive pronoun as its object (direct or indirect). The subject (which may, as with other verbs, be omitted) and the reflexive pronoun refer to the same person or thing:

La muchacha se llama Rosa.	The girl's name is Rosa.
(Ella) Se llama Rosa.	She calls herself Rosa *or* Her name is Rosa.

In some instances, a verb may have both a reflexive and a non-reflexive form. A verb that can be reflexive may be used without a reflexive pronoun if the action is performed *upon* or *for* someone else, in which case the verb is no longer considered reflexive.

Se llama Rosa.	She calls herself Rosa *or* Her name is Rosa.
Ella llama a Pedro.	She calls Pedro.
Ella te llama.	She calls you.

Some verbs that are generally not used reflexively may be made reflexive by adding the reflexive pronoun:

Yo miro la televisión.	I watch television.
Me miro en el espejo.	I look at myself in the mirror.

The following list includes some common reflexive verbs (bold letters indicate a spelling change or irregularity):

Verb	Meaning	Verb	Meaning
aburrirse	to become bored	hacerse	to become
ac**o**starse	to go to bed	irse	to go away, to leave
afeitarse	to shave	lavarse	to wash oneself
alegrarse	to be glad	levantarse	to get up (when the entire body is involved)
bañarse	to bathe oneself		
callarse	to be silent	llamarse	to be called, to be named
cansarse	to become tired	maquillarse	to put on makeup
cepillarse	to brush one's hair or teeth	marcharse	to go away
desp**e**rtarse	to wake up	peinarse	to comb one's hair
div**e**rtirse	to have fun	ponerse	to put on, to become, to place oneself
d**o**rmirse	to fall asleep		
enfadarse	to get angry	quedarse	to remain
engañarse	to be mistaken, to deceive oneself	resfriarse	to catch a cold
		romperse	to break (a part of one's body)
enojarse	to become angry	quitarse	to remove
equivocarse	to be mistaken	s**e**ntarse	to sit down
fijarse (en)	to notice	s**e**ntirse	to feel

141

Reflexive Pronouns

Reflexive verbs are always conjugated in all tenses with the reflexive pronoun that agrees with the subject. These pronouns generally, but not always, precede the conjugated verb. The verb is then conjugated according to the family to which it belongs, taking into account any irregularities or spelling and/or stem changes (bold letters indicate these irregularities and changes).

Infinitive	Subject	Reflexive Pronoun	Conjugation
div**e**rtirse (to have fun)	yo	me	me div**ie**rto
ac**o**starse (to go to bed)	tú	te	te ac**ue**stas
v**e**stirse (to get dressed)	él, ella, Ud.	se	se v**i**ste
levantarse (to get up)	nosotros	nos	nos levantamos
bañarse (to bathe)	vosotros	os	os bañáis
irse (to go away)	ellos, ellas, Uds.	se	se **van**

Here are two examples in sentences:

¿Se acuesta Ud. temprano?   Do you go to bed early?

Sí, generalmente me acuesto temprano.   Yes, I generally go to bed early.

To negate a reflexive verb, put *no* or the negative word before the reflexive pronoun:

¿Se levanta Ud. a las siete?   Do you get up at seven o'clock?

No, no me levanto a las siete.   No, I don't get up at seven o'clock.

Nunca me levanto a las siete.   I never get up at seven o'clock.

No me levanto nunca a las siete.   I never get up at seven o'clock.

Example Problems

Express what happens in the Ricardo household. Complete the sentences by filling in the reflexive pronoun where needed.

1. Nosotros ___ despertamos y entonces ___ despertamos a nuestros padres.

   Answer: Nosotros nos despertamos y entonces despertamos a nuestros padres.

   The reflexive pronoun is needed before the first verb because the subject, *nosotros*, is acting upon itself: "We" are waking up by "ourselves." The reflexive pronoun for *nosotros* is *nos*.

   The second verb is not used reflexively because the subject is acting upon someone else: "We" are waking up our parents.

2. Yo ___ acuesto a los niños a las ocho y yo ___ acuesto a las once.

   Answer: Yo acuesto a los niños a las ocho y yo me acuesto a las once.

   The first verb is not used reflexively because the subject is acting upon someone else: "I" am putting the children to bed at eight o'clock.

The reflexive pronoun is needed before the second verb because the subject, *yo*, is acting upon itself: "I" am putting myself to bed at eleven o'clock. The reflexive pronoun for *yo* is *me*.

Work Problems

The day continues in the Ricardo household. Complete the sentences by filling in the reflexive pronoun where needed.

1. Uds. ___ preparan el desayuno para los niños y rápidamente Uds. ___ preparan para ir al trabajo.

2. Yo ___ cepillo el pelo y luego yo ___ cepillo el pelo del perro.

3. Nosotros ___ lavamos el coche y después nosotros ___ lavamos.

4. Tú ___ bañas y más tarde tú ___ bañas a los niños.

5. Ella ___ maquilla primero antes de ir a la escuela y después ella ___ maquilla a su hermana.

6. Vosotros ___ miráis en el espejo y después vosotros ___ miráis la televisión.

Worked Solutions

1. **Uds. preparan el desayuno para los niños y rápidamente Uds. se preparan para ir al trabajo.** The first verb is not used reflexively because the subject is acting upon someone else: "You" are preparing breakfast for the children. The reflexive pronoun is needed before the second verb because the subject, *Uds.*, is acting upon itself: "You" are preparing yourself for work. The reflexive pronoun for *Uds.* is *se*.

2. **Yo me cepillo el pelo y luego yo cepillo el pelo del perro.** The reflexive pronoun is needed before the first verb because the subject, *yo*, is acting upon itself: "I" am brushing my hair. The reflexive pronoun for *yo* is *me*. The second verb is not used reflexively because the subject is acting upon someone else: "I" am brushing the dog's hair.

3. **Nosotros lavamos el coche y después nosotros nos lavamos.** The first verb is not used reflexively because the subject is not acting upon itself: "We" are washing the car. The reflexive pronoun is needed before the second verb because the subject, *nosotros*, is acting upon itself: "We" are washing ourselves. The reflexive pronoun for *nosotros* is *nos*.

4. **Tú te bañas y más tarde tú bañas a los niños.** The reflexive pronoun is needed before the first verb because the subject, *tú*, is acting upon itself: "You" are bathing yourself. The reflexive pronoun for *tú* is *te*. The second verb is not used reflexively because the subject is acting upon someone else: "You" are bathing the children.

5. **Ella se maquilla primero antes de ir a la escuela y después ella maquilla a su hermana.** The reflexive pronoun is needed before the first verb because the subject, *ella*, is acting upon itself: "She" is applying her own makeup. The reflexive pronoun for *ella* is *se*. The second verb is not used reflexively because the subject is acting upon someone else: "She" is applying makeup on her sister.

6. **Vosotros os miráis en el espejo y después vosotros miráis la televisión.**   The reflexive pronoun is needed before the first verb because the subject, *vosotros*, is acting upon itself: "You" are looking at yourself in the mirror. The reflexive pronoun for *vosotros* is *os*. The second verb is not used reflexively because the subject is not acting upon itself: "You" are watching television.

Reflexive Verbs with Infinitives and Gerunds

When a subject noun or pronoun, either stated or understood, is followed by a conjugated verb + an infinitive, or by a conjugated form of *estar* + a gerund (see Chapter 8), the reflexive pronoun may be placed either before the conjugated verb or after and attached to the infinitive to which its meaning is linked. When using the gerund, the stressed syllable is accented. In general, count back three vowels and add an accent to get the correct stress.

(Yo) Me voy a lavar el pelo.
(Yo) Voy a lavar**me** el pelo.   I'm going to wash my hair.

(Yo) Me estoy cepillando el pelo.
(Yo) Estoy cepillándo**me** el pelo.   I'm combing my hair.

Example Problems

Express in two ways what each person is going to do before going to bed.

Example: él/lavarse
  A. Él va a lavar<u>se</u>.
  B. (Él) <u>Se</u> va a lavar.

1. nosotros/cepillarse los dientes

   Answer: A. Nosotros vamos a cepillarnos los dientes. B. Nosotros nos vamos a cepillar los dientes.

   A. Use the *nosotros* form of the irregular verb *ir* to express "to go." The conjugated form of *ir* is followed by the preposition *a*. Because there is only one subject and two verbs, *ir* is conjugated and the second verb remains in the infinitive. The reflexive pronoun for *nosotros* is *nos*. Attach the reflexive pronoun to the infinitive of the verb, *cepillar*. Complete the rest of the sentence.

   B. The reflexive pronoun for *nosotros* is *nos*. Place the reflexive pronoun before the conjugated form of *ir (vamos)*. Add the preposition *a*, then the infinitive of the verb. Complete the rest of the sentence.

2. yo/ducharse

   Answer: A. Yo voy a ducharme. B. Yo me voy a duchar.

   A. Use the *yo* form of the irregular verb *ir* to express "to go." The conjugated form of *ir* is followed by the preposition *a*. Because there is only one subject and two verbs, *ir* is conjugated and the second verb remains in the infinitive. The reflexive pronoun for *yo* is *me*. Attach the reflexive pronoun to the infinitive of the verb, *duchar*.

B. The reflexive pronoun for *yo* is *me*. Place the reflexive pronoun before the conjugated form of *ir (voy)*. Add the preposition *a*, then the infinitive of the verb.

Work Problems

Express in two ways what each person is going to do on a day off.

Example: él/levantarse
A. Él va a levantar<u>se</u> tarde.
B. Él <u>se</u> va a levantar tarde.

1. tú/dormirse tarde

2. ella/pasearse en la playa

3. yo/quedarse en casa

4. nosotros/desayunarse en un café

5. Uds./divertirse en la fiesta

6. vosotros/aburrirse en la reunión

Worked Solutions

1. **A. Tú vas a dormirte tarde. B. Tú te vas a dormir tarde.**

   A. Use the *tú* form of the irregular verb *ir* to express "to go." The conjugated form of *ir* is followed by the preposition *a*. Because there is only one subject and two verbs, *ir* is conjugated and the second verb remains in the infinitive. The reflexive pronoun for *tú* is *te*. Attach the reflexive pronoun to the infinitive of the verb, *dormir*.

   B. The reflexive pronoun for *tú* is *te*. Place the reflexive pronoun before the conjugated form of *ir (vas)*. Add the preposition *a*, then the infinitive of the verb.

2. **A. Ella va a pasearse en la playa. B. Ella se va a pasear en la playa.**

   A. Use the *ella* form of the irregular verb *ir* to express "to go." The conjugated form of *ir* is followed by the preposition *a*. Because there is only one subject and two verbs, *ir* is conjugated and the second verb remains in the infinitive. The reflexive pronoun for *ella* is *se*. Attach the reflexive pronoun to the infinitive of the verb, *pasear*.

   B. The reflexive pronoun for *ella* is *se*. Place the reflexive pronoun before the conjugated form of *ir (va)*. Add the preposition *a*, then the infinitive of the verb.

3. **A. Yo voy a quedarme en casa. B. Yo me voy a quedar en casa.**

   A. Use the *yo* form of the irregular verb *ir* to express "to go." The conjugated form of *ir* is followed by the preposition *a*. Because there is only one subject and two verbs, *ir* is conjugated and the second verb remains in the infinitive. The reflexive pronoun for *yo* is *me*. Attach the reflexive pronoun to the infinitive of the verb, *quedar*. Complete the rest of the sentence.

B. The reflexive pronoun for *yo* is *me*. Place the reflexive pronoun before the conjugated form of *ir (voy)*. Add the preposition *a*, then the infinitive of the verb. Complete the rest of the sentence.

4.   **A. Nosotros vamos a desayunarnos en un café. B. Nosotros nos vamos a desayunar en un café.**

A. Use the *nosotros* form of the irregular verb *ir* to express "to go." The conjugated form of *ir* is followed by the preposition *a*. Because there is only one subject and two verbs, *ir* is conjugated and the second verb remains in the infinitive. The reflexive pronoun for *nosotros* is *nos*. Attach the reflexive pronoun to the infinitive of the verb, *desayunar*. Complete the rest of the sentence.

B. The reflexive pronoun for *nosotros* is *nos*. Place the reflexive pronoun before the conjugated form of *ir (vamos)*. Add the preposition *a*, then the infinitive of the verb. Complete the rest of the sentence.

5.   **A. Uds. van a divertirse en la fiesta. B. Uds. se van a divertir en la fiesta.**

A. Use the *Uds.* form of the irregular verb *ir* to express "to go." The conjugated form of *ir* is followed by the preposition *a*. Because there is only one subject and two verbs, *ir* is conjugated and the second verb remains in the infinitive. The reflexive pronoun for *Uds.* is *se*. Attach the reflexive pronoun to the infinitive of the verb, *divertir*.

B. The reflexive pronoun for *Uds.* is *se*. Place the reflexive pronoun before the conjugated form of *ir (van)*. Add the preposition *a*, then the infinitive of the verb.

6.   **A. Vosotros vais a aburriros en la reunión. B. Vosotros os vais a aburrir en la reunión.**

A. Use the *vosotros* form of the irregular verb *ir* to express "to go." The conjugated form of *ir* is followed by the preposition *a*. Because there is only one subject and two verbs, *ir* is conjugated and the second verb remains in the infinitive. The reflexive pronoun for *vosotros* is *os*. Attach the reflexive pronoun to the infinitive of the verb, *aburrir*.

B. The reflexive pronoun for *vosotros* is *os*. Place the reflexive pronoun before the conjugated form of *ir (vais)*. Add the preposition *a*, then the infinitive of the verb.

Verbs Used Reflexively in Spanish but Not in English

Some verbs are always reflexive in Spanish even though they are not necessarily used reflexively in English. Bold letters indicate a spelling change or irregularity:

Verb	Meaning
acercarse a	to approach
ac**o**rdarse (de)	to remember
apoderarse (de)	to take possession (of)
apresurarse (a)	to hurry
aprovecharse (de)	to take advantage of
asustarse	to get frightened
burlarse (de)	to make fun of
desayunarse	to breakfast

Verb	Meaning
empeñarse (en)	to insist (on)
enterarse de	to find out about
fiarse de	to trust
figurarse	to imagine
fijarse (en)	to notice
irse	to go away
n**eg**arse (de)	to refuse (to)
olvidarse de	to forget
pare**cer**se a	to resemble
quejarse de	to complain
r**eí**rse de	to laugh at
tratarse (de)	to be a matter of

Verbs with Special Reflexive Meanings

Some Spanish verbs have different meanings depending on whether or not they are used reflexively:

General Form	General Meaning	Reflexive Form	Reflexive Meaning
aburrir	to bore	aburrirse	to become bored
acordar	to agree	acordarse de	to remember
acostar	to put to bed	acostarse	to go to bed
bañar	to bathe (someone)	bañarse	to bathe oneself
cansar	to tire	cansarse	to become tired
colocar	to place (something)	colocarse	to place oneself; to get a job
dormir	to sleep	dormirse	to fall asleep
enfadar	to anger, to irritate	enfadarse (con)	to become angry or annoyed
engañar	to deceive	engañarse	to be mistaken, to deceive oneself
esconder	to hide (something)	esconderse	to hide oneself
ir	to go	irse	to go away
levantar	to raise (something)	levantarse	to get up
llamar	to call	llamarse	to be called, to call oneself
parar	to stop (something)	pararse	to stop oneself
poner	to put (something)	ponerse	to put (something on) to become, to place oneself
sentar	to seat	sentarse	to sit down

Idiomatic Reflexive Verbs

Some reflexive verbs are used idiomatically, which means that there is no logical grammatical explanation to account for their usage:

Expressions	Meaning
hacerse amigos	to become friends
darse cuenta de	to realize

Reflexive Verbs Expressing Reciprocal Action

Plural reflexive constructions may express reciprocal action, corresponding to *each other* and *one another* in English:

Nos amamos.	We love one another (each other).

Use *uno a otro (una a otra)* or *el uno al otro (la una a la otra)* (each other) to clarify or reinforce the meaning of the reflexive pronoun:

Ellas se hablan.	They speak to themselves *or* They speak to each other.
Ellas se hablan la una a la otra (una a otra).	They speak to each other.

Reflexive Pronoun *Se* Used to Express the Passive Voice

The reflexive pronoun *se* may be used to express the passive voice when the subject is a thing (not a person):

Aquí <u>se</u> habla español.	Spanish is spoken here.
<u>Se</u> vende carne hoy.	Meat is being sold today.

Example Problems

1. Express that they brush their teeth three times a day.

   Answer: Ellos se cepillan los dientes tres veces al día.

   The reflexive pronoun for *ellos* is *se*. Put the reflexive pronoun before the conjugated verb. Drop the *-ar* infinitive ending and add the ending for *ellos (-an)*. Use *los dientes* to express "the teeth." Note that the definite article, not the possessive adjective, is used with reflexive verbs because the possessor is clear. Use *tres* to express "three." *Vez* is the word for time in a series. In the plural, the *z* changes to *c*. Because the word ends in a consonant, *-es* is added to form the plural. Although words ending in *-a* tend to be feminine, *día* is masculine. Use the preposition *a*, which contracts with the masculine singular definite article *el* to express "a" (meaning "per") before *día*.

2. Express that Clara and Roberto write to each other every day.

Answer: Clara y Roberto se escriben todos los días.

Join the names of the two people with *y* to express "and." The phrase "each other" shows reciprocal action and calls for the use of a reflexive construction. The reflexive pronoun for *ellos* is *se*. Put the reflexive pronoun before the conjugated verb. Drop the *-ir* infinitive ending and add the ending for *ellos (-en)*. Although words ending in *-a* tend to be feminine, *días* is masculine. Use the masculine plural adjective *todos* (see Chapter 8) and the masculine plural definite article *los* to express "every" before *días*.

Work Problems
Express the following sentences in Spanish.

1. She can't remember his name.

2. These women don't trust those men.

3. The film bores the children.

4. I get tired after working.

5. They hug each other often.

6. Pictures are taken here.

Worked Solutions

1. **Ella no puede acordarse de su nombre. (Ella no se puede acordar de su nombre.)** Use *no* to express "not." Use the verb *poder* to express "can." *Poder* has an internal stem change from *o* to *ue* in all forms but *nosotros* and *vosotros*. Drop the *-er* infinitive ending and add the ending for *ella (-e)*. Because there is one subject and two verbs, the second verb remains in the infinitive. Attach the reflexive pronoun to the infinitive. The verb *acordarse* is followed by the preposition *de* before the name of a person or thing. Use the masculine singular possessive adjective *su* to express "his" before the word *nombre* (name). Alternatively, the reflexive pronoun *se* may be placed before the conjugated form of *poder*.

2. **Estas mujeres no se fían de esos hombres.** Use the feminine plural demonstrative adjective to express "these" before the word for "women" *(mujeres)*. Because *mujer* ends in a consonant, add *-es* to make it plural. Use *no* to express "not." The word for "do" is contained in the meaning of the conjugated verb. Drop the *-ar* infinitive ending and add third person plural ending *(-an)*. The verb *fiarse* is followed by the preposition *de* before the name of a person. Use the masculine plural demonstrative adjective to express "those" before the word for "men" *(hombres)*. Because *hombre* ends in a vowel, add *-s* to make it plural.

3. **La película aburre a los niños.** A reflexive construction is not called for in this question because the subject is not acting upon itself. Use *la película* to express "the movie." Conjugate the verb *aburrir* (to bore) by dropping the *-ir* infinitive ending and adding the third person singular ending *(-e)*. Use the personal *a* (see Chapter 7) to show that the direct object refers to people. Use *los niños* to express "the children."

4.   **Yo me canso después de trabajar.**   The reflexive pronoun for *yo* is *me*. Put the reflexive pronoun before the conjugated verb. Drop the -*ar* infinitive ending and add the ending for *yo* (-*o*). Use the adverbial phrase *después de* to express "after." Use *trabajar* to express "working."

5.   **Ellos se abrazan a menudo.**   The phrase "each other" shows reciprocal action and calls for the use of a reflexive construction. The reflexive pronoun for *ellos* is *se*. Put the reflexive pronoun before the conjugated verb. Drop the -*ar* infinitive ending and add the ending for *ellos* (-*an*). Use the adverbial phrase *a menudo* to express "often". Put the adverb at the end of the sentence (see Chapter 10).

6.   **Aquí se sacan fotografías.**   Use *aquí* to express "here." *Aquí* may be placed at either the beginning or the end of the sentence. Reflexive pronouns may be used to express the passive voice when the subject is a thing. Because "photographs" is plural, the third person plural form of the verb is needed. The third person plural reflexive pronoun is *se*. Conjugate the verb *sacar*. Drop the -*ar* infinitive and add the third person plural ending (-*an*). Add *fotografías* to express "photographs."

Chapter Problems

Problems

In problems 1–10, choose the appropriate phrase from the box to express what each person does in the following situations, then conjugate the verb to agree with the subject.

aburrirse	apresurarse	desayunarse	ponerse un abrigo	quejarse al camarero
alegrarse	asustarse	lavarse	quedarse en casa	quitarse el suéter

1.   Miguel tiene mucho frío.

2.   Yo recibo buenas noticias.

3.   Los alumnos no van a llegar a la escuela a tiempo.

4.   Hay una mosca en tu sopa.

5.   Los niños tienen las manos sucias.

6.   Vosotros tenéis hambre a las seis de la mañana.

7.   Ud. piensa que ha perdido su dinero.

8.   A ella no le gusta mucho el concierto.

9.   Yo estoy enfermo.

10.   Los muchachos tienen calor.

In problems 11–15, express what is done in each of the following places.

Example: supermercado/vender leche

En un supermercado se vende leche.

11. florería/vender flores

12. estadio/mirar partidos

13. banco/cambiar dinero

14. restaurante/preparar comidas

15. biblioteca/prestar libros

Answers and Solutions

1. **Answer: Él se pone un abrigo.**   When Miguel is cold, he puts on a coat. Use the third person singular reflexive pronoun *se* and place it before the conjugated verb. Drop the *-er* infinitive ending and add the third person singular ending *(-e)*.

2. **Answer: Yo me alegro.**   When I receive good news I become happy. The reflexive pronoun for *yo* is *me.* Place it before the conjugated verb. Drop the *-ar* infinitive ending and add the ending for *yo (-o).*

3. **Answer: Ellos se apresuran.**   When the students are not going to arrive at school on time, they hurry. Use the third person plural reflexive pronoun *se* and place it before the conjugated verb. Drop the *-ar* infinitive ending and add the ending for *ellos (-an).*

4. **Answer: Tú te quejas al camarero.**   When there's a fly in your soup, you complain to the waiter. The reflexive pronoun for *tú* is *te.* Place it before the conjugated verb. Drop the *-ar* infinitive ending and add the ending for *tú (-as).*

5. **Answer: Ellos se lavan las manos.**   When children have dirty hands, they wash them. Use the third person plural reflexive pronoun *se* and place it before the conjugated verb. Drop the *-ar* infinitive ending and add the ending for *ellos (-an).*

6. **Answer: Vosotros os desayunáis.**   When you're hungry at 6 a.m., you eat breakfast. The reflexive pronoun for *vosotros* is *os.* Place it before the conjugated verb. Drop the *-ar* infinitive ending and add the ending for *vosotros (-áis).*

7. **Answer: Ud. se asusta.**   When you think you've lost your money, you become frightened. The reflexive pronoun for *Ud.* is *se.* Place it before the conjugated verb. Drop the *-ar* infinitive ending and add the ending for *Ud. (-a).*

8. **Answer: Ella se aburre.**   If she doesn't like the concert, she becomes bored. The reflexive pronoun for *ella* is *se.* Place it before the conjugated verb. Drop the *-ir* infinitive ending and add the ending for *ella (-e).*

9. **Answer: Yo me quedo en casa.**   When I am sick, I stay home. The reflexive pronoun for *yo* is *me.* Place it before the conjugated verb. Drop the *-ar* infinitive ending and add the ending for *yo (-o).*

10. **Answer: Ellos se quitan el suéter.**   When the boys are warm, they remove their sweaters. Use the third person plural reflexive pronoun *se* and place it before the conjugated verb. Drop the *-ar* infinitive ending and add the ending for *ellos: (-an).*

11. **Answer: En una florería se venden flores.**   Use *una* to express "a" before the feminine singular noun, *florería*. Because *flores* (flowers) is plural, use the third person plural form of the verb. Drop the *-er* infinitive ending and add the third person plural ending *(-en)*.

12. **Answer: En un estadio se miran partidos.**   Use *un* to express "a" before the masculine singular noun, *estadio*. Because *partidos* (matches) is plural, use the third person plural form of the verb. Drop the *-ar* infinitive ending and add the third person plural ending *(-an)*.

13. **Answer: En un banco se cambia dinero.**   Use *un* to express "a" before the masculine singular noun, *banco*. Because *dinero* (money) is singular, use the third person singular form of the verb. Drop the *-ar* infinitive ending and add the third person singular ending *(-an)*.

14. **Answer: En un restaurante se preparan comidas.**   Words ending in *-e* tend to be masculine. Use *un* to express "a" before the masculine singular noun, *restaurante*. Because *comidas* (meals) is plural, use the third person plural form of the verb. Drop the *-ar* infinitive ending and add the third person plural ending *(-an)*.

15. **Answer: En una biblioteca se prestan libros.**   Use *una* to express "a" before the feminine singular noun, *biblioteca*. Because *libros* (books) is plural, use the third person plural form of the verb. Drop the *-ar* infinitive ending and add the third person plural ending *(-an)*

Supplemental Chapter Problems

Problems

In problems 1–10, choose the appropriate phrase from the box to express what each person does in the following situations, then conjugate the verb to agree with the subject.

acostarse	alegrarse	despertarse	prepararse limonada	quejarse
afeitarse	apresurarse	pasearse	preocuparse	resfriarse

1. Yo tengo sueño.

2. Nuestro despertador suena.

3. Ellos tienen sed.

4. A Rosa no le gusta su comida en el restaurante.

5. Tú tienes una cita a las nueve y son las ocho menos cinco.

6. Vosotros tenéis un examen hoy.

7. Ella sale bien en su clase.

8. Llueve mucho, hace frío y Ud. no tiene ni paraguas ni impermeable.

9. Él tiene una barba demasiado larga.

10. Hace buen tiempo y los Quevedo están en el parque.

In problems 11–15, express what the couple does every day.

    Example: hablar todos los días

            Se hablan todos los días.

11. ayudar

12. ver cada día

13. encontrar a menudo en la plaza

14. escribir cartas de amor

15. comprar regalos

In problems 16–20, express what takes place at school. Complete each sentence using the verb with or without its correct pronoun, according to its meaning.

16. (sentar/sentarse) El profesor _____ a los alumnos.

17. (ir/irse) Yo _____ de la escuela a las tres.

18. (aburrir/aburrirse) La lección no _____ a los estudiantes.

19. (levantar/levantarse) Nosotros _____ cuando contestamos las preguntas.

20. (cansar/cansarse) Tú _____ al final del día.

Answers

1. Yo me acuesto. (reflexive verbs, p. 141; stem-changing verbs, p. 97)

2. Nosotros nos despertamos. (reflexive verbs, p. 141; stem-changing verbs, p. 97)

3. Ellos se preparan una limonada. (reflexive verbs, p. 141; regular verbs, p. 92)

4. Ella se queja. (reflexive verbs, p. 141; regular verbs, p. 92)

5. Tú te apresuras. (reflexive verbs, p. 141; stem-changing verbs, p. 97)

6. Vosotros os preocupáis. (reflexive verbs, p. 141; regular verbs, p. 92)

7. Ella se alegra. (reflexive verbs, p. 141; regular verbs, p. 92)

8. Ud. se resfría. (reflexive verbs, p. 141; spelling-change verbs, p. 95)

9. Él se afeita. (reflexive verbs, p. 141; regular verbs, p. 92)

10. Ellos se pasean. (reflexive verbs, p. 141; regular verbs, p. 92)

11. Se ayudan. (reflexive verbs expressing reciprocal action, p. 148)

12. Se ven cada día. (reflexive verbs expressing reciprocal action, p. 148)

13. Se encuentran a menudo en la plaza. (reflexive verbs expressing reciprocal action, p. 148)

14. Se escriben cartas de amor. (reflexive verbs expressing reciprocal action, p. 148)

15. Se compran regalos. (reflexive verbs expressing reciprocal action, p. 148)

16. sienta (choosing the correct reflexive verb; p. 147, stem-changing verbs, p. 97)

17. me voy (choosing the correct reflexive verb, p. 147; irregular verbs, p. 100)

18. aburre (choosing the correct reflexive verb, p. 147; regular verbs, p. 92)

19. nos levantamos (choosing the correct reflexive verb, p. 147; regular verbs, p. 92)

20. te cansas (choosing the correct reflexive verb, p. 147; regular verbs, p. 92)

Chapter 7
Object Pronouns

Object pronouns are used so that an object noun doesn't have to be continuously repeated. Object nouns allow for a more free-flowing, conversational tone. When using object pronouns, make sure that the conjugated verb agrees with the subject and not with the object pronoun. Object pronouns are classified as either direct or indirect.

Direct Object Pronouns

Direct objects (which can be nouns or pronouns) answer the question "On whom or what is the subject acting?" and may refer to people, places, things, or ideas. A direct object pronoun replaces a direct object noun and, unlike in English, is usually placed before the conjugated verb.

The direct object pronouns in Spanish are shown in the following table:

Singular Pronouns	Meaning	Plural Pronouns	Meaning
me	me	nos	us
te	you (informal)	os (Spain)	you (informal)
le (Spain)	him, you (formal)		
lo	him, it, you (formal)	los	them, you
la	her, it, you (formal)	las	them, you

I watch the program.	Yo miro el programa.
I watch it.	Yo lo miro.
She reads the magazines.	Ella lee las revistas.
She reads them.	Ella las lee.
I adore you.	Yo te adoro.
You adore me.	Tú me adoras.
You look for us.	Ud. nos busca.
We look for you (informal plural).	Nosotros os buscamos.

In Latin America, the direct object pronoun *lo* is preferred to *le* to express "him" or "you":

Ella invita a Francisco.	She invites Francisco.
Ella le invita.	She invites him (in Spain).
Ella lo invita.	She invites him (in Latin America).

The Personal *A*

The personal *a* has no equivalent in English and is used only before a direct object noun (not before a pronoun) to indicate that the direct object is a person. Use the personal *a* when the direct object is:

- ❑ A person or persons:

  Conozco a tu hermano. (I know your brother.)

- ❑ A pet:

  Adiestra a su perro. (She tames her dog.)

- ❑ A pronoun referring to a person:

  ¿Buscas a alguien? (Are you looking for someone?)

- ❑ An unmodified geographic name (although modern usage tends to omit this):

  Quiero ver a España. (I want to see Spain.)

Do not use the personal *a* with the verb *tener:*

Tengo una hermana.   I have a sister.

Example Problems

Complete each dialogue by expressing the words in parentheses in Spanish.

Example: (the guys) ¿Ves <u>a los muchachos</u>?

(them) <u>Los</u> veo.

1. (Mr. Rosario) ¿Conoces_____?

   (him) No _____ conozco.

   Answer: ¿Conoces al señor Rosario? No lo (le) conozco.

   The personal *a* is used before the direct object when it refers to a person. The personal *a* contracts with the masculine singular definite article *el*, which must be used before the title *señor*. The direct object pronoun that replaces the name and refers to "him" is *lo* in Latin America and *le* in Spain.

2. (Luisa and Beatriz) ¿Buscas _____?

   (them) Sí, _____ busco.

   Answer: ¿Buscas a Luisa y a Beatriz? Sí, las busco.

   The personal *a* is used before each direct object when it refers to a person. The direct object pronoun that replaces the feminine "them" is *las*.

Work Problems

Complete each dialogue by expressing the words in parentheses in Spanish.

> Example: (the guys) ¿Busca <u>a los muchachos</u>?
>
> (them) Sí, <u>los</u> busco.

1.   (Gregorio and his brother) ¿Ve_____?

     (them) _____ veo.

2.   (you [informal plural]) ¿ _____ espera?

     (us) _____ espera.

3.   (you [informal singular]) ¿ _____ invita?

     (me) Sí _____ invita.

4.   (Carlota) ¿Visita _____?

     (her) No _____ visito.

5.   (Estela and Rafael) ¿Conoce _____?

     (them) Sí, _____ conozco.

6.   (Mauricio) ¿Escucha _____?

     (him) No _____ escucho.

Worked Solutions

1.   **¿Ve a Gregorio y a su hermano? Los veo.**   The personal *a* is used before each direct object when it refers to more than one person. The direct object pronoun that replaces the masculine "them" is *los*.

2.   **¿Os espera? Nos espera.**   Use the direct object pronoun *os* to express the informal plural "you." Use the direct object pronoun *nos* to express the informal singular "us."

3.   **¿Te invita? Me invita.**   Use the direct object pronoun *os* to express the informal singular "you." Use the direct object pronoun *me* to express the informal singular "me."

4.   **¿Visita a Carlota? No la visito.**   The personal *a* is used before the direct object when it refers to a person. The direct object pronoun that replaces the feminine name *Carlota* is *la*.

5.   **¿Conoce a Estela y a Rafael? Sí, los conozco.**   The personal *a* is used before each direct object when it refers to more than one person. The direct object pronoun that replaces the combined masculine and feminine subjects (them) is *los*.

6.   **¿Escucha a Mauricio? No lo escucho *or* No le escucho.**   The personal *a* is used before each direct object when it refers to a person. The direct object pronoun that replaces the name and refers to "him" is *lo* in Latin America and *le* in Spain.

Indirect Object Pronouns

Indirect objects (which can be nouns or pronouns) refer only to people (and pets) and answer the question "*To* or *for whom* is the subject doing something?" An indirect object pronoun replaces an indirect object noun but, in Spanish, it is also used even when the noun is mentioned. A clue to the correct usage of an indirect object pronoun is the use of the preposition *a* (*al, a la, a los,* or *a las*), which means "to" or "for" (unlike the personal *a*, which has no translation) followed by the name or reference to a person. Use *a él, a ella,* or *a Ud.* to clarify to whom you are referring.

The indirect object pronouns in Spanish are shown in the following table:

Singular Pronouns	*Meaning*	*Plural Pronouns*	*Meaning*
me	to me	nos	to us
te	to you (informal)	os	to you (informal)
le	to him, to her, to you, to it	les	to them, to you

The pronouns *me, te, nos,* and *os* are both direct and indirect object pronouns. They are also reflexive pronouns (see Chapter 6). In the third person, *a él (ellos), a ella (s),* or *a Ud.(s)* are used to distinguish to whom you are referring.

He reads to his son.	Él lee a su hijo.
He reads to him.	Él <u>le</u> lee (a él).
He writes to his girlfriend.	Él escribe a su novia.
He writes to her.	Él <u>le</u> escribe (a ella).
You buy a bracelet for me.	Ud. <u>me</u> compra una pulsera (a mí).
I buy a watch for you.	Yo <u>le</u> compro un reloj (a Ud.).

Although *a él (ellos), a ella(s),* or *a Ud.(s)* are generally placed immediately after the conjugated verb, in certain cases they may come at the end of a completed thought:

I ask my parents for permission.	Yo <u>les</u> pido permiso <u>a mis padres</u>.

In English, the prepositions "to" and "for" may or may not be used before a reference to a person. For example, you can say either of the following:

He showed his new car **to me.**	He showed **(to) me** his new car.

If these prepositions may be used in English, no matter how awkward the construction, an indirect (not a direct object) pronoun is called for in Spanish:

<u>Te</u> voy a comprar un regalo.	I am going to buy a gift **for you.**
	I am going to buy **(for) you** a gift.

Verbs requiring an indirect object in English do not necessarily require an indirect object in Spanish. These verbs take a direct object in Spanish because "to" or "for" is included in the meaning of the infinitive:

esperar	to wait for
buscar	to look for

escuchar	to listen to
esperar	to hope for (to)
llamar	to call, to name
pagar	to pay for (something)
mirar	to look at

Yo pago la cuenta.	I pay (for) the bill.
Yo la pago.	I pay (for) it.
Él busca a su hermana.	He looks for his sister.
Él la busca.	He looks for her.

Verbs requiring a direct object in English do not necessarily require a direct object in Spanish. These verbs take an indirect object in Spanish, regardless of the object used in English, because "to" or "for" is implied or because the verb is always followed by a when referring to a person (irregularities and spelling and stem changes are shown in bold):

aconsejar	to advise
contar	to relate, to tell
contestar	to answer
dar	to give
decir	to say, to tell
devolver	to return
enviar	to send
escribir	to write
explicar	to explain
mandar	to send
ofrecer	to offer
pagar	to pay (someone)
pedir	to ask
perdonar *	to forgive
preguntar	to ask
prestar	to lend
prohibir	to forbid
prometer	to promise
recordar *	to remind
regalar	to give a gift
telefonear	to phone

*Verbs with an asterisk take an indirect object only when a direct object is also present in the sentence:

| Explico el problema a mis amigas. | Les explico el problema. |
| I explain the problem to my friends. | I explain the problem to them. |

| Ella pide consejo a su hermano. | Ella le pide consejo. |
| She asks her brother for advice. | She asks him for advice. |

Lo recuerdo.	I remember him.
Le recuerdo de la fecha.	I remind him of the date.
La perdono.	I forgive her.
Le perdono su curiosidad.	I forgive her for her curiosity.

Example Problems

You are away at school and are talking to a friend on the phone. Rewrite each sentence, replacing all the nouns with the appropriate pronouns. Show clarity in your answer.

Example: yo digo todo/a mi mejor amiga.

Yo <u>le</u> digo todo (a mi mejor amiga).

1. mis padres envían paquetes/a mí

   Answer: Mis padres me envían paquetes (a mí).

   Use the pronoun *me* to express "to me." Put the pronoun before the conjugated verb form. Show clarity by including *a mí* at the end of the sentence.

2. yo escribo cartas electrónicas/a mis hermanos

   Answer: Yo les escribo cartas electrónicas (a mis hermanos).

   Use the pronoun *les* to express "to them." Put the pronoun before the conjugated verb form. Show clarity by including *a mis hermanos* at the end of the sentence.

Work Problems

Different people are giving gifts and exchanging good wishes. Rewrite each sentence, replacing all the nouns with the appropriate pronouns. Show clarity in your answer.

Example: tú envías ese regalo/a Jaime

Tú <u>le</u> envías (a Jaime) ese regalo.

1. yo regalo este dinero/a Rolando

2. nosotros ofrecemos estos CDs/a Beto y a Lorenzo

3. ellas dan esa carta/a ti

4. vosotros escribís este poema/a nosotros

5. ellos compran esas camisas/a vosotros

6. tú llevas muchas flores/a Rosa

Worked Solutions

1. **Yo le regalo (a Rolando) este dinero.**   Use the pronoun *le* to express "to him." Put the pronoun before the conjugated verb form. Show clarity by including *a Rolando* (to Roland) after the conjugated verb form or at the end of the sentence.

2. **Nosotros les ofrecemos (a Beto y a Lorenzo) estos CDs.**   Use the pronoun *les* to express "to them." Put the pronoun before the conjugated verb form. Show clarity by including *a Beto y a Lorenzo* (to Beto and Lorenzo) after the conjugated verb form or at the end of the sentence.

3. **Ellas te dan esa carta.**   Use the pronoun *te* to express "to you." Put the pronoun before the conjugated verb form.

4. **Vosotros nos escribís este poema.**   Use the pronoun *nos* to express "to us." Put the pronoun before the conjugated verb form.

5. **Ellos os compran esas camisas.**   Use the pronoun *os* to express "to you." Put the pronoun before the conjugated verb form.

6. **Tú le llevas (a Rosa) muchas flores.**   Use the pronoun *le* to express "to her." Put the pronoun before the conjugated verb form. Show clarity by including *a Rosa* (to Rosa) after the conjugated verb form or at the end of the sentence.

Gustar and Other Similar Verbs

Gustar (to please, to like) and a few other Spanish verbs use indirect objects to express the subject of their English counterparts. These verbs (irregularities and spelling and stem changes are in bold) include:

Verb	Meaning
agradar	to please, to be pleased with
bastar	to be enough
conv**e**nir	to be suitable, to be convenient
disgustar	to upset, to displease
d**o**ler	to be painful
encantar	to adore
faltar	to lack, to need
fascinar	to fascinate
importar	to matter, to care
interesar	to interest
pare**c**er	to seem
quedar	to have (something) left
to**c**ar	to be one's turn

Using These Verbs

Verbs requiring an indirect object follow these rules:

❑ The Spanish indirect object is the subject of the English sentence:

  <u>Les</u> gusta el chocolate. (They like chocolate.) [Chocolate is pleasing to them.]

  <u>Me</u> faltan dos dólares. (I need two dollars.) [Two dollars are lacking to me.]

❑ The third person singular form of *gustar* is used with one or more verbs:

Nos gusta leer y escribir. (We like to read and write.)

❑ The indirect object pronoun may be preceded by the preposition *a* + the corresponding prepositional pronoun (*mí, ti, él, ella, Ud., nosotros, vosotros, ellos, ellas,* or *Uds.*) for stress or clarification:

(A mí) me parece injusto. (It seems unfair to me.)

(A ellos) les interesan los deportes. (Sports interest them.)

❑ The indirect object pronoun may be preceded by the preposition *a* + the indirect object noun:

(A Rosita) no le gusta nada. (Rosita doesn't like anything.)

(A los muchachos) les gusta jugar. (The boys like to play.)

Example Problems

You are on a trip. Combine the elements to create sentences explaining what the people like.

Example: a ti/interesar los monumentos

(A ti) te interesan los monumentos.

1. a mí/encantar los mercados

Answer: (A mí) me encantan los mercados.

Use *a mí* to express "to me" at the beginning of the sentence for emphasis or clarity. Use the indirect object pronoun *me* to express "to me." The verb *encantar* must agree with the subject, *los mercados*. Drop the *-ar* ending and add the third person plural ending *(-an)*.

2. a ellos/gustar la comida

Answer: (A ellos) les gusta la comida.

Use *a ellos* to express "to them" at the beginning of the sentence for emphasis or clarity. Use the indirect object pronoun *les* to express "to them." The verb *gustar* must agree with the subject, *la comida*. Drop the *-ar* ending and add the third person singular ending *(-a)*.

Work Problems

Express how different people feel after a camping trip. Combine the elements to create sentences explaining what the people like.

Example: a él/interesar dormir

(A él) le interesa dormir.

1. a ti/gustar quedarte en casa

2. a nosotros/parecer una mala experiencia

3. a mí/faltar las comodidades de mi casa

4. a vosotros/disgustar los insectos

5. a Uds./convenir dormir en su cama

6. a ella/doler los pies

Worked Solutions

1. **(A ti) te gusta quedarte en casa.** Use *a ti* to express "to you" at the beginning of the sentence for emphasis or clarity. Use the indirect object pronoun *te* to express "to me." The verb *gustar* must agree with the subject, which happens to be a verb. Before the infinitive, *gustar* is used in the third person singular. Drop the *-ar* ending and add the third person singular ending *(-a)*.

2. **(A nosotros) nos parece una mala experiencia.** Use *a nosotros* to express "to us" at the beginning of the sentence for emphasis or clarity. Use the indirect object pronoun *nos* to express "to us." The verb *parecer* must agree with the subject, *una mala experiencia.* Drop the *-er* ending and add the third person singular ending *(-e)*.

3. **(A mí) me faltan las comodidades de mi casa.** Use *a mí* to express "to me" at the beginning of the sentence for emphasis or clarity. Use the indirect object pronoun *me* to express "to me." The verb *faltar* must agree with the subject, *las comodidades.* Drop the *-ar* ending and add the third person plural ending *(-an)*.

4. **(A vosotros) os disgustan los insectos.** Use *a vosotros* to express "to you" at the beginning of the sentence for emphasis or clarity. Use the indirect object pronoun *os* to express "to you." The verb *disgustar* must agree with the subject, *los insectos.* Drop the *-ar* ending and add the third person plural ending *(-an)*.

5. **(A Uds.) les conviene dormir en su cama.** Use *a Uds.* to express "to you" at the beginning of the sentence for emphasis or clarity. Use the indirect object pronoun *les* to express "to you." The verb *convenir* must agree with the subject, which happens to be a verb. Before the infinitive, *convenir* is used in the third person singular. *Convenir* has an internal stem change of *e* to *ie* in all forms except *nosotros* and *vosotros*. Drop the *-ir* ending and add the third person singular ending *(-e)*.

6. **(A ella) le duelen los pies.** Use *a ella* to express "to her" at the beginning of the sentence for emphasis or clarity. Use the indirect object pronoun *le* to express "to her." The verb *doler* must agree with the subject, *los pies. Doler* has an internal stem change of *o* to *ue* in all forms except *nosotros* and *vosotros*. Drop the *-er* ending and add the third person plural ending *(-en)*.

Position of Object and Reflexive Pronouns

Pronouns are placed as follows:

❑ Direct, indirect, and reflexive pronouns are placed before the verb:

Yo <u>lo</u> necesito. (I need it.)

Nosotros no <u>le</u> hablamos. (We don't speak to her.)

Ellos <u>se</u> bañan temprano. (They bathe themselves early.)

❑ The object or reflexive pronoun (see Chapter 6) may precede the conjugated verb or follow and be attached to an infinitive or gerund. It is necessary to add the required accent on the stressed vowel when the pronoun is attached to the gerund (in general, count back three vowels and add the accent):

<u>Lo</u> quiero ver.

Quiero ver<u>lo</u>.

        I want to see it.

<u>Me</u> estoy peinando.

Estoy peinándo<u>me</u>.
  3   2 1

        I'm combing my hair.

❑ The only time the object or reflexive pronoun follows the conjugated verb and is attached to it is in an affirmative command. An accent mark is normally required on the stressed vowel (count back three vowels and add the accent):

Affirmative: Escúche<u>lo</u>. (Listen to it.)
           3 2 1

BUT

Negative: No <u>lo</u> escuche. (Don't listen to it.)

Example Problems

Express what is happening at a picnic. Replace the underlined noun with a pronoun and put it in its correct position in the sentence.

    Example: La madre prepara <u>los sándwiches</u>.

           La madre <u>los</u> prepara.

1. Las muchachas quieren comer <u>helado</u>.

 Answer: Las muchachas quieren comerlo. (Las muchachas lo quieren comer.)

 Replace the masculine singular direct object noun *helado* with the masculine singular direct object pronoun *lo,* which expresses "it." Attach *lo* to the end of the infinitive. Alternatively, *lo* may be placed before the conjugated verb.

2. Ese muchacho no está obedeciendo <u>a sus padres</u>.

 Answer: Ese muchacho no está obedeciéndolos. (Ese muchacho no los está obedeciendo.)

 Replace the masculine plural indirect object noun phrase *a sus padres* with the masculine plural direct object pronoun *los,* which expresses "them." Attach *les* to the end of the gerund. Count back three vowels from the end and add an accent. Alternatively, *les* may be placed before the conjugated verb.

Work Problems

Express what is happening at home. Replace the underlined noun with a pronoun and put it in its correct position in the sentence.

> Example: El padre pasa <u>la aspiradora</u>.
>
> El padre <u>la</u> pasa.

1. Juan y Julio están cortando <u>el césped</u>.

2. Carlota no quiere sacar <u>la basura</u>.

3. Paco está escribiendo <u>a sus abuelos</u>.

4. La madre grita, "Telefonea <u>al electricista</u>."

5. El padre dice, "No sacudas <u>los muebles</u>."

6. Sarita no puede leer <u>a su hermana menor</u>.

Worked Solutions

1. **Juan y Julio están cortándolo. (Juan y Julio lo están cortando.)** Replace the masculine singular direct object noun *el césped* with the masculine singular direct object pronoun *lo*, which expresses "it." Attach *lo* to the end of the gerund. Count back three vowels from the end and add an accent. Alternatively, *lo* may be placed before the conjugated verb.

2. **Carlota no quiere sacarla. (Carlota no la quiere sacar.)** Replace the feminine singular direct object noun *la basura* with the feminine singular direct object pronoun *la*, which expresses "it." Attach *la* to the end of the infinitive. Alternatively, *la* may be placed before the conjugated verb.

3. **Paco está escribiéndoles. (Paco les está escribiendo.)** Replace the masculine plural indirect object noun phrase *a sus abuelos* with the masculine plural indirect object pronoun *les*, which expresses "to them." Attache *les* to the end of the gerund. Count back three vowels from the end and add an accent. Alternatively, *les* may be placed before the conjugated verb.

4. **La madre grita, "Telefonéale."** Replace the masculine singular indirect object noun phrase *al electricista* with the masculine singular indirect object pronoun *le*, which expresses "to him." In an affirmative command, attach *le* to the end of the command form. Count back three vowels and add an accent.

5. **El padre dice, "No los sacudas."** Replace the masculine plural direct object noun *los muebles* with the masculine plural direct object pronoun *los*, which expresses "them." In a negative command, place *los* before the conjugated verb.

6. **Sarita no puede leerle. (Sarita no le puede leer.)** Replace the feminine singular indirect object noun phrase *a su hermana menor* with the feminine singular indirect object pronoun *le*, which expresses "to her." Attach *le* to the end of the infinitive. Alternatively, *le* may be placed before the conjugated verb.

Double Object Pronouns

When a verb has two object pronouns, the indirect object pronoun (a person) precedes the direct object pronoun (usually a thing):

Ella <u>me lo</u> muestra. She shows it to me.

Él <u>se la</u> prepara. He prepares it for himself.

Note the following:

❑ The indirect object pronouns *le* and *les* change to *se* before the direct object pronouns *lo*, *la*, *los*, and *las*:

Yo <u>se la</u> escribo. I write it to you (him, her).

❑ The phrases *a Ud. (Uds.)*, *a él (ellos)*, and *a ella (ellas)* may be used to clarify the meaning of *se:*

Yo <u>se la</u> escribo a ella. I write it to her.

Also, note that the same rules for the position of single object pronouns apply for double object pronouns:

Infinitive: <u>Te la</u> quiere comprar.

Quiere comprár<u>tela</u>. He wants to buy it for you.

Gerund: <u>Se lo</u> está mostrando <u>a ella</u>.

Está mostrándo<u>selo</u> a ella. He's showing it to her.

Commands:

Affirmative: Escríba<u>melo</u>. Write it to me.

Negative: No <u>me lo</u> escriba. Don't write it to me.

All About Accents

When there are two pronouns with an infinitive, count back three vowels and then add an accent:

Él <u>se la</u> va a leer.

BUT He is going to read it to her.

Él va a leér<u>sela</u>.

Count back four vowels when a present participle or an affirmative command is used:

Nosotros <u>se lo</u> estamos mostrando.

BUT We are showing it to him.

Nosotros estamos mostrándo<u>selo</u>.

Cómpra<u>sela</u>. Buy it for her.

Example Problems

Use direct and indirect object pronouns to rewrite the sentences expressing what different people do to help others in their community.

Example: Tú das <u>dinero</u> <u>a los pobres</u>.

Tú <u>se lo</u> das.

1. Él lee <u>los libros</u> <u>al señor Colón</u>.

   Answer: Él se los lee.

   Replace the masculine plural direct object noun *los libros* with the masculine plural direct object pronoun *los*, which expresses "them." Replace the masculine singular indirect object noun phrase *al señor Colón* with the masculine singular indirect object pronoun *le*, which expresses "to him." When two third person direct (*lo, los, la, or las*) and indirect object (*le or les*) pronouns are used together, *le* (or *les*) becomes *se*. The indirect object pronoun precedes the direct object pronoun. Place both pronouns before the conjugated verb.

2. Nosotros podemos preparar <u>la cena</u> <u>a la señora López</u>.

   Answer: Nosotros podemos preparársela. Nosotros se la podemos preparar.

   Replace the feminine singular direct object noun *la cena* with the feminine singular direct object pronoun *la*, which expresses "it." Replace the feminine singular indirect object noun phrase *a la señora López* with the feminine singular indirect object pronoun *le*, which expresses "to her." When two third person direct (*lo, los, la, or las*) and indirect object (*le or les*) pronouns are used together, *le* becomes *se*. The indirect object pronoun precedes the direct object pronoun. Because there are two verbs and only one subject, the pronouns may be attached to the end of the infinitive. Count back three vowels and add an accent. Alternatively, place both pronouns before the conjugated verb.

Work Problems

Use direct and indirect object pronouns to rewrite the sentences expressing what different people do to celebrate the holidays.

> Example: Yo escribo <u>las cartas</u> <u>a mis amigas</u>.
> 　　　　　Yo <u>se las</u> escribo.

1. Ella da una camiseta (a mí).

2. Nosotros queremos enviar regalos a nuestras amigas.

3. ¡Manda juguetes a tu nieta!

4. Yo estoy ofreciendo un reloj (a ti).

5. ¡No regalen bufandas (a nosotros)!

6. Él va a pintar un retrato (a vosotros).

Worked Solutions

1. **Ella me la da.**　Replace the feminine singular direct object noun *una camiseta* with the feminine singular direct object pronoun *la*, which expresses "it." Use the indirect object noun *me* instead of *a mí* to express "to me." The indirect object pronoun precedes the direct object pronoun. Place both pronouns before the conjugated verb.

2. **Nosotros queremos enviárselos. (Nosotros se los queremos enviar.)**　Replace the masculine plural direct object noun *regalos* with the masculine plural direct object

pronoun *los*, which expresses "them." Replace the feminine plural indirect object noun phrase *a nuestras amigas* with the feminine plural object pronoun *les*, which expresses "to them." When two third person direct (*lo, los, la, or las*) and indirect object (*le* or *les*) pronouns are used together, *les* becomes *se*. The indirect object pronoun precedes the direct object pronoun. Because there are two verbs and only one subject, the pronouns may be attached to the end of the infinitive. Count back three vowels and add an accent. Alternatively, place both pronouns before the conjugated verb.

3. **¡Mándaselos!**   Replace the masculine plural direct object noun *juguetes* with the masculine plural direct object pronoun *los*, which expresses "them." Replace the feminine singular indirect object noun phrase *a su nieta* with the feminine singular indirect object pronoun *le*, which expresses "to her." When two third person direct (*lo, los, la, or las*) and indirect object (*le* or *les*) pronouns are used together, *le* becomes *se*. The indirect object pronoun precedes the direct object pronoun. With an affirmative command, attach the pronouns to the end of the command form. Count back four vowels and add an accent.

4. **Yo estoy ofreciéndotelo. (Yo te lo estoy ofreciendo.)**   Replace the masculine singular direct object noun *un reloj* with the masculine singular direct object pronoun *lo*, which expresses "it." Use the indirect object noun *te* instead of *a ti* to express "to you." The indirect object pronoun precedes the direct object pronoun. Because there are two verb forms in the progressive tense, the pronouns may be attached to the end of the gerund. Count back four vowels and add an accent. Alternatively, place both pronouns before the conjugated verb.

5. **¡No nos las regalen!**   Replace the feminine plural direct object noun *bufandas* with the feminine plural direct object pronoun *las*, which expresses "them." Use the indirect object noun *nos* instead of *a nosotros* to express "to us." With a negative command, place the pronouns before the conjugated verb.

6. **Él va a pintároslo. (Él os lo va a pintar.)**   Replace the masculine singular direct object noun *un retrato* with the masculine singular direct object pronoun *lo*, which expresses "it." Use the indirect object noun *os* instead of *a vosotros* to express "to you." The indirect object pronoun precedes the direct object pronoun. Because there are two verbs and only one subject, the pronouns may be attached to the end of the infinitive. Count back three vowels and add an accent. Alternatively, place both pronouns before the conjugated verb.

Chapter Problems

In problems 1–5, complete each sentence with the correct direct or indirect object pronoun.

1. (him) Yo ___ pago.

2. (her) Tú ___ aconsejas.

3. (them [feminine]) Nosotros ___ telefoneamos.

4. (them [masculine]) Tú ___ esperas.

5. (her) Su padres ___ llaman Susana.

In problems 6–12, express the following thoughts about school in Spanish.

6. ¿Julio? I see him.

7. ¿Los libros? They seem good to me.

8. ¿Las muchachas? The teacher (feminine) forgives them.

9. ¿José? The teacher (feminine) calls him.

10. ¿La profesora? He obeys her.

11. ¿La película? The class watches it.

12. ¿La muchacha? He looks for her.

In problems 13–16, express what people say to each other at a party. Select the correct pronouns and place them properly.

> Example: ella muestra (a nosotros/la sala)
>
> Ella <u>nos</u> <u>la</u> muestra.

13. él canta (a mí/esta canción)

14. ¡da! (a Juan/estas bebidas)

15. ¡no traigan! (a las muchachas/estos refrescos)

16. están sirviendo (a los invitados/postre)

Answers and Solutions

1. **Answer: le** The verb *pagar* takes an indirect object when it refers to a person.

2. **Answer: le** The verb *aconsejar* takes an indirect object because it is always followed by the preposition *a* (to).

3. **Answer: les** The verb *telefonear* takes an indirect object because it is always followed by the preposition *a* (to).

4. **Answer: los** The verb *esperar* (to wait for) takes a direct object because "for" is understood in the verb's meaning.

5. **Answer: la** The verb *llamar* takes a direct object in this case because the parents are not calling "to" the girl but are naming her Susana.

6. **Answer: Lo (Le) veo** The verb *ver* takes a direct object. The irregular *yo* form for *ver* is *veo*. Replace the masculine singular direct object noun *Julio* with the masculine singular direct object pronoun *lo,* which expresses "him." (In Spain, use *le*.) Place the direct object before the conjugated verb.

7. **Answer: Me parecen buenos** The verb *parecer* takes an indirect object and agrees with the subject that follows it: *los libros*. Because *los libros* is plural, use the third person plural form of the verb *parecer*. Use the indirect object *me* to express "to *me*"; place it before the verb. Use the masculine plural adjective *buenos* (see Chapter 9) to describe the masculine plural noun *los libros*.

8. **Answer: La profesora las perdona.** Use la *profesora* to express a female teacher. Use the verb *perdonar* to express "to forgive." Drop the *-ar* ending and add the third person

singular ending *(-a)*. The verb *perdonar* takes a direct object. Use the third person plural direct object *las* to express "them."

9. **Answer: La profesora lo (le) llama.** Use la *profesora* to express a female teacher. Use the verb *llamar* to express "to call." Drop the *-ar* ending and add the third person singular ending *(-a)*. The verb *llamar* takes a direct object. Use the third person singular direct object *lo* (or in Spain, *le)* to express "to him."

10. **Answer: Él la obedece.** Use the subject pronoun *él* to express "he." Use the verb *obedecer* to express "to obey." Drop the *-er* ending and add the third person singular ending *(-e)*. The verb *obedecer* takes a direct object. Use the third person singular indirect object *la* to express "her."

11. **Answer: La clase la mira.** Use *la clase* to express "the class." Use the verb *mirar* to express "to look at." Drop the *-ar* ending and add the third person singular ending *(-a)*. The verb *mirar* takes a direct object. Use the third person feminine singular direct object *la* to express "her."

12. **Answer: Él la busca.** Use the subject pronoun *él* to express "he." Use the verb *buscar* to express "to look for." Drop the *-ar* ending and add the third person singular ending *(-a)*. The verb *buscar* takes a direct object. Use the third person feminine singular direct object *la* to express "her."

13. **Answer: Me la canta.** Replace the feminine singular direct object noun *esta canción* with the feminine plural direct object pronoun *la*, which expresses "it." Use the indirect object noun *me* to express "to me." The indirect object pronoun precedes the direct object pronoun. Place both pronouns before the conjugated verb.

14. **Answer: ¡Dáselas!** Replace the feminine plural direct object noun *estas bebidas* with the feminine plural direct object pronoun *las*, which expresses "them." Replace the masculine singular indirect object noun phrase *a Juan* with the masculine singular indirect object pronoun *le*, which expresses "to him." When two third person direct (*lo, los, la,* or *las*) and indirect object (*le* or *les*) pronouns are used together, *le* becomes *se*. The indirect object pronoun precedes the direct object pronoun. In an affirmative command, attach the pronouns to the end of the command form. In this case, it is necessary to count back three vowels and add an accent to maintain the original stress.

15. **Answer: ¡No se los traigan!** Replace the masculine plural direct object noun *estos refrescos* with the masculine plural direct object pronoun *los*, which expresses "them." Replace the feminine plural indirect object noun phrase *a las muchachas* with the feminine plural indirect object pronoun *les*, which expresses "to them." When two third person direct (*lo, los, la,* or *las*) and indirect object pronouns (*le* or *les*) are used together, *les* becomes *se*. In a negative command, place the pronouns before the conjugated verb.

16. **Answer: Están sirviéndoselo. (Se lo están sirviendo.)** Nouns that end in *-e* tend to be masculine. Replace the masculine singular direct object noun *postre* with the masculine singular direct object pronoun *lo*, which expresses "it." Replace the masculine plural indirect object noun phrase *a los invitados* with the masculine plural indirect object pronoun *les*, which expresses "to them." *Les* changes to *se* before the third person direct object pronoun *lo*. The indirect object pronoun precedes the direct object pronoun. Because there are two verb forms in the progressive tense, the pronouns may be attached to the end of the gerund. Count back four vowels and add an accent. Alternatively, place both pronouns before the conjugated verb.

17. **Answer: Quiere sacártelas. (Te las quiere sacar.)** Replace the feminine plural direct object noun *fotografías* with the feminine plural direct object pronoun *las*, which

expresses "them." Use the indirect object *te* to express "to you." The indirect object pronoun precedes the direct object pronoun. Because there are two verbs and only one subject, the pronouns may be attached to the end of the infinitive. Count back three vowels and add an accent. Alternatively, place both pronouns before the conjugated verb.

18. **Answer: No puede mostrároslos. (No os los puede mostrar.)** Replace the masculine plural direct object noun *los regalos* with the masculine plural direct object pronoun *los*, which expresses "them." Use the indirect object *os* to express "to you." The indirect object pronoun precedes the direct object pronoun. Because there are two verbs and only one subject, the pronouns may be attached to the end of the infinitive. Count back three vowels and add an accent. Alternatively, place both pronouns before the conjugated verb.

19. **Answer: Se los compro.** Replace the masculine plural direct object noun phrase *vestidos de última moda* with the masculine plural direct object pronoun *los*, which expresses "them." Replace the feminine singular indirect object noun phrase *a mi amiga* with the feminine singular indirect object pronoun *le*, which expresses "to her." The indirect object *le* becomes *se* before the third person direct object pronoun *los*. Place both pronouns before the conjugated verb.

20. **Answer: No están ofreciéndonosla. (No nos la están ofreciendo.)** Replace the feminine singular direct object noun *comida* with the feminine singular direct object pronoun *la*, which expresses "it." Use the indirect object *nos* to express "to us." The indirect object pronoun precedes the direct object pronoun. Because there are two verb forms in the progressive tense, the pronouns may be attached to the end of the gerund. Count back four vowels and add an accent. Alternatively, place both pronouns before the conjugated verb.

Supplemental Chapter Problems

In problems 1–5, complete each sentence with the correct direct or indirect object pronoun.

1. (him) Tú ___ pides ayuda.

2. (them [masculine]) Ella ___ contesta.

3. (them [feminine]) Nosotros no ___ escuchamos.

4. (her) Él ___ recuerda de una cita.

5. (him) Yo ___ busco.

In problems 6–15, express the following thoughts in Spanish about working in a hospital.

6. ¿Las pastillas? I look for them.

7. ¿Su número de teléfono? I don't remember it.

8. ¿Los pacientes? The doctor advises them.

9. ¿Las curas? We find them.

10. ¿Los servicios? We pay for them.

11. ¿Las enfermeras? I ask them for a drink.

12. ¿Los ojos? They hurt Carlos.

13. ¿La dentista? He calls her.

In problems 14–16, express what people say to each other at the office. Select the correct pronouns and place them properly.

> Example: muestra (a mí/el papel)
>
> Muéstramelo.

14. ¿puedo prestar? (a Ud./mi bolígrafo)

15. ellos no explican (a nosotros/las reglas)

16. ¡traiga! (a mí/estos folletos)

Answers

1. le (indirect object pronouns, p. 158)

2. les (indirect object pronouns, p. 158)

3. las (direct object pronouns, p. 155)

4. le (indirect object pronouns, p. 158)

5. lo (direct object pronouns, p. 155)

6. Las busco. (direct object pronouns, p. 155)

7. No lo recuerdo. (direct object pronouns, p. 155)

8. El médico les aconseja. (indirect object pronouns, p. 158)

9. Nosotros las encontramos. (direct object pronouns, p. 155)

10. Nosotros los pagamos. (direct object pronouns, p. 155)

11. Les pido una bebida. (indirect object pronouns, p. 158)

12. Le duelen a Carlos. (indirect object pronouns, p. 158)

13. Él la llama. (direct object pronouns, p. 155)

14. ¿Puedo prestárselo? ¿Se lo puedo prestar? (double object pronouns, p. 166)

15. Ellos no nos las explican. (double object pronouns, p. 166)

16. ¡Tráigamelos! (double object pronouns, p. 166)

Chapter 8
Gerunds and the Present Progressive

Gerunds

A Spanish gerund *(un gerundio)* is derived from a verb. It may be the equivalent of an English present participle, which is used as an adjective that ends in *-ing*. A Spanish gerund may also be the equivalent of the English *by* or *while* + present participle.

Ese niño, quien está comiendo helado, es mi hermano.	That boy eating the ice cream is my brother.
Estudiando, se aprende mucho.	By (While) studying, one learns a lot.

An English gerund is used as a noun. A Spanish gerund may not be used as a noun subject; an infinitive is used instead:

Beber agua es importante.	Drinking water is important.

Forming Gerunds of Regular Verbs

Gerunds of regular verbs are formed as follows:

Drop *-ar* from *-ar* verb infinitive and add *-ando*.

Drop *-er* or *-ir* from *-er* and *-ir* verb infinitives, respectively, and add *-iendo*.

The following table shows how to create gerunds:

Ending	Verb	Meaning	Past Participle	Meaning
-ar	viajar	to travel	viajando	traveling
-er	beber	to drink	bebiendo	drinking
-ir	escribir	to write	escribiendo	writing

If an *-er* or *-ir* verb stem ends in a vowel, add *-yendo:*

caer (to fall)	cayendo
construir (to build)	construyendo
creer (to believe)	creyendo

leer (to read)	le<u>y</u>endo
oír (to hear)	o<u>y</u>endo
traer (to bring)	tra<u>y</u>endo

Example Problems

Give the correct form of the gerund to express what can be done.

Example:(estudiar) _____ mucho, se sale bien en los exámenes.
<u>Estudiando</u> mucho, se sale bien en los exámenes.

1. (viajar) _____ se puede aprender mucho.

   Answer: Viajando

   To form the gerund of an *-ar* verb infinitive, drop the *-ar* ending and add *-ando*.

2. (aprender) _____ una lengua extranjera se puede comunicar con los hispanohablantes.

   Answer: Aprendiendo

   To form the gerund of an *-er* verb infinitive, drop the *-er* ending and add *-iendo*.

3. (vivir) _____ en la América del Sur, se puede aprender el español rápidamente.

   Answer: Viviendo

   To form the gerund of an *-ir* verb infinitive, drop the *-ir* ending and add *-iendo*.

Work Problems

Give the correct form of the gerund to express what happens to or what happened to Olivia.

Example: Ella habla por su teléfono celular (conducir) _____ al centro.
Ella habla por su teléfono celular <u>conduciendo</u> al centro.

1. Ella se divierte (jugar) _____ al tenis.

2. Ella se cae (correr) _____ en la sala.

3. Ella se hace daño en la espalda (abrir) _____ la ventana.

4. Ella empieza a llorar (oír) _____ las noticias.

5. Ella se echa a reír (leer) _____ el periódico.

6. Ella telefonea a su mejor amiga (creer) _____ el chisme.

7. Ella se moja (huir) _____ de la tormenta.

8. Ella se quema (cocina) _____ la cena.

Worked Solutions

1. **jugando**   *Jugar* is an *-ar* verb that has an internal stem change from *u* to *ue*. To form the gerund of an *-ar* verb infinitive, drop the *-ar* ending and add *-ando*.

2. **corriendo**   To form the gerund of an *-er* verb infinitive, drop the *-er* ending and add *-iendo*.

3. **abriendo**   To form the gerund of an *-ir* verb infinitive, drop the *-ir* ending and add *-iendo*.

4. **oyendo**   *Oír* is irregular in the present tense. To form the gerund of an *-ir* verb whose stem ends in a vowel, add *-yendo*.

5. **leyendo**   To form the gerund of an *-er* verb whose stem ends in a vowel, add *-yendo*.

6. **creyendo**   To form the gerund of an *-er* verb whose stem ends in a vowel, add *-yendo*.

7. **huyendo**   To form the gerund of an *-ir* verb whose stem ends in a vowel, add *-yendo*.

8. **cocinando**   To form the gerund of an *-ar* verb infinitive, drop the *-ar* ending and add *-ando*.

Forming Gerunds of Stem-Change and Irregular Verbs

Here is a list of stem-change *-ir* verbs that change the stem vowel from *e* to *i* and from *o* to *u*:

corregir (to correct)	corrigiendo
decir (to say, to tell)	diciendo
divertir (to divert, to have fun)	divirtiendo
mentir (to lie)	mintiendo
pedir (to ask)	pidiendo
repetir (to repeat)	repitiendo
sentir (to feel)	sintiendo
servir (to serve)	sirviendo
venir (to come)	viniendo
vestir (to dress)	vistiendo
dormir (to sleep)	durmiendo
morir (to die)	muriendo

Verbs with irregular gerunds are:

ir (to go)	yendo
poder (to be able)	pudiendo
reír (to laugh)	riendo

Example Problems

Use a gerund to complete each sentence.

> Example: Jorge aprendió el vocabulario (repetir) _____ los verbos.
> Jorge aprendió el vocabulario <u>repitiendo</u> los verbos.

1. Juan escondió su miedo (reírse) _____.

   Answer: riendo

   Reír is an irregular verb. To form the gerund of *reír*, drop the *-ír* ending and add *-iendo*.

2. Gloria se hizo feliz (divertir) _____ a los niños.

   Answer: divirtiendo

   Divertir is an *-ir* verb with an internal stem change. Stem-change *-ir* verbs change the stem vowel from *e* to *i*. To form the gerund, change *e* to *i*, drop the *-ir* ending, and add *-iendo*.

3. María satisfizo a sus invitados (servir) _____ comida rica.

   Answer: sirviendo

   Servir is an *-ir* verb with an internal stem change. Stem-change *-ir* verbs change the stem vowel from *e* to *i*. To form the gerund, change *e* to *i*, drop the *-ir* ending, and add *-iendo*.

Work Problems

Express what happened to María at school.

> Example: Ella perdió el respeto de sus amigos (mentir) _____.
> Ella perdió el respeto de sus amigos <u>mintiendo.</u>

1. Ella salió bien en sus exámenes (pedir) _____ ayuda.

2. Ella ganó mucho dinero (poder) _____ trabajar el sábado.

3. Ella recibió el respeto de sus amigos (decir) _____ la verdad.

4. Ella mostró su felicidad (sonreír) _____.

5. Ella encontró algunos errores (corregir) _____ su trabajo.

6. Ella perdió su tren (dormir) _____ hasta tarde.

Worked Solutions

1. **pidiendo**   *Pedir* is an *-ir* verb with an internal stem change. For the gerund, stem-change *-ir* verbs change the stem vowel from *e* to *i*. To form the gerund, change *e* to *i*, drop the *-ir* ending, and add *-iendo*.

2. **podiendo**   The gerund for *poder* is irregular and must be memorized.

3. **diciendo**   *Decir* is an -*ir* verb with an internal stem change. For the gerund, stem-change -*ir* verbs change the stem vowel from *e* to *i*. To form the gerund, change *e* to *i*, drop the -*ir* ending, and add -*iendo*.

4. **sonriendo**   The gerund for *sonreír* is irregular and must be memorized.

5. **corrigiendo**   *Corregir* is an -*ir* verb with an internal stem change. For the gerund, stem-change -*ir* verbs change the stem vowel from *e* to *i*. To form the gerund, change *e* to *i*, drop the -*ir* ending, and add -*iendo*.

6. **durmiendo**   *Dormir* is an -*ir* verb with an internal stem change. For the gerund, stem-change -*ir* verbs change the stem vowel from *o* to *u*. To form the gerund, change *o* to *u*, drop the -*ir* ending, and add -*iendo*.

Progressive Tenses

The present tense (see Chapter 4) expresses an action or event that the subject generally **does** at a given time or that is habitual. The present progressive expresses an action or event that **is** in progress or that **is** continuing at a given time.

Él estudia a las ocho.	He studies (does study) at eight o'clock (every day).
Él está estudiando inglés.	He is studying English (at the present time).

Forming the Present Progressive

The two elements necessary for the formation of present progressive are:

❑ The present tense of the verb *estar,* which expresses that something is taking place:

yo estoy	nosotros estamos
tú estás	vosotros estáis
él (ella, Ud.) está	ellos (ellas, Uds.) están

❑ The gerund of the verb, which expresses what the action is.

The formula for the formation of the present progressive is:

> subject noun or pronoun + *estar* (in present tense) + gerund

For example:

Ellos están durmiendo.	They are sleeping.

For reflexive verbs, the reflexive pronoun may precede the conjugated verb form or may be attached to the gerund, in which case an accent mark is placed on the stressed vowel (in general, count back three vowels to find the stressed vowel):

Se está afeitando.	He's shaving.
Está afeitándose.	

The present progressive can also be formed by using the present tense of the verbs *seguir* (to keep on, to continue), *continuar* (to continue), *ir* (to go), *venir* (to come), *salir* (to go out), and *andar* (to walk) and adding a gerund:

Ella sigue hablando.	She continues speaking.
Yo continúo leyendo.	I continue reading.
El tiempo va cambiando.	The weather is changing.
Yo salgo llorando.	I leave crying.
Ellos andan buscando a su perro.	They walk looking for their dog.

Other progressive tenses can be formed by using the proper tense of the verb (preterit [see Chapter 13 and Chapter 14] or imperfect [see Chapter 15]), *will be* (future [see Chapter 17]), or *would be* (conditional [see Chapter 18]):

Él estaba leyendo.	He was reading (imperfect).
Ella siguió hablando.	She continued speaking (preterit).
El tiempo iba cambiando.	The weather was changing (imperfect).
Él llegará corriendo.	He will arrive running (future).
Yo saldría llorando.	I would leave crying (conditional).

Example Problems

Express what the people are doing.

> Example: tú/estar/estudiar
> Tú estás estudiando.

1. ellas/estar/divertirse

   Answer: Ellas están divirtiéndose. (Ellas se están divirtiendo.)

   The *ellas* form of *estar* is irregular. Drop the *-ar* ending and add *-án*. *Divertirse* is an *-ir* verb with an internal stem change. For the gerund, stem-change *-ir* verbs change the stem vowel from *e* to *i*. To form the gerund, change *e* to *i*, drop the *-ir* ending, and add *-iendo*. The reflexive pronoun may be attached to the gerund. Count back three vowels and add an accent. Alternatively, the reflexive pronoun may precede the conjugated verb.

2. yo/salir de mi casa/repetir un poema

   Answer: Yo salgo de mi casa repitiendo un poema.

   The *yo* form of *salir* is irregular. Drop the *-ir* ending and add *-go*. *Repetir* is an *-ir* verb with an internal stem change. For the gerund, stem-change *-ir* verbs change the stem vowel from *e* to *i*. To form the gerund, change *e* to *i*, drop the *-ir* ending, and add *-iendo*.

3. él/continuar/traer libros a casa

   Answer: Él continúa trayendo libros a casa.

Continuar is an *-ar* verb with an accented *u* in all forms except *nosotros* and *vosotros*. Drop the *-ar* ending and add *-a*. To form the gerund of an *-er* verb whose stem ends in a vowel, add *-yendo*.

Work Problems

Express what the people are doing or what is happening to them.

> Example: ellas/estar/bailando
> 　　　　　Ellas están bailando.

1.　yo/salir/despedirse de mis amigos

2.　nosotros/estar/morirse de sed

3.　Uds./seguir/atraer al público

4.　ellas/estar/pedir ayuda a sus amigos

5.　tú/continuar/reírse

6.　él/estar/mentir

7.　Ud./estar/dormir

8.　nosotros/seguir/ir al centro

Worked Solutions

1.　**Yo salgo despidiéndome de mis amigos.**　The *yo* form of *salir* is irregular. Drop the *-ir* ending and add *-go*. *Despedir* is an *-ir* verb with an internal stem change. For the gerund, stem-change *-ir* verbs change the stem vowel from *e* to *i*. To form the gerund, change *e* to *i*, drop the *-ir* ending, and add *-iendo*. The reflexive pronoun may be attached to the gerund. Count back three vowels and add an accent.

2.　**Nosotros estamos muriéndonos de sed.**　The *nosotros* form of *estar* is regular. Drop the *-ar* ending and add *-amos*. *Morirse* is an *-ir* verb with an internal stem change. For the gerund, stem-change *-ir* verbs change the stem vowel from *o* to *u*. To form the gerund, change *o* to *u*, drop the *-ir* ending, and add *-iendo*. The reflexive pronoun may be attached to the gerund. Count back three vowels and add an accent.

3.　**Uds. siguen atrayendo al público.**　The *Uds.* form of *seguir* is irregular. *Seguir* has an internal change of *e* to *i* in all forms except *nosotros* and *vosotros*. Drop the *-ir* ending and add *-en*. For the gerund, when the stem of a verb ends in a vowel, change the *i* of *iendo* to *y* (*-yendo*).

4.　**Ellas están pidiendo ayuda a sus amigos.**　The *ellas* form of *estar* is irregular. Drop the *-ar* ending and add *-án*. For the gerund, stem-change *-ir* verbs change the stem vowel from *e* to *i*. To form the gerund, drop the *-ir* ending and add *-iendo*.

5. **Tú continúas riéndote.** *Continuar* is an -*ar* verb with an accented *u* in all forms except *nosotros* and *vosotros*. Drop the -*ar* ending and add -*a*. The gerund for *reírse* is irregular and must be memorized.

6. **Él está mintiendo.** The *él* form of *estar* is irregular. Drop the -*ar* ending and add -*á*. For the gerund, stem-change -*ir* verbs change the stem vowel from *e* to *i*. To form the gerund, change *e* to *i*, drop the -*ir* ending, and add -*iendo*.

7. **Ud. está durmiendo.** The *Ud.* form of *estar* is irregular. Drop the -*ar* ending and add -*á*. For the gerund, stem-change -*ir* verbs change the stem vowel from *o* to *u*. To form the gerund, change *o* to *u*, drop the -*ir* ending, and add -*iendo*.

8. **Nosotros seguimos yendo al centro.** The *nosotros* form of *seguir* is regular. Drop the -*ir* ending and add -*imos*. The gerund for *ir* is irregular and must be memorized.

Chapter Problems

Problems

In problems 1–12, express what each person is doing after work or school.

> Example: ella/comer en un restaurante
> Ella está comiendo en un restaurante.

1. yo/jugar a los naipes

2. la madre/servir la cena

3. ellos/pedir ayuda a sus hermanas

4. ellas/oír la radio

5. nosotros/hacer las tareas

6. Ud./construir un coche en miniatura

7. el padre/escribir cheques

8. vosotros/comer galletas

9. Rogelio/conseguir datos para su amigo

10. Uds./divertirse

11. yo/leer el periódico

12. tú/vestirse para salir

In problems 13–20, describe the scene by combining the elements.

> Example: ella/estar/hablar
>
> Ella está hablando.

13. nosotros/llegar/gritar

14. ellos/entrar/hablar

15. tú/seguir/leer

16. yo/continuar/escribir cartas

17. vosotros/salir/sonreír

18. ella/ir/llorar

19. Uds./andar/caminar a su perro

20. nosotros/seguir/tocar el piano

Answers and Solutions

1. **Answer: Yo estoy jugando a los naipes.** The *yo* form of *estar* is irregular. Drop the *-ar* ending and add *-oy*. To form the gerund of an *-ar* verb infinitive, drop the *-ar* ending and add *-ando*.

2. **Answer: La madre está sirviendo la cena.** The *ella* form of *estar* is irregular. Drop the *-ar* ending and add *-á*. For the gerund, stem-change *-ir* verbs change the stem vowel from *e* to *i*. To form the gerund, change *e* to *i*, drop the *-ir* ending, and add *-iendo*.

3. **Answer: Ellos están pidiendo ayuda a sus hermanas.** The *ellos* form of *estar* is irregular. Drop the *-ar* ending and add *-án*. For the gerund, stem-change *-ir* verbs change the stem vowel from *e* to *i*. To form the gerund, change *e* to *i*, drop the *-ir* ending, and add *-iendo*.

4. **Answer: Ellas están oyendo la radio.** The *ellas* form of *estar* is irregular. Drop the *-ar* ending and add *-án*. To form the gerund or an *-ir* verb whose stem ends in a vowel, add *-yendo*.

5. **Answer: Nosotros estamos haciendo las tareas.** The *nosotros* form of *estar* is regular. Drop the *-ar* ending and add *-amos*. To form the gerund of an *-er* verb infinitive, drop the *-er* ending and add *-iendo*.

6. **Answer: Ud. está construyendo un coche en miniatura.** The *Ud.* form of *estar* is irregular. Drop the *-ar* ending and add *-á*. To form the gerund of an *-ir* verb whose stem ends in a vowel, add *-yendo*.

7. **Answer: El padre está escribiendo cheques.** The *él* form of *estar* is irregular. Drop the *-ar* ending and add *-á*. To form the gerund of an *-ir* verb infinitive, drop the *-ir* ending and add *-iendo*.

8.   **Answer: Vosotros estáis comiendo galletas.** The *vosotros* form of *estar* is regular. Drop the *-ar* ending and add *-áis*. To form the gerund of an *-er* verb infinitive, drop the *-er* ending and add *-iendo*.

9.   **Answer: Rogelio está consiguiendo datos para su amigo.** The *él* form of *estar* is irregular. Drop the *-ar* ending and add *-á*. For the gerund, stem-change *-ir* verbs change the stem vowel from *e* to *i*. To form the gerund, change *e* to *i*, drop the *-ir* ending, and add *-iendo*.

10. **Answer: Uds. están divirtiéndose. (Uds. se están divirtiendo.)** The *Uds.* form of *estar* is irregular. Drop the *-ar* ending and add *-án*. For the gerund, stem-change *-ir* verbs change the stem vowel from *e* to *i*. To form the gerund, change *e* to *i*, drop the *-ir* ending, and add *-iendo*.

11. **Answer: Yo estoy leyendo el periódico.** The *yo* form of *estar* is irregular. Drop the *-ar* ending and add *-oy*. To form the gerund or an *-ir* verb whose stem ends in a vowel, add *-yendo*. Alternatively, the reflexive pronoun may precede the conjugated verb.

12. **Answer: Tú estás vistiéndote para salir. (Tú te estás vistiendo para salir.)** The *tú* form of *estar* is irregular. Drop the *-ar* ending and add *-ás*. For the gerund, stem-change *-ir* verbs change the stem vowel from *e* to *i*. To form the gerund, change *e* to *i*, drop the *-ir* ending and add *-iendo*. Alternatively, the reflexive pronoun may precede the conjugated verb.

13. **Answer: Nosotros llegamos gritando.** For the *nosotros* form of *llegar*, drop the *-ar* ending and add *-amos*. To form the gerund of an *-ar* verb infinitive, drop the *-ar* ending, and add *-ando*.

14. **Answer: Ellos entran hablando.** For the *ellos* form of *entrar*, drop the *-ar* ending and add *-an*. To form the gerund of an *-ar* verb infinitive, drop the *-ar* ending and add *-ando*.

15. **Answer: Tú sigues leyendo.** The *tú* form of *seguir* is irregular. *Seguir* has an internal change of *e* to *i* in all forms except *nosotros* and *vosotros*. For the *tú* form of *seguir*, drop the *-ir* ending and add *-es*. To form the gerund of an *-er* verb whose stem ends in a vowel, add *-yendo*.

16. **Answer: Yo continúo escribiendo cartas.** *Continuar* is an *-ar* verb with an accented *u* in all forms except *nosotros* and *vosotros*. For the *yo* form of *continuar*, drop the *-ar* ending and add *-o*. To form the gerund of an *-ir* verb infinitive, drop the *-ir* ending and add *-iendo*.

17. **Answer: Vosotros salís sonriendo.** For the *vosotros* form of *salir*, drop the *-ir* ending and add *-ís*. The gerund of *sonreír* is irregular and must be memorized.

18. **Answer: Ella va llorando.** *Ir* is an irregular verb. The form for *ella* is *va*. To form the gerund of an *-ar* verb infinitive, drop the *-ar* ending and add *-ando*.

19. **Answer: Uds. andan caminando a su perro.** For the *Uds.* form of *andar*, drop the *-ar* ending and add *-an*. To form the gerund of an *-ar* verb infinitive, drop the *-ar* ending and add *-ando*.

20. **Answer: Nosotros seguimos tocando el piano.** For the *nosotros* form of *seguir*, drop the *-ir* infinitive ending and add *-imos*. To form the gerund of an *-ar* verb infinitive, drop the *-ar* ending and add *-ando*.

Supplemental Chapter Problems

Problems

In problems 1–12, express what each person is doing at the gym.

> Example: ellos/comer zanahorias
> Ellos están comiendo zanahorias.

1. nosotros/nadar en la piscina

2. tú/oír música

3. yo/repetir los ejercicios

4. vosotros/pedir ayuda a vuestro entrenador

5. ellas/hablar con sus amigas

6. Ud./desvestirse

7. nosotros/morirse de fatiga

8. Uds./correr en la pista

9. ella/seguir los consejos de sus amigos

10. ellos/bajar de peso

11. un muchacho/dormir en un rincón

12. yo/concluir mi entrenamiento

In problems 13–20, describe the scene by combining the elements.

> Example: tú/estar/mirar la televisión
> Tú estás mirando la televisión.

13. yo/llegar/correr

14. ellos/entrar/repetir el chisme

15. ella/seguir/vestirse

16. nosotros/continuar/hacer nuestro trabajo

17. tú/ir/comer

18. Uds./salir/reírse

19. vosotros/andar/distribuir folletos

20. ella y yo/seguir/dormir

Answers

1. Nosotros estamos nadando en la piscina. (forming gerunds of regular verbs, p. 173)

2. Tú estás oyendo música. (forming gerunds of irregular verbs, p. 175)

3. Yo estoy repitiendo los ejercicios. (forming gerunds of stem-change verbs, p. 175)

4. Vosotros estáis pidiendo ayuda a vuestro entrenador. (forming gerunds of stem-change verbs, p. 175)

5. Ellas están hablando con sus amigas. (forming gerunds of regular verbs, p. 173)

6. Ud. está desvistiéndose. (Ud. se está desvistiendo.) (forming gerunds of stem-change verbs, p. 175)

7. Nosotros estamos muriéndonos de fatiga. (Nosotros nos estamos muriendo de fatiga.) (forming gerunds of stem-change verbs, p. 175)

8. Uds. están corriendo en la pista. (forming gerunds of regular verbs, p. 173)

9. Ella está siguiendo los consejos de sus amigos. (forming gerunds of stem-change verbs, p. 175)

10. Ellos están bajando de peso. (forming gerunds of regular verbs, p. 173)

11. Un muchacho está durmiendo en un rincón. (forming gerunds of stem-change verbs, p. 175)

12. Yo estoy concluyendo mi entrenamiento. (forming gerunds of spelling-change verbs, p. 175)

13. Yo llego corriendo. (forming the present progressive, p. 177; forming gerunds of regular -er verbs, p. 173; regular verbs, p. 92)

14. Ellos entran repitiendo el chisme. (forming the present progressive, p. 177; forming gerunds of stem-change verbs, p. 175)

15. Ella sigue vistiéndose. (forming the present progressive, p. 177; forming gerunds of stem-change verbs, p. 175; spelling-change verbs, p. 95)

16. Nosotros continuamos haciendo nuestro trabajo. (forming the present progressive, p. 177; forming gerunds of irregular verbs; p. 175, spelling-change verbs, p. 95)

17. Tú vas comiendo. (forming the present progressive, p. 177; forming gerunds of regular -er verbs, p. 173; irregular verbs, p. 100)

18. Uds. salen riéndose. (forming the present progressive, p. 177; forming gerunds of irregular verbs, p. 175; regular verbs, p. 92)

19. Vosotros andáis distribuyendo folletos. (forming the present progressive, p. 177; forming gerunds of spelling-change verbs, p. 175)

20. Ella y yo seguimos durmiendo. (forming the present progressive, p. 177; forming gerunds of stem-change verbs, p. 175; spelling-change verbs, p. 95; stem-change verbs, p. 97)

Chapter 9
Adjectives

An adjective modifies a noun or a pronoun. All Spanish adjectives agree in number (singular or plural) and gender (masculine or feminine) with the nouns they describe. If the noun or pronoun is singular, its verb and any adjectives describing it must also be in the singular form. If the noun or pronoun is feminine, the adjective describing it must also be in the feminine form.

Unlike English, most Spanish adjectives are placed after the nouns they modify. A few adjectives, however, precede the noun. In addition, when more than one adjective is used to describe a noun, certain rules for placement must be followed.

The Gender of Adjectives

An adjective that ends in an -o is always masculine. Masculine adjectives can, however, end in other letters.

Masculine Adjectives Ending in -o

Masculine singular adjectives ending in -o form the feminine by changing -o to -a. Some common adjectives are in the following list:

Masculine	Feminine	Meaning
aburrido	aburrida	boring
afortunado	afortunada	fortunate
agradecido	agradecida	thankful
alto	alta	tall
atractivo	atractiva	attractive
bajo	baja	short
bondadoso	bondadosa	kind
bonito	bonita	pretty
bueno	buena	good
delgado	delgada	thin
delicioso	deliciosa	delicious
divertido	divertida	fun
enfermo	enferma	sick
enojado	enojada	angry
famoso	famosa	famous
feo	fea	ugly

flaco	flaca	thin
generoso	generosa	generous
gordo	gorda	fat
guapo	guapa	pretty, good-looking
listo	lista	ready
magnífico	magnífica	magnificent
malo	mala	bad
moderno	moderna	modern
moreno	morena	dark-complexioned
necesario	necesaria	necessary
negro	negra	black
nuevo	nueva	new
ordinario	ordinaria	ordinary
orgulloso	orgullosa	proud
pardo	parda	brown
pequeño	pequeña	small
perezoso	perezosa	lazy
perfecto	perfecta	perfect
rico	rica	rich, delicious
romántico	romántica	romantic
rubio	rubia	blond
serio	seria	serious
simpático	simpática	nice
sincero	sincera	sincere
tímido	tímida	shy
todo	toda	all
tonto	tonta	foolish
viejo	vieja	old

Masculine Adjectives Ending in Other Letters

Masculine singular adjectives ending in *-a, -e,* or a consonant require no change to get the feminine form:

Masculine	Feminine	Meaning
egoísta	egoísta	selfish
materialista	materialista	materialistic
optimista	optimista	optimistic
pesimista	pesimista	pessimistic
realista	realista	realistic
alegre	alegre	happy
amable	amable	nice
eficiente	eficiente	efficient
elegante	elegante	elegant
excelente	excelente	excellent

grande	grande	big
horrible	horrible	horrible
importante	importante	important
inteligente	inteligente	intelligent
interesante	interesante	interesting
pobre	pobre	poor
responsable	responsable	responsible
sociable	sociable	sociable
triste	triste	sad
valiente	valiente	brave
cortés	cortés	courteous
azul	azul	blue
débil	débil	weak
fácil	fácil	easy
genial	genial	brilliant, great
leal	leal	loyal
puntual	puntual	punctual
tropical	tropical	tropical
joven	joven	young
popular	popular	popular
feroz	feroz	ferocious

Exceptions to the Rules

Some adjectives of nationality whose masculine form ends in a consonant add -a to form the feminine. Note that *frances* and *aleman* also drop the accent on the final vowel to maintain original stress:

español	española	Spanish
francés	francesa	French
alemán	alemana	German

Some adjectives whose masculine form ends in -or add -a to form the feminine:

encantador	encantadora	enchanting
hablador	habladora	talkative
trabajador	trabajadora	hardworking

Example Problems

Describe the members of the Marcos family by filling in the blank with an adjective that means the opposite of the one given.

Example: Pablo es flaco y Linda es _____.

Pablo es flaco y Linda es <u>gorda</u>.

1. Héctor es alto e Hilda es ____.

   Answer: Héctor es alto e Hilda es baja.

   Alto means "tall." To describe Hilda, the opposite *(bajo)* must be changed to the feminine singular form by changing the *-o* to *-a.*

2. Fernando es fuerte y Bárbara es ____.

   Answer: Fernando es fuerte y Bárbara es débil.

   Fuerte means "strong." The opposite *(débil)* remains unchanged in the feminine form because masculine singular adjectives ending in a consonant require no change to get the feminine form.

Work Problems

Describe the members of the Adolfo family by filling in the blank with an adjective that means the opposite of the one given.

   Example: Alfonso es serio y Cristina es ____.
   Alfonso es serio y Cristina es <u>cómica</u>.

1. Alberto es <u>antipático</u> e Isabel es ____.

2. El abuelo es <u>viejo</u> y la abuela es ____.

3. Eva está <u>alegre</u> y Gregorio está ____.

4. El tío es <u>pobre</u> y la tía es ____.

5. Francisco es <u>descortés</u> y Alicia es ____.

6. La prima es <u>callada</u> y el primo es ____.

Worked Solutions

1. **Alberto es antipático e Isabel es simpática.** *Antipático* means "unpleasant." To describe Isabel, the opposite *(simpático)* must be changed to the feminine singular form by changing the *-o* to *-a.*

2. **El abuelo es viejo y la abuela es joven.** *Viejo* means "old." The opposite *(joven)* remains unchanged in the feminine form because masculine singular adjectives ending in a consonant require no change to get the feminine form.

3. **Eva está alegre y Gregorio está triste.** *Alegre* means "cheerful." The opposite *(triste)* remains unchanged in the feminine form because masculine singular adjectives ending in *-e* require no change to get the feminine form.

4. **El tío es pobre y la tía es rica.** *Pobre* means "poor." To describe *la tía,* the opposite *(rico)* must be changed to the feminine singular form by changing the *-o* to *-a.*

5. **Francisco es descortés y Alicia es cortés.** *Descortés* means "discourteous." The opposite *(cortés)* remains unchanged in the feminine form because masculine singular adjectives ending in a consonant require no change to get the feminine form.

6. **La prima es callada y el primo es hablador.** *Callada* means "quiet." The masculine singular form of the opposite *(hablador)* ends in *-or*.

Plural of Adjectives

Add *-s* to form the plural of adjectives ending in a vowel:

Singular	Plural	Meaning
bajo	bajo**s**	short
sincera	sincera**s**	sincere
inteligente	inteligente**s**	intelligent

Add *-es* to form the plural of adjectives ending in a consonant:

Singular	Plural	Meaning
difícil	difícil**es**	difficult
hablador	hablador**es**	talkative

Exceptions to the Rule

Singular adjectives ending in *-z* change the *z* to *c* in the plural and add *-es:*

Singular	Plural	Meaning
feliz	feli**ces**	happy
atroz	atro**ces**	atrocious
sagaz	saga**ces**	astute

Some adjectives add or drop an accent mark to maintain the original stress:

Singular	Plural	Meaning
joven	j**ó**venes	young
francés	franc**e**ses	French
inglés	ingl**e**ses	English
alemán	alem**a**nes	German
cortés	cort**e**ses	courteous

When an adjective modifies two or more nouns of different genders, the masculine plural form of the adjective is used:

El hombre y la mujer son trabajadores.   The man and the woman are hardworking.

Example Problems

Select the adjective that best describes the animal. Then change it to its plural form.

astuto	feroz	fuerte	trabajador

Example: Los zorros son ____.
Los zorros son <u>astutos</u>.

1. Los bueyes (oxen) son ____.

   Answer: Los bueyes son fuertes.

   Fuerte means "strong." To form the plural of an adjective ending in *-e*, add *-s*.

2. Los castores (beavers) son ____.

   Answer: Los castores son trabajadores.

   Trabajador means "hardworking." To form the plural of an adjective ending in a consonant, add *-es*.

Work Problems

Describe each subject with the adjective that makes the most sense. Then change the adjective to the plural.

alemán	feliz	joven	cortés	
francés	puntual	diligente	hablador	sincero

Example: Esos muchachos siempre dicen la verdad. Ellos son ____.
Esos muchachos siempre dicen la verdad. Ellos son <u>sinceros</u>.

1. Ellas son de Alemania. Ellas son ____.

2. Ellos son de Francia. Ellos son ____.

3. Las muchachas hablan todo el tiempo. Ellas son ____.

4. Ellas siempre llegan a tiempo. Ellas son ____.

5. Ellas trabajan mucho. Ellas son ____.

6. Ellas siempre dicen "por favor" y "de nada." Ellas son ____.

Worked Solutions

1. **Ellas son de Alemania. Ellas son alemanas.**   *Alemán* means "German." First, change the masculine singular adjective to its feminine singular form by adding *-a*. Then, form the plural of this adjective that ends in a vowel by adding *-s*. *Alemán* is an adjective that drops its accent in the feminine singular and in all plural forms to maintain the original stress.

2. **Ellos son de Francia. Ellos son franceses.** *Francés* means "French." *Francés* is an adjective that drops its accent in the feminine singular and in all plural forms to maintain the original stress. To form the plural of an adjective ending in a consonant, add *-es.*

3. **Las muchachas hablan todo el tiempo. Ellas son habladoras.** *Hablador* means "talkative." First, change the masculine singular adjective to its feminine singular form by adding *-a.* Then, form the plural of this adjective that ends in a vowel by adding *-s.*

4. **Ellas siempre llegan a tiempo. Ellas son puntuales.** *Puntual* means "punctual." Masculine singular adjectives ending in a consonant require no change to get the feminine form. Form the plural of this adjective that ends in a consonant by adding *-es.*

5. **Ellas trabajan mucho. Ellas son diligentes.** *Diligente* means "hardworking." Masculine singular adjectives ending in an *-e* require no change to get the feminine form. Form the plural of this adjective that ends in a vowel by adding *-s.*

6. **Ellas siempre dicen "por favor" y "de nada." Ellas son corteses.** *Cortés* means "courteous." Masculine singular adjectives ending in a consonant require no change to get the feminine form. Form the plural of this adjective that ends in a consonant by adding *-es.*

Position of Adjectives

In Spanish, adjectives may precede or follow the noun they modify, depending on the type of adjective being used, the connotation the speaker wishes to convey, and the emphasis being used.

Adjectives That Follow the Noun

Unlike in English, in Spanish, most descriptive adjectives usually follow the noun they modify:

mi coche <u>nuevo</u>	my new car
una casa <u>grande</u>	a big house

Adjectives That Precede the Noun

Adjectives that impose limits (numbers, possessive adjectives, demonstrative adjectives, and adjectives of quantity) usually precede the noun:

<u>tres</u> muchachos perezosos	three lazy boys
<u>nuestros</u> padres	our parents
<u>esta</u> película	that film
<u>algunas</u> personas	some people
<u>tal</u> cosa	such a thing
<u>otra</u> mujer	another woman
(el) <u>último</u> día	(the) last day

Descriptive adjectives that emphasize qualities or inherent characteristics may be placed before the noun:

Admiro esa isla, con sus <u>bellas</u> playas.   I admire that island with its beautiful beaches.
(The speaker is implying that all the beaches on the island are beautiful.)

Tengo <u>malos</u> recuerdos de ese día.   I have bad memories of that day.
(The speaker is emphasizing the quality of the memories.)

Example Problems

Rearrange the words into logical order to express what you see in the city.

Veo . . .

> Example: interesantes/cosas/otras
>> Veo otras cosas interesantes.

1. edificios/altos/muchos

   Answer: Veo muchos edificios altos.

   Muchos means "much" or "many" and, because it imposes a limit, precedes the noun. *Edificios* is a noun meaning "buildings" and logically follows the adjective *muchos*. *Altos* is a descriptive adjective and follows the noun it modifies.

2. modernas/tiendas/varias

   Answer: Veo varias tiendas modernas.

   Varias means "several" and, because it imposes a limit, precedes the noun. *Tiendas* is a feminine noun meaning "stores" and logically follows the adjective *varias*. *Modernas* is a feminine descriptive adjective and follows the noun it modifies.

Work Problems

Rearrange the words into logical order to express what there is on the tropical island by.

Hay . . .

> Example: comida/deliciosa/mucha
>> Hay mucha comida deliciosa.

1. blancas/dos/playas

2. americana/gente/poca

3. agua/azul/tanta

4. numerosas/magníficas/plantas

5. exóticos/animales/unos

6. grandes/árboles/algunos

Worked Solutions

1. **Hay dos playas blancas.**   *Dos* means "two" and, because it imposes a limit, precedes the noun. *Playas* is a feminine plural noun meaning "beaches" and logically follows the adjective *dos*. *Blancas* is a feminine plural descriptive adjective and follows the noun it modifies.

2. **Hay poca gente americana.** *Poca* means "a little" and, because it imposes a limit, precedes the noun. *Gente* is a feminine singular noun meaning "people" and logically follows the feminine singular adjective *poca*. *Americana* is a feminine singular descriptive adjective and follows the noun it modifies.

3. **Hay tanta agua azul.** *Tanta* means "so much" and, because it imposes a limit, precedes the noun. *Agua* is a feminine singular noun meaning "water" and logically follows the feminine singular adjective *tanta*. *Azul* is a descriptive adjective and follows the noun it modifies.

4. **Hay numerosas plantas magníficas.** *Numerosas* means "numerous" and, because it imposes a limit, precedes the noun. *Plantas* is a feminine plural noun meaning "plants" and logically follows the feminine plural adjective *numerosas*. *Magníficas* is a feminine plural descriptive adjective and follows the noun it modifies.

5. **Hay unos animales exóticos.** *Unos* means "some" and, because it imposes a limit, precedes the noun. *Animales* is a masculine plural noun meaning "animals" and logically follows the masculine plural adjective *unos*. *Exóticos* is a masculine plural descriptive adjective and follows the noun it modifies.

6. **Hay algunos árboles grandes.** *Algunos* means "a few" and, because it imposes a limit, precedes the noun. *Árboles* is a masculine plural noun meaning "trees" and logically follows the masculine plural adjective *algunos*. *Grandes* is a descriptive adjective and follows the noun it modifies.

Adjectives with Different Meanings

The meaning of some adjectives changes depending on whether they are positioned before or after the noun they modify. Adjectives before the noun tend to have a more literal meaning, while those following the noun are more figurative.

una tradición antigua	an old (ancient) tradition
una antigua tradición	an old (former) tradition
una cosa cierta	a sure thing
una cierta cosa	a certain (indefinite) thing
una mujer grande	a tall (large, big in size) woman
una gran mujer	a great woman (in moral character)
la idea misma	the idea itself
la misma idea	the same idea
un coche nuevo	a new car (brand new)
un nuevo coche	a new car (new to the owner, different)
el hombre pobre	the poor man (without money)
el pobre hombre	the unfortunate man
un remedio simple	a silly remedy
un simple remedio	a simple remedy

| un muchacho triste | a sad (unhappy) boy |
| un triste muchacho | a sad (sorry, wretched) boy |

| una amiga vieja | an old friend (elderly) |
| una vieja amiga | an old friend (dear, long-time) |

The adjectives *bueno* and *malo* have the same meanings whether they are used before or after the nouns they modify:

| unos muchachos buenos | some good boys |
| unos buenos muchachos | some good boys |

| unas muchachas malas | some bad girls |
| unas malas muchachas | some bad girls |

Example Problems

Place the adjective in its proper place to express the meaning indicated.

> Example: (poor) Es una mujer.
>> Es una mujer <u>pobre</u>.

1. (ancient) Vamos a ver las ruinas.

   Answer: Vamos a ver las ruinas antiguas.

   Antiguas connotes "ancient" or "old" when it follows the noun it modifies. Before the noun, it has the connotation of "former."

2. (simple) Es una formalidad.

   Answer: Es una simple formalidad.

   Simple connotes "simple" or "mere" when it precedes the noun it modifies. After the noun, it has the connotation of "silly."

Work Problems

Place the adjective in its proper place to express the meaning indicated.

> Example: (bad) Es una idea.
>> Es una <u>mala</u> idea.

1. (brand new) Compran una casa.

2. (sure) Le espera una muerte.

3. (good) Son hombres.

4. (same) Tengo el problema.

5. (great) Es un presidente.

6. (former) Habla con su novio.

Worked Solutions

1. **Compran una casa nueva.** *Nueva* connotes "brand new" when it follows the noun it modifies. Before the noun, it has the connotation of "different."

2. **Le espera una muerta cierta.** *Cierta* connotes "sure" when it follows the noun it modifies. Before the noun, it has the connotation of "certain" when it conveys something indefinite.

3. **Son buenos hombres. Son hombres buenos.** *Bueno* connotes "good" whether it precedes or follows the noun it modifies.

4. **Tengo el mismo problema.** *Mismo* connotes "same" when it precedes the noun it modifies. After the noun, it has the connotation of "itself."

5. **Es un gran presidente.** *Grande* becomes *gran* and connotes "great" when it precedes the noun it modifies. After the noun, it has the connotation of "tall" or "big in size."

6. **Habla con su antiguo novio.** *Antiguo* connotes "former" when it precedes the noun it modifies. After the noun, it has the connotation of "ancient."

One Noun and Two Adjectives

A noun may be modified by more than one adjective. Each adjective must be positioned either before or after the noun, according to the previously mentioned rules. Two adjectives in the same position are joined by *y* (and):

muchas flores amarillas	many yellow flowers
una muchacha alta y bonita	a tall, pretty girl
mis buenos amigos	my good friends

Shortened Forms of Adjectives

Some Spanish adjectives take on shortened forms in the following situations:

❏ Some adjectives drop the final *-o* before a masculine singular noun:

uno	un día	a day
bueno	un buen ejemplo	a good example
malo	un mal hombre	a bad man
primero	el primer mes	the first month
tercero	el tercer año	the third year
alguno	algún niño	some child
ninguno	ningún muchacho	no boy

An accent is placed on the *u* of *algún* and *ningún* when the *-o* is dropped.

The original adjective is used if a preposition separates the adjective from its noun:

uno de mis hermanos	one of my brothers
el primero de los muchachos	the first of the boys

❑ *Grande* becomes *gran* (important, famous) **before** (but not after) a singular masculine or feminine noun:

un gran científico	a great scientist (male)
una gran científica	a great scientist (female)
BUT	
un vaso grande	a large glass
una taza grande	a large cup

❑ *Ciento* becomes *cien* before nouns and before the numbers *mil* and *millones:*

cien libros	100 books
cien páginas	100 pages
cien mil dólares	100,000 dollars
cien millones de dólares	100 million dollars
BUT	
trescientos dólares	300 dollars
ciento cuarenta personas	140 people

❑ The masculine *Santo* becomes *San* before the name of a saint whose name does NOT begin with *To-* or *Do-:*

San Juan	Saint John
San Francisco	Saint Francis
BUT	
Santo Domingo	Saint Dominick
Santo Tomás	Saint Thomas

Example Problems

Complete each sentence about a play with the correct form of the adjective.

1. El _____ acto es aburrido.

   A. tercera B. tercero C. tercer D. terceros

   Answer: C

Use the shortened form of *tercero* before a masculine singular noun.

2. Es ___ de mis libros favoritos.

    A. una B. uno C. un D. unas

    Answer: B

    The original adjective *(uno)* is used if a preposition separates the adjective from its noun.

Work Problems

Complete each sentence about a famous man with the correct form of the adjective.

1. Es un _____ hombre.

    A. buen B. bueno C. buena D. buenos

2. Es el _____ científico que gana un premio.

    A. tercera B. terceras C. tercer D. tercero

3. Es el _____ de su familia en graduarse de la universidad.

    A. primer B. primero C. primera D. primeras

4. _____ biólogo es tan famoso como él.

    A. Ninguna B. Ninguna C. Ningunos D. Ningún

5. _____ científicos tienen celos de él.

    A. Algún B. Algunos C. Algunas D. Alguno

6. Gana _____ mil dólares al año.

    A. cientos B. ciento C. cien D. doscientas

Worked Solutions

1. **A** Use the shortened form of *bueno* before a masculine singular noun.

2. **C** Use the shortened form of *tercero* before a masculine singular noun.

3. **B** The original adjective *(primero)* is used if a preposition separates the adjective from its noun.

4. **D** Use the shortened form of *ninguno* before a masculine singular noun.

5. **B** Use the plural form of *alguno* before a masculine plural noun.

6. **C** Use the shortened form of *ciento* before the number *mil*. Note that the answer cannot be *doscientas* because *dólares* is masculine.

Chapter Problems

Problems

In problems 1–15, complete the story about a proud mother by filling in the correct form of the adjective in parentheses.

Soy una mujer muy (fortunate) _____ porque tengo dos hijos (brilliant) _____ pero
                                    1   2

(different) _____. El mayor, Enrique, es (thin)_____; ¡pesa solamente (100) _____
              3   4   5

treinta libras! Él es muy (shy) _____ pero es muy (nice) _____. Tiene el pelo (blond)
                                 6   7

_____. Pero mi hijo (younger) _____, Miguel, es más (fat) _____. Tiene el pelo (black)
  8   9   10

_____. Él es (brave) _____ y muy (talkative) _____. Mis dos hijos son muy (kind)
  11   12   13

_____. Mi esposo y yo estamos (proud) _____ de nuestros hijos.
  14   15

Answers and Solutions

1. **Answer: afortunada.** Use the feminine singular adjective *afortunada* to describe the feminine singular noun *mujer*.

2. **Answer: geniales.** Use the masculine plural adjective *geniales* to describe the masculine plural noun *hijos*. When a masculine adjective ends in a consonant, add -*es* to form the masculine plural.

3. **Answer: diferentes.** Use the masculine plural adjective *diferentes* to describe the masculine plural noun *hijos*.

4. **Answer: flaco.** Use the masculine singular adjective *flaco* to describe the masculine singular noun *Enrique*.

5. **Answer: ciento.** Use the number *ciento* to express 100 before another number.

6. **Answer: tímido.** Use the masculine singular adjective *tímido* to describe the masculine singular pronoun *él*.

7. **Answer: amable.** Use the masculine singular adjective *amable* to describe the masculine singular pronoun *él*.

8. **Answer: rubio.** Use the masculine singular adjective *rubio* to describe the masculine singular noun *pelo*.

9. **Answer: menor.** Use the masculine singular adjective *menor* to describe the masculine singular noun *hijo*.

10. **Answer: gordo.** Use the masculine singular adjective *gordo* to describe the masculine singular noun *Miguel*.

11. **Answer: negro.** Use the masculine singular adjective *negro* to describe the masculine singular noun *pelo*.

12. **Answer: valiente.** Use the masculine singular adjective *valiente* to describe the masculine singular pronoun *él*.

13. **Answer: hablador.** Use the masculine singular adjective *hablador* to describe the masculine singular pronoun *él*.

14. **Answer: bondadosos.** Use the masculine plural adjective *bondadosos* to describe the masculine plural noun *los dos*.

15. **Answer: orgullosos.** Use the masculine plural adjective *orgullosos* to describe a male and a female: *mi esposo y yo*.

Supplemental Chapter Problems

Problems

In problems 1–15, complete the letter from a son to his parents by filling in the correct form of the adjective in parentheses.

Queridos padres:

Acabo de encontrar a la mujer de mis sueños. Fue amor a (first) _____ vista. Se llama
$_1$

Dominique. Ella es (French) _____. Viene de una (small) _____ isla (tropical) _____
$_2$ $_3$ $_4$

llamada San Martín, pero vive ahora en (Saint) _____ Domingo. Ella tiene el pelo (long)
$_5$

_____ y (black) _____, los ojos (blue) _____ y una (big) _____ sonrisa (enchanting)
$_6$ $_7$ $_8$ $_9$

_____. Además de esas calidades (important) _____, ella es (faithful) _____,
$_{10}$ $_{11}$ $_{12}$

(hardworking) _____ y (courteous) _____. Ella es (magnificent) _____. ¿No
$_{13}$ $_{14}$ $_{15}$

creen Uds.?

Answers

1. primera (gender of adjectives, p. 185)

2. francesa (gender of adjectives, p. 185)

3. pequeña (gender of adjectives, p. 185)

4. tropical (gender of adjectives, p. 185)

5. Santo (gender of adjectives, p. 185)

6. largo (gender of adjectives, p. 185)

7. negro (gender of adjectives, p. 185)

8. azules (plural of adjectives, p. 189)

9. gran (shortened forms of adjectives, p. 195)

10. encantadora (gender of adjectives, p. 185)

11. importantes (plural of adjectives, p. 189)

12. leal (gender of adjectives, p. 185)

13. trabajadora (gender of adjectives, p. 185)

14. cortés (gender of adjectives, p. 185)

15. magnífica (gender of adjectives, p. 185)

Chapter 10
Adverbs

An adverb is a word that modifies a verb, an adjective, or another adverb. Adverbs often express how the subject performs an action. Many English adverbs end in *-ly* and many Spanish adverbs end in *-mente*. Because adverbs modify verbs, not nouns or pronouns, they do not require agreement.

Formation of Adverbs

Adverbs are formed by adding *-mente* to the **feminine singular** form of an adjective. Masculine singular adjectives that end in an *-e* or in a consonant require no change to get the feminine form, as shown in the following table:

Masculine Adjective	Feminine Adjective	Adverb	Meaning
completo	completa	completamente	completely
lento	lenta	lentamente	slowly
rápido	rápida	rápidamente	quickly
alegre	alegre	alegremente	happily
breve	breve	brevemente	briefly
frecuente	frecuente	frecuentemente	frequently
especial	especial	especialmente	especially
final	final	finalmente	finally
atroz	atroz	atrozmente	atrociously

Adverbial Phrases

The preposition *con* + a noun may be used to form an adverbial phrase. For example, *con cuidado* means "with care." Adverbial phrases function like adverbs and can be translated as an adverb:

Él trabaja con cuidado.　　　He works with care *or* He works carefully.
Él trabaja cuidadosamente.　　He works carefully.

Here are some common adverbial phrases with the equivalent adverb and the meaning in English:

Con + Noun	Adverb	Meaning
con alegría	alegremente	happily
con claridad	claramente	clearly
con cortesía	cortésmente	courteously
con energía	enérgicamente	energetically
con entusiasmo	entusiásticamente	enthusiastically
con habilidad	hábilmente	skillfully
con felicidad	felizmente	happily
con ferocidad	ferozmente	ferociously
con lealtad	lealmente	loyally
con lentitud	lentamente	slowly
con paciencia	pacientemente	patiently
con rapidez	rápidamente	quickly
con respeto	respetuosamente	respectfully

Example Problems

Use an adverb and the equivalent adverbial phrase to express how animals behave.

Example: (rápido) La pantera corre <u>rápidamente</u>. La pantera corre <u>con rapidez</u>.

1. (feroz) El león grita _____.

   Answer: El león grita ferozmente. El león grita con ferocidad.

   Masculine singular adjectives that end in a consonant require no change to get the feminine form. Add -mente to feroz to get the adverb expressing "ferociously." Alternatively, use the preposition con with the noun expressing "ferociousness," ferocidad.

2. (lento) La tortuga se mueve _____.

   Answer: La tortuga se mueve lentamente. La tortuga se mueve con lentitud.

   To change a masculine singular adjective to its feminine form, replace the final -o with -a. Add -mente to lenta to get the adverb expressing "slowly." Alternatively, use the preposition con with the noun expressing "slowness," lentitud.

Work Problems

Use an adverb and the equivalent adverbial phrase to express how people do things.

Example: (triste) Yo salgo <u>tristemente</u>. Yo salgo <u>con tristeza</u>.

1. (cortés) Ella habla ____.

2. (enérgico) Nosotros trabajamos ____.

3. (hábil) Uds. pintan ____.

4. (paciente) Yo escucho ____.

5. (feliz) Vosotros jugáis ____.

6. (cuidadoso) Tú conduces ____.

Worked Solutions

1. **Ella habla cortésmente. Ella habla con cortesía.** Masculine singular adjectives that end in a consonant require no change to get the feminine form. Add *-mente* to *cortés* to get the adverb expressing "courteously." Alternatively, use the preposition *con* with the noun expressing "courtesy," *cortesía*.

2. **Nosotros trabajamos enérgicamente. Nosotros trabajamos con energía.** To change a masculine singular adjective to its feminine form, replace the final *-o* with *-a*. Add *-mente* to *enérgica* to get the adverb expressing "energetically." Alternatively, use the preposition *con* with the noun expressing "energy," *energía*.

3. **Uds. pintan hábilmente. Uds. pintan con habilidad.** Masculine singular adjectives that end in a consonant require no change to get the feminine form. Add *-mente* to *hábil* to get the adverb expressing "skillfully." Alternatively, use the preposition *con* with the noun expressing "skill," *habilidad*.

4. **Yo escucho pacientemente. Yo escucho con paciencia.** Masculine singular adjectives that end in *-e* require no change to get the feminine form. Add *-mente* to *paciente* to get the adverb expressing "patiently." Alternatively, use the preposition *con* with the noun expressing "patience," *paciencia*.

5. **Vosotros jugáis felizmente. Vosotros jugáis con felicidad.** Masculine singular adjectives that end in a consonant require no change to get the feminine form. Add *-mente* to *feliz* to get the adverb expressing "happily." Alternatively, use the preposition *con* with the noun expressing "happiness," *felicidad*.

6. **Tú conduces cuidadosamente. Tú conduces con cuidado.** To change a masculine singular adjective to its feminine form, replace the final *-o* with *-a*. Add *-mente* to *cuidadosa* to get the adverb expressing "carefully." Alternatively, use the preposition *con* with the noun expressing "care," *cuidado*.

Adjectives versus Adverbs

Spanish words have distinct forms for adjectives and adverbs. For example:

❏ Adjective:

   bueno (good): Tengo buenos recuerdos. (I have good memories.)

   malo (bad): Tengo mala suerte. (I have bad luck.)

❏ Adverb:

   bien (well): Cocino bien. (I cook well.)

   mal (badly): Dibujo mal. (I draw poorly.)

Some Spanish words may be used as adjectives or adverbs. For example:

❑ As adjectives:

    Mucho, poco, and *demasiado* agree in number and gender with the nouns they modify.

    Mejor and *peor* only agree with the plural of the nouns they modify by adding *-es.*

    Más and *menos* do not change.

❑ As adverbs, all of these words remain invariable, as shown in the following table:

	Adjective	*Adverb*
más (more)	Tengo más ideas. (I have more ideas.)	Trabajo más lentamente. (I work more slowly.)
menos (less, fewer)	Tengo menos ideas. (I have fewer ideas.)	Trabajo menos lentamente. (I work less slowly.)
poco (few, little)	Tengo pocas ideas. (I have few ideas.)	Trabajo poco. (I work a little.)
mucho (much, many)	Tengo muchas ideas. (I have many ideas.)	Trabajo mucho. (I work a lot.)
mejor (better)	Tengo mejores ideas. (I have better ideas.)	Trabajo mejor. (I work better.)
peor (worse)	Tengo peores ideas. (I have worse ideas.)	Trabajo peor. (I work worse.)
demasiado (as much, many)	Tengo demasiadas ideas. (I have too many ideas.)	Trabajo demasiado. (I work too much.)

Example Problems

Complete each sentence with the correct form of the adjective or adverb indicated.

    Example: (mucho) Él sale _____ porque tiene _____ amigos.
        Él sale <u>mucho</u> porque tiene <u>muchos</u> amigos.

1. (poco) Él tiene _____ energía porque come ___.

    Answer: Él tiene poca energía porque come poco.

    In the first blank, use the feminine singular adjective to describe the feminine singular noun, *energía.* In the second blank, use the adverb *poco* to modify the verb *comer* (to eat).

2. (mal) Él sale _____ en sus exámenes y por eso tiene _____ notas.

    Answer: Él sale mal en sus exámenes y por eso tiene malas notas.

    In the first blank, use the adverb *mal* to modify the verb *salir* (to turn out). In the second blank, use the feminine plural adjective to describe the feminine plural noun, *notas.*

Work Problems

Describe the people by completing each sentence with the correct form of the adjective or adverb indicated.

> Example: (peor) Él se encuentra ____ porque tiene ____ problemas.
>
> Él se encuentra <u>peor</u> porque tiene <u>peores</u> problemas.

1. (mal) Elena trabaja ____ porque tiene una ____ supervisora.

2. (mejor) Eduardo toca ___ el piano porque tiene ____ profesores.

3. (bien/bueno) El señor Gómez es un ____ jefe porque trata ____ a sus empleados.

4. (más) Alma gana ____ dinero porque trabaja ___ rápidamente.

5. (demasiado) Víctor tiene ____ pesadillas porque duerme ____.

6. (poco) La señora Martínez pesa ____ porque come ____ postres.

Worked Solutions

1. **Elena trabaja mal porque tiene una mala supervisora.**   In the first blank, use the adverb *mal* to modify the verb *trabajar* (to work). In the second blank, use the feminine singular adjective to describe the feminine singular noun, *supervisora*.

2. **Eduardo toca mejor el piano porque tiene mejores profesores.**   In the first blank, use the adverb *mejor* to modify the verb *tocar* (to play). In the second blank, use the masculine plural adjective to describe the masculine plural noun, *profesores*.

3. **El señor Gómez es un buen jefe porque trata bien a sus empleados.**   Nouns ending in *-e* tend to be masculine. In the first blank, use the masculine singular adjective to describe the masculine singular noun, *jefe*. Use the short form of *bueno (buen)* before a masculine singular adjective. In the second blank, use the adverb *bien* to modify the verb *tratar* (to treat).

4. **Alma gana más dinero porque trabaja más rápidamente.**   In both blanks, use the word *más*, which acts as both an adjective and an adverb and is invariable.

5. **Víctor tiene demasiadas pesadillas porque duerme demasiado.**   In the first blank, use the feminine plural adjective to describe the feminine plural noun, *pesadillas*. In the second blank, use the adverb *demasiado* to modify the verb *dormir* (to sleep).

6. **La señora Martínez pesa poco porque come pocos postres.**   In the first blank, use the adverb *poco* to modify the verb *pesar* (to weigh). Nouns ending in *-e* tend to be masculine. In the second blank, use the masculine plural adjective to describe the masculine plural noun, *postres*.

Exceptions to the Rules

Some adverbs of time, order, and quantity and some adverbial expressions are not formed from adjectives. Some common adverbs are:

Meaning	Adverb
afterward	después
again	de nuevo
almost	casi
already	ya
also, too	también
always	siempre
as	tan
as soon as possible	cuanto antes
better	mejor
consequently	por consiguiente
every day	todos los días
excessively (too)	demasiado, excesivamente
far	lejos
from time to time	de vez en cuando
finally	al fin
here	aquí
however	sin embargo
immediately	enseguida
late	tarde
later	más tarde
less	menos
little	poco
meanwhile	mientras
more	más
near	cerca
nevertheless	sin embargo
no longer	ya no
now	ahora
nowadays	hoy (en) día
of course	por supuesto
often	a menudo, muchas veces
perhaps	tal vez
quite, enough	bastante
rather	bastante
right now	ahora mismo
seldom	rara vez
shortly	dentro de poco
slowly	despacio
so	tan
sometimes	a veces
soon	pronto
soon, early	temprano

still, yet	todavía
suddenly	de repente, de pronto
sufficiently	bastante, suficientemente
there	allá
thoroughly	a fondo
unwillingly	de mala gana
very	muy
willingly	de buena gana
worse	peor

Position of Adverbs

In simple tenses, adverbs are generally placed directly after the verbs they modify. Sometimes, however, the position of the adverb is variable and is usually placed where you would logically put an English adverb:

Ud. habla elocuentemente.

You speak eloquently.

Generalmente, llega temprano.

Generally, he arrives early.

Note that you cannot have two adverbs ending in *-mente* connected by *y* or in the same sentence. You may avoid this problem by using *con* + noun (see above) for one of the adverbs or, in a series of two or more adverbs, adding *-mente* only to the last one:

Generalmente, ella trabaja con cuidado.

Generally, she works carefully.

Él habla clara y lentamente.

He speaks clearly and slowly.

Example Problems

Rafael is learning how to drive. Rewrite each sentence by placing the adverbs in their correct position.

Example: (generalmente/con habilidad) Él conduce.

<u>Generalmente</u>, él conduce <u>con habilidad</u>.

1. (pacientemente/ya no) Su padre le habla.

Answer: Su padre ya no le habla pacientemente.

Because adverbs are generally placed directly after the verbs they modify, *pacientemente* follows the verb *habla*. Adverbs of doubt or negation, however, are placed before the verb. Thus, *ya no* must be placed before the verb and the direct object that precedes it to negate the action that no longer exists or takes place.

2. (impulsivamente/muy) Él frena.

Answer: Él frena muy impulsivamente.

Because adverbs are generally placed directly after the verbs they modify, *impulsivamente* follows the verb *frena*. *Muy* is placed before the adverb *impulsivamente* because it is an adverb of quantity.

Work Problems

Teresa is learning how to play tennis. Rewrite each sentence by placing the adverbs in their correct position.

Example: (pacientemente/muy) El instructor le habla.

El instructor le habla muy pacientemente.

1. (por supuesto/rápidamente) Ella comprende.

2. (enérgicamente/muy) Ella juega.

3. (atentamente/siempre) Ella escucha.

4. (brevemente/de vez en cuando) Ella descansa.

5. (impulsivamente/tan) Ella se mueve.

Worked Solutions

1. **Por supuesto ella comprende rápidamente.**   Because adverbs are generally placed directly after the verbs they modify, *rápidamente* follows the verb *comprende*. *Por supuesto* may be placed before the verb, as in English.

2. **Ella juega muy enérgicamente.**   Because adverbs are generally placed directly after the verbs they modify, *enérgicamente* follows the verb *juega*. *Muy* is placed before the adverb it modifies *(enérgicamente),* as in English.

3. **Ella siempre escucha atentamente.**   Because adverbs are generally placed directly after the verbs they modify, *atentamente* follows the verb *escucha*. *Siempre* can be placed anywhere in the sentence (before or after the verb, or at the beginning or end of the sentence) because it is an adverb of time.

4. **De vez en cuando ella descansa brevemente.**   Because adverbs are generally placed directly after the verbs they modify, *brevemente* follows the verb *descansa*.

5. **Ella se mueve tan impulsivamente.**   Because adverbs are generally placed directly after the verbs they modify, *impulsivamente* follows the verb se *mueve*. *Tan* is placed before the adverb it modifies *(impulsivamente),* as in English.

Chapter Problems

Problems

Fill in the correct form of the adverb indicated to complete the story.

(Suddenly) _____, una tarde, Miguel toma una decisión. Decide (willingly) _____
               1   2

hacerse oficial de la marina. (As soon as possible) _____ se inscribe en una escuela
                                                      3

especializada para marinos para aprender su nuevo oficio. (Shortly) _____ podrá trabajar
                                                                      4

en un submarino. Estudia (diligently) _____ todos los días. Escucha (very) _____
                                         5   6

(attentively) _____ y (carefully) _____. (Always) _____ habla (respectfully) _____ y
              7   8   9   10

(courteously) _____ a sus superiores. Tiene que aprender y comprender todo
              11

(thoroughly) _____. Por eso, les hace preguntas a los oficiales (frequently) _____. (Of
             12   13

course) _____, él es un muchacho (completely) _____ serio y (consequently) _____
        14   15   16

aprende (quickly) _____. Trabaja (a lot) _____ y descansa (rarely) _____. (At times)
                  17   18   19

_____ hace ejercicios y (almost) _____ nunca duerme porque está (too) _____
20   21   22

ocupado. Es (rather) _____ difícil ser oficial de la marina. (However) _____, él va a
                     23   24

hacer realidad sus sueños muy (soon) _____.
                                     25

Answers and Solutions

1. **Answer: De repente.** Some adverbs and adverbial expressions are not formed from adjectives and must be memorized.

2. **Answer: de buena gana.** Some adverbs and adverbial expressions are not formed from adjectives and must be memorized.

3. **Answer: Cuanto antes.** Some adverbs and adverbial expressions are not formed from adjectives and must be memorized.

4. **Answer: Dentro de poco.** Some adverbs and adverbial expressions are not formed from adjectives and must be memorized.

5. **Answer: diligentemente.** Adverbs are formed by adding -*mente* to the feminine form of the adjective. Masculine singular adjectives that end in -e require no change to get the feminine form. Add -*mente* to enégira = *diligente* to get the adverb expressing energetically = diligently. Alternatively, use the preposition *con* with the noun expressing energy = diligent, energia = diligente.

6. **Answer: muy.** Some adverbs and adverbial expressions are not formed from adjectives and must be memorized.

7. **Answer: atentamente.** Adverbs are formed by adding -*mente* to the feminine form of the adjective. To change a masculine singular adjective to its feminine form, replace the final -*o* with -*a*. Add -*mente* to *atenta* to get the adverb expressing "attentively." Alternatively, use the preposition *con* with the noun expressing "attention," *atención*. In this case, the preceding adverb *(muy)* would have to be changed to the adjective *mucha*, which modifies a feminine singular noun.

8. **Answer: con cuidado.** Because two adverbs ending in -mente can't be used in the same sentence, use the preposition *con* with the noun expressing "care," *cuidado*.

9. **Answer: Siempre.** Some adverbs and adverbial expressions are not formed from adjectives and must be memorized.

10. **Answer: respetuosamente.** Adverbs are formed by adding *-mente* to the feminine form of the adjective. To change a masculine singular adjective to its feminine form, replace the final *-o* with *-a*. Add *-mente* to *respetuosa* to get the adverb expressing "respectfully." Alternatively, use the preposition *con* with the noun expressing "respect," *respeto*.

11. **Answer: con cortesía.** Because two adverbs ending in *-mente* can't be used in the same sentence, use the preposition *con* with the noun expressing "courtesy," *cortesía*.

12. **Answer: a fondo.** Some adverbs and adverbial expressions are not formed from adjectives and must be memorized.

13. **Answer: frecuentemente.** Adverbs are formed by adding *-mente* to the feminine form of the adjective. Masculine singular adjectives that end in *-e* require no change to get the feminine form. Add *-mente* to *frecuente* to get the adverb expressing "frequently." Alternatively, use the preposition *con* with the noun expressing "frequency," *frecuencia*.

14. **Answer: Por supuesto.** Some adverbs and adverbial expressions are not formed from adjectives and must be memorized.

15. **Answer: completamente.** Adverbs are formed by adding *-mente* to the feminine form of the adjective. To change a masculine singular adjective to its feminine form, replace the final *-o* with *-a*. Add *-mente* to *completa* to get the adverb expressing "completely." This is one case in which you would not form an adverbial phrase by using the preposition *con* with a noun.

16. **Answer: por consiguiente.** Some adverbs and adverbial expressions are not formed from adjectives and must be memorized.

17. **Answer: rápidamente.** Adverbs are formed by adding *-mente* to the feminine form of the adjective. To change a masculine singular adjective to its feminine form, replace the final *-o* with *-a*. Add *-mente* to *rápida* to get the adverb expressing "quickly." Alternatively, use the preposition *con* with the noun expressing "rapidity," *rapidez*.

18. **Answer: mucho.** Some adverbs and adverbial expressions are not formed from adjectives and must be memorized.

19. **Answer: raramente.** Adverbs are formed by adding *-mente* to the feminine form of the adjective. To change a masculine singular adjective to its feminine form, replace the final *-o* with *-a*. Add *-mente* to *rara* to get the adverb expressing "rarely." Although quite awkward, you could alternatively use the preposition *con* with the noun expressing "rareness," *rareza*.

20. **Answer: A veces.** Some adverbs and adverbial expressions are not formed from adjectives and must be memorized.

21. **Answer: casi.** Some adverbs and adverbial expressions are not formed from adjectives and must be memorized.

22. **Answer: tan.** Some adverbs and adverbial expressions are not formed from adjectives and must be memorized.

23. **Answer: bastante.** Some adverbs and adverbial expressions are not formed from adjectives and must be memorized.

24. **Answer: Sin embargo.** Some adverbs and adverbial expressions are not formed from adjectives and must be memorized.

25. **Answer: pronto.** Some adverbs and adverbial expressions are not formed from adjectives and must be memorized.

Supplemental Chapter Problems

Fill in the correct form of the adjective indicated to complete the story.

Queridos padres:

(Nowadays) _____, (more) _____ que nunca, se dice que es (very) _____ importante
                 1   2   3

hacer ejercicios (frequently) _____ y (diligently) _____ para tener buena salud. Por
                                        4   5

eso, Alicia va (often) _____ al gimnasio cerca de su casa. Un día ella contrata a un
                           6

entrenador que le explica (clearly) _____ y (patiently) _____ los ejercicios y le dice que
                                             7   8

es necesario trabajar (very) _____ (energetically) _____. (Of course) _____ es
                                   9   10   11

importante comer (less) _____ y (slowly) _____. (Naturally) _____ ella tiene que
                             12   13   14

ingerir menos calorías y no comer dulces. Alicia siempre escucha (attentively) _____
                                                                                              15

sus instrucciones. Ella admite que (from time to time) _____ se siente culpable de
                                                                     16

comer (too much) _____, (especially) _____ cuando está (very) _____ nerviosa.
                        17   18   19

(Consequently) _____ ella promete empezar su plan (immediately) _____. Sabe que al
                         20   21

principio tiene que trabajar (enthusiastically) _____ y (skillfully) _____ si quiere bajar
                                                       22   23

de peso (quickly) _____. Ella le reafirma (respectfully) _____ a su entrenador que va
                        24   25

a hacer sus ejercicios (willingly) _____ todos los días.
                                         26

Answer:

1. Hoy día (exceptions to the rule, p. 206)

2. más (exceptions to the rule, p. 206)

3. muy (exceptions to the rule, p. 206)

4. frecuentemente (formation of adverbs, p. 201)

5. con diligencia (formation of adverbs, p. 201; position of adverbs, p. 207)

6. a menudo (exceptions to the rule, p. 206)

7. claramente (formation of adverbs, p. 201)

8. con paciencia (formation of adverbs, p. 201; position of adverbs, p. 207)

9. muy (exceptions to the rule, p. 206)

10. enérgicamente (formation of adverbs, p. 201)

11. Por supuesto (exceptions to the rule, p. 206)

12. menos (exceptions to the rule, p. 206)

13. lentamente (formation of adverbs, p. 201)

14. Naturalmente (formation of adverbs, p. 201)

15. atentamente (formation of adverbs, p. 201)

16. de vez en cuando (exceptions to the rule, p. 206)

17. demasiado (exceptions to the rule, p. 206)

18. especialmente (formation of adverbs, p. 201)

19. muy (exceptions to the rule, p. 206)

20. Por consiguiente (exceptions to the rule, p. 206)

21. inmediatamente (formation of adverbs, p. 201)

22. entusiásticamente (formation of adverbs, p. 201)

23. con habilidad (formation of adverbs, p. 201; position of adverbs, p. 207)

24. rápidamente (formation of adverbs, p. 201)

25. respetuosamente (formation of adverbs, p. 201)

26. de buena gana (exceptions to the rule, p. 206)

Chapter 11
Comparisons

In comparisons of inequality, one thing is deemed to be more superior or less superior than another. In comparisons of equality, both things are deemed to be equal. Comparisons are generally made using adjectives and adverbs. The superlative expresses the extreme degree, whether you are describing a positive or a negative condition.

In English, comparisons are made in the following ways:

❏ In the positive, stating the fact:

Adjective: Spanish is easy.

Adverb: She speaks Spanish quickly.

❏ The comparative states "more" or "less." In English, a comparative may end in -er.

Adjective: Spanish is easier than Russian.

Russian is harder than Spanish.

Adverb: She speaks more quickly than I.

I speak less quickly than she.

❏ The superlative states the most or the least — the extreme degree. In English, a superlative may end in -est.

Adjective: Spanish is the easiest language.

Russian is the hardest language.

Adverb: She speaks the most quickly of anyone I know.

I speak the least quickly of my friends.

In Spanish, comparisons are made in much the same way as they are made in English:

❏ In the positive, state the fact:

Adjective: El español es fácil.

Adverb: Ella habla rápidamente.

❏ The comparative shows that something is more or less equal to something else:

Adjective: El español es más fácil que el ruso.

El español es menos difícil que el ruso.

Adverb: Ella habla más rápidamente que yo.

Yo hablo menos rápidamente que ella.

❏ The superlative shows the extreme:

Adjective: El español es el más fácil de todas las lenguas.

El ruso es el menos fácil de todas las lenguas.

Adverb: Ella habla español más rápidamente de todos.

Yo hablo español menos rápidamente de todos.

Comparisons of Inequality

A comparison of inequality shows that two things or actions are of unequal value or importance. Comparisons of inequality can be made using adjectives and adverbs.

Comparison of Adjectives

Positive	optimistic optimista (optimistas)
Comparative	more (less) optimistic más (menos) optimista (optimistas)
Superlative	the most (least optimistic) el (la, los, las) . . . más (menos) optimista (optimistas)

To express the positive, merely state a fact, keeping in mind that your adjective must agree in gender and number with the noun or pronoun it modifies.

Ella es baja.   She is short.

In Spanish, make a comparison of inequality by stating "more" *(más)* or "less" *(menos)* and by introducing the second element with "than" *(que)*. The second element is generally a noun or a subject pronoun. When using adjectives to make a comparison, the adjective must agree in gender and number with the noun it modifies:

Ellos son menos atléticos que sus amigos.   They are less athletic than their friends.

Ella es más baja que tú.   She is shorter than you.

In the superlative, "in" or "of" is expressed by *de* + definite article + noun. The superlative is formed as follows: *el (la, los, las) más (menos)* + adjective + *de* + noun (or pronoun).

Ella es la muchacha más baja de la familia.   She is the shortest girl in the family.

Juan es el alumno menos inteligente de todos.   Juan is the least intelligent student of them all.

Agosto es el mes más caluroso del año.   August is the hottest month of the year.

Example Problems

Compare the people.

> Example: (+) un muchacho atlético (Domingo, Esteban, Pablo)
> Domingo es atlético.
> Esteban es más atlético.
> Pablo es el más atlético.

1. (+) una cantante popular (Christina Aguilera, Gloria Estefan, Jennifer López/ellas)

   Answer: Christina Aguilera es una cantante popular.

   Gloria Estefan es una cantante más popular.

   Jennifer López es la cantante más popular.

   The positive states the fact that Christina Aguilera is a popular singer. Use the comparative *más* before the adjective *popular* to show that Gloria Estefan is a more popular singer. To express the superlative, use the definite article *la* before the feminine singular noun *cantante* to express "the" and the adverb *más* to express "most" before the adjective *popular*.

2. (–) un artista conocido (Picasso, Velázquez, El Greco)

   Answer: Picasso es un artista muy conocido.

   Velázquez es un artista menos conocido.

   El Greco es el artista menos conocido.

   The positive states the fact that Picasso is a well-known artist. Use the comparative *menos* before the adjective *conocido* to show that Velázquez is a less well-known artist. To express the superlative, use the definite article *el* before the masculine singular noun *artista* to express "the" and the adverb *menos* to express "least" before the adjective *conocido*.

3. (+) un descubridor famoso (de Soto, Ponce de León, Cristóbal Colón)

   Answer: De Soto es un descubridor famoso.

   Ponce de León es un descubridor más famoso.

   Cristóbal Colón es el descubridor más famoso.

   The positive states the fact that de Soto is a famous discoverer. Use the comparative *más* before the adjective *famoso* to show that Ponce de León is a more famous discoverer. To express the superlative, use the definite article *el* before the masculine singular noun *descubridor* to express "the" and the adverb *más* to express "most" before the adjective *famoso*.

Work Problems

Compare the things.

> Example: (–) un deporte popular (el baloncesto, el tenis, el golf)
> El baloncesto es un deporte popular.
> El tenis es un deporte menos popular.
> El golf es el deporte menos popular.

1. (+) un baile divertido (la rumba, el mambo, la salsa)

2. (–) una tela rica (la seda, el lino, el algodón)

3. (+) una piedra preciosa (el topacio, el rubí, el diamante)

4. (–) una emoción importante (el amor, la felicidad, el orgullo)

5. (+) un color vivo (el blanco, el morado, el rojo)

6. (–) una enfermedad seria (la pulmonía, la bronquitis, la gripe)

Worked Solutions

1. **La rumba es un baile divertido.**

    El mambo es un baile más divertido.

    La salsa es el baile más divertido.

    The positive states the fact that *la rumba* is an amusing dance. Use the comparative *más* before the adjective *divertido* to show that *el mambo* is a more amusing dance. To express the superlative, use the definite article *el* before the masculine singular noun *baile* to express "the" and the adverb *más* to express "most" before the adjective *divertido*.

2. **La seda es una tela rica.**

    El lino es una tela menos rica.

    El algodón es la tela menos rica.

    The positive states the fact that *la seda* is a rich material. Use the comparative *menos* before the adjective *rica* to show that *el lino* is a less rich material. To express the superlative, use the definite article *la* before the feminine singular noun *tela* to express "the" and the adverb *menos* to express "least" before the adjective *rica*.

3. **El topacio es una piedra preciosa.**

    El rubí es una piedra más preciosa.

    El diamante es la piedra más preciosa.

    The positive states the fact that *el topacio* is a precious stone. Use the comparative *más* before the adjective *preciosa* to show that *el rubí* is a more precious stone. To express the superlative, use the definite article *la* before the feminine singular noun *piedra* to express "the" and the adverb *más* to express "most" before the adjective *preciosa*.

4. **El amor es una emoción importante.**

    La felicidad es una emoción menos importante.

    El orgullo es la emoción menos importante.

    The positive states the fact that *el amor* is an important emotion. Use the comparative *menos* before the adjective *importante* to show that *la felicidad* is a less important emotion. To express the superlative, use the definite article *la* before the feminine singular noun *emoción* to express "the" and the adverb *menos* to express "least" before the adjective *importante*.

5. **El blanco es un color vivo.**

    El morado es un color más vivo.

    El rojo es el color más vivo.

    The positive states the fact that *el blanco* is a vivid color. Use the comparative *más* before the adjective *vivo* to show that *el morado* is a more vivid color. To express the superlative, use the definite article *el* before the masculine singular noun *color* to express "the" and the adverb *más* to express "most" before the adjective *vivo*.

6. **La pulmonía es una enfermedad seria.**

    La bronquitis es una enfermedad menos seria.

    La gripe es la enfermedad menos seria.

    The positive states the fact that *la pulmonía* is a serious illness. Use the comparative *menos* before the adjective *seria* to show that *la bronquitis* is a less serious illness. To express the superlative, use the definite article *la* before the feminine singular noun *enfermedad* to express "the" and the adverb *menos* to express "least" before the adjective *seria*.

Irregular Comparatives

A few adjectives have irregular forms in the comparative and superlative:

Positive	*Comparative*	*Superlative*
bueno (-a, -os, -as)	mejor(es)	el (la) mejor los (las) mejores
(good)	(better)	(the best)
malo (-a, -os, -as)	peor(es)	el (la) peor los (las) peores
(bad)	(worse)	(the worst)

(continued)

Positive	Comparative	Superlative
grande(s)	mayor(es)	el (la) [los, las] mayor[es] dethe
(great, big)	(greater, older)	(the greatest, the oldest of)
	más grande(s)	el (la) [los, las] más grande[s] de
	(larger, bigger)	(the largest, the biggest)
	menos grande(s)	el (la) [los, las] menos grande[s]
	(less large, less big)	(the least large (big))
pequeño (-a, -os, -as)	menor(es)	el (la) [los, las] menor[es]
(small)	(minor, lesser, younger)	(the least, the youngest)
	más pequeño (-a, -os, -as)	el (la) [los, las] más pequeño (-a) [-os, -as]
	(smaller)	(the smallest)
	menos pequeño (-a, -os, -as)	el (la) [los, las] menos pequeño (-a) [-os, -as]
	(less small)	(the least small)

Mejor and *peor* generally precede the noun, while *mayor* and *menor* generally follow the noun:

Es el mejor libro.	It's the best book.
Es la peor película.	It's the worst film.

Es mi hermano mayor.	He's my older brother.
Soy su hermana menor.	I'm his younger sister.

Grande and *pequeño* have regular and irregular comparisons that connote different meanings. With *más* or *menos*, *grande* and *pequeño* refer to physical size or height. *Mayor* and *menor* compare differences in age or status.

Mi hermana menor es más grande que yo.
My younger sister is taller (bigger) than I.

Mi hermano mayor me visita con menos frecuencia.
My older brother visits me less frequently.

Example Problems
Compare the things.

Example: (good) (un apartamento, una casa, un palacio)
Un apartamento es bueno.
Una casa es mejor.
Un palacio es el mejor.

1. (good) (el drama, la telenovela, el misterio)

   Answer: Un drama es bueno.

        Una telenovela es mejor.

        Un misterio es el mejor.

   The positive states the fact that a drama is good. Use the irregular comparative *mejor . . . que* to express that a soap opera is better. To express the irregular superlative "best," use the masculine singular definite article *el,* which agrees with the masculine singular noun *misterio,* before the adjective *mejor.*

2. (bad) (la tristeza, la pobreza, la enfermedad)

   Answer: La tristeza es mala.

        La pobreza es peor.

        La enfermedad es la peor.

   The positive states the fact that unhappiness is bad. Use the irregular comparative *peor* to express that poverty is worse. To express the irregular superlative "worst," use the definite article *la,* which agrees with the feminine singular noun *enfermedad,* before the adjective *peor.*

Work Problems

Compare the things.

    Example: (big) (el mono, el oso, el elefante)
     El mono es grande.
     El oso es más grande.
     El elefante es el más grande.

1. (little) (el acordeón, el violín, la flauta)

2. (good) (el estofado, el rosbif, el bistec)

3. (bad) (el miedo, la envidia, el odio)

4. (big) (el mercado, el supermercado, el hipermercado)

Worked Solutions

1. **El acordeón es pequeño.**

   El violín es más pequeño.

   La flauta es la más pequeña.

   The positive states the fact that the accordion is little. Use the comparative *más* before the adjective *pequeño* to show that *el violín* is smaller. To express the superlative, use the definite article *la*, which agrees with the feminine singular noun *flauta*, to express "the" and the adverb *más* to express "most" before the adjective *pequeña*.

2. **El estofado es bueno.**

    El rosbif es mejor.

    El bistec es el mejor.

    The positive states the fact that stew is good. Use the irregular comparative *mejor* to express that roast beef is better. To express the irregular superlative "best," use the masculine singular definite article *el*, which agrees with the masculine singular noun *bistec*, before the adjective *mejor*.

3. **El miedo es malo.**

    La envidia es peor.

    El odio es el peor.

    The positive states the fact that fear is bad. Use the irregular comparative *peor* to express that envy is worse. To express the irregular superlative "worst," use the definite article *el*, which agrees with the masculine singular noun *odio*, before the adjective *peor*.

4. **El mercado es grande.**

    El supermercado es más grande.

    El hipermercado es el más grande.

    The positive states the fact that the market is big. Use the comparative *más* before the adjective *grande* to show that the supermarket is bigger. To express the superlative, use the definite article *el*, which agrees with the masculine singular noun *hipermercado*, to express "the" and the adverb *más* to express "most" before the adjective *grande*.

Comparison of Adverbs

In Spanish, there is no distinction between the comparative and superlative of adverbs:

Positive	quickly
	rápidamente
Comparative	more (less) quickly
	más (menos) rápidamente
Superlative	more (less) quickly
	más (menos) rápidamente de

To express the positive, merely state a fact, keeping in mind that because adverbs modify verbs, adverbs do not change.

Ella corre rápidamente.   She runs quickly.

In Spanish, make a comparison by stating "more" *(más)* or "less" *(menos)* and by introducing the second element with "than" *(que).* The second element is generally a noun or a subject pronoun.

> Ella corre más rápidamente que su hermana.   She runs faster than her sister.

In the superlative, "in" or "of" is expressed by *de* + noun (pronoun). The superlative is formed as follows: Definite article + noun + *más (menos)* + adverb + *de* + nouns (pronouns)

> Ella corre la más rápidamente de todas las muchachas.   She runs the fastest of all
>   the girls.

The adverbs *bien* (well) and *mal* (poorly) become *mejor* (better) and *peor* (worse) respectively in their comparative and superlative forms and follow the verb or verb phrase they modify:

Comparative:

> Él baila el tango mejor que yo.   He dances the tango better than I do.
> Yo canto peor que ella.   I sing worse than she does.

Superlative:

> Él baila el mejor de todos.   He dances the best of everyone.
> Yo canto el peor de todos.   I sing the worst of everyone.

Example Problems

Compare how the animals behave.

> Example: (nadar) La tortuga es menos rápida que el tiburón.
>   La tortuga nada menos rápidamente que el tiburón.

1. (gritar) El mono es menos feroz que el león.

   Answer: El mono grita menos ferozmente que el león.

   Conjugate the regular *-ar* verb *gritar* by dropping the *-ar* ending and adding *-a* for the third person singular subject, *el mono.* Use *menos* to express "less." Adverbs are formed by adding *-mente* to the feminine form of the adjective. Masculine singular adjectives that end in a consonant require no change to get the feminine form. Add *-mente* to *feroz* to get the adverb expressing "ferociously." Use *que* to express "than." Add the second animal being compared, *el león.*

2. (correr) El perro es más lento que la pantera.

   Answer: El perro corre más lentamente que la pantera.

   Conjugate the regular *-er* verb *correr* by dropping the *-er* ending and adding *-e* for the third person singular subject, *el perro.* Use *más* to express "more." Adverbs are formed by adding *-mente* to the feminine form of the adjective. To change a masculine singular adjective to its feminine form, replace the final *-o* with *-a.* Add *-mente* to *lenta* to get the adverb expressing "slowly." Use *que* to express "than." Add the second animal being compared, *la pantera.*

3.   (trabajar) El caballo es más diligente que el burro.

Answer: El caballo trabaja más diligentemente que el burro.

Conjugate the regular *-ar* verb *trabajar* by dropping the *-ar* ending and adding *-a* for the third person singular subject, *el caballo*. Use *más* to express "more." Adverbs are formed by adding *-mente* to the feminine form of the adjective. Masculine singular adjectives that end in an *-e* require no change to get the feminine form. Add *-mente* to *diligente* to get the adverb expressing "diligently." Use *que* to express "than." Add the second animal being compared, *el burro.*

Work Problems

Express how people do things.

Example: (conducir) Manuela es menos prudente que su hermana.
Manuela conduce menos prudentemente que su hermana.

1.   (trabajar) Nosotros somos menos pacientes que Uds.

2.   (vestirse) Yo soy más elegante que tú.

3.   (pensar) Ud. es más ingenioso que Rosa.

4.   (hablar) Él es menos cortés que su amigo.

5.   (estudiar) Ellos son menos cuidadosos que nosotros.

6.   (comportarse) Tú eres más respetuoso que ella.

Worked Solutions

1.   **Nosotros trabajamos menos pacientemente que Uds.**   Conjugate the regular *-ar* verb *trabajar* by dropping the *-ar* ending and adding *-amos* for the first person plural subject, *nosotros*. Use *menos* to express "less." Adverbs are formed by adding *-mente* to the feminine form of the adjective. Masculine singular adjectives that end in an *-e* require no change to get the feminine form. Add *-mente* to *paciente* to get the adverb expressing "patiently." Use *que* to express "than." Add the person being compared, *Uds.*

2.   **Yo me visto más elegantemente que tú.**   Conjugate the stem-change reflexive verb *vestirse* by changing the internal *e* to *i* and adding *-o* for the first person singular subject, *yo*. Additionally, place the reflexive pronoun *me*, which agrees with the subject, before the conjugated verb. Use *más* to express "more." Adverbs are formed by adding *-mente* to the feminine form of the adjective. Masculine singular adjectives that end in an *-e* require no change to get the feminine form. Add *-mente* to *elegante* to get the adverb expressing "elegantly." Use *que* to express "than." Add the person being compared, *tú.*

3.   **Ud. piensa más ingeniosamente que Rosa.**   Conjugate the stem-change verb *pensar* by changing the internal *e* to *ie* and adding *-a* for the third person singular subject, *Ud.* Use *más* to express "more." Adverbs are formed by adding *-mente* to the feminine form of the adjective. To change a masculine singular adjective to its feminine form, replace the final *-o* with *-a*. Add *-mente* to *ingeniosa* to get the adverb expressing "ingeniously." Use *que* to express "than." Add the person being compared, *Rosa.*

4. **Él habla menos cortésmente que su amigo.**   Conjugate the regular -ar verb *hablar* by dropping the -ar ending and adding -a for the third person singular subject, *él*. Use *menos* to express "less." Adverbs are formed by adding -mente to the feminine form of the adjective. Masculine singular adjectives that end in a consonant require no change to get the feminine form. Add -mente to *cortés* to get the adverb expressing "courteously." Use *que* to express "than." Add the person being compared, *su amigo*.

5. **Ellos estudian menos cuidadosamente que nosotros.**   Conjugate the regular -ar verb *estudiar* by dropping the -ar ending and adding -an for the third person singular subject, *ellos*. Use *menos* to express "less." Adverbs are formed by adding -mente to the feminine form of the adjective. To change a masculine singular adjective to its feminine form, replace the final -o with -a. Add -mente to *cuidadosa* to get the adverb expressing "attentively." Use *que* to express "than." Add the person being compared, *nosotros*.

6. **Tú te comportas más respetuosamente que ella.**   Conjugate the regular -ar reflexive verb *comportarse* by dropping the -ar ending and adding -as for the second person singular subject, *tú*. Additionally, place the reflexive pronoun *te*, which agrees with the subject, before the conjugated verb. Use *más* to express "more." Adverbs are formed by adding -mente to the feminine form of the adjective. To change a masculine singular adjective to its feminine form, replace the final -o with -a. Add -mente to *respetuosa* to get the adverb expressing "respectfully." Use *que* to express "than." Add the person being compared, *ella*.

Comparisons of Equality

Comparisons of equality show that two things are the same. The following formula works for adjectives and adverbs: *tan* + adjective or adverb + *como*.

Esas muchachas no son tan altas como esos muchachos.	Those girls aren't as tall as those boys.
Yo corro tan rápidamente como tú.	I run as quickly as you.

Use no to express the negative:

Ella no es tan bonita como su hermana.	She isn't as pretty as her sister.
Él no habla español tan bien como yo.	He doesn't speak Spanish as well as I do.

Example Problems

Express in Spanish that these people are equal to each other.

1. I am as intelligent as you are.

   Answer: Yo soy tan inteligente como tú (Ud.).

   Use the first person singular form of the irregular verb *ser* to express "I am." Use *tan* + the adjective *inteligente* (which is invariable for masculine or feminine subjects because it ends in -e) + *como* to express "as intelligent as." Use the informal subject pronoun *tú* or the formal subject pronoun *Ud.* to express "you." The "are" at the end of the sentence is implied and, therefore, requires no Spanish equivalent.

2. They write as well as we do.

Answer: Ellos escriben tan bien como nosotros.

Use the third person singular form of the regular -ir verb *escribir* to express "they write." Drop the -ir ending and add -en. Use *tan* + the adverb *bien* + *como* to express "as well as." Use *nosotros* to express "we." The "do" at the end of the sentence is implied and, therefore, requires no Spanish equivalent.

3. He isn't as tall as his sister.

Answer: Él no es tan grande como su hermana.

Use the third person singular form of the irregular verb *ser* to express "he is." Negate the sentence by putting *no* before the conjugated verb form. Use *tan* + the adjective *grande* (which is invariable for masculine or feminine subjects since it ends in -e) + *como* to express "as tall as." The possessive adjective *su* expresses "his" before the singular noun for "sister" *(hermana)*.

Work Problems

Express how these people compare to each other in Spanish.

1. You (informal) are as popular as she is.

2. They aren't as optimistic as we are.

3. My husband cooks as well as I do.

4. We don't dance as gracefully (elegantly) as they do.

5. She isn't as nice as her friends.

6. You (formal plural) work as seriously as he does.

Worked Solutions

1. **Tú eres tan popular como ella.**   Use the second person singular form of the irregular verb *ser* to express "you are." Use *tan* + the adjective *popular* (which is invariable for masculine or feminine subjects because it ends in a consonant) + *como* to express "as popular as." Use the subject pronoun *ella* to express "she." The "is" at the end of the sentence is implied and, therefore, requires no Spanish equivalent.

2. **Ellos no son tan optimistas como nosotros.**   Use the third person plural form of the irregular verb *ser* to express "they are." Negate the sentence by putting *no* before the conjugated verb form. Use *tan* + the plural adjective *optimistas* (which is invariable for masculine or feminine subjects because it ends in -a) + *como* to express "as optimistic as." Use the subject pronoun *nosotros* to express "we." The "are" at the end of the sentence is implied and, therefore, requires no Spanish equivalent.

3. **Mi esposo cocina tan bien como yo.**   The possessive adjective *mi* expresses "my" and is used before the noun for "husband" *(esposo)*. Use the third person singular form of the

regular -ar verb *cocinar* to express "cooks." Drop the -ar ending and add -a. Use *tan* + the adverb *bien* + *como* to express "as well as." Use *yo* to express "I." The "do" at the end of the sentence is implied and, therefore, requires no Spanish equivalent.

4. **Nosotros no bailamos tan elegantemente como ellos.** Use the second person plural form of the regular -ar verb *bailar* to express "we dance." Drop the -ar ending and add -amos. Negate the sentence by putting *no* before the conjugated verb form. Use *tan* + the adverb *elegantemente*+ *como* to express "as gracefully as." Use *ellos* to express "they." The "do" at the end of the sentence is implied and, therefore, requires no Spanish equivalent.

5. **Ella no es tan simpática como sus amigas.** Use the third person singular form of the irregular verb *ser* to express "she is." Negate the sentence by putting *no* before the conjugated verb form. Use *tan* + the adjective *simpática* (change the masculine singular form of the adjective *simpático* to its feminine form by changing the -o to -a) + *como* to express "as nice as." The possessive adjective *sus* expresses "her" and agrees in number with the plural noun for "friends" *(amigas)*.

6. **Uds. trabajan tan seriamente como él.** Use the third person polite plural form of the regular -ar verb *trabajar* to express "you work." Drop the -ar ending and add -an. Use *tan* + the adverb *seriamente* (change the adjective *serio* to the feminine [*seria*] and add -mente to form the adverb) + *como* to express "as seriously as." Use *él* to express "he." The "does" at the end of the sentence is implied and, therefore, requires no Spanish equivalent.

The Absolute Superlative

The absolute superlative is used when no comparison is made. Add *-ísimo, -ísima, -ísimos,* or *-ísimas* to the adjective according to the gender (masculine or feminine) and number (singular or plural) of the noun being described without any relation to a group. The meaning is the same as *muy* + adjective:

Esa mujer es bella.	Esa mujer es bellísima.
Los postres son grandes.	Los postres son grandísimos.

When forming the absolute superlative keep the following in mind:

❑ Drop the final vowel of an adjective before adding *-ísimo:*

El coche es barato.	El coche es baratísimo.

❑ Use *muchísimo* to express "very much":

Lo dudo muchísimo.	I doubt it very much.

❑ Adjectives ending in *-co (-ca), -go (-ga),* or *-z* change *c* to *qu, g* to *gu,* and *z* to *c* to keep the original sound before adding *-ísimo:*

La mujer es muy rica.	La mujer es riquísima.
Las calles son muy largas.	Las calles son larguísimas.
El león es muy feroz.	El león es ferocísimo.

Example Problems

You are in a restaurant in a Spanish-speaking country. Express how you feel about the restaurant by using the absolute superlative.

> Example: Los camareros son muy atentos.
>
> Los camareros son atentísimos.

1. El menú es muy grande.

   Answer: El menú es grandísimo.

   The singular definite article *el* indicates that *menú* is masculine. Drop the final *-e* from *grande* and add *-ísimo*.

2. Las frutas son muy frescas.

   Answer: Las frutas son fresquísimas.

   The plural definite article *las* indicates that *frutas* is feminine. Drop the final *-o* from *fresco*, change the *-c* to *-qu*, and add *-ísimas*.

3. Todo el mundo se divierte mucho.

   Answer: Todo el mundo se divierte muchísimo.

   Drop the final *-o* from *mucho* and use *muchísimo* to express "very much."

Work Problems

You return to the restaurant on a subsequent day with a friend. Express how you feel about the experience by using the absolute superlative.

> Example: El comedor es elegante.
>
> El comedor es elegantísimo.

1. Hay una cola muy larga.

2. Las porciones son muy generosas.

3. Tenemos apetitos muy grandes.

4. Todo el mundo come mucho.

5. Los postres son muy ricos.

6. Soy un muchacho muy feliz.

Worked Solutions

1. **Hay una cola larguísima.**   The singular indefinite article *una* indicates that *cola* is feminine. Drop the final *-a* from *larga*, change the *-g* to *-gu*, and add *-ísima*.

2.   **Las porciones son generosísimas.**   The plural definite article *las* indicates that *porciones* is feminine. Drop the final *-as* from *generosas* and add *-ísimas*.

3.   **Tenemos apetitos grandísimos.**   Nouns ending in *-o* tend to be masculine. The final *-s* on *apetitos* indicates that the word is plural. Drop the final *-es* from *grandes* and add *-ísimos*.

4.   **Todo el mundo come muchísimo.**   Drop the final *-o* from *mucho* and use *muchísimo* to express "very much."

5.   **Los postres son riquísimos.**   The plural definite article *los* indicates that *postres* is masculine. Drop the final *-o* from *rico*, change the *-c* to *-qu*, and add *-ísimo*.

6.   **Soy un muchacho felicísimo.**   Nouns ending in *-o* tend to be masculine. Change the final *-z* from *feliz* to *-c* and add *-ísimo*.

Chapter Problems

Problems

In problems 1–10, compare the people.

> Example: Gregorio es generoso. (+/Domingo)
> Gregorio es más generoso que Domingo.

1.   Luisa es ambiciosa (–/Diana)

2.   Ese doctor es malo. (–/el otro)

3.   Nosotros somos atléticos (+/Uds.)

4.   Ud. es franco. (=/Arturo)

5.   Tú eres impulsivo. (+/yo)

6.   Ella es bondadosa. (+/su hermana)

7.   Él es inteligente. (=/tú)

8.   Estela es curiosa. (–/Luz)

9.   El actor es bueno. (+/la actriz)

10. Luis es serio. (=/José)

In problems 11–20, describe the people.

> Example: (fuerte) mi hermano menor/gritar(+/yo)
> Mi hermano menor grita más fuertemente que yo.

11. (diligente) yo/estudiar(–/tú)

12. (bueno) mi madre/cocinar(+/mi padre)

13. (lento) Ud./conducir(=/su hermano)

14. (profundo) Elena/dormir(–/Adela)

15. (mal) Ud./pintar(–/su hermana)

16. (claro) tú/hablar(=/Mercedes)

17. (profesional) Jaime/bailar(–/Vicente)

18. (dulce) nosotros/cantar(+/ellos)

19. (silencioso) ellas/trabajar(=/Uds.)

20. (frecuente) yo/llorar(–/tú)

In problems 21–25, you are walking on the beach. Describe the scene by using the absolute superlative.

        Example: La vista es muy bella.
                     La vista es bellísima.

21. El aire es muy fresco.

22. La playa es muy hermosa.

23. Las olas son muy tranquilas.

24. Los niños se divierten mucho.

25. El agua es clara.

Answers and Solutions

1. **Answer: Luisa es menos ambiciosa que Diana.** Use *menos* to express "less" and place it before the adjective it modifies. Use *que* to express "than" when comparing two people.

2. **Answer: Ese doctor es peor que el otro.** Use the irregular comparative form of *mal: peor.* Use *que* to express "than" before the final noun.

3. **Answer: Nosotros somos más atléticos que Uds.** Use *más* to express "more" and place it before the adjective it modifies. Use *que* to express "than" when comparing two people.

4. **Answer: Ud. es tan franco como Arturo.** Use *tan* to express "as" and place it before the adjective it modifies. Use *como* to express "as" when comparing two people.

5. **Answer: Tú eres más impulsivo que yo.** Use *más* to express "more" and place it before the adjective it modifies. Use *que* to express "than" when comparing two people.

6. **Answer: Ella es más bondadosa que su hermana.** Use *más* to express "more" and place it before the adjective it modifies. Use *que* to express "than" before the final noun.

7. **Answer: Él es tan inteligente como tú.** Use *tan* to express "as" and place it before the adjective it modifies. Use *como* to express "as" when comparing two people.

8. **Answer: Estela es menos curiosa que Luz.** Use *menos* to express "less" and place it before the adjective it modifies. Use *que* to express "than" when comparing two people.

9. **Answer: El actor es mejor que la actriz.** Use the irregular comparative form of *bueno: mejor*. Use *que* to express "than" before the final noun.

10. **Answer: Luis es tan serio como José.** Use *tan* to express "as" and place it before the adjective it modifies. Use *como* to express "as" when comparing two people.

11. **Answer: Yo estudio menos diligentemente que tú.** Conjugate the regular -*ar* verb *estudiar* by dropping the -*ar* ending and adding -*o* for the first person singular subject, *yo*. Use the irregular comparative adverb *menos* to express "less." Use *que* to express "than." Add the person being compared, *tú*.

12. **Answer: Mi madre cocina mejor que mi padre.** Conjugate the regular -*ar* verb *cocinar* by dropping the -*ar* ending and adding -*a* for the third person singular subject, *mi madre*. Use *mejor* to express "better." Use *que* to express "than." Add the person being compared, *mi padre*.

13. **Answer: Ud. conduce tan lentamente como su hermano.** Conjugate the irregular -*ir* verb *conducir* by dropping the -*ir* ending and adding -*e* for the third person singular subject, *Ud*. Use *tan* to express "as." Adverbs are formed by adding -*mente* to the feminine form of the adjective. To change a masculine singular adjective to its feminine form, replace the final -*o* with -*a*. Add -*mente* to *lenta* to get the adverb expressing "slowly." Use *como* to express "as." Add the person being compared, *su hermano*.

14. **Answer: Elena duerme menos profundamente que Adela.** Conjugate the spelling-change verb *dormir* by changing the internal *o* to *ue*, then dropping the -*ir* ending and adding -*e* for the third person singular subject, *Elena*. Use *menos* to express "less." Adverbs are formed by adding -*mente* to the feminine form of the adjective. To change a masculine singular adjective to its feminine form, replace the final -*o* with -*a*. Add -*mente* to *profunda* to get the adverb expressing "deeply." Use *que* to express "than." Add the person being compared, *Adela*.

15. **Answer: Ud. pinta peor que su hermana.** Conjugate the regular -*ar* verb *pintar* by dropping the -*ar* infinitive ending and adding -*a* for the third person singular subject, *Ud*. Use the irregular comparative adverb *peor* to express "worse." Use *que* to express "than." Add the person being compared, *su hermana*.

16. **Answer: Tú hablas tan claramente como Mercedes.** Conjugate the regular -*ar* verb *hablar* by dropping the -*ar* ending and adding -*as* for the second person singular subject, *tú*. Use *tan* to express "as." Adverbs are formed by adding -*mente* to the feminine form of the adjective. To change a masculine singular adjective to its feminine form, replace the final -*o* with -*a*. Add -*mente* to *clara* to get the adverb expressing "clearly." Use *como* to express "as." Add the person being compared, *Mercedes*.

17. **Answer: Jaime baila menos profesionalmente que Vicente.** Conjugate the regular -*ar* verb *bailar* by dropping the -*ar* ending and adding -*a* for the third person singular subject, *Jaime*. Use *menos* to express "less." Adverbs are formed by adding -*mente* to the feminine form of the adjective. Masculine singular adjectives that end in a consonant require no change to get the feminine form. Add -*mente* to *profesional* to get the adverb expressing "professionally." Use *que* to express "than." Add the person being compared, *Vicente*.

18. **Answer: Nosotros cantamos más dulcemente que ellos.** Conjugate the regular *-ar* verb *cantar* by dropping the *-ar* ending and adding *-amos* for the second person plural subject, *nosotros*. Use *más* to express "more." Adverbs are formed by adding *-mente* to the feminine form of the adjective. Masculine singular adjectives that end in *-e* require no change to get the feminine form. Add *-mente* to *dulce* to get the adverb expressing "softly." Use *que* to express "than." Add the person being compared, *ellos*.

19. **Answer: Ellas trabajan tan silenciosamente como Uds.** Conjugate the regular *-ar* verb *trabajar* by dropping the *-ar* ending and adding *-an* for the third person plural subject, *ellas*. Use *tan* to express "as." Adverbs are formed by adding *-mente* to the feminine form of the adjective. To change a masculine singular adjective to its feminine form, replace the final *-o* with *-a*. Add *-mente* to *silenciosa* to get the adverb expressing "silently." Use *como* to express "as." Add the person being compared, *Uds*.

20. **Answer: Yo lloro menos frecuentemente que tú.** Conjugate the regular *-ar* verb *llorar* by dropping the *-ar* ending and adding *-o* for the first person singular subject, *yo*. Use *menos* to express "less." Adverbs are formed by adding *-mente* to the feminine form of the adjective. Masculine singular adjectives that end in *-e* require no change to get the feminine form. Add *-mente* to *frecuente* to get the adverb expressing "frequently." Use *que* to express "than." Add the person being compared, *tú*.

21. **Answer: El aire es fresquísimo.** The singular definite article *el* indicates that *aire* is masculine. Drop the final *-o* from *fresco*, change the *c* to *qu*, and add *-ísimo*.

22. **Answer: La playa es hermosísima.** The singular definite article *la* indicates that *playa* is feminine. Drop the final *-a* from *hermosa* and add *-ísima*.

23. **Answer: Las olas son tranquilísimas.** The plural definite article *las* indicates that *olas* is feminine. Drop the final *-as* from *tranquilas* and add *-ísimas*.

24. **Answer: Los niños se divierten muchísimo.** Drop the final *-o* from *mucho* and use *muchísimo* to express "very much."

25. **Answer: El agua es clarísima.** *Agua* is a feminine word that uses the definite article *el* in order to prevent two *a* sounds from clashing. Drop the final *-a* from *clara* and add *-ísima*.

Supplemental Chapter Problems

In problems 1–10, compare the things.

> Example: La biología es fácil. (+/la química)
>> La biología es más fácil que la química.

1. Un artista es creativo. (=/un escritor)

2. Una calculadora es útil. (–/una computadora)

3. El chocolate es bueno. (+/la vainilla)

4. Un pueblo es grande. (–/una ciudad)

5. La plata es preciosa. (–/el oro)

6. La influenza es mala. (+/un resfriado)

7. Un sillón es cómodo. (=/un sofá)

8. Una flor es bella. (=/una estrella)

9. El acero es duro. (+/la madera)

10. El español es difícil. (–/el ruso)

In problems 11–20, describe the things.

> Example: (rápido) el tren/correr(+/el autobús)
> El tren corre más rápidamente que el autobús.

11. (bien) un poeta/escribir(=/un novelista)

12. (hábil) un anciano/jugar(–/un joven)

13. (lento) la tortuga/caminar(+/el perro)

14. (rápido) el profesor/hablar español (+/los estudiantes)

15. (atento) un dentista/trabajar(=/un médico)

16. (mal) un radio/funcionar(+/un estéreo)

17. (profundo) un obrero/pensar(–/un filósofo)

18. (diligente) los atletas profesionales/entrenarse(+/los estudiantes)

19. (profesional) el juez/comportarse(=/el abogado)

20. (valiente) un cobarde/luchar(–/un héroe)

In problems 21–25, you are walking in the city. Describe the scene by using the absolute superlative.

> Example: Los restaurantes son muy lujosos.
> Los restaurantes son lujosísimos

21. La catedral es muy bella.

22. Las avenidas son muy anchas.

23. Los rascacielos son muy altos.

24. Los turistas están muy felices.

25. Yo camino muy poco.

Answers

1. Un artista es tan creativo como un escritor. (comparisons of equality, adjectives, p. 223)

2. La calculadora es menos útil que una computadora. (comparisons of inequality, adjectives, p. 214)

3. El chocolate es mejor que la vainilla. (comparisons of inequality, irregular adjectives, p. 214)

4. Un pueblo es menos grande que una ciudad. (comparisons of inequality, adjectives, p. 214)

5. La plata es menos preciosa que el oro. (comparisons of inequality, adjectives, p. 214)

6. La influenza es peor que un resfriado. (comparisons of inequality, irregular adjectives, p. 217)

7. Un sillón es tan cómodo como un sofá. (comparisons of equality, adjectives, p. 223)

8. Una flor es tan bella como una estrella. (comparisons of equality, adjectives, p. 223)

9. El acero es más duro que la madera. (comparisons of inequality, adjectives, p. 214)

10. El español es menos difícil que el ruso. (comparisons of inequality, adjectives, p. 214)

11. Un poeta escribe tan bien como un novelista. (comparisons of equality, adverbs, p. 223; adverbs, p. 201)

12. Un anciano juega menos hábilmente que un joven. (comparisons of inequality, adverbs, p. 220; adverbs, p. 201)

13. La tortuga camina más lentamente que el perro. (comparisons of inequality, adverbs, p. 220; adverbs, p. 201)

14. El profesor habla español más rápidamente que los alumnos. (comparisons of inequality, adverbs, p. 220; adverbs, p. 201)

15. Un dentista trabaja tan atentamente como un médico. (comparisons of equality, adverbs, p. 223; adverbs, p. 201)

16. Un radio funciona peor que un estéreo. (comparisons of inequality, irregular adverbs, p. 221)

17. Un obrero piensa menos profundamente que un filósofo. (comparisons of inequality, adverbs, p. 220; adverbs, p. 201)

18. Los atletas profesionales se entrena más diligentemente que los estudiantes. (comparisons of inequality, adverbs, p. 220; adverbs, p. 201)

19. El juez se comporta tan profesionalmente como el abogado. (comparisons of equality, adverbs, p. 223; adverbs, p. 201)

20. Un cobarde lucha menos valientemente que un héroe. (comparisons of inequality, adverbs, p. 220; adverbs, p. 201)

21. La catedral es bellísima. (absolute superlative, p. 225)

22. Las avenidas son anchísimas. (absolute superlative, p. 225)

23. Los rascacielos son altísimos. (absolute superlative, p. 225)

24. Los turistas están felicísimos. (absolute superlative, p. 225)

25. Yo camino poquísimo. (absolute superlative, p. 225)

Chapter 12
Prepositions

Prepositions are used to relate elements in a sentence: noun to noun, verb to verb, or verb to noun/pronoun:

❑ Noun to noun:

   Se cortó el dedo **de** la mano izquierda. (He cut a finger on his left hand.)

❑ Verb to verb:

   Comienza a hablar **en** voz alta. (He begins to speak in a loud voice.)

❑ Verb to noun:

   El bebé no juega **con** sus manos. (The baby doesn't play with his hands.)

❑ Verb to pronoun:

   Él habla bien **de** ella. (He speaks well of her.)

Prepositions may be used before and after nouns and verbs. Certain verbs are always followed by a preposition. In addition, prepositions are used before the names of geographical locations to refer to travel and location.

Note: Prepositions may contract with articles: *a + el = al, de + el = del* (see Chapter 2 for more on contractions).

Some common Spanish prepositions and prepositional phrases include:

English	Spanish
about	acerca de
about (time)	a eso de (+ time)
above, on top of	encima de
according to	según
across	a través de
after	después (de)
against	contra
around	alrededor de
at	a, en
at the house of	en casa de
before	antes (de)
behind	detrás de
beneath, under	debajo de
besides	además de

between	entre
by	en, por
by perservering	a fuerza
deduring	durante
far	lejos de
for	por, para
from	de, desde
from now on	de hoy en adelante
in	en
in front of	delante de, enfrente de
in spite of	a pesar de
inside, within	dentro de
instead of	en lugar de, en vez de, por
of	de
on, upon	en, sobre
on the other hand	en cambio,
on time	a tiempo
opposite	enfrente de
otherwise	de otro modo
outside of	fuera de
over, above	sobre,
near	cerca de
since	desde
through	a través de
to	a
toward	hacia
until	hasta
with	con
without	sin

Example Problems

Your friend is late for an appointment with you. Complete each sentence by filling in the appropriate preposition.

a eso	enfrente	hasta
a casa	entre	según

Yo espero a un amigo en un banco que está _____ el supermercado y la panadería. El

banco está también _____ del cine. Puedo esperarlo _____ las dos y diez. Él no llega a las

dos en punto; llega _____ de làs dos. _____ mi amigo, él puede explicar su retraso. ¡Fue

_____ de su novia primero!

Answer:

1. **entre**   The preposition *entre* means "between" and is not followed by the preposition *de*.

2. **enfrente**   The preposition *enfrente* followed by the preposition *de* means "in front of."

3. **hasta**   The preposition *hasta* means "until" and is not followed by the preposition *de*.

4. **a eso**   The preposition *a eso* followed by the preposition *de* means "at about."

5. **según**   The preposition *según* means "according to" and is not followed by the preposition *de*.

6. **a casa**   The preposition *a casa* followed by the preposition *de* means "at the house of."

Work Problems

Tonight, there is a surprise party for Alberto. Corréct the story by giving the opposite of the underlined preposition.

Alberto termina su trabajo <u>antes de</u> (1) las nueve. Él llega a casa <u>con</u> (2) su esposa. Él estaciona su coche <u>detrás de</u> (3) la casa. Él está <u>lejos de</u> (4) la puerta. Carlos abre la puerta y pone sus llaves <u>debajo de</u> (5) la mesa. Sus invitados ya están <u>fuera de</u> (6) su casa.

Worked Solutions

1. **después de**   The preposition *antes* followed by the preposition *de* means "before." The expression for "after" is *después de*.

2. **sin**   The preposition *con* means "with." The word for "without" is *sin*.

3. **enfrente de**   The preposition *detrás* followed by the preposition *de* means "behind." The expression for "in front of" is *enfrente de*.

4. **cerca de**   The preposition *lejos* followed by the preposition *de* means "far from." The expression for "near" is *cerca de*.

5. **sobre**   The preposition *debajo* followed by the preposition *de* means "under." The word for "on" is *sobre*.

6. **dentro de**   The preposition *fuera* followed by the preposition *de* means "outside." The expression for "inside" is *dentro de*.

Prepositional Distinctions

Some prepositions have distinct uses, as outlined in the sections that follow.

En and *A*

Both *en* and *a* may be used to express "at":

- ❏ *En* means "inside" or "within" an enclosed or specified place:

    Estoy en casa. (I'm at [inside my] home.)

- ❏ *A* refers to a general location where there are no suggested or implied boundaries:

    Viajo a Colombia el martes. (I'm going to Colombia on Tuesday.)

A and *De*

Both *a* (to) and *de* (from) are used when referring to places. It is important to contract *a* and *de* with the definite article *el* (the) before a masculine singular noun, as shown below. *A* and *de* do not contract with *la, los,* or *las*:

a + el = al	Vamos al teatro. (We are going to the theater.)
de + el = del	Salimos del teatro. (We are leaving the theater.)

De also expresses origin and possession:

Soy de España.	I am from Spain.
Es el carro de Pedro.	It's Peter's car.

Por and *Para*

Both *por* and *para* mean "for." Do not use *por* or *para* with the verbs *buscar* (to look for), *esperar* (to wait for), or *pedir* (to ask for) because the word "for" is already included in the meaning of the verb. The use of *por* and *para* is determined by the Spanish context:

Por shows:

- ❏ Motion:

    ¿Pasas por mi casa? (Are you passing **by** my house?)

    Salen por esa puerta. (They are leaving **through** that door.)

    Camina por esa calle. (He walks **along** that street.)

- ❏ Means or manner:

    ¿Lo necesitas por escrito? (Do you need it **in** writing?)

    Envío el paquete por avión. (I'm sending the package **by** plane.)

    When speaking about a means of transportation for a passenger, use *en* rather than *por* to express "by":

    Voy a viajar **en** barco. (I'm going to travel by boat.)

    Envío el paquete **por** barco. (I'm sending the package by boat.)

- ❏ In exchange for:

    Pago mucho por mi coche. (I'm paying a lot **for** my car.)

- ❏ The duration of an action:

    Trabajó allá por un año. (He worked there **for** a year.)

❑ An indefinite period of time:

Voy de compras por la mañana. (I'm going shopping **in** the morning.)

❑ For the sake of or on behalf of:

Lo hace por mí. (He does it **for my sake (on my behalf).**)

❑ A reason or motive:

Trabajamos por necesidad. (We work **out of** necessity.)

❑ "Per" or "by the":

Gana mucho por semana. (He earns a lot **per** week.)

Cuestan menos por docena. (They cost less **by the** dozen.)

❑ Opinion or estimation and is equivalent to "for" or "as":

Le toman por médico. (They take him **for** a doctor.)

Se le conoce por Julio. (He is known **as** Julio.)

❑ The agent (doer) in a passive construction:

Fue descubierto por Ana. (It was discovered **by** Ana.)

❑ "For" after the verbs *enviar* (to send), *ir* (to go), *mandar* (to order, to send), *preguntar* (to ask), *regresar* (to return), *venir* (to come), and *volver* (to return):

Fui (Envié, Pregunté) por la policía. (I **went for (sent for, asked for)** the police.)

Vino (Regresó, Volvió) por su dinero. (He **came for (returned for, came back for)** his money.)

Por is also used in the following adverbial expressions:

Spanish	English
por eso	therefore, so
por lo común	generally
por lo general	generally
por lo visto	apparently
por supuesto	of course

Para is used to show:

❑ Destination to a place or a direction:

Yo salgo para España. (I'm leaving **for** Spain.)

❑ Destination to a recipient:

Este dinero es para ella. (This money is **for** her.)

❑ A time limit in the future:

Voy a regresar para las dos. (I'm going to return **by** two o'clock.)

❑ A purpose or goal:

Trabajo mucho para hacerme rico. (I work a lot **(in order to)** become rich.)

❑ The use of an object:

Es un cepillo para los vestidos. (It's a brush **for** clothing.)

❑ Comparisons by expressing "for" or "considering that":

   Para ser muchacha, es muy fuerte. (**For** being a girl, she is very strong.)

Example Problems

Select the correct preposition to complete each sentence about Susana's evening.

1. Estudio _____ casa hasta las siete.

   A. a la **B.** en **C.** para **D.** de la

   Answer: B

   To express "in," select the preposition *en*.

2. Salgo _____ teatro a las siete y media.

   A. por el **B.** para el **C.** de **D.** a la

   Answer: B

   To express "for," select the preposition *para*, which expresses a destination. Use the definite article *el* to express "the" with the masculine singular noun ending in an *-o*, *teatro*.

3. Voy _____ concierto a las nueve.

   A. al **B.** en el **C.** del **D.** por el

   Answer: A

   To express "to," select the preposition *a*, which combines with the definite article *el* to become *al*.

Work Problems

Select the correct preposition to complete each sentence about a voice-mail message.

1. Ahora estoy ____ casa.

   A. a la **B.** por **C.** para **D.** en

2. Quiero ir ____ centro.

   A. del **B.** por **C.** al **D.** en el

3. Voy allá ____ la tarde.

   A. al **B.** en **C.** por **D.** para

4. Tengo que ir allá ____ comprar un regalo.

   A. por **B.** para **C.** de **D.** en

Worked Solutions

1. **D** To express "in," select the preposition *en*.

2. **C** To express "to," select the preposition *a*, which combines with the definite article *el* to become *al*.

3. **C** To express "for," select the preposition *por*, which expresses an indefinite period of time. Use the definite article *la* to express "the" with the feminine singular noun, *tarde*.

4. **B** To express "for," select the preposition *para*, which expresses a purpose or a goal.

Prepositions before Infinitives

In Spanish, the infinitive is the verb form that follows a preposition. Spanish verbs may require the preposition *a, de, en,* or *con* before the infinitive. Some Spanish verbs are followed immediately by the infinitive and no preposition should be used with them.

Spanish Verbs Requiring *A*

The following Spanish verbs are followed by *a* before an infinitive:

Spanish	English
acercarse	to approach
acostumbrarse	to become accustomed
aprender	to learn
apresurarse	to hurry
aspirar	to aspire
atreverse	to dare
ayudar	to help
comenzar	to begin
convidar	to invite
correr	to run
decidirse	to decide
dedicarse	to devote oneself
disponerse	to get ready
empezar	to begin
enseñar	to teach
ir	to go
llegar	to succeed in
negarse (ie)	to refuse
obligar	to force
ponerse	to begin
principiar	to begin
regresar	to return
resignarse	to resign oneself
salir	to go out

venir	to come
volver (ue)	to return (again)

Here is an example:

Los niños aprenden a nadar.   The children learn to swim.

Spanish Verbs Requiring *De*

The following Spanish verbs are followed by *de* before an infinitive:

Spanish	English
acabar	to have just
acordarse (ue)	to remember (to)
alegrarse	to be glad
cesar	to stop
dejar	to stop
encargarse	to take charge (of)
olvidarse	to forget
tratar	to try (to)

Here is an example:

Yo acabo de leer un buen libro.   I have just read a good book.

Spanish Verbs Requiring *En*

The following Spanish verbs are followed by *en* before an infinitive:

Spanish	English
consentir	to consent (to)
consistir	to consist (of)
convenir	to agree (to)
empeñarse	to insist (on)
fijarse	to notice
insistir	to insist (on)
tardar	to delay (in)

Here is an example:

¿Por qué tardan en llegar?   Why are they late in arriving?

Spanish Verbs Requiring *Con*

The following Spanish verbs are followed by *con* before an infinitive:

Spanish	English
contar	to count (on)
soñar	to dream (of)
amenazar	to threaten

Here is an example:

Yo cuento con recibir el cheque.   I'm counting on receiving the check.

Verbs Requiring No Preposition

The following verbs do not require a preposition before an infinitive that follows them:

Spanish	English
deber	must (to have to)
dejar	to allow
desear	to want, to wish
esperar	to hope
hacer	to make (to have something done)
lograr	to succeed in
necesitar	to need
oír	to hear
pensar	to intend
poder	to be able to
preferir	to prefer
pretender	to attempt
prometer	to promise
querer	to want, to wish
saber	to know (how)
ver	to see

Here is an example:

Él sabe hablar español.   He knows how to speak Spanish.

Example Problems

Complete each sentence about what each person does by filling in a preposition, if needed.

1. Una mujer insiste _____ trabajar.

    Answer: en

    The verb *insistir* is followed by the preposition *en*.

2. Un hombre acaba ____ hacer negocios.

Answer: de

The verb *acabar* is followed by the preposition *de*.

3. Unos empleados prefieren ____ ir a casa.

Answer: no preposition required

The verb *preferir* is not followed by a preposition.

Work Problems

Complete each sentence about what each student does by filling in a preposition, if needed.

1. Luisa debe ____ ayudar a su amiga.

2. Marco se olvida ____ estudiar para su examen.

3. Margarita tarda ____ hacer sus tareas.

4. Rogelio empieza ____ trabajar a las ocho.

5. Los muchachos cuentan ____ jugar en clase.

Worked Solutions

1. **no preposition required** The verb *deber* is not followed by a preposition.

2. **de** The verb *olvidarse* is followed by the preposition *de*.

3. **en** The verb *tardar* is followed by the preposition *en*.

4. **a** The verb *empezar* is followed by the preposition *a*.

5. **con** The verb *contar* is followed by the preposition *con*.

Prepositional Modifiers

The prepositions *para* (used mainly to express "for") or *de* (used mainly to express "of") + noun are used to express the use, the function, purpose, or the characteristic of an object:

una puerta de madera	a wooden door
la loción para broncearse	suntan lotion

The preposition *de* + noun is used to express the source, the goal, or the content of an object:

una taza de café	a cup of coffee

A preposition + a noun modifying another noun is equivalent to an adjective:

las gotas para la nariz   nose drops
los pañuelos de papel   paper handkerchiefs (tissues)

A preposition + a noun modifying a verb is equivalent to an adverb:

Él escribe con cuidado.   He writes carefully.

Example Problems

Complete each sentence describing the object by filling in the correct preposition.

1. Son cucharas ____ plástico.

    Answer: de

    The preposition *de* is used to express the characteristic of an object.

2. Es un vaso ____ el agua.

    Answer: para

    The preposition *para* is used to express the purpose of an object.

3. Son platos ____ la sopa.

    Answer: para

    The preposition *para* is used to express the purpose of an object.

Work Problems

Complete each sentence describing the object by filling in the correct preposition.

1. Son gotas ___ los ojos.

2. Es un anillo ___ oro.

3. Es una blusa ___ seda.

4. Son mesas ___ madera.

Worked Solutions

1. **para**   The preposition *para* (for) is used to express the purpose of an object.

2. **de**   The preposition *de* is used to express the characteristic of an object.

3. **de**   The preposition *de* is used to express the characteristic of an object.

4. **de**   The preposition *de* is used to express the characteristic of an object.

Prepositional Pronouns

A prepositional pronoun is used as the object of a preposition and always follows it:

¿Es para mí?	Is that for me?
No salgo con él.	I'm not going out with him.

The following pronouns are those used after prepositions:

Subject	Prepositional Pronoun	Meaning
yo	mí	I, me
tú	ti	you (informal singular)
él	él	he, him
ella	ella	she
Ud.	Ud.	you
nosotros	nosotros	we, us
vosotros	vosotros	you (informal plural)
ellos	ellos	they, them
ellas	ellas	they, them
Uds.	Uds.	you (formal plural)

The prepositional pronoun phrase *para sí* is used reflexively both in the singular and in the plural to express "yourself," "himself," "herself," "itself," "themselves," or "yourselves":

Ella lo quiere todo para sí.	She wants everything for herself.

The prepositional pronoun is used as the object of a preposition and always follows the preposition:

No es para él; es para ella.	It's not for him; it's for her.

The prepositional pronouns *mí, ti,* and *sí* combine with the preposition *con* as follows:

conmigo	with me
contigo	with you
consigo	with himself (herself, yourself, themselves, yourselves)

Here is an example in a sentence:

¿Quieres ir al cine conmigo?	Do you want to go to the movies with me?

Example Problems

Write reciprocal sentences expressing what each person does.

Example: Él habla por ellas.
Ellas hablan por él.

1. Nosotros venimos sin Uds.

Answer: Uds. vienen sin nosotros.

Make *Uds.* the subject of the sentence. Conjugate the irregular verb *venir* in the third person plural. Change the stem's internal *e* to *ie*, drop the *-ir* ending, and add *-en*. Add the first person plural prepositional pronoun *nosotros* after the preposition *sin*.

2. Tú compras un regalo para ella.

Answer: Ella compra un regalo para ti.

Make *ella* the subject of the sentence. Conjugate the regular *-ar* verb *comprar* in the third person singular by dropping the *-ar* ending and adding *-a*. Add the second person singular prepositional pronoun *ti* after the preposition *para*.

3. Yo salgo con mis amigos.

Answer: Mis amigos salen conmigo.

Make *mis amigos* the subject of the sentence. Conjugate the irregular *yo* form verb *salir* in the third person plural by dropping the *-ir* ending and adding *-en*. Attach the special first person singular prepositional pronoun *-migo* to the preposition *con*.

Work Problems

Write reciprocal sentences expressing what each person does.

Example: Ella tiene confianza en ellos.
Ellos tienen confianza en ella.

1. Ella vive cerca de mí.

2. Tú te enojas con él.

3. Nosotros pensamos en Uds.

4. Yo salgo sin ti.

Worked Solutions

1. **Yo vivo cerca de ella.** Make *yo* the subject of the sentence. Conjugate the regular *-ir* verb *vivir* in the first person singular by dropping the *-ir* ending and adding *-o*. Add the third person singular prepositional pronoun *ella* after the prepositional phrase *cerca de*.

2. **Él se enoja contigo.** Make *él* the subject of the sentence. Conjugate the regular reflexive *-ar* verb *enojarse* in the third person singular by dropping the *-ar* ending and adding *-a*. Add the reflexive pronoun *se*, which agrees with the subject, before the conjugated verb. Attach the special first person singular prepositional pronoun, *-tigo*, to the preposition *con*.

3. **Uds. piensan en nosotros.** Make *Uds.* the subject of the sentence. Conjugate the stem-changing verb *pensar* in the third person plural. Change the stem's internal *e* to *ie*, drop the *-ar* ending, and add *-an*. Add the first person plural prepositional pronoun *nosotros* after the preposition *en*.

4. **Tú sales sin mí.**   Make *tú* the subject of the sentence. Conjugate the irregular *yo* form verb *salir* in the second person singular by dropping the *-ir* ending and adding *-es*. Add the first person singular prepositional pronoun *mí* after the preposition *sin*.

Chapter Problems

Problems
Complete the story by filling in the correct form of the preposition indicated.

Estamos (in) ____₁___ invierno. Es domingo, el dos (of) ____₂___ septiembre. Santiago tiene

una cita (with) ____₃___ su amigo Roberto (at) ____₄___ las dos. Él quiere saber qué tiempo

hace. Mira (through) ____₅___ la ventana. Está nevando. (In spite of) ____₆___ eso, se prepara

(in order to) ____₇___ ir (to) ____₈___ casa de su amigo. Como Roberto vive bastante (far

from) ____₉___ él y como Santiago tiene que caminar (across) ____₁₀___ un parque, Santiago

decide ponerse un abrigo, botas, guantes, y una bufanda. Es la una y media y está casi

listo. Quiere salir pero no puede encontrar su bufanda. Busca (in) ____₁₁___ su cuarto,

(under) ____₁₂___ su cama, (behind) ____₁₃___ su cómoda, (on top of) ____₁₄___ su escritorio,

(inside) ____₁₅___ su ropero, pero no está (in) ____₁₆___ ninguna parte. No quiere salir

(without) ____₁₇___ su bufanda. (On the other hand) ____₁₈___ quiere llegar (on time) ____₁₉___.

Santiago se promete a sí mismo arreglar sus cosas (from now on) ____₂₀___. Tiene que

partir ahora mismo, (otherwise) ____₂₁___ va a llegar (with) ____₂₂___ diez minutos (of) ____₂₃___

retraso por lo menos. Finalmente Santiago le pregunta (to) ____₂₄___ su madre, "¿Has visto

mi bufanda?" Ella le contesta sonriendo, "¡Hijo mío, tu bufanda está (around) ____₂₅___ tu

cuello!"

Answers and Solutions

1. **Answer: en.** To express "in," select the preposition *en*.

2. **Answer: de.** To express "of," select the preposition *de*.

3. **Answer: con.** To express "with," select the preposition *con*.

4. **Answer: a.** To express "at," select the preposition *a*.

5. **Answer: por.** To express "through (out of)," select the preposition *por*.

6. **Answer: a pesar de.** To express "in spite of," select the prepositional phrase *a pesar de*.

7. **Answer: para.** To express "in order to," select the preposition *para*.

8. **Answer: a.** To express "to," select the preposition *a*.

9. **Answer: lejos de.** To express "far from," select the prepositional phrase *lejos de*.

10. **Answer: a través de.** To express "across," select the prepositional phrase *a través de*.

11. **Answer: en or por.** To express "in," select the preposition *en* or the preposition *por*.

12. **Answer: debajo de.** To express "under," select the prepositional phrase *debajo de*.

13. **Answer: detrás de.** To express "behind," select the prepositional phrase *detrás de*.

14. **Answer: encima de.** To express "on top of," select the preposition *encima de*.

15. **Answer: dentro de.** To express "inside," select the preposition *dentro de*.

16. **Answer: en or por.** To express "in," select the preposition *en* or the preposition *por*.

17. **Answer: sin.** To express "without," select the preposition *sin*.

18. **Answer: en cambio.** To express "on the other hand," select the prepositional phrase *en cambio*.

19. **Answer: a tiempo.** To express "on time," select the preposition *a tiempo*.

20. **Answer: de hoy en adelante.** To express "from now on," select the prepositional phrase *de hoy en adelante*.

21. **Answer: de otro modo.** To express "otherwise," select the prepositional phrase *de otro modo*.

22. **Answer: con.** To express "with," select the preposition *con*.

23. **Answer: de.** To express "of," select the preposition *de*.

24. **Answer: a.** To express "to," select the preposition *a*.

25. **Answer: alrededor de.** To express "around," select the prepositional phrase *alrededor de*.

Supplemental Chapter Problems

Problems

Complete the story by filling in the correct form of the preposition indicated.

Hoy es el cumpleaños (of) _____ Linda. Todos sus amigos están (in) _____ su casa (in
order to) _____ darle una fiesta. Es una sorpresa. Como Linda va (to) _____ llegar (at)
_____ casa (at about) _____ las ocho, todos sus amigos han llegado (with) _____
media hora (of) _____ anticipación. Todo el mundo se esconde. Raquel se pone
(beneath) _____ una mesa. Rodolfo y Bernardo se ponen (behind) _____ las cortinas.
Carlota se mete (in) _____ el cuarto de Linda y Julio se mete (inside) _____ un ropero.
Son las ocho (on) _____ punto. Linda llega (on time) _____. Ella anda (toward) _____
su casa. Cree que todo el mundo se ha olvidado (of) _____ su día especial. Se cree una
muchacha (without) _____ amigos y se echa (to) _____ llorar. Se para (outside) _____
su casa, (in front of) _____ la puerta (in order to) _____ secarse las lágrimas. (Instead
of) _____ llorar se decide (to) _____ celebrar su fiesta sola. Finalmente, pone su llave (in)
_____ la cerradura cuando de repente todo el mundo grita, "¡Feliz cumpleaños, Linda!"
Ahora ella llora (from) _____ felicidad.

Answers

1. de (prepositional distinctions, p. 236)

2. en (prepositional distinctions, p. 236)

3. para (prepositional distinctions, p. 236)

4. a (prepositional distinctions, p. 236)

5. a (prepositional distinctions, p. 236)

6. a eso de (prepositions, p. 233)

7. con (prepositions, p. 233)

8. de (prepositional distinctions, p. 236)

9. debajo de (prepositions, p. 233)

10. detrás de (prepositions, p. 233)

11. en (prepositional distinctions, p. 236)

12. dentro de (prepositions, p. 233)

13. en (prepositions, p. 233)

14. a tiempo (prepositions, p. 233)

15. hacia (prepositions, p. 233)

16. de (Spanish verbs requiring *de*, p. 240)

17. sin (prepositions, p. 233)

18. a (Spanish verbs requiring *a*, p. 239)

19. fuera de (prepositions, p. 233)

20. delante de (prepositions, p. 233)

21. para (prepositional distinctions, p. 236)

22. En vez de (prepositions, p. 233)

23. a (Spanish verbs requiring *de*, p. 240)

24. en (prepositional distinctions, p. 236)

25. de (prepositional distinctions, p. 236)

Chapter 13
The Preterit

The Preterit Tense of Regular Verbs

The preterit is a tense that expresses an action, event, or state of mind that occurred and was completed at a specific time in the past.

The preterit of regular verbs is formed by dropping the *-ar, -er,* or *-ir* infinitive endings and adding the preterit endings:

Person	*-ar* Verbs	*-er* Verbs	*-ir* Verbs
yo	-é	-í	-í
tú	-aste	-iste	-iste
él	-ó	-ió	-ió
ella	-ó	-ió	-ió
Ud.	-ó	-ió	-ió
nosotros	-amos	-imos	-imos
vosotros	-asteis	-isteis	-isteis
ellos	-aron	-ieron	-ieron
ellas	-aron	-ieron	-ieron
Uds.	-aron	-ieron	-ieron

Here are examples of conjugated verbs:

Subject	*-ar* Verbs *Hablar (to Speak)*	*-er* Verbs *Comer (to Eat)*	*-ir* Verbs *Vivir (to Live)*
yo	hablé	comí	viví
tú	hablaste	comiste	viviste
él	habló	comió	vivió
ella	habló	comió	vivió
Ud.	habló	comió	vivió
nosotros	hablamos	comimos	vivimos
vosotros	hablasteis	comisteis	vivisteis

(continued)

Subject	-ar Verbs Hablar (to Speak)	-er Verbs Comer (to Eat)	-ir Verbs Vivir (to Live)
ellos	hablaron	comieron	vivieron
ellas	hablaron	comieron	vivieron
Uds.	hablaron	comieron	vivieron

Example Problems

Express what each person did at the party.

Example: (cantar) Yo <u>canté.</u>

1. (bailar)

   Yo _____ la rumba, ellos _____ el tango, tú _____ el mambo, nosotros _____ el vals, vosotros _____ el merengue y ella _____ la samba.

   Answer: bailé, bailaron, bailaste, bailamos, bailasteis, bailó

   To conjugate regular -ar verbs in the preterit, drop the -ar ending and do the following:

   1. For *yo,* add -é as the ending.

   2. For *ellos,* add -aron as the ending.

   3. For *tú,* add -aste as the ending.

   4. For *nosotros,* add -amos as the ending.

   5. For *vosotros,* add -asteis as the ending.

   6. For *ella,* add -ó as the ending.

2. (beber)

   Ellas _____ una limonada, nosotras _____ té, Ud. _____ café, yo _____ chocolate, vosotros _____ vino y tú _____ cerveza.

   Answer: bebieron, bebimos, bebió, bebí, bebisteis, bebiste

   To conjugate regular -er verbs in the preterit, drop the -er ending and do the following:

   1. For *ellas,* add -ieron as the ending.

   2. For *nosotras,* add -imos as the ending.

   3. For *Ud.,* add -ió as the ending.

   4. For *yo,* add -í as the ending.

5. For *vosotros*, add *-isteis* as the ending.

6. For *tú*, add *-iste* as the ending.

3. (recibir)

Wigberto _____ un reloj, vosotras _____ dinero, yo _____ una cámara, Uds. _____ vestidos, tú _____ cartas y nosotros _____ libros.

Answer: recibió, recibisteis, recibí, recibieron, recibiste, recibimos

To conjugate regular *-ir* verbs in the preterit, drop the *-ir* ending and do the following:

1. For the masculine name Wigberto *(él)*, add *-ió* as the ending.

2. For *vosotras*, add *-isteis* as the ending.

3. For *yo*, add *-í* as the ending.

4. For *Uds.*, add *-ieron* as the ending.

5. For *tú*, add *-iste* as the ending.

6. For *nosotras*, add *-imos* as the ending.

Work Problems
Express what each person did yesterday on a day off.

1. (comer) Yo _____ en un restaurante.

2. (abrir) Tú _____ una cuenta de ahorros.

3. (mirar) Vosotros _____ la televisión por la tarde.

4. (insistir) Ella _____ en tocar el piano.

5. (pretender) Uds. _____ convencerme de ir al cine.

6. (responder) Nosotros _____ el correo.

7. (limpiar) Yo _____ la casa.

8. (meter) Vosotros _____ dinero en el banco.

9. (correr) Tú _____ en el parque.

10. (escribir) Nosotros _____ cartas.

11. (ayudar) Él _____ a su amigo.

12. (partir) Ellos _____ para España.

13. (asistir) Yo _____ a un concierto.

14. (caminar) Nosotros _____ por el bosque.

15. (aprender) Ud. _____ a conducir un coche.

16. (comprar) Ellas _____ regalos.

17. (recibir) Vosotros _____ muchos paquetes.

18. (cocinar) Tú _____.

Worked Solutions

1. **comí**   To conjugate regular -er verbs in the preterit, drop the -er ending and add -í as the ending.

2. **abriste**   To conjugate regular -ir verbs in the preterit, drop the -ir ending and add -iste the ending.

3. **mirasteis**   To conjugate regular -ar verbs in the preterit, drop the -ar ending and add -asteis as the ending.

4. **insistió**   To conjugate regular -ir verbs in the preterit, drop the -ir ending and add -ió as the ending.

5. **pretendieron**   To conjugate regular -er verbs in the preterit, drop the -er ending and add -ieron as the ending.

6. **respondimos**   To conjugate regular -er verbs in the preterit, drop the -er ending and add -imos as the ending.

7. **limpié**   To conjugate regular -ar verbs in the preterit, drop the -ar ending and add -é as the ending.

8. **metisteis**   To conjugate regular -er verbs in the preterit, drop the -er ending and add -isteis as the ending.

9. **corriste**   To conjugate regular -er verbs in the preterit, drop the -er ending and add -iste as the ending.

10. **escribimos**   To conjugate regular -ir verbs in the preterit, drop the -ir ending and add -imos as the ending.

11. **ayudó**   To conjugate regular -ar verbs in the preterit, drop the -ar infinitive and add -ó as the ending.

12. **partieron**   To conjugate regular -ir verbs in the preterit, drop the -ir ending and add -ieron as the ending.

13. **asistí**   To conjugate regular -ir verbs in the preterit, drop the -ir infinitive and add -í as the ending.

14. **caminamos**   To conjugate regular -ar verbs in the preterit, drop the -ar ending and add -amos as the ending.

15. **aprendió**   To conjugate regular *-er* verbs in the preterit, drop the *-er* ending and add *-ió* as the ending.

16. **compraron**   To conjugate regular *-ar* verbs in the preterit, drop the *-ar* ending and add *-aron* as the ending.

17. **recibisteis**   To conjugate regular *-ir* verbs in the preterit, drop the *-ir* ending and add *-isteis* as the ending.

18. **cocinaste**   To conjugate regular *-ar* verbs in the preterit, drop the *-ar* ending and add *-aste* as the ending.

The Preterit Tense of Spelling-Change Verbs

Some verbs that follow the regular rules of verb conjugation in the present tense require a spelling change in the preterit.

Verbs Ending in *-car, -gar,* and *-zar*

Verbs ending in *-car, -gar,* and *-zar* have the following changes only in the *yo* form of the preterit, to preserve the original sound of the verb:

c changes to *qu*	buscar (to look for)	yo busqué
g changes to *gu*	llegar (to arrive)	yo llegué
z changes to *c*	empezar (to begin)	yo empecé

Common verbs ending in *-car* include:

Verb	Meaning
aplicar	to apply
buscar	to look for
clarificar	to clarify
complicar	to complicate
comunicar	to communicate
confiscar	to confiscate
criticar	to criticize
educar	to educate
equivocarse	to be mistaken
explicar	to explain
identificar	to identify
indicar	to indicate
marcar	to designate, to label, to dial
notificar	to notify
platicar	to chat
practicar	to practice
sacar	to take out
significar	to mean
tocar	to touch, to play (music)
verificar	to verify

Common verbs ending in -gar include:

Verb	Meaning
apagar	to put out, to turn off
castigar	to punish
colgar	to hang
delegar	to delegate
entregar	to deliver
interrogar	to interrogate
jugar	to play (a sport or game)
llegar	to arrive
pagar	to pay
rogar	to ask, to beg

Common verbs ending in -zar include:

Verb	Meaning
almorzar	to eat lunch
aterrizar	to land
comenzar	to begin
cruzar	to cross
empezar	to begin
forzar	to force
gozar	to enjoy
lanzar	to throw
memorizar	to memorize
organizar	to organize
utilizar	to use

Example Problems

Use the preterit of the verbs in parentheses to express what each person did yesterday.

1. (tocar) Yo _____ la guitarra, él _____ el piano y Uds. _____ la flauta.

   Answer: toqué, tocó, tocaron

   To conjugate spelling-change -car verbs in the preterit, drop the -ar ending and do the following: For yo, change c to qu and add -é as the ending; for él, add -ó as the ending; for Uds., add -aron as the ending.

2. (jugar) Tú _____ a los naipes, nosotros _____al fútbol y yo _____ al tenis.

   Answer: jugaste, jugamos, jugué

   To conjugate spelling-change -gar verbs in the preterit, drop the -ar ending and do the following: For tú, add -aste as the ending; for nosotros, add -amos as the ending; for yo, change g to gu and add -é as the ending.

3. (almorzar) Vosotros _____ a la una, yo _____ a las once, y Ud. _____ al mediodía.

   Answer: almorzasteis, almorcé, almorzó

   To conjugate spelling-change *-zar* verbs in the preterit, drop the *-ar* ending and do the following: For *vosotros*, add *-asteis* as the ending; for *yo*, change *z* to *c* and add *-é* as the ending; for *Ud.*, add *-ó* as the ending.

Work Problems

Use the verb in parentheses to express what each person did yesterday to study for a test.

1. (memorizar) Yo _____ los verbos y Uds. _____ el vocabulario.

2. (explicar) Yo te _____ la gramática y Uds. me _____ las tareas.

3. (jugar) Yo no _____ al fútbol y Uds. _____ con la computadora.

4. (comenzar) Yo _____ a estudiar a las siete y Uds. _____ a las nueve.

5. (llegar) Yo _____ a casa temprano y Uds. _____ tarde.

6. (buscar) Yo _____ mi libro y Uds. _____ su diccionario.

Worked Solutions

1. **memoricé/memorizaron** To conjugate spelling-change *-zar* verbs in the preterit, drop the *-zar* ending. For *yo*, change *z* to *c* and add *-é* as the ending. For *Uds.*, add *-aron* as the ending.

2. **expliqué/explicaron** To conjugate spelling-change *-car* verbs in the preterit, drop the *-ar* ending. For *yo*, change *c* to *qu* and add *-é* as the ending. For *Uds.*, add *-aron* as the ending.

3. **jugué/jugaron** To conjugate spelling-change *-gar* verbs in the preterit, drop the *-ar* ending. For *yo*, change *g* to *gu* and add *-é* as the ending. For *Uds.*, add *-aron* as the ending.

4. **comencé/comenzaron** To conjugate spelling-change *-zar* verbs in the preterit, drop the *-zar* ending. For *yo*, change *z* to *c* and add *-é* as the ending. For *Uds.*, add *-aron* as the ending.

5. **llegué/llegaron** To conjugate spelling-change *-gar* verbs in the preterit, drop the *-ar* ending. For *yo*, change *g* to *gu* and add *-é* as the ending. For *Uds.*, add *-aron* as the ending. For *Uds.*, add *-aron* as the ending.

6. **busqué/buscaron** To conjugate spelling-change *-car* verbs in the preterit, drop the *-ar* ending. For *yo*, change *c* to *qu* and add *-é* as the ending. For *Uds.*, add *-aron* as the ending.

Verbs That Change *i* to *y*

Except for the verb *traer* (to bring) and all verbs ending in *-guir* (which follow the rules for regular verbs for the formation of the preterit), verbs ending in a vowel when the infinitive *-er* or *-ir* ending is dropped change *i* to *y* in the third person singular (*él, ella, Ud.*) and third person plural (*ellos, ellas, Uds.*) forms. All other forms have an accented *i*: **í**. Verbs ending in *-uir* (*construir, contribuir, distribuir, incluir,* and so on) follow the *i* to *y* change but do not accent the *i* in the *tú, nosotros,* or *vosotros* forms.

Subject	Caer (to Fall)	Creer (to Believe)	Oír (to Hear)	Incluir (to Include)
yo	caí	creí	oí	incluí
tú	caíste	creíste	oíste	incluiste
él, ella, Ud.	ca**y**ó	cre**y**ó	o**y**ó	inclu**y**ó
nosotros	caímos	creímos	oímos	incluimos
vosotros	caísteis	creísteis	oísteis	incluisteis
ellos, ellas, Uds.	ca**y**eron	cre**y**eron	o**y**eron	inclu**y**eron

The Preterit of Stem-Change Verbs

Verbs ending in *-ir* that undergo a stem change in the present tense also do so in the preterit. In the third person singular and plural forms, *e* changes to *i* and *o* changes to *u*.

e to ie in the present e to i in the preterit Preferir (to Prefer)	e to i in the present e to i in the preterit Servir (to Serve)	o to ue in the present o to u in the preterit Dormir (to Sleep)
yo preferí	yo serví	yo dormí
tú preferiste	tú serviste	tú dormiste
él, ella, Ud. prefirió	él, ella, Ud. sirvió	él, ella, Ud. durmió
nosotros preferimos	nosotros servimos	nosotros dormimos
vosotros preferisteis	vosotros servisteis	vosotros dormisteis
ellos, ellas, Uds. prefirieron	ellos, ellas, Uds. sirvieron	ellos, ellas, Uds. durmieron

The verbs *reír* (to laugh) and *sonreír* (to smile) drop *e* in the stem of the third person singular (*él, ella, Ud.*) and third person plural (*ellos, ellas, Uds.*) forms and add accents to the *tú, nosotros,* and *vosotros* forms, where usually no accents are present:

yo (son)reí	nosotros (son)reímos
tú (son)reíste	vosotros (son)reísteis
él (son)rió	ellos (son)rieron

Example Problems

Express what Guillermo did yesterday.

1. (dormir) Él _____ hasta las siete.

   Answer: durmió

   For present-tense stem-change verbs ending in *-ir*, *o* changes to *u* in the third person singular form.

2. (construir) Él _____ un aeromodelo.

   Answer: construyó

   For present-tense verbs ending in *-uir*, change *i* to *y* in the third person singular form.

3. (oír) Él _____ las quejas de su amigo.

   Answer: oyó

   Verbs ending in a vowel when the infinitive *-ir* ending is dropped change *i* to *y* in the third person singular.

4. (leer) Él _____ una revista.

   Answer: leyó

   Verbs ending in a vowel when the infinitive *-er* ending is dropped change *i* to *y* in the third person singular.

5. (caerse) Él _____ al suelo.

   Answer: se cayó

   Verbs ending in a vowel when the infinitive *-er* ending is dropped change *i* to *y* in the third person singular. Add the reflexive pronoun *se*, which agrees with the subject pronoun.

6. (reírse) Él _____ mucho.

   Answer: se rió

   The verb *reír* drops *e* in the stem of the third person singular and adds *–ió* to form the preterit. Add the reflexive pronoun *se*, which agrees with the subject pronoun.

7. (vestirse) Él _____ elegantemente.

   Answer: se vistió

   For present-tense stem-change verbs ending in *-ir*, *e* changes to *i* in the third person singular form. Add the reflexive pronoun *se*, which agrees with the subject pronoun.

8. (mentir) Él _____.

   Answer: mintió

   For present-tense stem-change verbs ending in *-ir*, *e* changes to *i* in the third person singular form.

Work Problems

Express what didn't happen to the soldiers.

1. (sonreír) Ellos no_____.

2. (creer) Ellos no _____ las mentiras del enemigo.

3. (caerse) Ellos no _____ al agua.

4. (sentir) Ellos no _____ pena por sus enemigos.

5. (morir) Los soldados no _____.

6. (oír) Ellos no _____ más que el silencio.

7. (destruir) Ellos no _____ nada.

8. (gemir) Ellos no _____.

Worked Solutions

1. **sonrieron**   The verb *sonreír* drops *e* in the stem of the third person plural and adds *–ieron* to form the preterit.

2. **creyeron**   Verbs ending in a vowel when the infinitive *-er* ending is dropped change *i* to *y* in the third person plural.

3. **se cayeron**   Verbs ending in a vowel when the infinitive *-er* ending is dropped change *i* to *y* in the third person plural. Add the reflexive pronoun *se*, which agrees with the subject pronoun.

4. **sintieron**   For present-tense stem-change verbs ending in *-ir*, *e* changes to *i* in the third person plural form.

5. **murieron**   For present-tense stem-change verbs ending in *-ir*, *o* changes to *u* in the third person plural form.

6. **oyeron**   Verbs ending in a vowel when the infinitive *-ir* ending is dropped change *i* to *y* in the third person plural.

7. **destruyeron**   For present-tense verbs ending in *-uir*, change *i* to *y* in the third person plural form.

8. **gimieron**   For present-tense stem-change verbs ending in *-ir*, *e* changes to *i* in the third person plural form.

The Preterit of Irregular Verbs

Many high-frequency verbs are irregular in the present tense and also in the preterit. Many of these verbs may be grouped according to the changes they undergo in the preterit. A small number of verbs are completely irregular and must be memorized.

Most irregular verbs in the preterit have the following endings:

yo	-e	nosotros	-imos
tú	-iste	vosotros	-isteis
él, ella, Ud.	-o	ellos, ellas, Uds.	-ieron (or -jeron)

Verbs with *I* in the Preterit Stem

	Decir (to Say)	*Venir* (to Come)	*Querer* (to Want)	*Hacer* (to Make)	*Satisfacer* (to Satisfy)
yo	dije	vine	quise	hice	satisfice
tú	dijiste	viniste	quisiste	hiciste	satisficiste
él, ella, Ud.	dijo	vino	quiso	hizo*	satisfizo*
nosotros	dijimos	vinimos	quisimos	hicimos	satisficimos
vosotros	dijisteis	vinisteis	quisisteis	hicisteis	satisficisteis
ellos, ellas, Uds.	dijeron	vinieron	quisieron	hicieron	satisficieron

* In these verbs -c changes to -z to maintain the original sound of the verb.

Verbs with *U* in the Preterit Stem

	Caber (to Fit)	*Haber (as an auxiliary verb) (to Have)*	*Saber* (to Know)	*Poner* (to Put)	*Poder* (to Be Able)
yo	cupe	hube	supe	puse	pude
tú	cupiste	hubiste	supiste	pusiste	pudiste
él, ella, Ud.	cupo	hubo	supo	puso	pudo
nosotros	cupimos	hubimos	supimos	pusimos	pudimos
vosotros	cupisteis	hubisteis	supisteis	pusisteis	pudisteis
ellos, ellas, Uds.	cupieron	hubieron	supieron	pusieron	pudieron

Verbs with *Uv* in the Preterit Stem

	Andar (to Walk)	*Estar (to Be)*	*Tener (to Have)*
yo	anduve	estuve	tuve
tú	anduviste	estuviste	tuviste
él, ella, Ud.	anduvo	estuvo	tuvo
nosotros	anduvimos	estuvimos	tuvimos
vosotros	anduvisteis	estuvisteis	tuvisteis
ellos, ellas, Uds.	anduvieron	estuvieron	tuvieron

Verbs with *J* in the Preterit Stem

These verbs include all those that end in *-ducir* and in the verb *decir* (see above).

	Traer (to Bring)	*Reducir (to Reduce)*
yo	traje	reduje
tú	trajiste	redujiste
él, ella, Ud.	trajo	redujo
nosotros	trajimos	redujimos
vosotros	trajisteis	redujisteis
ellos, ellas, Uds.	trajeron	redujeron

The Preterit of *Dar* and *Ver*

Dar and *ver* have the same irregular preterit endings, which are added to *d-* and *v-*:

	Dar (to Give)	*Ver (to See)*
yo	di	vi
tú	diste	viste
él, ella, Ud.	dio	vio
nosotros	dimos	vimos
vosotros	disteis	visteis
ellos, ellas, Uds.	dieron	vieron

The Preterit of *Ser* and *Ir*

Ser (to be) and *ir* (to go) have the exact same preterit forms. In order to distinguish which verb is being used, the context of the sentence must be understood. The highly irregular forms of these two verbs are:

yo	fui	nosotros	fuimos
tú	fuiste	vosotros	fuisteis
él, ella, Ud.	fue	ellos, ellas, Uds.	fueron

Example Problems

Use the preterit of the verb in parentheses to express what the members of the Ruíz family did yesterday.

1. (hacer) Yo _____ muchas tareas.

Answer: hice

In the preterit stem, *hacer* changes the *a* from the infinitive stem to *i*. The first person singular preterit ending for an irregular *-er* verb is *-e*.

2. (poner) Nosotros _____ la mesa.

   Answer: pusimos

   In the preterit stem, *poner* changes the *o* from the infinitive stem to *u*. The *n* from the infinitive stem changes to *s* in the preterit. The first person plural preterit ending for an *-er* verb is *-imos*.

3. (tener) Ellas _____ que limpiar la casa.

   Answer: tuvieron

   In the preterit stem, *tener* changes the *en* from the infinitive stem to *uv*. The third person plural preterit ending for an *-er* verb is *-ieron*.

4. (traer) Tú _____ comestibles a casa.

   Answer: trajiste

   In the preterit stem, *traer* adds a *j* after the *a*. The second person plural preterit ending for a verb that has *j* in its stem is *-eron*. Note that the *i* that is normally used is dropped.

5. (conducir) Ud. _____ al centro.

   Answer: condujo

   In the preterit stem, *conducir* (and other verbs ending in *-ucir*) adds a *j* after the *u* and drops the *c*. The third person singular preterit ending for this stem-change verb is *-o*. Note that the accent that is normally used in the preterit is dropped.

6. (dar) Vosotros _____ de comer al perro.

   Answer: disteis

   Dar has irregular preterit endings that are added to the *d-* in the infinitive. The preterit ending for *vosotros* is *-isteis*.

Work Problems

Use the preterit of the verbs in parentheses to express what happened to cause the subjects to have a bad day.

1. (ponerse/venir) Ellos _____ furiosos cuando ella no _____.

2. (satisfacer/traerse) El resultado no le _____ a él por lo tanto _____ los reportes.

3. (querer/poder) Nosotros _____ hacer el trabajo pero no _____.

4. (deducir/decir) Tú _____ que ellos _____ mentiras.

5. (ver/estar) Yo no _____ que unos empleados no _____ en la oficina.

6. (ir/tener) Vosotros _____al café cuando _____ que hacer algo muy importante.

Worked Solutions

1. **se pusieron/vino**   In the preterit stem, *ponerse* changes the *o* from the infinitive stem to *u*. The *n* from the infinitive stem changes to *s* in the preterit. The third person plural preterit ending for an -*er* verb is -*ieron*. The -*se* at the end of the infinitive indicates a reflexive verb. Place the pronoun *se*, which agrees with the subject, before the conjugated form of the verb. In the preterit stem, *venir* changes the *e* from the infinitive stem to *i*. The third person singular preterit ending for an irregular -*ir* verb is -*o*.

2. **satisfizo/se trajo**   In the preterit stem, *satisfacer* changes the second *a* from the infinitive stem to *i*. In the third person singular preterit form, the *c* from the stem changes to *z* to maintain the original sound of the verb. The third person plural preterit ending for an irregular -*er* verb is -*o*. In the preterit stem, *traerse* adds a *j* after the *a*. The third person singular preterit ending for an irregular -*er* verb is -*o* (without an accent). Note that the -*i* that is normally used for regular verbs is dropped. The *se* at the end of the infinitive indicates a reflexive verb. Place the pronoun -*se*, which agrees with the subject, before the conjugated form of the verb.

3. **quisimos/pudimos**   In the preterit stem, *querer* changes the *e* from the infinitive stem to *i*. The *r* from the infinitive stem changes to *s* in the preterit. The first person plural preterit ending for an -*er* verb is -*imos*. In the preterit stem, *poder* changes the *o* from the infinitive stem to *u*. The first person plural preterit ending for an -*er* verb is -*imos*.

4. **dedujiste/dijeron**   In the preterit stem, *deducir* (and other verbs ending in -*ucir*) adds a *j* after the *u* and drops the *c*. The second person singular preterit ending for this stem-change verb is -*iste*. In the preterit stem, *decir* changes the *e* from the infinitive stem to *i*. A *j* is added after the *i*. The third person plural preterit ending is -*eron*.

5. **vi/estuvieron**   *Ver* has irregular preterit endings that are added to the *v*- from the infinitive. The preterit ending for *yo* is an unaccented -*i*. In the preterit stem, *estar* adds the *uv* to the infinitive stem, *est*-. The third person plural preterit ending for an irregular verb is -*ieron*.

6. **fuisteis/tuvisteis**   The verb *ir* is irregular in the preterit and must be memorized. All forms start with *fu*-. The preterit ending for *vosotros* is -*isteis*. In the preterit stem, *tener* changes the *en* from the infinitive stem to *uv*. The second person plural preterit ending for an -*er* verb is -*isteis*.

Using the Preterit

Use the preterit:

❑ To express an action or event that began at a specific time in the past:

Ella llegó a las dos. (She arrived at two o'clock.)

❑ To express an action or event that was completed at a specific time in the past:

Fuimos al centro ayer. (We went downtown yesterday.)

❑ To express an action that was completed in the past:

Le envié un regalo a mi hijo. (I sent a gift to my son.)

❑ To express a series of events that were complete within a definite time period in the past:

Preparé la cena, comí, lavé los platos, y después descansé. (I made dinner, I ate, I washed the dishes, and afterwards I rested.)

Example Problems

Using the preterit, talk about your morning. Express the following statements in Spanish.

1. Say that you woke up early.

    Answer: Yo me desperté temprano.

    The verb *despertarse* is a regular *-ar* reflexive verb in the preterit. Drop the *-ar* ending and add the first person singular preterit ending *(-é)*. The *-se* at the end of the infinitive indicates a reflexive verb. Place the pronoun *me,* which agrees with the subject, before the conjugated form of the verb. Use the adverb *temprano* to express "early."

2. Say that you went to the supermarket at 10 a.m.

    Answer: Yo fui al supermercado a las diez de la mañana.

    The verb *ir* is irregular in the preterit and must be memorized. All forms start with *fu-.* The preterit ending for the *yo* form of this irregular verb is *-i.* Nouns ending in *-o* tend to be masculine. Use the contraction *al (a + el)* to express "to the." Use *supermercado* to express "supermarket." To express the time of day, use the cardinal number *diez* preceded by *a las.* "In the morning" is expressed by *de la mañana.*

3. Say that before lunch you played on the computer and read the newspaper.

    Answer: Antes del almuerzo yo jugué en la computadora y leí el periódico.

    The adverb *antes de* expresses "before." Nouns ending in *-o* tend to be masculine. Use the contraction *del (de + el)* before the word for lunch, *almuerzo.* The stem-change *-gar* verb *jugar* changes *g* to *gu* in all forms of the preterit. Add the first person singular ending *(é).* Use *en la computadora* to express "on the computer." The verb *leer* drops its *-er* ending and adds the first person singular ending *(-i).* The words for "the newspaper" are *el periódico.*

4. Say that you prepared lunch at home.

    Answer: Yo preparé el almuerzo en casa.

    The verb *preparar* is a regular *-ar* verb. Drop the *-ar* ending and add the first person singular preterit ending *(-é).* Use *el almuerzo* to express "lunch." Use the expression *en casa* to express "at home."

Work Problems

Now talk about your afternoon. Express the following statements in Spanish.

1. Say that you ate lunch at 1 p.m.

2. Say that you went to the gym at 3:30 p.m.

3. Say that you did exercises until 4:30 p.m.

4. Say that you returned home, showered, and prepared dinner.

5. Say that you had to wash the dishes.

6. Say that you took out the garbage.

7. Say that you paid your bills.

8. Say that you went to bed at midnight.

Worked Solutions

1. **Yo almorcé a la una.** To conjugate spelling-change *-zar* verbs in the preterit, drop the *-zar* ending. For *yo* change *z* to *c* and add *-é* as the ending. To express the time of day, use the cardinal number *una,* which is singular, preceded by *a la.*

2. **Yo fui al gimnasio a las tres y media de la tarde.** The verb *ir* is irregular in the preterit and must be memorized. All forms start with *fu-.* The preterit ending for the *yo* form of this irregular verb is *-i.* Nouns ending in *-o* tend to be masculine. Use the contraction *al (a + el)* to express "to the." Use *gimnasio* to express "gym." To express the time of day, use the cardinal number *tres* preceded by *a las.* Use *y media* to express half past the hour. "In the afternoon" is expressed by *de la tarde.*

3. **Yo hice ejercicios hasta las cuatro y media de la tarde.** In the preterit stem, *hacer* changes the *a* from the stem to *i.* The first person singular preterit ending for an irregular *-er* verb is *-e.* Use the word *ejercicios* to express "exercises." *Hasta* expresses "until." To express the time of day, use the cardinal number *cuatro* preceded by *a las.* Use *y media* to express half past the hour. "In the afternoon" is expressed by *de la tarde.*

4. **Yo regresé a casa, me duché, y preparé la cena.** To conjugate regular *-ar* verbs in the preterit, drop the *-ar* ending and add *-é* as the ending. The verb *ducharse* is a regular *-ar* reflexive verb. Drop the *-ar* ending and add the first person singular preterit ending *(-é).* The *-se* at the end of the infinitive indicates a reflexive verb. Place the pronoun *me,* which agrees with the subject, before the conjugated form of the verb. The verb *preparar* is a regular *-ar* verb. Drop the *-ar* ending and add the first person singular preterit ending *(-é).* Use *la cena* to express "dinner."

5. **Yo tuve que lavar los platos.** Use the expression *tener que* to express "to have to." In the preterit stem, *tener* changes the *en* from the infinitive stem to *uv.* The first person singular preterit ending for an irregular *-er* verb is *-e. Lavar,* the infinitive of "to wash," follows *tener que* in the preterit. *Los platos* expresses "the dishes."

6. **Yo saqué la basura.** To conjugate spelling-change *-car* verbs in the preterit, drop the *-ar* ending. For *yo,* change *c* to *qu* and add *-é* as the ending. *La basura* expresses "the garbage."

7. **Yo pagué las cuentas.** To conjugate spelling-change *-gar* verbs in the preterit, drop the *-ar* ending. For *yo,* change *g* to *gu* and add *-é* as the ending. *Las cuentas* expresses "the bills."

8. **Yo me acosté a la medianoche.** The verb *acostarse* is a regular *-ar* reflexive verb in the preterit. Drop the *-ar* ending and add the first person singular preterit ending *(-é).* The *-se* at the end of the infinitive indicates a reflexive verb. Place the pronoun *me,* which agrees with the subject, before the conjugated form of the verb. Use *a la medianoche* to express "at midnight."

Chapter Problems

Problems

In problems 1–10, express what Julia did and didn't do by looking at the checkmarks on her list of chores.

1. telefonear al plomero ✓

2. barrer el suelo

3. escribir cheques

4. pagar el alquiler ✓

5. ir a la carnicería ✓

6. sacar dinero del cajero automático

7. poner la mesa ✓

8. concluir los quehaceres

9. comenzar a limpiar la casa.

10. hacer las tareas escolares ✓

In problems 11–15, use the preterit of the verbs in parentheses to express what people did and didn't do in situations they encountered at a specific time.

> Example: (beber agua/comer) Yo hice muchos ejercicios y por eso tenía sed.
>
> Yo bebí agua. Yo no comí.

11. (hacer un error/dar la respuesta correcta) Yo contesté que uno y uno son dos.

12. (salir bien/fracasar) Nosotros estudiamos mucho para un examen.

13. (caminar lentamente/conducir rápidamente) Tú tuviste cuarenta minutos de retraso.

14. (ponerse el abrigo/quitarse el sombrero) Nevó anoche.

15. (sentirse bien/tomar medicamentos) Le dolió a Ud. la garganta.

Answers and Solutions

1. **Answer: Ella telefoneó al plomero.** To conjugate regular -ar verbs in the preterit, drop the -ar ending and add -ó as the ending.

2. **Answer: Ella no barrió el suelo.** To conjugate regular -er verbs in the preterit, drop the -er ending and add -ió as the ending.

3. **Answer: Ella no escribió cheques.** To conjugate regular -ir verbs in the preterit, drop the -ir ending and add -ió as the ending.

4. **Answer: Ella pagó el alquiler.** To conjugate spelling-change -gar verbs in the preterit, drop the -ar ending. For the third person singular form, there is no spelling change. Add -ó as the ending.

5. **Answer: Ella fue a la carnicería.** The verb ir is irregular in the preterit and must be memorized. All forms start with fu-. The preterit ending for ella is -e.

6. **Answer: Ella no sacó dinero del cajero automático.** To conjugate spelling-change -car verbs in the preterit, drop the -ar ending. For the third person singular form, there is no spelling change. Add -ó as the ending.

7. **Answer: Ella puso la mesa.** In the preterit stem, poner changes the o from the stem to u. The n from the stem changes to s in the preterit. Add -o as the ending.

8. **Answer: Ella no concluyó los quehaceres.** In the preterit stem, concluir (and other verbs ending in -uir) adds a y after the u in the third person singular form. Add -ó as the ending.

9. **Answer: Ella no comenzó a limpiar la casa.** To conjugate spelling-change -zar verbs in the preterit, drop the -zar ending. For the third person singular form, there is no spelling change. Add -ó as the ending.

10. **Answer: Ella hizo las tareas escolares.** In the preterit stem, hacer changes the a from the stem to i. In the third person singular preterit form, the c from the stem changes to z to maintain the original sound of the verb. The third person plural preterit ending for an irregular -er verb is -o.

11. **Answer: Yo no hice un error. Yo di la respuesta correcta.** In the preterit stem, hacer changes the a from the stem to i. There are no other stem changes in the first person singular form. For yo add -e as the ending. Dar has irregular preterit endings that are added to the d- from the infinitive. The preterit ending for yo is an unaccented -i.

12. **Answer: Nosotros salimos bien. Nosotros no fracasamos.** To conjugate regular -ir verbs in the preterit, drop the -ir ending and add -imos as the ending. To conjugate regular -ar verbs in the preterit, drop the -ar infinitive ending and add -amos as the ending.

13. **Answer: Tú no caminaste lentamente. Tú condujiste rápidamente.** To conjugate regular -ar verbs in the preterit, drop the -ar ending and add -aste as the ending. In the preterit stem, conducir (and other verbs ending in -ucir) adds a j after the u and drops the c. The second person singular preterit ending for this stem-change verb is -iste.

14. **Answer: Ellas se pusieron el abrigo. Ellas no se quitaron el sombrero.** In the preterit stem, ponerse changes the o from the stem to u. The n from the stem changes to s in the preterit. The third person plural preterit ending for an -er verb is -ieron. The -se at the end of the infinitive indicates a reflexive verb. Place the pronoun se, which agrees with the subject, before the conjugated form of the verb. The verb quitarse is a regular -ar reflexive verb. Drop the -ar infinitive ending and add the third person plural preterit ending (-aron). The -se at the end of the infinitive indicates a reflexive verb. Place the pronoun se, which agrees with the subject, before the conjugated form of the verb.

15. **Answer: Ud. no se sintió bien. Ud. tomó medicamentos.** Present-tense stem-change verbs ending in -ir also undergo a stem change in the preterit. In the third person singular form, e changes to i. Drop the -ir ending and add the preterit -ió ending. The -se at the end of the infinitive indicates a reflexive verb. Place the pronoun se, which agrees with the subject, before the conjugated form of the verb. To conjugate regular -ar verbs in the preterit, drop the -ar ending and add -ó as the ending.

Supplemental Chapter Problems

Problems

In problems 1–10, express what certain people did and didn't do at work by looking at the checkmarks on the employee list of chores.

1.   Daniel y Antonio/ayudar al jefe ✓

2.   nosotros/responder a los mensajes electrónicos

3.   vosotros/escribir informes ✓

4.   Pilar/leer el correo ✓

5.   yo/verificar unos documentos

6.   tú/ver a unos clientes ✓

7.   Luisa y Juana/decir la verdad a todo el mundo

8.   yo/organizar una conferencia

9.   Ud./tener que trabajar muy duro

10. yo/entregar el correo a los otros empleados ✓

Answers

1.   Daniel y Antonio ayudaron al jefe. (preterit of regular -ar verbs, p. 249)

2.   Nosotros no respondimos a los mensajes electrónicos. (preterit of regular -er verbs, p. 249)

3.   Vosotros escribisteis informes. (preterit of regular -ir verbs, p. 249)

4.   Pilar leyó el correo. (preterit of verbs that change i to y, p. 256)

5.   Yo no verifiqué unos documentos. (preterit of -car verbs, p. 253)

6.   Tú viste a unos clientes. (preterit of stem-change verbs, p. 256)

7.   Luisa y Juana no dijeron la verdad a todo el mundo. (preterit of irregular verbs, p. 259)

8.   Yo no organicé una conferencia. (preterit of -zar verbs, p. 253)

9.   Ud. no tuvo que trabajar muy duro. (preterit of irregular verbs, p. 259)

10. Yo entregué el correo a los otros empleados. (preterit of -gar verbs, p. 253)

Chapter 14
The Imperfect

The imperfect is a past tense that has no English grammatical equivalent. It expresses a continuing state or action in the past; an action that was taking place or that used to happen repeatedly over an indefinite period of time. The imperfect is used to describe scenes, settings, situations, or states in the past.

La ventana estaba abierta.	The window was open.
Yo jugaba al tenis.	I was playing tennis.

The Imperfect of Regular Verbs

The imperfect of regular verbs is formed by dropping the *-ar, -er,* and *-ir* infinitive endings and adding the imperfect endings:

	-ar Verbs *Cantar (to Sing)*	*-er Verbs* *Comer (to Eat)*	*-ir Verbs* *Vivir (to Live)*
Yo	cant**aba**	com**ía**	viv**ía**
Tú	cant**abas**	com**ías**	viv**ías**
Él, Ella, Ud.	cant**aba**	com**ía**	viv**ía**
Nosotros	cant**ábamos**	com**íamos**	viv**íamos**
Vosotros	cant**abais**	com**íais**	viv**íais**
Ellos, Ellas, Uds.	cant**aban**	com**ían**	viv**ían**

The Imperfect of Irregular Verbs

There are only three Spanish verbs that are irregular in the imperfect:

	Ir (to Go)	*Ser (to Be)*	*Ver (to See)*
Yo	iba	era	veía
Tú	ibas	eras	veías
Él, Ella, Ud.	iba	era	veía
Nosotros	íbamos	éramos	veíamos
Vosotros	ibais	erais	veíais
Ellos, Ellas, Uds.	iban	eran	veían

Example Problem

Express what each person did as a youth.

Example: (bailar) Yo bailaba.

(jugar)

Yo _____ al tenis, ellos _____ al fútbol, tú _____ al vóleibol, nosotros _____ al hockey, vosotros _____ al béisbol y ella _____ al golf.

Answer: jugaba, jugaban, jugabas, jugábamos, jugabais, jugaba

To conjugate regular -ar verbs in the imperfect, drop the -ar ending and do the following:

1. For *yo*, add -aba as the ending.

2. For *ellos*, add -aban as the ending.

3. For *tú*, add -abas as the ending.

4. For *nosotros*, add -ábamos as the ending.

5. For *vosotros*, add -abais as the ending.

6. For *ella*, add -aba as the ending.

Work Problems

Express what each person habitually did as a youth.

1. (estudiar) Nosotros _____ el arte, yo _____ la música, tú _____ el francés, ellas _____ el inglés, Ud. _____ las ciencias y vosotros _____ la historia.

2. (comer) Tú no_____carne, vosotros no _____ legumbres, Uds. no _____postres, nosotros no _____ frutas, él no _____ pescado y yo no _____ pollo.

3. (escribir) Ellas _____ artículos escolares, tú _____ cartas de amor, vosotras _____ diálogos, Ud. _____ tarjetas postales, yo _____ cuentos y nosotros _____ programas de computación.

4. (ir) Vosotros _____ al campo, nosotros _____ a la montaña, él _____ al teatro, ellos _____ al museo, yo _____ a la playa y tú _____ a la ópera.

5. (ser) Ella _____ optimista, Uds. _____ atléticos, nosotros _____ serios, vosotros _____ egoístas, tú _____ pesimista y yo _____ ingenuo.

6. (ver) Ud. _____ a su familia, ellos _____ a sus amigos, tú _____ a tus compañeros de clase, vosotros _____ a vuestros profesores nosotros _____ a nuestro jefe y yo _____ a mis niños.

Worked Solutions

1. **estudiábamos, estudiaba, estudiabas, estudiaban, estudiaba, estudiabais**   To conjugate regular *-ar* verbs in the imperfect, drop the *-ar* ending and do the following:

    1. For *nosotros,* add *-ábamos* as the ending.

    2. For *yo,* add *-aba* as the ending.

    3. For *tú,* add *-abas* as the ending.

    4. For *ellas,* add *-aban* as the ending.

    5. For *Ud.,* add *-aba* as the ending.

    6. For *vosotros,* add *-abais* as the ending.

2. **comías, comíais, comían, comíamos, comía, comía**   To conjugate regular *-er* verbs in the imperfect, drop the *-er* ending and do the following:

    1. For *tú,* add *-ías* as the ending.

    2. For *vosotros,* add *-íais* as the ending.

    3. For *Uds.,* add *-ían* as the ending.

    4. For *nosotros,* add *-íamos* as the ending.

    5. For *él,* add *-ía* as the ending.

    6. For *yo,* add *-ía* as the ending.

3. **escribían, escribías, escribíais, escribía, escribía, escribíamos**   To conjugate regular *-ir* verbs in the imperfect, drop the *-ir* ending and do the following:

    1. For *ellas,* add *-ían* as the ending.

    2. For *tú,* add *-ías* as the ending.

    3. For *vosotras,* add *-íais* as the ending.

    4. For *Ud.,* add *-ía* as the ending.

    5. For *yo,* add *-ía* as the ending.

    6. For *nosotros,* add *-íamos* as the ending.

4. **ibais, íbamos, iba, iban, iba, ibas**   To conjugate the verb *ir* in the imperfect, drop the *-r* from the infinitive ending and do the following:

    1. For *vosotros,* add *-bais* as the ending.

    2. For *nosotros,* add *-bamos* as the ending. Add an accent to the *i.*

3. For *él*, add *-ba* as the ending.

4. For *ellos*, add *-ban* as the ending.

5. For *yo*, add *-ba* as the ending.

6. For *tú*, add *-bas* as the ending.

5. **era, eran, éramos, erais, eras, era**   To conjugate the verb *ser* in the imperfect, use *er-* as the stem and do the following:

1. For *ella*, add *-a* as the ending.

2. For *Uds.*, add *-an* as the ending.

3. For *nosotros*, add *-amos* as the ending. Add an accent to the *e*.

4. For *vosotros*, add *-ais* as the ending.

5. For *tú*, add *-as* as the ending.

6. For *yo*, add *-a* as the ending.

6. **veía, veían, veías, veíais, veíamos, veía**   To conjugate the verb *ver* in the imperfect, drop the *-r* from the ending and do the following:

1. For *Ud.*, add *-ía* as the ending.

2. For *ellos*, add *-ían* as the ending.

3. For *tú*, add *-ías* as the ending.

4. For *vosotros*, add *-íais* as the ending.

5. For *nosotros*, add *-íamos* as the ending.

6. For *yo*, add *-ía* as the ending.

Using the Imperfect

Use the imperfect to:

❏ Describe ongoing or continuous actions in the past (which may or may not have been completed):

   Ella hablaba con su amiga. (She was talking with her friend.)

❏ Describe repeated or habitual actions that took place in the past:

   Yo conducía al centro. (I used to drive downtown.)

❏ Describe an action that continued for an unspecified period of time:

   Vivíamos en España. (We used to live in Spain.)

❏ Describe a person, place, thing, weather, time, day of the week, state of mind, or emotion in the past:

El niño lloraba porque llovía y no podía ir al parque. (The child was crying because it was raining and he couldn't go to the park.)

❏ Describe simultaneous actions taking place at the same time in the past:

Ernesto tocaba la guitarra mientras Elena cantaba. (Ernesto was playing the guitar while Elena was singing.)

❏ Describe a situation that was going on in the past when another action or event, expressed by the preterit, took place:

Estudiaba cuando ella me hizo una pregunta. (I was studying when she asked me a question.)

❏ Express an event or action that began in the past and continued in the past, by using *hacía . . . (que)* or *desde hacía,* which means "for" or "since":

¿Cuánto tiempo hacía que vivías en esa ciudad?   How long had you been living in
                                                                                that city?

Hacía dos años que vivía en esa ciudad.   I'd been living in that city for two years.

Example Problems

Use the imperfect to talk about what used to happen or to describe a scene in the past.

1.   Say that you used to visit your family every weekend.

Answer: Yo visitaba a mi familia todos los fines de semana.

To conjugate the regular *-ar* verb *visitar* in the imperfect, drop the *-ar* ending, and add *-aba* as the ending for *yo.* Use the personal *a* before the direct object noun that refers to people. Use the possessive adjective *mi* to express "my." The word for "family" is *familia. El fin de semana* expresses "the weekend." To make the expression plural, change the masculine singular definite article to *los.* Because *fin* ends in a consonant, add *-es* to form the plural. Use the masculine plural adjective *todos* to express "every."

2.   Say that the girl was smiling because it was Saturday and she didn't have to go to school.

Answer: La muchacha sonreía porque era sábado y no tenía que ir a la escuela.

Use *la muchacha* to express "the girl." The verb *sonreír* is regular in the imperfect. Drop the *-ir* ending and add the third person singular ending *(-ía). Porque* expresses "because." Use the third personal singular of the irregular verb *ser (era)* to express "it was." *Sábado* expresses "Saturday." Join the clauses with the word for "and" *(y).* Negate the next clause by using *no.* Use the expression *tener que* to express "to have to." The verb *tener* is regular in the imperfect. Drop the *-er* ending and add the third person singular ending *(-ía).* The conjugated verb is then followed by the infinitive expressing "to go" *(ir).* Use *a la escuela* to express "to school."

Work Problems

Use the imperfect and, where necessary, the preterit to talk about what used to happen or to describe a scene in the past.

1. Explain that you were happy because it was Friday, it was five o'clock, and you were going to eat in a restaurant.

2. Say that your sister was opening the door when the telephone rang.

3. Say that they used to travel to Europe every summer.

4. Express that a man was speaking and that you couldn't understand him.

5. Ask an acquaintance how long she had been studying music.

6. Give the acquaintance's answer: I had been studying music for six months.

Worked Solutions

1. **Yo estaba contento porque era viernes, eran las cinco, e iba a comer en un restaurante.**   Use the verb *estar* in the imperfect to describe a temporary state. Drop the *-ar* ending and add the first person singular imperfect ending *(-aba)*. *Contento* expresses "happy." (For the feminine form, drop the final *-o* from *contento* and add an *-a: contenta*.) *Porque* expresses "because." Use the third personal singular of the irregular verb *ser (era)* to express "it was." *Viernes* expresses "Friday." Use the third personal plural of the irregular verb *ser (eran)* to express "it was" with the plural time. *Las cinco* expresses "five o'clock." Join the clauses with the word for "and" (*y* becomes *e* before *iba* because it starts with an *i*). Use the irregular verb *ir* to express "to go." Drop the *-r* and add the first person singular ending *(-ba)*. The verb *ir* is followed by the preposition *a*. The conjugated verb is followed by the infinitive that expresses "to eat" *(comer)*. Use *en un restaurante* to express "in a restaurant."

2. **Mi hermana abría la puerta cuando el teléfono sonó.**   Use the possessive adjective *mi* to express "my" before the singular noun *hermana*, which expresses "sister." Use the verb *abrir* to express "to open." Drop the *-ir* ending and add the third person singular imperfect ending *(-ía)*. Use *la puerta* to express "the door." Use *cuando* to express "when." Use *el teléfono* to express "the telephone." The preterit is used to express a situation that took place while another situation was going on. The preterit is needed for the verb *sonar* (to ring). To form the preterit of *sonar*, drop the *-ar* ending and add the third person singular ending *(-ó)*.

3. **Ellos viajaban a Europa cada verano.**   To conjugate the regular *-ar* verb *viajar* in the imperfect, drop the *-ar* ending and add *-aban* as the ending for *ellos*. Use the expression *a Europa* to express "to Europe." *Cada verano* expresses "every summer."

4. **Un hombre hablaba y yo no podía comprenderlo.**   To conjugate the regular *-ar* verb *hablar* in the imperfect, drop the *-ar* ending and add *-aba* as the ending for *un hombre* (*él*). Join the clauses with the word for "and" (*y*). Negate the next clause by using *no*. The verb *poder* is in the imperfect. Drop the *-er* ending and add the first person singular imperfect ending *(-ía)*. After the conjugated verb, use the infinitive *comprender* to express "to understand." Attach the direct object pronoun *lo* to the infinitive. Alternatively, put *lo* before *podía* (see Chapter 7).

5. **¿Cuánto tiempo hacía que tú estudiabas la música? ¿Desde cuándo estudiabas la música?**   The expression *¿Cuánto tiempo hacía que . . . ?* inquires how long the subject had been doing something. Use the verb *estudiar* to express "to study." Drop the *-ar* ending and add the second person singular imperfect ending *(-abas)*. Alternatively, you may use the expression *¿Desde cuándo . . . ?* followed by the verb in the imperfect. "Music" is expressed by *música*.

6. **Hacía seis meses que yo estudiaba la música. Estudiaba la música desde hacía seis meses.**   The expression *hacía* + time + *que* expresses how long the subject had been doing something. Use the verb *estudiar* to express "to study." Drop the *-ar* ending and add the first person singular imperfect ending *(-aba)*. Alternatively, the expression *desde hacía* may follow the verbal phrase and precede the time period.

The Preterit versus the Imperfect

The preterit expresses an action that was completed at a specific time in the past. The preterit represents an action that could be captured by an instamatic camera — the action happened and was completed.

The imperfect expresses an action that continued in the past over an indefinite period of time. The imperfect represents an action that could be captured by a video camera — the action continued over a period of time, it *was* happening, it *used to* happen, or it *would* (meaning used to) happen.

The imperfect expresses what "was" going on when another action (in the preterit) took place:

> Yo miraba la televisión cuando mi mejor amiga me llamó.   I was watching television when my best friend called me.

Compare the two:

Preterit	Imperfect
Expresses specific actions or events that were started and completed at a definite time in the past (even if the time isn't mentioned). *Ella cantó.* (She sang.)	Describes ongoing or continuous actions or events (what **was** happening) in the past (which may or may not have been completed). *Ella cantaba.* (She was singing.)
Expresses a specific action or event that occurred at a specific point in the past. *Yo estudié ayer.* (I studied yesterday.)	Describes habitual or repeated actions in the past. *Generalmente yo estudiaba todos los días.* (Generally, I used to study every day.)
Expresses a specific action or event that was repeated a stated number of times. *La niña se cayó tres veces.* (The girl fell three times.)	Describes a person, place, thing, or state of mind in the past. *Nosotros estábamos contentos.* (We were happy.)
	Expresses the time of day in the past: *Eran las cinco.* (It was five o'clock.)

When *would* means "used to" the imperfect is used:

> Me levantaba a las seis todos los días.   I would get up at six o'clock every day.

When *would* means what the subject "would do" under specific conditions, the conditional is used (see Chapter 16).

Clues to the Preterit and the Imperfect

The preterit is often used with the following words and expressions that specify a time period:

Spanish	Meaning
anteayer	day before yesterday
ayer	yesterday
anoche	last night
ayer por la noche	last night
de repente	suddenly
el año pasado	last year
el otro día	the other day
el verano pasado	last summer
finalmente	finally
la semana pasada	last week
por fin	finally
primero	at first
un día	one day
una vez	one time

The imperfect is often used with the following words and expressions that imply repetition:

Spanish	Meaning
a menudo	often
a veces	sometimes
cada día	each day, every day
con frecuencia	frequently
de vez en cuando	from time to time
en ese momento	at that time
en general	generally
frecuentemente	frequently
generalmente	generally
habitualmente	habitually
normalmente	normally
siempre	always
todo el tiempo	all the time
todos los días (meses, años, veranos)	every day (month, year, summer)
usualmente	usually

In some instances, either the preterit or the imperfect is acceptable, depending on the meaning the speaker wishes to convey:

Él trabajó duro.	He worked hard.	The action is completed.
Él trabajaba duro.	He was working hard.	The action was ongoing or continuous in the past.

Example Problems

Express the misfortunes of these people by giving the correct form of the verb in the preterit or in the imperfect.

1. Amalia (cruzar) _____ la calle cuando un coche la (atropellar) _____.

Answer: cruzaba/atropelló

The first phrase expresses what Amalia "was doing"; therefore, the imperfect is required. To conjugate the regular -ar verb *cruzar* in the imperfect, drop the -ar ending and add -aba as the ending for *ella*. The second phrase expresses what happened at a specific moment in time; therefore, the preterit is required. To conjugate the regular -ar verb *atropellar* in the preterit, drop the -ar ending and add -ó as the ending for *un coche*.

2. Gonzalo (caerse) _____ cuando él (correr) _____.

Answer: se cayó/corría

The first phrase expresses what happened and was completed; therefore, the preterit is required. To conjugate the -er verb *caer* in the preterit, drop the -er ending, add a *y* in the third person singular to separate the two vowels, and add -ó as the ending for *Gonzalo*. The -se attached to the infinitive indicates a reflexive verb. Put the third person singular reflexive pronoun *(se)* before the conjugated verb form. The second phrase expresses what Gonzalo "was doing"; therefore, the imperfect is required. To conjugate the regular -er verb *correr* in the imperfect, drop the -er ending and add -ía as the ending for *él*.

Work Problems

Express the misfortunes of these people by giving the correct form of the verb in the preterit or in the imperfect.

1. Cristina (viajar) _____ a Europa cuando su esposo (ponerse) _____ enfermo.

2. El señor Blanco (morir) _____ cuando (hacer) _____ ejercicios.

3. Los señores Padilla (salir) _____ de su casa cuando una tormenta (desatarse) _____.

4. Dolores (prepararse) _____ para su boda cuando su novio le (romper) _____ el corazón.

5. La señora Martínez (despedirse) _____ de Pedro cuando él (partir) _____ para España.

6. Un perro (morder) _____ a Eduardo cuando él lo (acariciar) _____.

Worked Solutions

1. **viajaba/se puso**   The first phrase expresses what *Cristina* "was doing"; therefore, the imperfect is required. To conjugate the regular -ar verb *viajar* in the imperfect, drop the -ar ending, and add -aba as the ending for *ella*. The second phrase expresses what happened at a specific moment in time; therefore, the preterit is required. To conjugate the verb *ponerse* in the preterit, change the internal *o* to *u* and change the internal *n* to *s*. Add -o as the ending for *su esposo*. The -se attached to the infinitive indicates a reflexive verb. Put the third person singular reflexive pronoun *(se)* before the conjugated verb form.

2. **murió/hacía**   The first phrase expresses what happened and was completed; therefore, the preterit is required. To conjugate the spelling-change -*ir* verb *morir* in the preterit, change the internal *o* to *u* for the third person singular, drop the -*ir* ending and add the third person singular ending (-*ió*) as the ending for *el señor Blanco*. The second phrase expresses what *el señor Blanco* "was doing"; therefore, the imperfect is required. To conjugate *hacer* in the imperfect, drop the -*er* ending, and add -*ía* as the ending for *él*.

3. **salían/se desató**   The first phrase expresses what *los señores Padilla* "were doing"; therefore, the imperfect is required. To conjugate the regular -*ir* verb *salir* in the imperfect, drop the -*ir* ending, and add -*ían* as the ending for *ellos*. The second phrase expresses what happened at a specific moment in time; therefore, the preterit is required. To conjugate the verb *desatarse* in the preterit, drop the -*ar* ending and add -*ó* as the ending for *una tormenta*. The -*se* attached to the infinitive indicates a reflexive verb. Put the third person singular reflexive pronoun (*se*) before the conjugated verb form.

4. **se preparaba/rompió**   The first phrase expresses what *Dolores* "was doing"; therefore, the imperfect is required. To conjugate the regular -*ar* verb *preparar* in the imperfect, drop the -*ar* ending, and add -*aba* as the ending for *ella*. The -*se* attached to the infinitive indicates a reflexive verb. Put the third person singular reflexive pronoun (*se*) before the conjugated verb form. The second phrase expresses what happened at a specific moment in time; therefore, the preterit is required. To conjugate the verb *romper* in the preterit, drop the -*er* ending and -*ió* as the ending for *su novio*.

5. **se despidió/partía**   The first phrase expresses what happened and was completed. The preterit is required. To conjugate the spelling-change -*ir* verb *despedir* in the preterit, change the second internal -*e* to -*i* for the third person singular, drop the -*ir* infinitive ending and add the third person singular ending: -*ió* as the ending for *la señora Martínez*. The -*se* attached to the infinitive indicates a reflexive verb. Put the third person singular reflexive pronoun: *se* before the conjugated verb form. The second phrase expresses what *Pedro* "was doing" and, therefore, the imperfect is required. To conjugate the regular -*ir* verb *partir* in the imperfect, drop the -*ir* infinitive ending, and add -*ía* as the ending for *él*.

6. **mordió/acariciaba**   The first phrase expresses what happened and was completed; therefore, the preterit is required. To conjugate the regular -*er* verb *morder* in the preterit, drop the -*er* ending and add the third person singular ending (-*ió*) as the ending for *un perro*. The second phrase expresses what *Eduardo* "was doing"; therefore, the imperfect is required. To conjugate the regular -*ar* verb *acariciar* in the imperfect, drop the -*ar* ending, and add -*aba* as the ending for *él*.

Chapter Problems

Problems

Express what a young boy saw from his window by changing the verbs indicated into the preterit or the imperfect according to the meaning of the sentence.

1. (ser) _____ sábado por la tarde.

2. (hacer) _____ frío.

3. (estar) Yo _____ enfermo.

4. (mirar) Yo _____ la televisión.

5.   (aburrirse) Finalmente, yo _____.

6.   (querer) Yo ya no _____ mirar ese programa.

7.   (levantarse) Yo _____ de la cama.

8.   (ir) Yo _____ a la ventana.

9.   (abrir) Yo la _____.

10. (ver) Yo _____ a mis amigos.

11. (jugar) Ellos _____ en la nieve.

12. (divertirse) Ellos _____ mucho.

13. (construir) Ellos _____ un muñeco de nieve.

14. (tener) Ese muñeco _____ como nariz una zanahoria.

15. (lanzar) De repente Alfredo _____ una bola de nieve.

16. (pegar) La bola le _____ a Guillermo.

17. (devolver) Guillermo le _____ el golpe.

18. (caerse) Alfredo _____.

19. (poder) Alfredo no _____ levantarse.

20. (decir) Primero no _____ nada.

Answers and Solutions

1.   **Answer: Era.** The imperfect is used to express a day in the past. The verb *ser* is used with the days of the week. To conjugate the verb *ser* in the imperfect, use *er-* as the stem and add *-a* as the ending for "it."

2.   **Answer: Hacía.** The imperfect is used to describe the weather. To conjugate *hacer* in the imperfect, drop the *-er* ending and add *-ía* to express "it."

3.   **Answer: estaba.** The imperfect is used to describe a condition. To conjugate *estar* in the imperfect, drop the *-ar* ending and add the first person singular ending *(-aba)*.

4.   **Answer: miraba.** The imperfect is used to describe what a person was doing. To conjugate the regular *-ar* verb *mirar* in the imperfect, drop the *-ar* ending and add the first person singular ending *(-aba)*.

5.   **Answer: me aburrí.** The preterit is used to tell what happened at a particular moment of time. To conjugate the regular *-ir* verb *aburrir* in the preterit, drop the *–ir* ending and add *-í* as the ending for *yo*.

6.   **Answer: quería.** The imperfect is used to describe a state of mind. To conjugate *querer* in the imperfect, drop the *-er* ending and add the first person singular ending *(-ía)*.

7. **Answer: me levanté.** The preterit is used to express an action that was completed in the past. To conjugate the regular -ar verb *levantarse* in the preterit, drop the -ar ending and add -é as the ending for *yo*. The -se attached to the infinitive indicates a reflexive verb. Put the first person singular reflexive pronoun *(me)* before the conjugated verb form.

8. **Answer: fui.** The preterit is used to express an action that was completed. The verb *ir* is irregular in the preterit and must be memorized. All forms start with *fu-*. The preterit ending for *yo* is -i.

9. **Answer: abrí.** The preterit is used to express an action that was completed. To conjugate the regular -ir verb *abrir* in the preterit, drop the -ir ending and add -í as the ending for *yo*.

10. **Answer: vi.** The preterit is used to express an action that was completed. *Ver* has irregular preterit endings that are added to the *v-* from the infinitive. The preterit ending for *yo* is an unaccented -i.

11. **Answer: jugaban.** The imperfect is used to describe what was happening. To conjugate the -ar verb *jugar* in the imperfect, drop the -ar ending and add the third person plural ending *(-aban)*.

12. **Answer: se divertían.** The imperfect is used to describe what was happening. To conjugate the -ir verb *divertir* in the imperfect, drop the -ir ending and add the third person plural ending *(-ían)*. The -se attached to the infinitive indicates a reflexive verb. Put the third person plural reflexive pronoun *(se)* before the conjugated verb form.

13. **Answer: construían.** The imperfect is used to describe what was happening. To conjugate the -ir verb *construir* in the imperfect, drop the -ir ending and add the third person plural ending *(-ían)*.

14. **Answer: tenía.** The imperfect is used to describe a person or thing. To conjugate the -er verb *tener* in the imperfect, drop the -er ending and add the third person singular ending *(-ía)*.

15. **Answer: lanzó.** The preterit is used to express an action that was completed. To conjugate *lanzar* in the preterit, drop the -ar infinitive ending and add the third person singular ending *(-ó)*.

16. **Answer: pegó.** The preterit is used to express an action that was completed. To conjugate the -gar verb *pegar* in the preterit, drop the -ar ending and add the third person singular ending *(-ó)*.

17. **Answer: devolvió.** The preterit is used to express an action that was completed. To conjugate the regular -er verb *devolver* in the preterit, drop the -er ending and add -ió as the ending.

18. **Answer: se cayó.** The preterit is used to express an action that was completed. To conjugate *caer* in the preterit, drop the -er ending, add a *y* in the third person singular to separate the two vowels, and add -ó as the ending for *Alfredo*.

19. **Answer: podía.** The imperfect is used to describe a condition. To conjugate the -er verb *poder* in the imperfect, drop the -er ending and add the third person singular ending *(-ía)*.

20. **Answer: dijo.** The preterit is used to express an action that was completed. In the preterit stem, *decir* changes the *e* in the stem to *i*. A *j* is added after the *i*. The third person singular preterit ending is -o.

Supplemental Chapter Problems

Express what happened to a young girl by changing the verbs indicated into the preterit or the imperfect according to the meaning of the sentence.

1. (ser) En 1968 yo _____ una alumna en la universidad.

2. (tomar) Yo _____ una clase de baile.

3. (haber) Desafortunadamente, _____ solamente tres muchachos en esa clase.

4. (llamarse) Uno de ellos _____ Ramón.

5. (ser) Él _____ muy alto y guapo.

6. (tener) Él _____ pelo negro y ojos azules.

7. (querer) Muchas veces él _____ bailar conmigo.

8. (decir) Yo siempre le _____, "Con mucho gusto."

9. (bailar) A decir verdad, él no _____ muy bien.

10. (pisar) Generalmente él me _____ los pies.

11. (estar) Un día, Ramón _____ ausente.

12. (tener) Ese día yo _____ que bailar con una muchacha.

13. (gustar) No me _____ esa experiencia.

14. (regresar) Unos días más tarde Ramón _____.

15. (hacer) El último día de clases Ramón y yo _____ nuestro examen final juntos.

16. (recibir) Nosotros _____ una A.

17. (ver) Yo no _____ más a Ramón después de ese día.

18. (poder) Recientemente yo no _____ ir al trabajo.

19. (sentirse) Yo no _____ bien.

20. (decidir) Yo _____ mirar la televisión.

Answers

1. era (uses of the imperfect, p. 272)

2. tomaba (uses of the imperfect, p. 272)

3. había (uses of the imperfect, p. 272)

4. se llamaba (uses of the imperfect, p. 272)

5.   era (uses of the imperfect, p. 272)

6.   tenía (uses of the imperfect, p. 272)

7.   quería (uses of the imperfect, p. 272)

8.   decía (uses of the imperfect, p. 272)

9.   bailaba (uses of the imperfect, p. 272)

10.   pisaba (uses of the imperfect, p. 272)

11.   estuvo (uses of the preterit, p. 275)

12.   tuve (uses of the preterit, p. 275)

13.   gustó (uses of the preterit, p. 275)

14.   regresó (uses of the preterit, p. 275)

15.   hicimos (uses of the preterit, p. 275)

16.   recibimos (uses of the preterit, p. 275)

17.   vi (uses of the preterit, p. 275)

18.   podía (uses of the imperfect, p. 272)

19.   me sentía (uses of the imperfect, p. 272)

20.   decidí (uses of the preterit, p. 275)

Chapter 15
The Present Perfect

The present perfect tense, also referred to as the past indefinite, describes an action that started in the past (at no definite time) and that continues to the present. It may also describe an action that happened in the past but is in some manner connected to the present:

I haven't been there lately.

Have you seen my keys?

The present perfect is a compound tense, which means that it contains two elements: a helping verb and a past participle. In Spanish, the helping verb, *haber* (to have), expresses that something "has" taken place. The past participle expresses the specific action that occurred.

Formation of the Present Perfect

The present perfect is formed by conjugating the helping verb *haber* in the present tense, then adding the past participle of the verb expressing the action: subject (noun or pronoun) + helping verb + past participle.

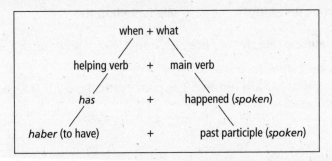

The helping verb *haber* must be conjugated because it is the first verb to follow the subject. Because *haber* may be used as a helping verb in other compound tenses, it must be conjugated in the present tense to form the present perfect tense.

yo he	nosotros hemos
tú has	vosotros habéis
él, ella, Ud. ha	ellos, ellas, Uds. han

A past participle must then be added to form the present perfect tense.

Past Participles of Regular Verbs

To form the past participle of regular verbs, drop the *-ar, -er,* or *-ir* infinitive ending and add *-ado* for *-ar* verbs or *-ido* for *-er* and *-ir* verbs:

hablar	hablado	spoken
vender	vendido	sold
decidir	decidido	decided

If an *-er* or *-ir* stem ends in a vowel, add an accent mark to the *i* as follows:

oír	oído	heard
caer	caído	fallen
creer	creído	believed
leer	leído	read
traer	traído	brought

The past participle remains the same for every subject. Only the helping verb changes:

Yo he hablado.	Nosotros hemos hablado.
Tú has hablado.	Vosotros habéis hablado.
Él/ella/Ud. ha hablado.	Ellos/ellas/Uds. han hablado.

There are no changes for stem-changing or spelling-change verb past participles:

Yo he almorzado.	I have eaten lunch.
Nosotros hemos escogido el rojo.	We have chosen the red one.

When a reflexive verb is used, place the reflexive pronoun before the conjugated form of the helping verb *haber:*

Él se ha despertado temprano.	He has awakened early.
Nosotros nos hemos divertido.	We have had fun.

Note: The reflexive pronouns (*me, te, se, nos, os,* and *se*) are never attached to the past participle.

The past participles for *ir* and *ser* are regular: The past participle for *ir* (to go) is *ido*, and the past participle for *ser* (to be) is *sido*.

Example Problems

Use the present perfect to express what each person has done on a trip.

Example: él/hablar español

Él ha hablado español.

1. yo/visitar muchos castillos

   Answer: Yo he visitado muchos castillos.

   To form the present perfect of a regular *-ar* verb, take the *yo* form of the present tense of the verb *haber (he)*. Form the past participle of the verb *visitar* by dropping the *-ar* ending and adding *-ado.*

2. nosotros/asistir a una corrida de toros

   Answer: Nosotros hemos asistido a una corrida de toros.

   To form the present perfect of a regular *-ir* verb, take the *nosotros* form of the present tense of the verb *haber (hemos)*. Form the past participle of the verb *asistir* by dropping the *-ir* ending and adding *-ido*.

3. Uds./aprender muchas palabras

   Answer: Uds. han aprendido muchas palabras.

   To form the present perfect of a regular *-er* verb, take the *Uds.* form of the present tense of the verb *haber (han)*. Form the past participle of the verb *aprender* by dropping the *-er* ending and adding *-ido*.

Work Problems

Use the present perfect to express what has happened when people haven't seen each other in a long time.

   Example: él/engordar
   Él ha engordado.

1. ella/crecer

2. yo/adelgazar

3. nosotros/leer mucho

4. Uds./vivir en México

5. tú/graduarse

6. vosotros/decidir estudiar en España

Worked Solutions

1. **Ella ha crecido.** To form the present perfect of a regular *-er* verb, take the *ella* form of the present tense of the verb *haber (ha)*. Form the past participle of the verb *crecer* by dropping the *-er* ending and adding *-ido*.

2. **Yo he adelgazado.** Spelling-change *-zar* verbs are regular in the present perfect. To form the present perfect of a regular *-ar* verb, take the *yo* form of the present tense of the verb *haber (he)*. Form the past participle of the verb *adelgazar* by dropping the *-ar* ending and adding *-ado*.

3. **Nosotros hemos leído mucho.** To form the present perfect of a regular *-er* verb, take the *nosotros* form of the present tense of the verb *haber (hemos)*. Form the past participle of the verb *leer* by dropping the *-er* ending and adding *-ido*. Because the stem of *leer* ends in a vowel, add an accent mark on the *i*.

4. **Uds. han vivido en México.**   To form the present perfect of a regular -ir verb, take the Uds. form of the present tense of the verb haber (han). Form the past participle of the verb vivir by dropping the -ir ending and adding -ido.

5. **Tú te has graduado.**   To form the present perfect of a regular -ar verb, take the tú form of the present tense of the verb haber (has). Form the past participle of the verb graduarse by dropping the -ar ending and adding -ado. The -se attached to the infinitive indicates that the verb is reflexive. Put the reflexive pronoun te, which agrees with the subject, before the conjugated form of haber.

6. **Vosotros habéis decidido estudiar en España.**   To form the present perfect of a regular -ir verb, take the vosotros form of the present tense of the verb haber (habéis). Form the past participle of the verb decidir by dropping the -ir ending and adding -ido.

Past Participles of Irregular Verbs

The following verbs and their compounds (descubrir, describir, componer, and so on) have irregular past participles that must be memorized:

Infinitive	Past Participle	Meaning
abrir (to open)	abierto	opened
cubrir (to cover)	cubierto	covered
decir (to say)	dicho	said
escribir (to write)	escrito	written
hacer (to do)	hecho	done
morir (to die)	muerto	died
poner (to put)	puesto	put
resolver (to resolve)	resuelto	resolved
romper (to break)	roto	broken
ser (to be)	sido	been
ver (to see)	visto	seen
volver (to return)	vuelto	returned

Example Problems

Use the present perfect to express what has happened when people have talked to friends.

Example: él/creer las mentiras
　　　　　Él ha creído las mentiras.

1. yo/abrirse a mi mejor amigo.

Answer: Yo me he abierto a mi mejor amigo.

To form the present perfect of abrir, take the yo form of the present tense of the verb haber (he). The past participle of the verb abrir is irregular and must be memorized: abierto. The -se attached to the infinitive indicates that the verb is reflexive. Put the reflexive pronoun me, which agrees with the subject, before the conjugated form of haber.

2. nosotros/ponerse tristes

   Answer: Nosotros nos hemos puesto tristes.

   To form the present perfect of *poner,* take the *nosotros* form of the present tense of the verb *haber (hemos).* The past participle of the verb *poner* is irregular and must be memorized: *puesto.* The *-se* attached to the infinitive indicates that the verb is reflexive. Put the reflexive pronoun *nos,* which agrees with the subject, before the conjugated form of *haber.*

3. ellas/descubrir el secreto de su amiga

   Answer: Ellas han descubierto el secreto de su amiga.

   To form the present perfect of *descubrir,* take the *ellas* form of the present tense of the verb *haber (han).* The past participle of the verb *descubrir* is irregular and must be memorized: *descubierto.*

Work Problems

Use the present perfect to express what people have done.

> Example: él/trabajar duro.
> > Él ha trabajado duro.

1. él/romper su juguete favorito

2. yo/leer muchas novelas

3. Uds./resolver sus problemas

4. nosotros/ver a nuestros abuelos

5. tú/escribir muchas cartas

6. vosotros/hacer experimentos

7. ella/cubrir a su novio de besos

8. Ud./decir la verdad

Worked Solutions

1. **Él ha roto su juguete favorito.**   To form the present perfect of *romper,* take the *él* form of the present tense of the verb *haber (ha).* The past participle of the verb *romper* is irregular and must be memorized: *roto.*

2. **Yo he leído muchas novelas.**   To form the present perfect of *leer,* take the *yo* form of the present tense of the verb *haber (he).* Form the past participle of the verb *leer* by dropping the *-er* ending and adding *-ido.* Because the stem of *leer* ends in a vowel, add an accent mark to the *i.*

3. **Uds. han resuelto sus problemas.**   To form the present perfect of *resolver*, take the *Uds.* form of the present tense of the verb *haber (han)*. The past participle of the verb *resolver* is irregular and must be memorized: *resuelto*.

4. **Nosotros hemos visto a nuestros abuelos.**   To form the present perfect of *ver*, take the *nosotros* form of the present tense of the verb *haber (hemos)*. The past participle of the verb *ver* is irregular and must be memorized: *visto*.

5. **Tú has escrito muchas cartas.**   To form the present perfect of *escribir*, take the *tú* form of the present tense of the verb *haber (has)*. The past participle of the verb *escribir* is irregular and must be memorized: *escrito*.

6. **Vosotros habéis hecho experimentos.**   To form the present perfect of *hacer*, take the *vosotros* form of the present tense of the verb *haber (habéis)*. The past participle of the verb *hacer* is irregular and must be memorized: *hecho*.

7. **Ella ha cubierto a su novio de besos.**   To form the present perfect of *cubrir*, take the *ella* form of the present tense of the verb *haber (ha)*. The past participle of the verb *cubrir* is irregular and must be memorized: *cubierto*.

8. **Ud. ha dicho la verdad.**   To form the present perfect of *decir*, take the *Ud.* form of the present tense of the verb *haber (ha)*. The past participle of the verb *decir* is irregular and must be memorized: *dicho*.

Using the Present Perfect

The present perfect is used to express an action that took place at no definite time in the past:

He preparado la comida.	I have prepared the meal.

Although English usage often omits the helping verb (which is implied), in Spanish, the helping verb must be used:

Ya he leído ese libro.	I (have) already read that book.

The past participle cannot be separated from the helping verb:

Ella no ha vuelto.	She hasn't returned.
Le he telefoneado dos veces.	I have called him two times.
¿Ya ha escrito la carta?	Have you already written the letter?
¿Todavía no ha llegado el avión?	Hasn't the plane arrived yet?

Example Problems

Use the present perfect tense to express what has happened.

1. She has seen that film.

   Answer: Ella ha visto esa película.

   To form the present perfect of *ver*, take the *ella* form of the present tense of the verb *haber (ha)*. The past participle of the verb *ver* is irregular and must be memorized: *visto*. Words that end in *-a* tend to be feminine. Use the feminine singular demonstrative adjective *esa* to express "that." Use *película* to express "film."

2. You (informal singular) have contradicted your friend.

    Answer: Tú has contradicho a tu amigo.

    To form the present perfect of *contradecir*, take the *tú* form of the present tense of the verb *haber (has)*. The past participle of the verb *contradecir* is irregular and must be memorized: *contradicho*. Use the personal *a* before the direct object, *tu amigo,* which refers to a person. Use the singular possessive adjective *tu* to express "your." Use *amigo* to express "friend."

3. They (masculine) have returned early.

    Answer: Ellos han vuelto temprano.

    To form the present perfect of *volver*, take the *ellos* form of the present tense of the verb *haber (han)*. The past participle of the verb *volver* is irregular and must be memorized: *vuelto*. Use *temprano* to express "early."

Work Problems

Use the present perfect to express what people have done regarding an accident.

1. He covered his back.

2. You (informal plural) described the scene.

3. We believed the boy.

4. They heard the accident.

5. She died because of the accident.

6. You (informal singular) saw two cars.

Worked Solutions

1. **Él se ha cubierto la espalda.**   To form the present perfect of *cubrir*, take the *él* form of the present tense of the verb *haber (ha)*. The past participle of the verb *cubrir* is irregular and must be memorized: *cubierto*. The *-se* attached to the infinitive indicates that the verb is reflexive. Put the reflexive pronoun *se*, which agrees with the subject, before the conjugated form of *haber*. Use *la espalda* to express "his back." Note that the definite article is used to show possession when the possessor is made clear by the reflexive pronoun (see Chapter 2).

2. **Vosotros habéis descrito la escena.**   To form the present perfect of *describir*, take the *vosotros* form of the present tense of the verb *haber (habéis)*. The past participle of the verb *describir* is irregular and must be memorized: *descrito*. Use *la escena* to express "the scene."

3. **Nosotros le hemos creído al muchacho.**   To form the present perfect of *creer*, take the *nosotros* form of the present tense of the verb *haber (hemos)*. Form the past participle of

the verb *creer* by dropping the *-er* ending and adding *-ido*. Because the stem of *creer* ends in a vowel, add an accent mark to the *i*. Use *el muchacho* to express "the boy." Because *muchacho* is a direct object referring to a person, the personal *a* is required before the definite article *el*. *A* contracts with *el* to become *al*.

4. **Ellos han oído el accidente.**   To form the present perfect of *oír*, take the *ellos* form of the present tense of the verb *haber (han)*. Form the past participle of the verb *oír* by dropping the *-ir* ending and adding *-ido*. Because the stem of *oír* ends in a vowel, add an accent mark to the *i*. Use *el accidente* to express "the accident."

5. **Ella ha muerto a causa del accidente.**   To form the present perfect of *morir*, take the *ella* form of the present tense of the verb *haber (ha)*. The past participle of the verb *morir* is irregular and must be memorized: *muerto*. Use *a causa de* to express "because of." Use *el accidente* to express "the accident."

6. **Tú has visto dos coches.**   To form the present perfect of *hacer*, take the *tú* form of the present tense of the verb *haber (has)*. The past participle of the verb *ver* is irregular and must be memorized: *visto*. Use *dos coches* to express "two cars."

Chapter Problems

Use the present perfect tense to express what people have done to prepare for a trip.

1. Ella (sacar) _____ el pasaporte.

2. Nosotros (escribir) _____ un itinerario.

3. Vosotros (hacer) _____ una reservación en un hotel.

4. Uds. (escoger) _____ las fechas del viaje.

5. Yo (invitar) _____ a mi amigo a acompañarme.

6. Él (cambiar) _____ dinero.

7. Ellas (comprar) _____ los billetes de avión.

8. Tú (ahorrar) _____ dinero.

9. Ud. (lavar) _____ la ropa.

10. Ellos (leer) _____ las guías turísticas.

11. Yo (hablar) _____ con personas de ese país.

12. Ellas (estar) _____ contentas.

13. Nosotros (alquilar) _____ un coche.

14. Uds. (verificar) _____ las reservaciones.

15. Él le (decir) _____ sus planes a su familia.

16. Vosotros (resolver) _____ escuchar los consejos de vuestros padres.

17. Ella (ir) _____ a la oficina de turismo de ese país.

18. Tú (investigar) _____ sitios web.

19. Ellos (disponer) _____ divertirse lo más posible.

20. Ud. (ver) _____ documentales sobre ese país.

Answers and Solutions

1. **Answer: ha sacado.** Spelling-change -car verbs are regular in the present perfect. To form the present perfect of *sacar*, take the *ella* form of the present tense of the verb *haber (ha)*. Form the past participle of the verb *sacar* by dropping the -ar ending and adding -ado.

2. **Answer: hemos escrito.** To form the present perfect of *escribir*, take the *nosotros* form of the present tense of the verb *haber (hemos)*. The past participle of the verb *escribir* is irregular and must be memorized: *escrito*.

3. **Answer: habéis hecho.** To form the present perfect of *hacer*, take the *vosotros* form of the present tense of the verb *haber (habéis)*. The past participle of the verb *hacer* is irregular and must be memorized: *hecho*.

4. **Answer: han escogido.** Spelling-change -ger verbs are regular in the present perfect. To form the present perfect of *escoger*, take the *Uds.* form of the present tense of the verb *haber (han)*. Form the past participle of the verb *escoger* by dropping the -er ending and adding -ido.

5. **Answer: he invitado.** To form the present perfect of *invitar*, take the *yo* form of the present tense of the verb *haber (he)*. Form the past participle of the verb *invitar* by dropping the -ar ending and adding -ado.

6. **Answer: ha cambiado.** To form the present perfect of *cambiar*, take the *él* form of the present tense of the verb *haber (ha)*. Form the past participle of the verb *cambiar* by dropping the -ar ending and adding -ado.

7. **Answer: han comprado.** To form the present perfect of *comprar*, take the *ellas* form of the present tense of the verb *haber (han)*. Form the past participle of the verb *comprar* by dropping the -ar infinitive ending and adding -ado.

8. **Answer: has ahorrado.** To form the present perfect of *ahorrar*, take the *tú* form of the present tense of the verb *haber (has)*. Form the past participle of the verb *ahorrar* by dropping the -ar ending and adding -ado.

9. **Answer: ha lavado.** To form the present perfect of *lavar*, take the *Ud.* form of the present tense of the verb *haber (ha)*. Form the past participle of the verb *lavar* by dropping the -ar ending and adding -ado.

10. **Answer: han leído.** To form the present perfect of *leer*, take the *ellos* form of the present tense of the verb *haber (han)*. Form the past participle of the verb *leer* by dropping the -er ending and adding -ido. Because the stem of *leer* ends in a vowel, add an accent mark to the *i*.

11. **Answer: he hablado.** To form the present perfect of *hablar*, take the *yo* form of the present tense of the verb *haber (he)*. Form the past participle of the verb *hablar* by dropping the *-ar* ending and adding *-ado*.

12. **Answer: han estado.** To form the present perfect of *estar*, take the *ella* form of the present tense of the verb *haber (han)*. Form the past participle of the verb *estar* by dropping the *-ar* ending and adding *-ado*.

13. **Answer: hemos alquilado.** To form the present perfect of *alquilar*, take the *nosotros* form of the present tense of the verb *haber (hemos)*. Form the past participle of the verb *alquilar* by dropping the *-ar* ending and adding *-ado*.

14. **Answer: han verificado.** Spelling-change *-car* verbs are regular in the present perfect. To form the present perfect of *verificar*, take the *Uds.* form of the present tense of the verb *haber (han)*. Form the past participle of the verb *verificar* by dropping the *-ar* ending and adding *-ado*.

15. **Answer: ha dicho.** To form the present perfect of *decir*, take the *él* form of the present tense of the verb *haber (ha)*. The past participle of the verb *decir* is irregular and must be memorized: *dicho*.

16. **Answer: habéis resuelto.** To form the present perfect of *resolver*, take the *vosotros* form of the present tense of the verb *haber (habéis)*. The past participle of the verb *resolver* is irregular and must be memorized: *resuelto*.

17. **Answer: ha ido.** To form the present perfect *ir*, take the *ella* form of the present tense of the verb *haber (ha)*. The past participle of the verb *ir* is irregular and must be memorized: *ido*.

18. **Answer: has investigado.** Spelling-change *-gar* verbs are regular in the present perfect. To form the present perfect of *investigar*, take the *tú* form of the present tense of the verb *haber (has)*. Form the past participle of the verb *investigar* by dropping the *-ar* ending and adding *-ado*.

19. **Answer: han dispuesto.** To form the present perfect of *disponer*, take the *ellos* form of the present tense of the verb *haber (han)*. The past participle of the verb *disponer* is irregular and must be memorized: *dispuesto*.

20. **Answer: ha visto.** To form the present perfect of *ver*, take the *Ud.* form of the present tense of the verb *haber (ha)*. The past participle of the verb *ver* is irregular and must be memorized: *visto*.

Supplemental Chapter Problems

Problems

Use the present perfect to express what different children have done at camp.

1. Ellas (nadar) _____ en el lago.

2. Vosotros (comer) _____ muchas hamburguesas.

3. Ellos (escribir) _____ cartas a su familia.

4.   Uds. (ir) _____ al bosque.

5.   Ud. (hacer) _____ tonterías.

6.   Ella (tener) _____ miedo de la oscuridad.

7.   Él (jugar) _____ muchos deportes.

8.   Yo (despertarse) _____ temprano.

9.   Tú (divertirse) _____ mucho.

10. Nosotros (ser) _____ responsables.

11. Ud. (pescar) _____.

12. Ella (decir) _____ mentiras.

13. Tú (resolver) _____ regresar el año próximo.

14. Yo (ver) _____ a mis amigos.

15. Él (leer) _____ las cartas de sus amigos.

16. Uds. (bañarse) _____ en el lago.

17. Vosotros (dormir) _____ al aire libre.

18. Nosotros (competir) _____ en muchos partidos.

19. Ellas (contar) _____ historias de fantasmas.

20. Ellos (comportarse) _____ bien.

Answers

1.   han nadado (the helping verb *haber,* p. 283; past participles of regular *-ar* verbs, p. 284)

2.   habéis comido (the helping verb *haber,* p. 283; past participles of regular *-er* verbs, p. 284)

3.   han escrito (the helping verb *haber,* p. 283; past participles of irregular verbs, p. 286)

4.   han ido (the helping verb *haber,* p. 283; past participles of irregular verbs, p. 286)

5.   ha hecho (the helping verb *haber,* p. 283; past participles irregular verbs, p. 286)

6.   ha tenido (the helping verb *haber,* p. 283; past participles of regular *-er* verbs, p. 284)

7.   ha jugado (the helping verb *haber,* p. 283; past participles of regular *-ar* verbs, p. 284)

8.   me he despertado (the helping verb *haber,* p. 283; past participles of regular *-ar* reflexive verbs, p. 284)

9. te has divertido (the helping verb *haber*, p. 283; past participles of regular *-ir* reflexive verbs, p. 284)

10. hemos sido (the helping verb *haber*, p. 283; past participles of regular *-er* verbs, p. 284)

11. ha pescado (the helping verb *haber*, p. 283; past participles of regular *-ar* verbs, p. 284)

12. ha dicho (the helping verb *haber*, p. 283; past participles of irregular verbs, p. 286)

13. has resuelto (the helping verb *haber*, p. 283; past participles of irregular verbs, p. 286)

14. he visto (the helping verb *haber*, p. 283; past participles of irregular verbs, p. 286)

15. ha leído (the helping verb *haber*, p. 283; past participles of regular *-er* verbs, p. 284)

16. se han bañado (the helping verb *haber*, p. 283; past participles of regular *-ar* reflexive verbs, p. 284)

17. habéis dormido (the helping verb *haber*, p. 283; past participles of regular *-ir* verbs, p. 284)

18. hemos competido (the helping verb *haber*, p. 283; past participles of regular *-ir* verbs, p. 284)

19. han contado (the helping verb *haber*, p. 283; past participles of regular *-ar* verbs, p. 284)

20. se han comportado (the helping verb *haber*, p. 283; past participles of regular *-ar* reflexive verbs, p. 284)

Chapter 16
The Future and the Conditional

The Future

In Spanish, the future may be expressed as follows:

❑ By using the present + expression of time indicating future (*mañana, más tarde, después,* and so on)

❑ By using *ir* (to go) + *a* + infinitive

❑ By using the future tense

Expressing the Future by Using the Present

The present tense may be used to imply the future when asking for instructions or when the proposed action will take place in the not so distant future. Words and phrases such as *mañana* (tomorrow), *más tarde* (later), *después* (afterwards), and *a las ocho* (at eight o'clock) follow a phrase in the present to indicate that the action is going to take place shortly.

¿Dejo los papeles aquí?	Shall I leave the papers here?
Él viene más tarde.	He will come later.

The present may also be used to imply the future in response to a question about a future action:

¿Qué haces mañana?	What are you doing tomorrow?
Voy al cine.	I'm going to the movies.

Ir + A + Infinitive

The present tense of the verb *ir* (to go) + *a* + the infinitive expresses a near future action or event.

The present tense of *ir* is irregular and is conjugated as follows:

yo voy	nosotros vamos
tú vas	vosotros vais
él, ella, Ud. va	ellos, ellas, Uds. van

Add the preposition *a* + an infinitive to express something that is imminent, or something that is going to happen soon:

Voy a descansarme.   I'm going to rest.

Van a trabajar esta noche.   They're going to work tonight.

Example Problems

Using the present and *ir* + *a* + infinitive, express what people are going to do after work today.

Example: él/mirar la televisión
Él mira la televisión.
Él va a mirar la televisión.

1. ella/bañarse

   Answer: Ella se baña.
   Ella va a bañararse. (Ella se va a bañar.)

   Use the present tense of the regular reflexive -*ar* verb *bañarse*. Drop the -*ar* ending and add the third person singular ending (-*a*). The -*se* attached to the infinitive indicates that the verb is reflexive. Put the reflexive pronoun *se*, which agrees with the subject, before the conjugated form of the verb. Alternatively, conjugate the irregular verb *ir* in the third person singular (*va*) and add the preposition *a*. Because *ir* is conjugated, the verb showing the action, *bañar*, remains in the infinitive. (The reflexive pronoun may remain attached to the infinitive or may be placed before the conjugated form of *ir*.)

2. nosotros/asistir a un concierto

   Answer: Nosotros asistimos a un concierto.
   Nosotros vamos a asistir a un concierto.

   Use the present tense of the regular -*ir* verb *asistir*. Drop the -*ir* ending and add the second person plural ending (-*imos*). Alternatively, conjugate the irregular verb *ir* in the first person plural (*vamos*) and add the preposition *a*. Because *ir* is conjugated, the verb showing the action, *asisitir*, remains in the infinitive.

Work Problems

Using the present and *ir* + *a* + infinitive, express what people are going to do upon awakening.

Example: ella/levantarse
Ella se levanta.
Ella va a levantarse. (Ella se va a levantar.)

1. vosotros/bañarse

2. yo/hacer la cama

3. ellos/desayunarse

4. nosotros/partir para la oficina

Worked Solutions

1. **Vosotros os bañáis. Vosotros vais a bañaros. Vosotros os vais a bañar.**   Use the present tense of the regular reflexive -ar verb *bañarse*. Drop the -ar ending and add the second person plural ending *(-áis)*. The -se attached to the infinitive indicates that the verb is reflexive. Put the reflexive pronoun *os*, which agrees with the subject, before the conjugated form of the verb. Alternatively, conjugate the irregular verb *ir* in the second person plural *(vais)* and add the preposition *a*. Because *ir* is conjugated, the verb showing the action, *bañar*, remains in the infinitive. The reflexive pronoun may remain attached to the infinitive or may be placed before the conjugated form of *ir*.

2. **Yo hago la cama. Yo voy a hacer la cama.**   Use the present tense of the irregular verb *hacer (hago)*. Alternatively, conjugate the irregular verb *ir* in the first person singular *(voy)* and add the preposition *a*. Because *ir* is conjugated, the verb showing the action, *hacer*, remains in the infinitive.

3. **Ellos se desayunan. Ellos van a desayunarse. Ellos se van a desayunar.**   Use the present tense of the regular reflexive -ar verb *desayunarse*. Drop the -ar ending and add the third person plural ending *(-an)*. The -se attached to the infinitive indicates that the verb is reflexive. Put the reflexive pronoun *se*, which agrees with the subject, before the conjugated form of the verb. Alternatively, conjugate the irregular verb *ir* in the third person plural *(van)* and add the preposition *a*. Because *ir* is conjugated, the verb showing the action, *descansar*, remains in the infinitive. The reflexive pronoun may remain attached to the infinitive or may be placed before the conjugated form of *ir*.

4. **Nosotros partimos para la oficina. Nosotros vamos a partir para la oficina.**   Use the present tense of the regular -ir verb *partir*. Drop the -ir ending and add the second person plural ending *(-imos)*. Alternatively, conjugate the irregular verb *ir* in the first person plural *(vamos)* and add the preposition *a*. Because *ir* is conjugated, the verb showing the action, *partir*, remains in the infinitive.

Using the Future Tense

Use the future:

❑ To express what will happen:

Yo saldré esta noche. (I will go out tonight.)

❑ To express wonder and probability in the present:

¿Cuánto ganará? (I wonder how much he earns.)

Será la una. (It's probably one o'clock.)

Estará contento. (He must be happy.) (He is probably happy.)

❑ To predict a future action or event:

Lloverá esta tarde. (It will rain this afternoon.)

The Future Tense of Regular Verbs

The future tense tells what the subject will do or what action or event will take place in future time. In Spanish, all verbs, whether they have regular or irregular stems, have the same endings. In addition, there are no spelling or stem changes in the future tense.

To form the future of regular verbs, add the future endings to the infinitive of the verb:

	-ar Verbs Comprar (to Buy)	-er Verbs Comer (to Eat)	-ir Verbs Abrir (to Open)
Yo	compraré	comeré	abriré
Tú	comprarás	comerás	abrirás
Él, Ella, Ud.	comprará	comerá	abrirá
Nosotros	compraremos	comeremos	abriremos
Vosotros	compraréis	comeréis	abriréis
Ellos, Ellas, Uds.	comprarán	comerán	abrirán

Here are a couple examples in sentences:

Yo compraré un coche nuevo el año próximo.   I will buy a new car next year.

Nosotros no comeremos en ese restaurante.   We won't eat in that restaurant.

Verbs such as *oír* and *reír*, whose infinitive contains an accent mark, drop that accent in the future:

Él no oirá las noticias.   He won't hear the news.

Yo reiré.   I will laugh.

Example Problem

Using the present tense, express what each person will do in the future.

Example: (comprar) Él _____ un coche nuevo.

Él <u>comprará</u> un coche nuevo.

(trabajar)

Yo _____ en una oficina, ellos _____ en una escuela, tú _____ en un hospital, nosotros _____ en una tienda, vosotros _____ en una farmacia y ella _____ en un país extranjero.

Answer: trabajaré, trabajarán, trabajarás, trabajaremos, trabajaréis, trabajará

To conjugate regular -ar verbs in the future, keep the -ar ending and:

1. For *yo*, add -é as the ending.

2. For *ellos*, add -án as the ending.

3. For *tú*, add -ás the ending.

4. For *nosotros*, add -emos as the ending.

5. For *vosotros*, add -éis as the ending.

6. For *ella*, add -á as the ending.

Work Problems

Using the future tense, express what each person will do to lose weight.

1. (tomar) Yo no _____ chocolate.

2. (beber) Tú _____ mucha agua.

3. (decidir) Vosotros _____ no comer mucho.

4. (contratar) Ella _____ a un entrenador.

5. (cocer) Uds. _____ alimentos sin grasa animal.

6. (andar) Nosotros _____ mucho.

Worked Solutions

1. **tomaré**   To conjugate regular -ar verbs in the future, keep the -ar ending and add -é as the ending for *yo*.

2. **beberás**   To conjugate regular -er verbs in the future, keep the -er ending and add -ás as the ending for *tú*.

3. **decidiréis**   To conjugate regular -ir verbs in the future, keep the -ir ending and add -éis as the ending for *vosotros*.

4. **contratará**   To conjugate regular -ar verbs in the future, keep the -ar ending and add -á as the ending for *ella*.

5. **cocerán**   To conjugate regular -er verbs in the future, keep the -er ending and add -án as the ending for *Uds*.

6. **andaremos**   To conjugate regular -ar verbs in the future, keep the -ar ending and add -emos as the ending for *nosotros*.

The Future Tense of Irregular Verbs

There are a few verbs that are irregular in the future. They have irregular future stems, which always end in -r or -rr. To form the future of irregular verbs do one of three things:

❏ Drop e from the infinitive ending before adding the future endings:

Infinitive	Meaning	Future Stem
caber	to fit	cabr-
haber	to have	habr-
poder	to be able	podr-
querer	to want	querr-
saber	to know	sabr-

❏ Drop *e* or *i* from the infinitive ending and replace the vowel with a *d* before adding the future endings:

Infinitive	Meaning	Future Stem
poner	to put	pondr-
salir	to leave	saldr-
tener	to have	tendr-
valer	to be worth	valdr-
venir	to come	vendr-

❏ Memorize the completely irregular stem and add the future endings:

Infinitive	Meaning	Future Stem
decir	to say	dir-
hacer	to make, to do	har-

Compounds of verbs that are irregular in the future (*componer, contener,* and so on) are also irregular.

Example Problems

Using the future tense, express what each person will do to improve in school.

Example: Él/estudiar más
Él estudiará más.

1. yo/no hacer las tareas en clase

   Answer: Yo no haré las tareas en clase.

   The verb *hacer* is irregular in the future and must be memorized. Use *har-* as the future stem and add the first person singular future ending *(-é).*

2. nosotros/venir a la escuela todos los días

   Answer: Nosotros vendremos a la escuela todos los días.

   The verb *venir* is irregular in the future. Drop *i* from the infinitive ending and replace it with a *d.* Add the first person plural future ending *(-emos).*

Work Problems

Complete the e-mail message by expressing what will happen. Use the future tense.

Ernesto me (decir) _____ sus planes para mañana, por la tarde. Él (poder) _____ estar

1   2

en mi casa a las dos. Yo sé que tu familia y tú (querer) _____ ir con nosotros al cine

3

pero tantas personas no (caber) _____ en su coche. Él (tener) _____ que hacer dos
                                    4   5

viajes pero los (hacer) _____ sin quejarse. ¿(saber) _____ tú como ir al cine? (valer)
                              6   7

_____ la pena llegar allí temprano porque (haber) _____ mucha gente a esa hora. Yo te
      8   9

(ver) _____ pronto.
          10

Worked Solutions

1. **dirá**   The verb *decir* is irregular in the future and must be memorized. Use *dir-* as the future stem and add the third person singular future ending *(-á)*.

2. **podrá**   The verb *poder* is irregular in the future and must be memorized. Drop the *e* from the infinitive ending and add the third person singular future ending for *él (-á)*.

3. **querréis**   The verb *querer* is irregular in the future and must be memorized. Drop the *e* from the infinitive ending and add the second person plural future ending *(-éis)* for *vosotros*. (*Note: tu familia y tú* combines to form the familiar plural subject *vosotros*.)

4. **cabrán**   The verb *caber* is irregular in the future and must be memorized. Drop the *e* from the infinitive ending and add the third person plural future ending *(-án)*.

5. **tendrá**   The verb *tener* is irregular in the future. Drop the *e* from the infinitive ending and replace it with a *d*. Add the third person singular ending for *él (-á)*.

6. **hará**   The verb *hacer* is irregular in the future and must be memorized. Use *har-* as the future stem and add the third person singular future ending *(-é)*.

7. **Sabrás**   The verb *saber* is irregular in the future and must be memorized. Drop the *e* from the infinitive ending and add the third person singular future ending for *tú (-ás)*.

8. **Valdrá**   The verb *valer* is irregular in the future. Drop *e* from the infinitive ending and replace it with a *d*. Add the third person singular future ending *(-á)* to express "it will be worth."

9. **habrá**   The verb *haber* is irregular in the future and must be memorized. Drop the *e* from the infinitive ending and add the third person singular future ending *(-á)* to agree with the subject *mucha gente*.

10. **veré**   *Ver* is regular in the future tense. To conjugate regular *-er* verbs in the future, keep the *-er* ending and add *-é* as the ending for *yo*.

The Conditional

The conditional expresses what the speaker would do or what would happen under certain circumstances or conditions. The conditional is formed by using the same stem that is used to form the future and by adding the same endings that are used for the imperfect. Just as in the future, there are no spelling or stem changes in the future tense.

	-ar Verbs Comprar (to Buy)	-er Verbs Comer (to Eat)	-ir Verbs Abrir (to Open)
Yo	compraría	comería	abriría
Tú	comprarías	comerías	abrirías
Él, Ella, Ud.	compraría	comería	abriría
Nosotros	compraríamos	comeríamos	abriríamos
Vosotros	compraríais	comeríais	abriríais
Ellos, Ellas, Uds.	comprarían	comerían	abrirían

Here are a couple of examples:

Yo sabía que ella no podría visitarnos hoy.   I knew that she couldn't visit us today.

¿Qué te gustaría hacer ahora?   What would you like to do now?

Verbs such as *oír* and *reír*, whose infinitive contains an accent mark, drop that accent in the conditional:

Yo no te oiría.   I wouldn't hear you.

Ellos sonreirían.   They would smile.

The Conditional of Irregular Verbs

The verbs that are irregular in the conditional have the same stem as they do for the future (see the minitables in "The Future Tense of Irregular Verbs," above). To form the conditional of irregular verbs do one of three things:

❑ Drop *e* from the infinitive ending before adding the conditional endings.

❑ Drop *e* or *i* from the infinitive ending and replace the vowel with a *d* before adding the conditional endings.

❑ Memorize the completely irregular stem and add the conditional endings.

Compounds of verbs that are irregular in the conditional (*componer, contener,* and so on) are also irregular.

Example Problem

Using the conditional tense, express what each person would do to prepare for a party.

Example: (comprar) Él _____ comestibles.

Él <u>compraría</u> comestibles.

(preparar) Yo _____ la ensalada, ellos _____ los pasteles, tú _____ los sándwiches, nosotros _____ los postres, vosotros _____ los dulces y ella _____ las galletitas.

Answer: prepararía, prepararían, prepararías, prepararíamos, prepararíais, prepararía

To conjugate regular -ar verbs in the conditional, keep the -ar ending and:

1. For *yo*, add -ía as the ending.

2. For *ellos*, add -ían as the ending.

3. For *tú*, add -ías as the ending.

4. For *nosotros*, add -íamos as the ending.

5. For *vosotros*, add -íais as the ending.

6. For *ella*, add -ía as the ending.

Work Problems

Using the conditional tense, express what might happen at the office on a sunny day.

1. (trabajar) Julio no _____.

2. (beber) Roberto y yo _____ mucha agua.

3. (abrir) Vosotros no _____ las ventanas.

4. (valer) _____ la pena trabajar lentamente.

5. Los empleados no (hacer) _____ mucho.

6. Todo el mundo (salir) _____ para almorzar.

Worked Solutions

1. **trabajaría**   To conjugate regular -ar verbs in the conditional, keep the -ar ending and add -ía as the ending for *Julio*.

2. **beberíamos**   To conjugate regular -er verbs in the conditional, keep the -er ending and add -íamos as the ending for *Roberto y yo*, which is the equivalent of *nosotros*.

3. **abriríais**   To conjugate regular -ir verbs in the conditional, keep the -ir ending and add -íais as the ending for *vosotros*.

4. **Valdría**   The verb *valer* is irregular in the conditional. Drop *e* from the infinitive ending and replace it with a *d*. Add the third person singular conditional ending (-ía) to express "it will be worth."

5. **harían**   The verb *hacer* is irregular in the conditional and must be memorized. Use *har-* as the conditional stem and add the third person plural conditional ending (-ían).

6. **saldría**   The verb *salir* is irregular in the conditional. Drop *i* from the infinitive ending and replace it with a *d*. Add the third person singular conditional ending (-ía).

Uses of the Conditional

Use the conditional:

❏ To express what would happen under certain conditions:

Si hiciera mal tiempo, yo me quedaría en casa. Yo no iría al parque.

(If the weather were bad, I would stay home. I wouldn't go to the park.)

When "would" means "used to," use the imperfect:

Nosotros viajábamos mucho. (We would [used to] travel a lot.)

When "would" means "to be willing" or "to want," use the preterit of *querer:*

Ellos no quisieron pagar la cuenta. (They wouldn't [weren't willing to] pay the bill.)

❏ To express wonder, speculation and probability in the past: (A subordinate clause in the past tense may be used or implied.

¿Qué hora sería cuando él llegó? (I wonder what time it was when he arrived.)

Sería la una (cuando llegó). (It was probably one o'clock.)

Estaría contento. (He must have been happy.)

Example Problems

Complete the following problems by using the appropriate form of the verb.

1. Complete the sentence: Si hiciera buen tiempo (I would go to the beach).

   Answer: Si hiciera buen tiempo yo iría a la playa.

   The verb *ir* is regular in the conditional. To conjugate *ir* in the conditional, keep the *ir* infinitive and add *-ía* as the ending for *yo*. Use *la playa* to express "the beach."

2. Complete the sentence: Cuando era joven, (I would always visit my grandparents on Saturdays).

   Answer: Cuando era joven, yo siempre visitaba a mis abuelos los sábados.

   In this sentence, use the imperfect because "would" means "used to." To conjugate regular *-ar* verbs in the imperfect, drop the *-ar* ending and add *-aba* as the ending for *yo*. (See Chapter 14.) Use the adverb *siempre* to express "always" and place it before the conjugated verb. Use the personal *a* before the direct object, *mis abuelos,* which refers to a person (or persons). Use the plural possessive adjective *mis* to express "my" before a plural noun. Use *abuelos* to express "grandparents." Use *los sábados* to express "on Saturdays."

3. Express that you were not willing to pay more.

   Answer: Yo no quise pagar más.

   When "would" means "to be willing to," use the preterit of *querer*. The irregular preterit stem of *querer* is *quis-*. Add the preterit ending for *yo (-é)*. Because *querer* is conjugated, the verb immediately following it must be in the infinitive. Use *pagar* to express "to pay." Use *más* to express "more."

Work Problems

Complete the following problems by using the appropriate form of the verb.

1. Complete the sentence: Si hiciera calor (we would go out).

2. Express that you wonder what time it was when Clarita called.

3. Express that it was probably 3:15 p.m.

4. Say that you would (be willing to, want to) eat in a Cuban restaurant.

5. Complete the sentence: Cuando era joven (I would go bike riding after leaving school).

6. Say that you wonder where the dog went.

Worked Solutions

1. **Si hiciera calor nosotros saldríamos.** The verb *salir* is irregular in the conditional. Drop *i* from the infinitive ending and replace it with a *d*. Add the first person plural conditional ending *(-íamos)*.

2. **¿Qué hora sería cuando Clarita llamó?** Use *¿qué?* to ask "what?" Use *hora* to express "time." To express wonder or speculation, use the conditional of the verb showing the action *(ser)*. The verb *ser* is regular in the conditional. Add the third personal singular conditional ending *(-ía)*, which agrees with the subject, *hora*. Use *cuando* to express "when." Use the verb *llamar* (to call) in the preterit to express that the action took place and was completed. To conjugate *llamar* in the preterit, drop the *-ar* ending and add *-ó* to agree with the subject, *Clarita*.

3. **Serían las tres y cuarto de la tarde.** To express wonder or speculation, use the conditional of the verb showing the action *(ser)*. The verb *ser* is regular in the conditional. Add the third personal plural conditional ending *(-ían)*, which agrees with the subject, *las tres y cuarto*. Use *de la tarde* to express "in the afternoon."

4. **Quise comer en un restaurante cubano.** When "would" means "to be willing to," use the preterit of *querer*. The irregular preterit stem of *querer* is *quis-*. Add the preterit ending for *yo (-e)*. Because *querer* is conjugated, the verb immediately following it must be in the infinitive. Use *comer* to express "to eat." Use *en* to express "in." Nouns ending in *-e* tend to be masculine. Use *un restaurante* to express "a restaurant." The adjective *cubano* must agree in number and gender with the noun it modifies: *un restaurante*. Adjectives in Spanish generally follow the nouns they modify.

5. **Cuando era joven yo montaba en bicicleta después de salir de la escuela.** In this sentence, use the imperfect because "would" means "used to." To conjugate regular *-ar* verbs in the imperfect, drop the *-ar* ending and add *-aba* as the ending for *yo*. (See Chapter 14.) Use the expression *montar en bicicleta* to express "to go bicycle riding." Use the prepositional phrase *después de* to express "after." Use the infinitive *salir* after the preposition *de*. Use *de la escuela* to express "from school."

6. **¿Dónde iría el perro?** Use *¿dónde?* to ask "where?" To express wonder or speculation, use the conditional of the verb showing the action *(ir)*. The verb *ir* is regular in the conditional. To conjugate *ir* in the conditional, keep the *ir* infinitive and add *-ía* as the ending for *el perro*.

Chapter Problems

Problems

In problems 1–6, express what the children will do so that Santa will bring them toys. Use the future.

1. ellas/ayudar a sus padres

2. tú/tener éxito en tus estudios

3. vosotros/decir la verdad

4. Ud./ir a la escuela todos los días

5. yo/hacer todas mis tareas

6. ellos/cuidar a sus hermanos

In problems 7–9, express what the people would do if they could do anything they wanted. Use the conditional.

7. nosotros/conducir un coche deportivo

8. él/ir a Europa

9. yo/hacerse actor

Answers and Solutions

1. **Answer: Ellas ayudarán a sus padres.** To conjugate regular -ar verbs in the future, keep the -ar ending and add -án as the ending for ellas.

2. **Answer: Tú tendrás éxito en tus estudios.** The verb tener is irregular in the future. Drop the e from the infinitive ending and replace it with a d. Add the second person singular ending for tú (-ás).

3. **Answer: Vosotros diréis la verdad.** The verb decir is irregular in the future and must be memorized. Use dir- as the future stem and add the second person plural future ending (-éis) for vosotros.

4. **Answer: Ud. irá a la escuela todos los días.** The verb ir is regular in the future. To conjugate ir in the future, keep the ir infinitive and add -á as the ending for Ud.

5. **Answer: Yo haré todas mis tareas.** The verb hacer is irregular in the future and must be memorized. Use har- as the future stem and add the first person singular conditional ending (-é) for yo.

6. **Answer: Ellos cuidarán a sus hermanos.** To conjugate regular -ar verbs in the future, keep the -ar ending and add -án as the ending for ellos.

7. **Answer: Nosotros conduciríamos un coche deportivo.** Spelling-change -cir verbs are regular in the conditional. To conjugate regular -ir verbs in the conditional, keep the -ir ending and add the first person plural ending (-íamos) for nosotros.

8. **Answer: Él iría a Europa.** The verb *ir* is regular in the conditional. To conjugate *ir* in the conditional, keep the *ir* infinitive and add *-ía* as the ending for *él*.

9. **Answer: Yo me haría actor.** The verb *hacer* is irregular in the conditional and must be memorized. Use *har-* as the conditional stem and add the first person singular conditional ending *(-ía)* for *yo*. The *-se* attached to the infinitive indicates that the verb is reflexive. Put the reflexive pronoun *me*, which agrees with the subject, before the conjugated form of the verb.

Supplemental Chapter Problems

Problems

In problems 1–6, express what New Year's resolutions people make. Use the future.

1. Uds./no conducir rápidamente

2. vosotros/no beber cerveza

3. él/no fumar cigarrillos

4. ellas/bajar de peso

5. tú/hacer más ejercicios

6. Ud./no acostarse tarde

In problems 7–12, express what people would want if they could have their wish. Use the conditional.

7. yo/querer ser rico

8. ellas/tener solamente veinte años

9. Ud./hacerse rico

10. vosotros/dar la vuelta al mundo

11. mi colección de sellos/valer un millón de dólares

12. nosotros/poder correr en un maratón

Answers

1. Uds. no conducirán rápidamente. (the future of regular verbs, p. 297)

2. Vosotros no beberéis cerveza. (the future of regular verbs, p. 297)

3. Él no fumará cigarrillos. (the future of regular verbs, p. 297)

4. Ellas bajarán de peso. (the future of regular verbs, p. 297)

5. Tú harás más ejercicios. (the future of irregular verbs, p. 299)

6. Ud. no se acostará tarde. (the future of regular verbs, p. 297)

7. Yo querría ser rico. (the conditional of irregular verbs, p. 302)

8. Ellas tendrían solamente veinte años. (the conditional of irregular verbs, p. 302)

9. Ud. se haría rico. (the conditional of irregular verbs, p. 302)

10. Vosotros daríais la vuelta al mundo. (the conditional of regular verbs, p. 301)

11. Mi colección de sellos valdría un millón de dólares. (the conditional of irregular verbs, p. 302)

12. Nosotros podríamos correr en un maratón. (the conditional of irregular verbs, p. 302)

Chapter 17
The Subjunctive

The subjunctive is a mood that is used far more frequently in Spanish than it is in English. The present subjunctive expresses actions or events that take place in the present or the future. The subjunctive mood expresses unreal, hypothetical, or unsubstantiated conditions or situations resulting from doubt, wishes, needs, desires, feelings, emotions, speculation, and supposition.

Forming the Subjunctive

The present subjunctive of regular verbs is formed by dropping the *-o* from the *yo* form of the present tense and adding the subjunctive endings:

	-ar Verbs	*-er Verbs*	*-ir Verbs*
Yo Form of the Present	ayudo (I help)	como (I eat)	decido (I decide)
Yo	ayud**e**	com**a**	decid**a**
Tú	ayud**es**	com**as**	decid**as**
Él, Ella, Ud.	ayud**e**	com**a**	decid**a**
Nosotros	ayud**emos**	com**amos**	decid**amos**
Vosotros	ayud**éis**	com**áis**	decid**áis**
Ellos, Ellas, Uds.	ayud**en**	com**an**	decid**an**

Here are some examples in sentences:

Es necesario que yo le compre un regalo.	It is necessary that I buy her a gift.
Es importante que tú bebas mucho.	It is important that you drink a lot.
Es posible que ellos asistan a la fiesta.	It is possible that they will come to the party.

Example Problems

Express what is necessary to do for school by using the present subjunctive.

> Example: (estudiar) Es necesario que él _____ mucho.
> Es necesario que él <u>estudie</u> mucho.

1. (comprar)

Es necesario que yo _____ plumas, ellos _____ una mochila, tú _____ un diccionario, nosotros _____ una regla, vosotros _____ una calculadora y ella _____ un calendario.

Answer: compre, compren, compres, compremos, compréis, compre

To conjugate regular -ar verbs in the present subjunctive, drop the -ar infinitive ending and add:

1. For *yo,* add -e as the ending.

2. For *ellos,* add -en as the ending.

3. For *tú,* add -es as the ending.

4. For *nosotros,* add -emos as the ending.

5. For *vosotros,* add -éis as the ending.

6. For *ella,* add -e as the ending.

2. (prometer)

Es necesario que ellas _____ hacer sus tareas, nosotras _____ estudiar más, Ud. _____ escribir buenas notas, yo _____ no salir por la noche, vosotros _____ ir a la escuela y tú _____ escuchar en clase.

Answer: prometan, prometamos, prometa, prometa, prometáis, prometas

To conjugate regular -er verbs in the present subjunctive, drop the -er infinitive ending and add:

1. For *ellas,* add -an as the ending.

2. For *nosotras,* add -amos as the ending.

3. For *Ud.,* add -a as the ending.

4. For *yo,* add -a as the ending.

5. For *vosotros,* add -áis as the ending.

6. For *tú,* add -as as the ending.

Work Problems

Express the advice being given to and by retired people. Use the subjunctive.

Es necesario que . . .

1. (disfrutar) yo _____ de la vida.

2. (depender) tú no _____ de tus hijos.

3. (aceptar) vosotros _____ vuestras limitaciones.

4. (admitir) ella _____ su edad al doctor.

5. (abonarse) Uds. _____ a muchas revistas.

6. (discutir) nosotros _____ nuestros problemas.

7. (comer) yo _____ bien.

8. (vivir) vosotros _____ lentamente.

9. (consumir) tú _____ menos carne.

10. (andar) nosotros _____ para mantener la buena salud.

Worked Solutions

1. **disfrute**   To conjugate regular -*ar* verbs in the present subjunctive, drop the -*ar* infinitive ending and add -*e* as the ending for *yo*.

2. **dependas**   To conjugate regular -*er* verbs in the present subjunctive, drop the -*er* infinitive ending and add -*as* as the ending for *tú*.

3. **aceptéis**   To conjugate regular -*ar* verbs in the present subjunctive, drop the -*ar* infinitive ending and add -*éis* as the ending for *vosotros*.

4. **admita**   To conjugate regular -*ir* verbs in the present subjunctive, drop the -*ir* infinitive ending and add -*a* as the ending for *ella*.

5. **se abonen**   To conjugate regular -*ar* verbs in the present subjunctive, drop the -*er* infinitive ending and add -*en* as the ending for *Uds*. Additionally, the -*se* ending indicates that the verb *abonarse* is reflexive. Place the reflexive pronoun *se*, which agrees with the subject, before the conjugated verb.

6. **discutamos**   To conjugate regular -*ir* verbs in the present subjunctive, drop the -*ir* infinitive ending and add -*amos* as the ending for *nosotros*.

7. **coma**   To conjugate regular -*er* verbs in the present subjunctive, drop the -*er* infinitive ending and add -*a* as the ending for *yo*.

8. **viváis**   To conjugate regular -*ir* verbs in the present subjunctive, drop the -*ir* infinitive ending and add -*áis* as the ending for *vosotros*.

9. **consumas**   To conjugate regular -*ir* verbs in the present subjunctive, drop the -*ir* infinitive ending and add -*as* as the ending for *tú*.

10. **andemos**   To conjugate regular -*ar* verbs in the present subjunctive, drop the -*ar* infinitive ending and add -*emos* as the ending for *nosotros*.

Irregular in the Present Tense Yo Form Verbs

Some verbs that are irregular in the *yo* form of the present tense form the subjunctive in the same manner as regular verbs: They drop the final -*o* from the irregular *yo* form and add the appropriate subjunctive ending:

Verb	Meaning	Yo Form	Subjunctive Forms
caber	to fit	quepo	quepa, quepas, quepa, quepamos, quepáis, quepan
caer	to fall	caigo	caiga, caigas, caiga, caigamos, caigáis, caigan
decir	to say, to tell	digo	diga, digas, diga, digamos, digáis, digan
hacer	to make, to do	hago	haga, hagas, haga, hagamos, hagáis, hagan
incluir	to include	incluyo	incluya, incluyas, incluya, incluyamos, incluyáis, incluyan
oír	to hear	oigo	oiga, oigas, oiga, oigamos, oigáis, oigan
poner	to put	pongo	ponga, pongas, ponga, pongamos, pongáis, pongan
salir	to go out	salgo	salga, salgas, salga, salgamos, salgáis, salgan
tener	to have	tengo	tenga, tengas, tenga, tengamos, tengáis, tengan
traer	to bring	traigo	traiga, traigas, traiga, traigamos, traigáis, traigan
valer	to be worth	valgo	valga, valgas, valga, valgamos, valgáis, valgan
venir	to come	vengo	venga, vengas, venga, vengamos, vengáis, vengan
ver	to see	veo	vea, veas, vea, veamos, veáis, vean

Example Problems

There is an important meeting. Using the present subjunctive, express what Geraldo has to do.

Example: venir a la cita a tiempo
Más vale que él venga a la cita a tiempo.

1. poner sus papeles importantes en su cartera

   Answer: Más vale que él ponga sus papeles importantes en su cartera.

   Poner is a verb that is irregular in its present tense *yo* form. To form the subjunctive, take the *yo* form (*pongo*), drop the -*o*, and add -*a* as the ending for *él*.

2. traer todo lo necesario

    Answer: Más vale que él traiga todo lo necesario

    Traer is a verb that is irregular in its present tense *yo* form. To form the subjunctive, take the *yo* form (*traigo*), drop the *-o*, and add *-a* as the ending for *él*.

Work Problems

Use the present subjunctive to express what the teacher tells the students it is better for them to do.

> Example: no destruir nada
> Es mejor que Uds. no destruyan nada.

1. oírme bien

2. poner sus mochilas debajo de sus pupitres

3. venir a mi clase a tiempo

4. traer sus libros a clase

5. hacer todas las tareas

6. siempre decir la verdad

Worked Solutions

1. **Es mejor que Uds. me oigan bien.**   *Oír* is a verb that is irregular in its present tense *yo* form. To form the subjunctive, take the *yo* form (*oigo*), drop the *-o*, and add *-an* as the ending for *Uds.*

2. **Es mejor que Uds. pongan sus mochilas debajo de sus pupitres.**   *Poner* is a verb that is irregular in its present tense *yo* form. To form the subjunctive, take the *yo* form (*pongo*), drop the *-o*, and add *-an* as the ending for *Uds.*

3. **Es mejor que Uds. vengan a mi clase a tiempo.**   *Venir* is a verb that is irregular in its present tense *yo* form. To form the subjunctive, take the *yo* form (*vengo*), drop the *-o*, and add *-an* as the ending for *Uds.*

4. **Es mejor que Uds. traigan sus libros a clase.**   *Traer* is a verb that is irregular in its present tense *yo* form. To form the subjunctive, take the *yo* form (*traigo*), drop the *-o*, and add *-an* as the ending for *Uds.*

5. **Es mejor que Uds. hagan todas las tareas.**   *Hacer* is a verb that is irregular in its present tense *yo* form. To form the subjunctive, take the *yo* form (*hago*), drop the *-o*, and add *-an* as the ending for *Uds.*

6. **Es mejor que Uds. siempre digan la verdad.**   *Decir* is a verb that is irregular in its present tense *yo* form. To form the subjunctive, take the *yo* form (*digo*), drop the *-o*, and add *-an* as the ending for *Uds.*

Spelling Changes in the Present Subjunctive

In the present subjunctive, verbs ending in *-car, -gar,* and *-zar* undergo the same change that occurs in the *yo* form of the preterit:

-*car* verbs: $c \rightarrow qu$
-*gar* verbs: $g \rightarrow gu$
-*zar* verbs: $z \rightarrow c$

Infinitive	Preterit *Yo* Form	Stem	Subjunctive Endings
sacar	saqué	saqu-	-e, -es, -e, -emos, -éis, -en
llegar	llegué	llegu-	-e, -es, -e, -emos, -éis, -en
utilizar	utilicé	utilic-	-e, -es, -e, -emos, éis, -en

Verbs ending in *-cer/-cir, -ger/-gir,* and *-guir* (but not *-uir*) undergo the same change that occurs in the *yo* form of the present:

consonant + *-cer/-cir* verbs: $c \rightarrow z$
vowel + *-cer/-cir* verbs: $c \rightarrow zc$
-*ger/-gir* verbs: $g \rightarrow j$
-*guir* verbs: $gu \rightarrow g$

Infinitive	Present *Yo* Form	Stem	Subjunctive Endings
convencer	convenzo	convenz-	-a, -as, -a, -amos, -áis, -an
esparcir	esparzo	esparz-	-a, -as, -a, -amos, -áis, -an
conocer	conozco	conozc-	-a, -as, -a, -amos, -áis, -an
conducir	conduzco	conduzc-	-a, -as, -a, -amos, -áis, -an
escoger	escojo	escoj-	-a, -as, -a, -amos, -áis, -an
dirigir	dirijo	dirij-	-a, -as, -a, -amos, -áis, -an
distinguir	distingo	disting-	-a, -as, -a, -amos, -áis, -an

Example Problems

Company will be arriving soon. Using the present subjunctive, express what different people need to do.

Example: Ud./organizarse
Es preciso que Ud. se organice.

1. tú/sacar la basura

   Answer: Es preciso que tú saques la basura.

   Sacar is a spelling-change verb that is irregular in its preterit tense *yo* form: -*c* changes to -*qu*. To form the subjunctive, take the *yo* form (*saqué*), drop the -*é,* and add -*es* as the subjunctive ending for *tú.*

2.   yo/escoger los mejores vinos para la cena

Answer: Es preciso que yo escoja los mejores vinos para la cena.

Escoger is a stem-changing *-ger* verb that is irregular in its present tense *yo* form: *-g* changes to *-j*. To form the subjunctive, take the *yo* form (*escojo*), drop the *-o*, and add *-a* as the subjunctive ending for *yo*.

Work Problems

Express what a parent tells a babysitter is imperative.

> Example: tú/llegar a tiempo
> Es imperativo que tú llegues a tiempo.

1.   yo/explicar las reglas

2.   tú/no castigar a los niños

3.   los niños/obedecer las reglas

4.   Manuel/no tocar nada

5.   Adela/no lanzar sus juguetes

6.   los niños/no te convencer de mirar la televisión toda la noche

Worked Solutions

1.   **Es imperativo que yo explique las reglas.**   *Explicar* is a spelling-change verb that is irregular in its preterit tense *yo* form: *-c* changes to *-qu*. To form the subjunctive, take the *yo* form (*expliqué*), drop the *-é*, and add *-e* as the subjunctive ending for *yo*.

2.   **Es imperativo que tú no castigues a los niños.**   *Castigar* is a spelling-change verb that is irregular in its preterit tense *yo* form: *-g* changes to *-gu*. To form the subjunctive, take the *yo* form (*castigué*), drop the *-é*, and add *-es* as the subjunctive ending for *tú*.

3.   **Es imperativo que los niños obedezcan las reglas.**   *Obedecer* is a spelling-change "vowel + *-cer*" verb that is irregular in its present tense *yo* form: *-c* changes to *-zc*. To form the subjunctive, take the *yo* form (*obedezco*), drop the *-o*, and add *-an* as the subjunctive ending for *los niños (ellos)*.

4.   **Es imperativo que Manuel no toque nada.**   *Tocar* is a spelling-change verb that is irregular in its preterit tense *yo* form: *-c* changes to *-qu*. To form the subjunctive, take the *yo* form (*toqué*), drop the *-é*, and add *-e* as the subjunctive ending for *yo*.

5.   **Es imperativo que Adela no lance sus juguetes.**   *Lanzar* is a spelling-change verb that is irregular in its preterit tense *yo* form: *-z* changes to *-c*. To form the subjunctive, take the *yo* form (*lancé*), drop the *-é*, and add *-e* as the subjunctive ending for *Adela (ella)*.

6.   **Es imperativo que los niños no te convenzan de mirar la televisión toda la noche.**   *Convencer* is a spelling-change "consonant + *-cer*" verb that is irregular in its present

tense *yo* form: *-c* changes to *-z*. To form the subjunctive, take the *yo* form (*convenzo*), drop the *-o*, and add *-an* as the subjunctive ending for *los niños (ellos)*.

Stem Changes in the Present Subjunctive

The changes that stem-changing *-ar*, *-er*, and *-ir* verbs undergo in the present subjunctive are often, but not always, the same changes they undergo in the present. Changes in the stem occur in all persons but *nosotros* and *vosotros*.

Verb Type	Stem Change	Subjunctive Stems	
-ar and -er	*e to ie*	*Yo, Tú, Él, Ellos*	*Nosotros/Vosotros*
cerrar (to close)	yo cierro	cierr-	cerr-
querer (to want)	yo quiero	quier-	quer-
	o to ue	*Yo, Tú, Él, Ellos*	*Nosotros/Vosotros*
contar (to tell)	yo cuento	cuent-	cont-
volver (to return)	yo vuelvo	vuelv-	volv-
-ir	*e to ie*	*Yo, Tú, Él, Ellos*	*Nosotros/Vosotros*
sentir (to feel, regret)	yo siento	sient-	sint-
	o to ue	*Yo, Tú, Él, Ellos*	*Nosotros/Vosotros*
dormir (to sleep)	yo duermo	duerm-	durm-
	e to i	*Yo, Tú, Él, Ellos*	*Nosotros/Vosotros*
pedir (to ask)	yo pido	pid-	pid-

Accent marks are used in the *-iar* and *-uar* verbs listed below, in all forms but *nosotros*:

enviar (to send)   yo envío   env-   -íe, -íes, -íe, -iemos, -iéis, -íen

Verbs like *enviar* include:

confiar (en)	to rely (on), to confide (in)
espiar	to spy
fiarse (de)	to trust
guiar	to guide
resfriarse	to catch a cold
variar	to vary

continuar (to continue)   yo continúo   contin-   -úe, -úes, -úe, -uemos, -uéis, -úen

Verbs like *continuar* include:

actuar	to act
graduarse	to graduate

For verbs ending in *-uir* (but not *-guir*), a *y* is inserted after the *u* in all forms of the present subjunctive:

distribuir (to distribute)   yo distribu**y**o   distribu**y**-   -a, -as, -a, -amos, -áis, -an

Irregular Verbs in the Present Subjunctive

Verbs that follow no rules for the formation of the subjunctive must be memorized. The most common irregular verbs are:

dar (to give): dé, des, dé, demos, deis, den

estar (to be): esté, estés, esté, estemos, estéis, estén

haber (to have): haya, hayas, haya, hayamos, hayáis, hayan

ir (to go): vaya, vayas, vaya, vayamos, vayáis, vayan

saber (to know): sepa, sepas, sepa, sepamos, sepáis, sepan

ser (to be): sea, seas, sea, seamos, seáis, sean

Example Problems

Mr. Rueda is ill. Using the present subjunctive, express what is important for him to do.

Example: continuar tomando las pastillas
Es importante que Ud. continúe tomando las pastillas.

1. no ir al trabajo

   Answer: Es importante que Ud. no vaya al trabajo.

   Ir has an irregular subjunctive stem (*vay-*), which must be memorized. Add *-a* as the subjunctive ending for *Ud.*

2. dormir mucho

   Answer: Es importante que Ud. duerma mucho.

   Dormir is a spelling-change verb that has an internal change from *-o* to *-ue* in the *yo* form of the present. To form the subjunctive, take the *yo* form (*duermo*), drop the *–o,* and add *-a* as the subjunctive ending for *Ud.*

Work Problems

Using the present subjunctive, express what a person has to do to prepare for a big exam.

Example: querer tener éxito
Es menester que Ud. quiera tener éxito.

1. dormir mucho antes del examen

2. pedir ayuda a sus profesores

3. contar con sus propios conocimientos

4.   no sentirse mal antes de presentar el examen.

5.   darse cuenta de la importancia del examen

6.   ir a la biblioteca a menudo

Worked Solutions

1.   **Es menester que Ud. duerma mucho antes del examen.**   *Dormir* is a stem-changing verb that has an internal change from *-o* to *-ue* in the *yo* form of the present. To form the subjunctive, take the *yo* form (*duermo*), drop the *-o*, and add *-a* as the subjunctive ending for *Ud*.

2.   **Es menester que Ud. pida ayuda a sus profesores.**   *Pedir* is a stem-changing verb that has an internal change from *-e* to *-i* in the *yo* form of the present. To form the subjunctive, take the *yo* form (*pido*), drop the *-o*, and add *-a* as the subjunctive ending for *Ud*.

3.   **Es menester que Ud. cuente con sus propios conocimientos.**   *Contar* is a stem-changing verb that has an internal change from *-o* to *-ue* in the *yo* form of the present. To form the subjunctive, take the *yo* form (*cuento*), drop the *-o*, and add *-e* as the subjunctive ending for *Ud*.

4.   **Es menester que Ud. no se sienta mal antes de presentar el examen.**   *Sentir* is a stem-changing verb that has an internal change from *-e* to *-ie* in the *yo* form of the present. To form the subjunctive, take the *yo* form (*siento*), drop the *-o*, and add *-a* as the subjunctive ending for *Ud*. Additionally, the *-se* ending indicates that the verb *sentirse* is reflexive. Place the reflexive pronoun *se*, which agrees with the subject, before the conjugated verb.

5.   **Es menester que Ud. se dé cuenta de la importancia del examen.**   *Dar* has irregular subjunctive forms that must be memorized. Drop the *-ar* ending from the infinitive and add *-é* as the subjunctive ending for *Ud*.

6.   **Es menester que Ud. vaya a la biblioteca a menudo.**   *Ir* has an irregular subjunctive stem (*vay-*), which must be memorized. Add *-a* as the subjunctive ending for *Ud*.

Using the Subjunctive

The subjunctive is used if:

☐ The sentence contains two different clauses with two different subjects.

☐ The clauses are joined by *que* (that), which is followed by the subjunctive.

☐ The main clause shows wishing, need, emotion, or doubt, among other things.

A *clause* is a group of words (containing a subject and a verb) that is part of a sentence. An independent, or main, clause can stand by itself as a simple sentence. A dependent, or subordinate, clause cannot stand by itself.

The Subjunctive after Expressions of Wishing, Emotion, Need, and Doubt

The subjunctive is used after impersonal expressions that show wishing, emotion, need, and doubt. Impersonal expressions begin with *es* (it is), followed by an adjective, and then *que* (to express "that" before the dependent clause):

Expression	Spanish
it is absurd that	es absurdo que
it is amazing that	es asombroso que
it is amusing that	es divertido que
it is bad that	es malo que
it is better that	es mejor que
it is curious that	es curioso que
it is doubtful that	es dudoso que
it is essential that	es esencial que
it is fair that	es justo que
it is imperative that	es imperativo que
it is important that	es importante que
it is impossible that	es imposible que
it is improbable that	es improbable que
it is incredible that	es increíble que
it is indispensable that	es indispensable que
it is necessary that	es necesario que
it is possible that	es posible que
it is preferable that	es preferible que
it is probable that	es probable que
it is regrettable that	es lamentable que
it is unfair that	es injusto que
it is urgent that	es urgente que
it is useful that	es útil que

When using the subjunctive in English, people often omit the word "that." In Spanish, however, *que* must always be used to join the two clauses:

Es importante que ellos lleguen a tiempo.	It is important (that) they arrive on time.
Es urgente que Ud. me llame.	It is urgent (that) you call me.

Certain impersonal expressions show certainty and, therefore, require the indicative:

English	Spanish
it is certain, it is sure	es cierto
it is clear	es claro
it is evident	es evidente
it is exact	es exacto
it is sure	es seguro
it is true	es verdad

Es claro que él es muy inteligente.   It is clear that he is very inteligent.

Es cierto que ellas vendrán.   It is certain that they will come.

In the negative, however, these expressions show doubt or denial and, thus, require the subjunctive:

No es claro que él sea muy inteligente.   It is not clear that he is very intelligent.

No es cierto que ellas vengan.   It is uncertain that they will come.

Example Problems

Describe a business trip. Combine the clauses by using the subjunctive, if necessary.

> Example: es urgente/nosotros/encontrar al presidente de la sociedad
> Es urgente que nosotros encontremos al presidente de la sociedad.

1. es probable/yo/ir a la conferencia

   Answer: Es probable que yo vaya a la conferencia.

   Add *que* after *es probable,* which requires the subjunctive because it shows doubt. *Ir* has an irregular subjunctive stem (*vay-*), which must be memorized. Add *-a* as the subjunctive ending for *yo.*

2. es seguro/Uds./querer asistir a las reuniones

   Answer: Es seguro que Uds. quieren asistir a las reuniones.

   Add *que* after *es seguro,* which requires the indicative because it shows certainty. *Querer* has an internal stem change in the present tense: *-i* changes to *-ie* in all forms but *nosotros* and *vosotros.* Drop the *-er* infinitive ending and add *-en* for *Uds.*

Work Problems

Describe a surprise party. Combine the clauses by using the subjunctive, if necessary.

> Example: es importante/todo el mundo/divertirse mucho
> Es importante que todo el mundo se divierta mucho.

1. es dudoso/Mercedes/llegar a tiempo

2. es asombroso/Arturo/cocer algo para la fiesta

3. es seguro/yo/te ayudar

4. es lamentable/ellos/no venir

5. es esencial/tú/contribuir a la fiesta

6. es probable/nosotros/estar en tu casa temprano

Worked Solutions

1. **Es dudoso que Mercedes llegue a tiempo.** Add *que* after *es dudoso*, which requires the subjunctive because it shows doubt. *Llegar* is a spelling-change verb that is irregular in its preterit tense *yo* form: *-g* changes to *-gu*. To form the subjunctive, take the *yo* form (*llegué*), drop the *-é*, and add *-e* as the subjunctive ending for *Mercedes (ella)*.

2. **Es asombroso que Arturo cueza algo para la fiesta.** Add *que* after *es asombroso*, which requires the subjunctive because it shows doubt. *Cocer* is a spelling-change "vowel + -cer" verb that is irregular in its present tense *yo* form: *-c* changes to *-z*. To form the subjunctive, take the *yo* form (*cuezo*), drop the *-o*, and add *-a* as the subjunctive ending for *Arturo (él)*.

3. **Es seguro que yo te ayudaré.** Add *que* after *es seguro*, which requires the indicative because it shows certainty. Because the future is implied in this sentence, add the future ending for *yo* (*-é*) to this regular *-ar* verb infinitive.

4. **Es lamentable que ellos no vengan.** Add *que* after *es lamentable*, which requires the subjunctive because it shows doubt. *Venir* is a verb that is irregular in its present tense *yo* form. To form the subjunctive, take the *yo* form (*vengo*), drop the *-o*, and add *-an* as the ending for *ellos*.

5. **Es esencial que tú contribuyas a la fiesta.** Add *que* after *es esencial*, which requires the subjunctive because it shows doubt. *Contribuir* is a stem-changing verb. A *y* is inserted after the *u* in all forms of the present subjunctive for verbs ending in *-uir*. Add *-as* as the subjunctive ending for *tú*.

6. **Es probable que nosotros estemos en tu casa temprano.** Add *que* after *es probable*, which requires the subjunctive because it shows doubt. *Estar* has irregular subjunctive forms that must be memorized. Drop the *-ar* infinitive ending and add *-emos* as the subjunctive ending for *nosotros*.

The Subjunctive after Verbs of Wishing, Emotion, Need, and Doubt

The subjunctive is used in the dependent clause introduced by *que* when the main clause expresses not only wishing, emotion, need, and doubt, but also other related activities, such as advice, command, demand, desire, hope, permission, preference, prohibition, request, suggestion, and wanting, as shown below:

Spanish	English
aconsejar	to advise
alegrarse (de)	to be glad, to be happy
desear	to desire, to wish, to want
dudar	to doubt
enfadarse	to become angry
enojarse	to become angry
esperar	to hope
exigir	to require, to demand
insistir	to insist
lamentar	to regret
mandar	to command, to order

necesitar	to need
negar	to deny
ordenar	to order
pedir	to ask for, to request
permitir	to permit
preferir	to prefer
prohibir	to forbid
querer	to wish, to want
recomendar	to recommend
rogar	to beg, to request
sorprenderse de	to be surprised
sugerir	to suggest
temer	to fear
tener miedo de	to fear

Here are a couple of examples in sentences:

Ella quiere que yo vaya al supermercado.	She wants me to go to the supermarket.
Mi madre insiste en que yo haga mi tarea ahora.	My mother insists that I do my homework now.

Example Problems

Using the subjunctive, express how people feel in the following situations, using the appropriate verb from the box below.

alegrarse de	lamentar	sorprenderse de	temer

Example: Yo ganaré mucho dinero trabajando. Mi familia . . .
     Mi familia se alegra de que yo gane mucho dinero trabajando.

1. Un huracán se formará mañana. Nosotros . . .

   Answer: Nosotros tememos que un huracán se forme mañana.

   Add *temer* after the subject to express "we fear that the hurricane will break out tomorrow." To conjugate the regular *-er* verb *temer,* drop the *-er* ending and add *-emos* for the subject, *nosotros.* Add *que* to join the two clauses. To conjugate regular *-ar* verbs in the present subjunctive, drop the *-ar* ending and add *-e* as the ending for *un huracán (él).*

2. El número de robos disminuye. La policía . . .

   Answer: La policía se sorprende de que el número de robos disminuya.

   Add *sorprenderse de* after the subject to express "the police are surprised that the number of robberies has diminished." To conjugate the regular *-er* verb *sorprenderse,* drop the *-er* ending and add *-e* for the subject, *la policía (ellas).* The *-se* ending indicates that the verb *sorprenderse* is reflexive. Place the reflexive pronoun *se,* which agrees with the subject, before the conjugated verb. Add *que* to join the two clauses. Because *disminuir* is a stem-changing verb, a *y* is inserted after the *u* in all forms of the present subjunctive for verbs ending in *-uir.* Add *-a* as the subjunctive ending for *el número (él).*

Work Problems

Using the subjunctive, express how people feel in the following situations.

> Example: Hay clases pero Carlos no va a la escuela. (sus padres/mandar)
> Sus padres mandan que él vaya a la escuela.

1. Ernesto no dice la verdad. (su madre/insistir en)

2. Los niños no sacan la basura. (sus padres/mandar)

3. Tú haces una fiesta pero yo no puedo venir. (tú/lamentar)

4. Estamos en un restaurante y mi amigo no escoge una comida saludable. (yo/recomendar)

5. Julio no hace sus tareas de español. (su amigo/aconsejarle de)

Worked Solutions

1. **Su madre insiste en que él diga la verdad.**   To conjugate the regular *-ir* verb *insistir*, drop the *-ir* ending and add *-e* for the subject, *su madre (ella)*. Add *que* to join the two clauses. *Decir* is a verb that is irregular in its present tense *yo* form. To form the subjunctive, take the *yo* form (*digo*), drop the *-o*, and add *-a* as the ending for *él*.

2. **Sus padres mandan que ellos saquen la basura.**   To conjugate the regular *-ar* verb *mandar*, drop the *-ar* ending and add *-an* for the subject, *sus padres (ellos)*. Add *que* to join the two clauses. *Sacar* is a spelling-change verb that is irregular in its preterit tense *yo* form: *-c* changes to *-qu*. To form the subjunctive, take the *yo* form (*saqué*), drop the *-é*, and add *-en* as the subjunctive ending for *ellos*.

3. **Tú lamentas que yo no pueda venir.**   To conjugate the regular *-ar* verb *lamentar*, drop the *-ar* ending and add *-as* for the subject, *tú*. Add *que* to join the two clauses. *Poder* is a stem-changing verb that has an internal change from *-o* to *-ue* in the *yo* form of the present. To form the subjunctive, take the *yo* form (*puedo*), drop the *-o*, and add *-a* as the subjunctive ending for *yo*.

4. **Yo recomiendo que él escoja una comida saludable.**   *Recomendar* is a stem-changing verb that has an internal change from *-e* to *-ie* in the *yo* form of the present. Add *que* to join the two clauses. *Escoger* is a spelling-change *-ger* verb that is irregular in its present tense *yo* form: *-g* changes to *-j*. To form the subjunctive, take the *yo* form (*escojo*), drop the *-o*, and add *-a* as the subjunctive ending for *él*.

5. **Su amigo le aconseja de que él haga sus tareas de español.**   To conjugate the regular *-ar* verb *aconsejar*, drop the *-ar* ending and add *-a* for the subject, *su amigo (él)*. Add *que* to join to the two clauses. *Hacer* is a verb that is irregular in its present tense *yo* form. To form the subjunctive, take the *yo* form (*hago*), drop the *-o*, and add *-a* as the ending for *él*.

Chapter Problems and Solutions

Problems

Complete the story by filling in the correct form of the verb in the indicative, the subjunctive, or the infinitive.

Es la Navidad y los señores Moreno preparan una comida muy deliciosa. Es cierto que

(ser) _____ una fiesta magnífica. Todos los miembros de la familia tienen que (ayudar)
$\quad\quad$ 1

_____ a la madre. El señor Moreno le aconseja a su esposa de que (empezar) _____ a
$\quad$ 2 $\quad\quad\quad\quad\quad\quad\quad\quad\quad\quad\quad\quad\quad\quad\quad\quad\quad\quad\quad\quad$ 3

hacer planes con dos días de antelación. Es una buena idea porque hay mucho que

(hacer) _____. Es necesario que la señora Moreno (ir) _____ de compras y es dudoso
$\quad\quad$ 4 $\quad\quad\quad\quad\quad\quad\quad\quad\quad\quad\quad\quad\quad$ 5

que ella (poder) _____ comprar todos los comestibles en una sola tienda. Además, su
$\quad\quad\quad\quad\quad$ 6

esposo insiste en que ella (buscar) _____ todo en rebaja. Por eso, la señora Moreno
$\quad\quad\quad\quad\quad\quad\quad\quad$ 7

recomienda que él la (acompañar) _____. Él prefiere (quedar) _____ en casa pero su
$\quad\quad\quad\quad\quad\quad\quad\quad\quad$ 8 $\quad\quad\quad\quad\quad\quad\quad\quad\quad$ 9

esposa le exige que él la (conducir) _____ al centro. Es injusto que él (descansar)
$\quad\quad\quad\quad\quad\quad\quad\quad\quad\quad$ 10

_____ cuando ella tiene tantas cosas que hacer. Más vale que el señor Moreno (decir)
$\quad$ 11

_____ "sí" y que no (quejarse) _____.
$\quad$ 12 $\quad\quad\quad\quad\quad\quad\quad\quad$ 13

Answers and Solutions

1. **Answer: será.** The expression *es cierto que* takes the indicative because it shows certainty. The future is implied, so use the infinitive of the verb *ser* and add the future ending *-á* for *la fiesta*.

2. **Answer: ayudar.** The expression *tener que* takes the infinitive despite the fact that it shows necessity. Thus, *ayudar* remains in its infinitive form.

3. **Answer: empiece.** The verb *aconsejar* takes the subjunctive because it expresses advice. *Empezar* is a spelling-change verb that is irregular in its preterit tense *yo* form: *-z* changes to *-c*. Additionally, *empezar* is a stem-changing verb that has an internal change from *-e* to *-ie* in the *yo* form of the present. To form the subjunctive, take the *yo* form (*empiezo*), change *-z* to *-c*, and add *-e* as the subjunctive ending for *su esposa (ella)*.

4. **Answer: hacer.** The expression *hay . . . que* takes the infinitive despite the fact that it shows necessity. Thus, *hacer* remains in its infinitive form.

5. **Answer: vaya.** The expression *es necesario que* takes the subjunctive because it shows need. *Ir* has an irregular subjunctive stem (*vay-*), which must be memorized. Add *-a* as the subjunctive ending for *la señora Moreno (ella)*.

6. **Answer: pueda.** The expression *es dudoso que* takes the subjunctive because it shows doubt. *Poder* is a stem-changing verb that has an internal change from *-o* to *-ue* in the *yo* form of the present. To form the subjunctive, take the *yo* form (*puedo*), drop the *-o,* and add *-a* as the subjunctive ending for *ella*.

7. **Answer: busque.** The verb *insistir* takes the subjunctive because it shows demand. *Buscar* is a spelling-change verb that is irregular in its preterit tense *yo* form: *-c* changes to *-qu*. To form the subjunctive, take the *yo* form (*busqué*), drop the *-é*, and add *-e* as the subjunctive ending for *ella*.

8. **Answer: acompañe.** The verb *recomendar* takes the subjunctive because it shows a request. To conjugate regular *-ar* verbs in the present subjunctive, drop the *-ar* ending and add *-e* as the ending for *él*.

9. **Answer: quedarse.** The verb *preferir* takes the infinitive in this case because there is only one clause. Thus, the verb *quedarse* remains in its infinitive form.

10. **Answer: conduzca.** The verb *exigir* takes the subjunctive because it shows demand. *Conducir* is a spelling-change "vowel + *-cir*" verb that is irregular in its present tense *yo* form: *-c* changes to *-zc*. To form the subjunctive, take the *yo* form (*conduzco*), drop the *-o*, and add *-a* as the subjunctive ending for *él*.

11. **Answer: descanse.** The expression *es injusto que* takes the subjunctive because it shows an opinion. To conjugate regular *-ar* verbs in the present subjunctive, drop the *-ar* ending and add *-e* as the ending for *él*.

12. **Answer: diga.** The expression *es increíble que* takes the subjunctive because it shows doubt. *Decir* is a verb that is irregular in its present tense *yo* form. To form the subjunctive, take the *yo* form (*digo*), drop the *-o*, and add *-a* as the ending for *el señor Moreno (él)*.

13. **Answer: se queje.** The expression *es asombroso que* takes the subjunctive because it shows emotion. To conjugate regular *-ar* verbs in the present subjunctive, drop the *-ar* ending and add *-e* as the ending for *él*. The *-se* ending indicates that the verb *quejarse* is reflexive. Place the reflexive pronoun *se*, which agrees with the subject, before the conjugated verb.

Supplemental Chapter Problems

Complete the story by filling in the correct form of the verb in parentheses.

Es probable que hoy (ser) _____ un día horrible para Teresa. Es imperativo que ella

(despertarse) _____ temprano. Ella tiene que (vestirse) _____ rápidamente. Es malo

que ella no (comer) _____ nada antes de partir. Es urgente que ella (ir) _____ al

consultorio de su doctor. Es esencial que ella (hacerse) _____ examinar la garganta. Es

evidente que ella (estar) _____ enferma pero es dudoso que ella (tener) _____ fiebre.

Es urgente que ella (llegar) _____ a su trabajo hoy. Es lamentable que ella no (sentirse)

_____ bien porque su jefe quiere que ella (venir) _____ a la oficina temprano. Él insiste

en que ella (explicar) _____ ciertas reglas a los otros empleados y que ella (comenzar)

_____ un proyecto bastante importante.

Answers

1. sea (the subjunctive after expressions of doubt, p. 319; the present of irregular verbs, p. 100)

2. se despierte (the subjunctive after expressions of need, p. 319; the subjunctive of stem-changing verbs, p. 316)

3. vestirse (the uses of the subjunctive, p. 318)

4. coma (the subjunctive after expressions of emotion, p. 319; the subjunctive of regular -er verbs, p. 309)

5. vaya (the subjunctive after expressions of need, p. 319; the subjunctive of irregular verbs, p. 317)

6. se haga (the subjunctive after expressions of need, p. 319; the subjunctive of irregular verbs, p. 317)

7. está (the subjunctive after expressions of doubt, p. 319; the present of irregular verbs, p. 100)

8. tenga (the subjunctive after expressions of doubt, p. 319; the subjunctive of irregular verbs, p. 317)

9. llegue (the subjunctive after expressions of need, p. 319; the subjunctive of spelling-change verbs, p. 314)

10. se sienta (the subjunctive after expressions of emotion, p. 319; the subjunctive of stem-changing verbs, p. 316)

11. venga (the subjunctive after verbs of wanting, p. 321; the subjunctive of irregular verbs, p. 317)

12. explique (the subjunctive after verbs of need, p. 321; the subjunctive of spelling-change verbs, p. 314)

13. comience (the subjunctive after verbs of need, p. 321; the subjunctive of stem-changing verbs, p. 316; the subjunctive of spelling-change verbs, p. 314)

Chapter 18
The Imperative

The imperative is a mood used to give a command. Just as in English, the subject of most commands is understood to be "you." There are four ways to express "you" in Spanish, depending on whether the speaker is being formal (polite) or informal (familiar) or whether the speaker is addressing one or more than one person.

	Singular	**Plural**
Informal (Familiar)	tú	vosotros
Formal (Polite)	usted (Ud.)	(ustedes) Uds.

Formal Commands

A speaker addresses formal, or polite, commands to people who are older or who are unfamiliar to the speaker. The subject of the command is *Ud.* (if one person is being addressed) or *Uds.* (if more than one person is being addressed.)

In Spanish, the use of the subject pronoun in the command is optional. When the subject pronoun is not used, the verb form being used identifies the subject.

Regular Verbs

To form an affirmative or a negative command with any verb when *Ud.* or *Uds.* is the subject, use the present subjunctive of the *Ud.* or *Uds.* form of that verb. To form the present subjunctive:

1. Drop the final *-o* from the *yo* form of the present tense.

2. For infinitives ending in *-ar*, add *-e* for *Ud.* and *-en* for *Uds.* For infinitives ending in *-er* or *-ir*, add *-a* for *Ud.* and *-an* for *Uds.*

Infinitive	*Affirmative*	*Negative*	*Meaning*
-ar: escuchar (to listen)	escuche(n) (Ud.)(s)	no escuche(n) (Ud.)(s)	(don't) listen
-er: beber (to drink)	beba(n) (Ud.)(s)	no beba(n) (Ud.)(s)	(don't) drink
-ir: abrir (to open)	abra(n) (Ud.)(s)	no abra(n) (Ud.)(s)	(don't) open

An inverted exclamation mark (¡) may be placed at the beginning of an emphasized command with a regular exclamation mark (!) placed at the end:

¡Abra la puerta!	Open the door!
¡No hablen (Uds.)!	Don't talk!

Example Problems

Express what a tutor asks her adult student to do.

1. Please open your book.

   Answer: Abra (Ud.) su libro, por favor.

   To form a command with *Ud.*, use the present subjunctive of the verb. To form the present subjunctive for regular -*ir* verbs, drop the final -*o* from the *yo* form of the present tense and add -*a*. Use the singular possessive adjective *su* to express "your" before the singular noun *libro* that expresses "book." Use *por favor* to express "please."

2. Please don't speak English.

   Answer: No hable (Ud.) inglés, por favor.

   To form a command with *Ud.*, use the present subjunctive of the verb. To form the present subjunctive for regular -*ar* verbs, drop the final -*o* from the *yo* form of the present tense and add -*e*. To negate the command, put *no* before the conjugated verb. Use *inglés* to express "English." Use *por favor* to express "please."

3. Please learn the rules.

   Answer: Aprenda (Ud.) las reglas, por favor.

   To form a command with *Ud.*, use the present subjunctive of the verb. To form the present subjunctive for regular -*er* verbs, drop the final -*o* from the *yo* form of the present tense and add -*a*. Use the plural definite article *las* to express "the" before the plural noun *reglas* that expresses "rules." Use *por favor* to express "please."

Work Problems

Express what a counselor says to children at camp.

1. Eat your vegetables.

2. Write to your parents.

3. Don't talk.

4. Don't open the windows.

5. Listen.

6. Don't drink too much soda.

Worked Solutions

1. **Coman (Uds.) sus legumbres.**   To form a command with *Uds.*, use the present subjunctive of the verb. To form the present subjunctive for regular -*er* verbs, drop the final -*o* from the *yo* form of the present tense and add -*an*. Use the plural possessive adjective *sus* to express "your" before the plural noun *legumbres*, which expresses "vegetables."

2. **Escriban (Uds.) a sus padres.** To form a command with *Uds.*, use the present subjunctive of the verb. To form the present subjunctive for regular *-ir* verbs, drop the final *-o* from the *yo* form of the present tense and add *-an*. Use the personal *a*, which refers to people, before the direct object *sus padres*. Use the plural possessive adjective *sus* to express "your" before the plural noun *padres*, which expresses "parents."

3. **No hablen (Uds.).** To form a command with *Uds.*, use the present subjunctive of the verb. To form the present subjunctive for regular *-ar* verbs, drop the final *-o* from the *yo* form of the present tense and add *-en*. To negate the command, put *no* before the conjugated verb.

4. **No abran (Uds.) las ventanas.** To form a command with *Uds.*, use the present subjunctive of the verb. To form the present subjunctive for regular *-ir* verbs, drop the final *-o* from the *yo* form of the present tense and add *-an*. To negate the command, put *no* before the conjugated verb. Use the definite article *las* to express "the" before the plural noun *ventanas*, which expresses "windows."

5. **Escuchen (Uds.).** To form a command with *Uds.*, use the present subjunctive of the verb. To form the present subjunctive for regular *-ar* verbs, drop the final *-o* from the *yo* form of the present tense and add *-e*.

6. **No beban (Uds.) demasiados refrescos.** To form a command with *Uds.*, use the present subjunctive of the verb. To form the present subjunctive for regular *-er* verbs, drop the final *-o* from the *yo* form of the present tense and add *-an*. To negate the command, put *no* before the conjugated verb. Use the plural adjective *demasiados* to express "too many" before the plural noun *refrescos*, which expresses "soft drinks."

Spelling-Change, Stem-Changing, and Irregular Verbs

Most spelling-change, all stem-changing, and all verbs with irregular *yo* forms form the affirmative and negative imperative by using the present subjunctive of the *Ud.* or *Uds.* form of that verb. Exceptions to this rule include spelling-change verbs that end in *-car*, *-gar*, or *-zar*. For these verbs only, the present subjunctive is formed by dropping the final *-é* from the *yo* form of the preterit tense and adding *-e* for *Ud.* and *-en for Uds.*

¡Saquen los libros!	Take out your books!
¡Apague la luz!	Turn off the light!
¡No cruce la calle!	Don't cross the street!

Formal Commands for Verbs with Irregular *Yo* Forms			
Infinitive	*Affirmative*	*Negative*	*Meaning*
decir	diga(n) (Ud.)(s)	no diga(n) (Ud.)(s)	(don't) tell
hacer	haga(n) (Ud.)(s)	no haga(n) (Ud.)(s)	(don't) do
oír	oiga(n) (Ud.)(s)	no oiga(n) (Ud.)(s)	(don't) hear
poner	ponga(n) (Ud.)(s)	no ponga(n) (Ud.)(s)	(don't) put
salir	salga(n) (Ud.)(s)	no salga(n) (Ud.)(s)	(don't) leave

(continued)

Formal Commands for Verbs with Irregular *Yo* Forms *(continued)*

Infinitive	Affirmative	Negative	Meaning
tener	tenga(n) (Ud.)(s)	no tenga(n) (Ud.)(s)	(don't) have (don't) be
traer	traiga(n) (Ud.)(s)	no traiga(n) (Ud.)(s)	(don't) bring
valer	valga(n) (Ud.)(s)	no valga(n) (Ud.)(s)	(don't) be worth
venir	venga(n) (Ud.)(s)	no venga(n) (Ud.)(s)	(don't) come

Formal Commands for Spelling-Change Verbs

Infinitive	Affirmative	Negative	Meaning
tocar	toque(n) (Ud.)(s)	no toque(n) (Ud.)(s)	(don't) touch
pagar	pague(n) (Ud.)(s)	no pague(n) (Ud.)(s)	(don't) pay
lanzar	lance(n) (Ud.)(s)	no lance(n) (Ud.)(s)	(don't) throw
convencer	convenza(n) (Ud.)(s)	no convenza(n) (Ud.)(s)	(don't) convince
ofrecer	ofrezca(n) (Ud.)(s)	no ofrezca(n) (Ud.)(s)	(don't) offer
esparcir	esparza(n) (Ud.)(s)	no esparza(n) (Ud.)(s)	(don't) spread
traducir	traduzca(n) (Ud.)(s)	no traduzca(n) (Ud.)(s)	(don't) translate
coger	coja(n) (Ud.)(s)	no coja(n) (Ud.)(s)	(don't) seize
exigir	exija(n) (Ud.)(s)	no exija(n) (Ud.)(s)	(don't) demand
distinguir	distinga(n) (Ud.)(s)	no distinga(n) (Ud.)(s)	(don't) distinguish

Formal Commands for Stem-Changing Verbs

Infinitive	Affirmative	Negative	Meaning
pensar	piense(n) (Ud.)(s)	no piense(n) (Ud.)(s)	(don't) think
contar	cuente(n) (Ud.)(s)	no cuente(n) (Ud.)(s)	(don't) count
defender	defienda(n) (Ud.)(s)	no defienda(n) (Ud.)(s)	(don't) defend
volver	vuelva(n) (Ud.)(s)	no vuelva(n) (Ud.)(s)	(don't) return
mentir	mienta(n) (Ud.)(s)	no mienta(n) (Ud.)(s)	(don't) lie
dormir	duerma(n) (Ud.)(s)	no duerma(n) (Ud.)(s)	(don't) sleep
repetir	repita(n) (Ud.)(s)	no repita(n) (Ud.)(s)	(don't) repeat
enviar	envíe(n) (Ud.)(s)	no envíe(n) (Ud.)(s)	(don't) send
continuar	continúe(n) (Ud.)(s)	no continúe(n) (Ud.)(s)	(don't) continue
sustituir	sustituya(n) (Ud.)(s)	no sustituya(n) (Ud.)(s)	(don't) substitute

Formal Commands for Irregular Verbs			
Infinitive	**Affirmative**	**Negative**	**Meaning**
dar	dé (den) (Ud.)(s)	no dé (den) (Ud.)(s)	(don't) give
estar	esté(n) (Ud.)(s)	no esté(n) (Ud.)(s)	(don't) be
ir	vaya(n) (Ud.)(s)	no vaya(n) (Ud.)(s)	(don't) go
saber	sepa(n) (Ud.)(s)	no sepa(n) (Ud.)(s)	(don't) know
ser	sea(n) (Ud.)(s)	no sea(n) (Ud.)(s)	(don't) be

Here are two examples:

¡(No) Toque(n) eso!   (Don't) touch that!

¡(No) Vuelva(n) tarde!   (Don't) return late!

Example Problems

Express the rules of a museum.

Example: no poner nada en las estatuas

No ponga nada en las estatuas.

1. no sacar fotografías

   Answer: No saque (Ud.) fotografías.

   To form a command with *Ud.*, use the present subjunctive of the verb. To form the present subjunctive for the spelling-change verb *sacar*, drop the final *-é* from the *yo* form of the preterit tense *(saqué)* and add *-e*. To negate the command, put *no* before the conjugated verb. Use *fotografías* to express "photographs."

2. ir solamente a las salas abiertas

   Answer: Vaya (Ud.) solamente a las salas abiertas.

   To form a command with *Ud.*, use the present subjunctive of the verb. To form the present subjunctive for the irregular verb *ir*, use the irregular subjunctive stem *vay-* and add *-a*. Use *solamente* to express "only." Use the preposition *a* to express "go to." Use the plural definite article *las* to express "the." Use *salas* to express "rooms." Use the feminine plural adjective *abiertas*, which agrees with the feminine plural noun *salas*, to express "open."

3. traer comida al museo

   Answer: No traiga (Ud.) comida al museo.

   To form a command with *Ud.*, use the present subjunctive of the verb. To form the present subjunctive for the irregular verb *traer*, drop the final *-o* from the *yo* form of the present tense *(traigo)* and add *-a*. To negate the command, put *no* before the conjugated verb. Use *al museo* to express "into the museum."

Work Problems

Express the advice a traveler needs.

　　　Example: dormir en el avión
　　　　　　　Duerma (Ud.) en el avión.

1. pagar con una tarjeta de crédito

2. no volver a su hotel tarde

3. no traer mucho dinero

4. siempre tener cuidado

5. no ser impaciente

6. dar una propina a su guía

7. no salir solo

8. saber el número de teléfono de su hotel

9. no perder su billete de avión

10. seguir las instrucciones de su guía

Worked Solutions

1. **Pague (Ud.) con una tarjeta de crédito.**　To form a command with *Ud.*, use the present subjunctive of the verb. To form the present subjunctive for the spelling-change verb *pagar*, drop the final *-é* from the *yo* form of the preterit tense *(pagué)* and add *-e*.

2. **No vuelva (Ud.) a su hotel tarde.**　To form a command with *Ud.*, use the present subjunctive of the verb. The present tense of the stem-changing verb *volver* changes the internal *o* to *ue*. To form the present subjunctive for volver, drop the final *-o* from the *yo* form of the present tense *(vuelvo)* and add *-a*. To negate the command, put *no* before the conjugated verb.

3. **No traiga (Ud.) mucho dinero.**　To form a command with *Ud.*, use the present subjunctive of the verb. To form the present subjunctive for the irregular verb *traer*, drop the final *-o* from the *yo* form of the present tense *(traigo)* and add *-a*. To negate the command, put *no* before the conjugated verb.

4. **Siempre tenga (Ud.) cuidado.**　To form a command with *Ud.*, use the present subjunctive of the verb. To form the present subjunctive for the irregular verb *tener*, drop the final *-o* from the *yo* form of the present tense *(tengo)* and add *-a*.

5. **No sea (Ud.) impaciente.**　To form a command with *Ud.*, use the present subjunctive of the verb. To form the present subjunctive for the irregular verb *ser*, use the irregular subjunctive stem *se-* and add *-a*.

6. **Dé (Ud.) una propina a su guía.**   To form a command with *Ud.*, use the present subjunctive of the verb. The present subjunctive for the verb *dar* is irregular and must be memorized. Note that the *Ud.* form has an accented *-é*.

7. **No salga (Ud.) solo.**   To form a command with *Ud.*, use the present subjunctive of the verb. To form the present subjunctive for the irregular verb *salir*, drop the final *-o* from the *yo* form of the present tense *(salgo)* and add *-a*. To negate the command, put *no* before the conjugated verb.

8. **Sepa (Ud.) el número de teléfono de su hotel.**   To form a command with *Ud.*, use the present subjunctive of the verb. To form the present subjunctive for the irregular verb *saber*, use the irregular subjunctive stem *(sep-)* and add *-a*.

9. **No pierda (Ud.) su billete de avión.**   To form a command with *Ud.*, use the present subjunctive of the verb. The present tense of the stem-changing verb *perder* changes the internal *e* to *ie*. To form the present subjunctive for *perder*, drop the final -o from the *yo* form of the present tense *(pierdo)* and add *-a*. To negate the command, put *no* before the conjugated verb.

10. **Siga (Ud.) las instrucciones de su guía.**   To form a command with *Ud.*, use the present subjunctive of the verb. The present tense of the stem-changing verb *seguir* changes the internal *e* to *i*. Additionally, the *gu* changes to *g* in the *yo* form of the present tense. To form the present subjunctive for *seguir*, drop the final -o from the *yo* form of the present tense *(sigo)* and add *-a*.

Informal Commands

A speaker addresses informal, or familiar, commands to friends, peers, family members, or pets. The subject of the command is *tú* (if one person is being addressed) or *vosotros* (if more than one person is being addressed). Note that the *vosotros* command is used primarily in Spain. In Latin American countries, the *Uds.* form is used for plural informal commands.

Singular Informal Commands with *Tú*

To form an affirmative command with any verb when *tú* is the subject, use the *tú* form of the present indicative without the final *-s* (the result of which is the equivalent of the *él* form of the present indicative). A few irregular verbs have irregular familiar affirmative command forms and must be memorized.

To form a negative command with any verb when *tú* is the subject, use the present subjunctive *tú* form. To form the present subjunctive:

1. Drop the final *-o* from the *yo* form of the present tense.

2. For infinitives ending in *-ar*, add *-es* for the *tú* form. For infinitives ending in *-er* or *-ir*, add *-as* for the *tú* form.

Singular Informal Commands for Regular Verbs			
Infinitive	*Affirmative*	*Negative*	*Meaning*
escuchar	escucha (tú)	no escuches (tú)	(don't) listen
beber	bebe (tú)	no bebas (tú)	(don't) drink
abrir	abre (tú)	no abras (tú)	(don't) open

Singular Informal Commands for Verbs with Irregular *Yo* Forms

Infinitive	Affirmative	Negative	Meaning
oír	oye (tú)	no oigas (tú)	(don't) hear
traer	trae (tú)	no traigas (tú)	(don't) bring

Singular Informal Commands for Spelling-Change Verbs

Infinitive	Affirmative	Negative	Meaning
tocar	toca (tú)	no toques (tú)	(don't) touch
pagar	paga (tú)	no pagues (tú)	(don't) pay
lanzar	lanza (tú)	no lances (tú)	(don't) throw
convencer	convence (tú)	no convenzas (tú)	(don't) convince
ofrecer	ofrece (tú)	no ofrezcas (tú)	(don't) offer
esparcir	esparce (tú)	no esparzas (tú)	(don't) spread
traducir	traduce (tú)	no traduzcas (tú)	(don't) translate
coger	coge (tú)	no cojas (tú)	(don't) seize
exigir	exige (tú)	no exijas (tú)	(don't) demand
distinguir	distingue (tú)	no distingas (tú)	(don't) distinguish

Singular Informal Commands for Stem-Changing Verbs

Infinitive	Affirmative	Negative	Meaning
pensar	piensa (tú)	no pienses (tú)	(don't) think
contar	cuenta (tú)	no cuentes (tú)	(don't) count
defender	defiende (tú)	no defiendas (tú)	(don't) defend
volver	vuelve (tú)	no vuelvas (tú)	(don't) return
mentir	miente (tú)	no mientas (tú)	(don't) lie
dormir	duerme (tú)	no duermas (tú)	(don't) sleep
repetir	repite (tú)	no repitas (tú)	(don't) repeat
enviar	envía (tú)	no envíes (tú)	(don't) send
continuar	continúa (tú)	no continúes (tú)	(don't) continue
sustituir	sustituye (tú)	no sustituyas (tú)	(don't) substitute

Singular Informal Commands for Irregular Verbs			
Infinitive	*Affirmative*	*Negative*	*Meaning*
decir	di (tú)	no digas (tú)	(don't) tell
hacer	haz (tú)	no hagas (tú)	(don't) do
ir	ve (tú)	no vayas (tú)	(don't) go
poner	pon (tú)	no pongas (tú)	(don't) put
salir	sal (tú)	no salgas (tú)	(don't) leave
ser	sé (tú)	no seas (tú)	(don't) be
tener	ten (tú)	no tengas (tú)	(don't) have, (don't) be
valer	val *or* vale (tú)	no valgas (tú)	(don't) be worth
venir	ven (tú)	no vengas (tú)	(don't) come

Here are two examples, using both affirmative and negative commands. Note that *tú* is generally not used when issuing a familiar command.

¡Repite la frase!   ¡No repitas la frase!   (Don't) repeat the sentence!

¡Sal!   ¡No salgas!   (Don't) go out!

Example Problems

Express the advice that one friend gives another.

Example: no tocar el piano/tocar la guitarra

No toques el piano, toca la guitarra.

1. no contar secretos/contar chistes

    Answer: No cuentes secretos, cuenta chistes.

    To form a negative command with *tú*, use the present subjunctive *tú* form. To form the present subjunctive for the stem-changing verb *contar*, change the internal *o* to *ue* (the same change made for the present indicative *yo* form). Drop the final *-ar* infinitive ending and add the present subjunctive ending for *tú (-es)*. To negate the command, put *no* before the conjugated verb. To form an affirmative command with *tú*, drop the final *-s* from the second person singular present indicative form of *tú (cuentas)*.

2. pagar con líquido/no pagar con una tarjeta de crédito

    Answer: Paga con líquido, no pagues con una tarjeta de crédito.

    To form an affirmative command with *tú*, drop the final *-s* from the second person singular present indicative form of *tú (pagas)*. To form a negative command with *tú*, use the present subjunctive *tú* form. To form the present subjunctive for the spelling-change verb *pagar*, change *g* to *gu* (the same change made for the preterit indicative *yo* form).

Drop the final *-ar* infinitive ending and add the present subjunctive ending for *tú (-es)*. To negate the command, put *no* before the conjugated verb.

3. no ofrecer consejos a tus amigos/ofrecer consejos a tu familia

   Answer: No ofrezcas consejos a tus amigos, ofrece consejos a tu familia.

   To form a negative command with *tú*, use the present subjunctive *tú* form. To form the present subjunctive for the spelling-change verb *ofrecer*, change the *c* to *zc* (the same change made for the present indicative *yo* form). Drop the final *-er* infinitive ending and add the present subjunctive ending for *tú (-as)*. To negate the command, put *no* before the conjugated verb. To form an affirmative command with *tú*, drop the final *-s* from the second person singular present indicative form of *tú (ofreces)*.

Work Problems

Express the advice you give to a friend.

   Example: obedecer a tus padres/no obedecer a tus amigos
   Obedece a tus padres, no obedezcas a tus amigos.

1. poner dinero en el banco/no poner dinero en tu cuarto

2. no tener prisa/tener cuidado

3. no ser tonto/ser inteligente

4. venir temprano/no venir tarde

5. hacer lo bueno/no hacer lo malo

6. no decir mentiras/decir la verdad

7. volver a casa antes de la medianoche/no volver después de la medianoche

8. no exigir mucho de tus amigos/exigir poco

Worked Solutions

1. **Pon dinero en el banco, no pongas dinero en tu cuarto.** The informal affirmative command form of *poner* is irregular and must be memorized: *pon*. To form a negative command with *tú*, use the present subjunctive *tú* form. Take the irregular *yo* form of the present tense *(pongo)*. Drop the *-o* and add the *tú* form subjunctive ending *(-as)*. To negate the command, put *no* before the conjugated verb.

2. **No tengas prisa, ten cuidado.** To form a negative command with *tú*, use the present subjunctive *tú* form. Take the irregular *yo* form of the present tense *(tengo)*. Drop the *-o* and add the *tú* form subjunctive ending *(-as)*. To negate the command, put *no* before the conjugated verb. The informal affirmative command form of *tener* is irregular and must be memorized: *ten*.

3. **No seas tonto, sé inteligente.**   To form a negative command with *tú*, use the present subjunctive *tú* form. Take the irregular *stem* of the subjunctive *(se-)*. Add the *tú* form subjunctive ending *(-as)*. To negate the command, put *no* before the conjugated verb. The informal affirmative command form of *ser* is irregular and must be memorized: *sé.*

4. **Ven temprano, no vengas tarde.**   The informal affirmative command form of *venir* is irregular and must be memorized: *ven.* To form a negative command with *tú*, use the present subjunctive *tú* form. Take the irregular *yo* form of the present tense *(vengo)*. Drop the *-o* and add the *tú* form subjunctive ending *(-as)*. To negate the command, put *no* before the conjugated verb.

5. **Haz lo bueno, no hagas lo malo.**   The informal affirmative command form of *hacer* is irregular and must be memorized: *haz.* To form a negative command with *tú*, use the present subjunctive *tú* form. Take the irregular *yo* form of the present tense *(hago)*. Drop the *-o* and add the *tú* form subjunctive ending *(-as)*. To negate the command, put *no* before the conjugated verb.

6. **No digas mentiras, di la verdad.**   To form a negative command with *tú*, use the present subjunctive *tú* form. Take the irregular *yo* form of the present tense *(digo)*. Drop the *-o* and add the *tú* form subjunctive ending *(-as)*. To negate the command, put *no* before the conjugated verb. The informal affirmative command form of *decir* is irregular and must be memorized: *di.*

7. **Vuelve a casa antes de la medianoche, no vuelvas después de la medianoche.**   To form an affirmative command with *tú*, drop the final *-s* from the second person singular present indicative form of *tú (vuelves)*. To form a negative command with *tú*, use the present subjunctive *tú* form. To form the present subjunctive for the stem-changing verb *volver*, change the internal *o* to *ue* (the same change made for the present indicative *yo* form). Drop the final *-er* infinitive ending and add the present subjunctive ending for *tú (-as)*. To negate the command, put *no* before the conjugated verb.

8. **No exijas mucho de tus amigos, exige poco.**   To form a negative command with *tú*, use the present subjunctive *tú* form. To form the present subjunctive for the spelling-change verb *exigir*, change the *g* to *j* (the same change made for the present indicative *yo* form). Drop the final *-ir* infinitive ending and add the present subjunctive ending for *tú (-as)*. To negate the command, put *no* before the conjugated verb. To form an affirmative command with *tú*, drop the final *-s* from the second person singular present indicative form of *tú (exiges)*.

Plural Informal Commands with *Vosotros (Vosotras)*

To form an affirmative command with any verb when *vosotros* is the subject, drop the final *-r* of the infinitive and add *-d.*

To form a negative command with any verb when *vosotros* is the subject, use the present subjunctive *vosotros* form. To form the present subjunctive:

1. Drop the final *-o* from the *yo* form of the present tense.

2. For infinitives ending in *-ar*, add *-éis* for the *vosotros* form. For infinitives ending in *-er* or *-ir*, add *-áis* for the *vosotros* form.

The tables that follow illustrate how this is done:

Plural Informal Commands for Regular Verbs			
Infinitive	*Affirmative*	*Negative*	*Meaning*
escuchar	escuchad (vosotros)	no escuchéis (vosotros)	(don't) listen
beber	bebed (vosotros)	no bebáis (vosotros)	(don't) drink
abrir	abrid (vosotros)	no abráis (vosotros)	(don't) open

Plural Informal Commands for Verbs with Irregular *Yo* Forms			
Infinitive	*Affirmative*	*Negative*	*Meaning*
oír	oíd	no oigáis	(don't) hear
traer	traed	no traigáis	(don't) bring

Plural Informal Commands for Spelling-Change Verbs			
Infinitive	*Affirmative*	*Negative*	*Meaning*
tocar	tocad	no toquéis	(don't) touch
pagar	pagad	no paguéis	(don't) pay
lanzar	lanzad	no lancéis	(don't) throw
convencer	convenced	no convenzáis	(don't) convince
ofrecer	ofreced	no ofrezcáis	(don't) offer
esparcir	esparcid	no esparzáis	(don't) spread
traducir	traducid	no traduzcáis	(don't) translate
coger	coged	no cojáis	(don't) seize
exigir	exigid	no exijáis	(don't) demand
distinguir	distinguid	no distingáis	(don't) distinguish

Plural Informal Commands for Stem-Changing Verbs			
Infinitive	*Affirmative*	*Negative*	*Meaning*
pensar	pensad	no penséis	(don't) think
contar	contad	no contéis	(don't) count
defender	defended	no defendáis	(don't) defend
volver	volved	no volváis	(don't) return
mentir	mentid	no mintáis	(don't) lie
dormir	dormid	no durmáis	(don't) sleep
repetir	repetid	no repitáis	(don't) repeat

Infinitive	Affirmative	Negative	Meaning
enviar	enviad	no enviéis	(don't) send
continuar	continuad	no continuéis	(don't) continue
sustituir	sustituid	no sustituyáis	(don't) substitute

Plural Informal Commands for Irregular Verbs			
Infinitive	Affirmative	Negative	Meaning
decir	decid	no digáis	(don't) tell
hacer	haced	no hagáis	(don't) do
ir	id	no vayáis	(don't) go
poner	poned	no pongáis	(don't) put
salir	salid	no salgáis	(don't) leave
ser	sed	no seáis	(don't) be
tener	tened	no tengáis	(don't) have (don't) be
valer	valed	no valgáis	(don't) be worth
venir	venid	no vengáis	(don't) come

Here are two examples, using both affirmative and negative commands:

¡Continuad leyendo!	¡No continuéis leyendo!	(Don't) Continue reading!
¡Venid conmigo!	¡No vengáis conmigo!	(Don't) Come with me!

Example Problems

A person is lost with some friends. Express what is said.

Examples: decir dónde estamos
Decid dónde estamos.

no perder paciencia
No perdáis paciencia.

1. traducir esta señal

   Answer: Traducid esta señal.

   To form an affirmative command with *vosotros*, drop the final *-r* from the infinitive and add *-d*.

2. no dejarme solo

   Answer: No me dejéis solo.

   To form a negative command with *vosotros*, use the present subjunctive *vosotros* form. To form the present subjunctive, drop the final *-o* from the *yo* form of the present tense and, for infinitives ending in *-ar*, add *-éis*.

3. buscar un agente

Answer: Buscad un agente.

To form an affirmative command with *vosotros*, drop the final *-r* from the infinitive and add *-d*.

Work Problems

Some friends are going to the country. Tell them what to do and what not to do there.

Examples: correr por el campo   no montar a caballo
           Corred por el campo.   No montéis a caballo.

1. jugar al fútbol

2. dar un paseo

3. no ir al bosque

4. no tocar las plantas exóticas

5. almorzar al aire libre

6. no seguir caminos peligrosos

Worked Solutions

1. **Jugad al fútbol.**   To form an affirmative command with *vosotros*, drop the final *-r* from the infinitive and add *-d*.

2. **Dad un paseo.**   To form an affirmative command with *vosotros*, drop the final *-r* from the infinitive and add *-d*.

3. **No vayáis al bosque.**   To form a negative command with *vosotros*, use the present subjunctive *vosotros* form. To form the present subjunctive of the irregular verb *ir*, use *vay-* as the subjunctive stem. This stem is irregular and must be memorized. Add the *vosotros* subjunctive ending *(-áis)*.

4. **No toquéis las plantas exóticas.**   To form a negative command with *vosotros*, use the present subjunctive *vosotros* form. To form the present subjunctive of the stem-changing verb *tocar*, drop the final *-é* from the *yo* form of the preterit, in which the *c* changes to *qu* *(toqué)*. Add the subjunctive ending for infinitives ending in *-ar (-éis)*.

5. **Almorzad al aire libre.**   To form an affirmative command with *vosotros*, drop the final *-r* from the infinitive and add *-d*.

6. **No sigáis caminos peligrosos.**   To form a negative command with *vosotros*, use the present subjunctive *vosotros* form. The present tense of the stem-changing verb *seguir* changes the internal *e* to *i*. Additionally, the *gu* changes to *g* in the *yo* form of the present tense. To form the present subjunctive for *seguir*, drop the final *-o* from the *yo* form of the present tense *(sigo)* and add the ending for *vosotros (-áis)*.

Object Pronouns with Commands

In Spanish, direct objects, indirect objects, and reflexive pronouns precede negative commands and follow and are attached to affirmative commands.

Hágalo (Ud.).	Do it.	No lo haga (Ud.).	Don't do it.
Háganlo (Uds.).	Do it.	No lo hagan (Uds.).	Don't do it.
Hazlo (tú).	Do it.	No lo hagas (tú).	Don't do it.
Hacedlo (vosotros).	Do it.	No lo hagáis (vosotros).	Don't do it

The stressed vowel normally requires an accent mark when the command form (not including any pronoun that may be attached to the end of it) has more than one syllable:

Affirmative: Dígame la verdad.	Dime la verdad.	Tell me the truth.
Despiértese.	Despiértate.	Wake up.

Note that diphthongs (two vowels that are pronounced as one sound) count as one vowel:

Sáquelo.	Sácalo.	Take it out.

Note further than when two object pronouns are attached to a multisyllabic verb, it is necessary to count back 4 vowels to add an accent:

Dígamelo.   Tell it to me.

BUT:

Negative: No me diga mentiras. No me digas mentiras. (Don't tell me lies.)

When forming the plural informal *(vosotros)* command, the final *-d* is dropped before adding *-os* for all verbs except *ir:*

lavarse	→	lavad – *d* + *os*	→	¡Lavaos!	Wash up!
sentarse	→	sentad – *d* + *os*	→	¡Sentaos!	Sit!

BUT:

irse	→	id + *os*	→	¡Idos!	Go!

When forming the plural informal *(vosotros)* command when *os* is added to an *-ir* reflexive verb, an accent mark must be added:

despedirse	→	despedid – *d* + *os*	→	¡Despedíos!	Say goodbye!

Example Problems

People are always in a hurry. Express what they should and shouldn't do.

Example: ¿Ud. va a llegar tarde? (no bañarse/ducharse)
No se bañe. Dúchese.

1. ¿Tú vas a perder el tren? (no desayunarse/apresurarse)

   Answer: No te desayunes. Apresúrate.

   To form a negative command with *tú*, use the present subjunctive *tú* form. To form the present subjunctive for regular -*ar* verbs, drop the -*ar* infinitive ending and add the present subjunctive ending for *tú* (-*es*). The -*se* attached to the infinitive indicates a reflexive verb. Use the reflexive pronoun *te*, which agrees with the subject. To negate the command, put the reflexive pronoun before the conjugated verb and put *no* before the reflexive pronoun. To form an affirmative command with *tú*, drop the final -*s* from the second person singular present indicative form of *tú* (*apresuras*). Attach the reflexive pronoun to the end of the command form. To find the stressed vowel, count back three vowels and add an accent to the *u*.

2. ¿Ud. no escuchó el despertador? (no afeitarse/cepillarse el pelo solamente)

   Answer: No se afeite. Cepíllese el pelo solamente.

   To form a negative command with *Ud.*, use the present subjunctive of the verb. To form the present subjunctive for regular -*ar* verbs, drop the final -*o* from the *yo* form of the present tense and add -*e*. The -*se* attached to the infinitive indicates a reflexive verb. Use the reflexive pronoun *se*, which agrees with the subject. To negate the command, put the reflexive pronoun before the conjugated verb and put *no* before the reflexive pronoun. To form the affirmative command for the second verb, drop the final -*o* from the *yo* form of the present tense and add -*e*. Attach the reflexive pronoun to the end of the command form. To find the stressed vowel, count back three vowels and add an accent to the *i*.

3. ¿Vosotros preferís llegar a tiempo? (no dormirse tarde/levantarse temprano)

   Answer: No os durmáis tarde. Levantaos temprano.

   To form a negative command with *vosotros*, use the present subjunctive *vosotros* form. The present subjunctive of the stem-changing verb *dormir* changes the internal *o* to *u*, reflecting the change that is made in the *vosotros* form of the present indicative. Add the *vosotros* subjunctive ending (*áis*). The -*se* attached to the infinitive indicates a reflexive verb. Use the reflexive pronoun *os*, which agrees with the subject. To negate the command, put the reflexive pronoun before the conjugated verb and put *no* before the reflexive pronoun. To form an affirmative command with *vosotros*, drop the final -*r* from the infinitive and add -*d*. The -*d* is dropped when the reflexive pronoun *os* is added and attached to the end of the command form. No accent is necessary.

Work Problems

Some people are taking a trip. Tell them what to do and what not to do.

> Example: ¿Tú vas al extranjero? (divertirse/aburrirse)
> Diviértete. No te aburras.

1. ¿Uds. hacen un viaje? (acordarse de todo/no olvidarse de nada)

2. ¿Tú tienes frío en el avión? (ponerse un abrigo/no quitarse el suéter)

3. ¿Vosotros no queréis perder el vuelo? (despertarse temprano/no acostarse tarde)

4. ¿Ud. necesita ayuda? (asegurarse de buscar un portero/no hacerse daño)

5. ¿Tú no entiendes al aeromozo? (atreverse a hablar/no callarse)

6. ¿Uds. no tienen problemas? (alegrarse/no apurarse)

Worked Solutions

1. **Acuérdense de todo. No se olviden de nada.**   To form a command with *Uds.*, use the present subjunctive of the verb. The present subjunctive of the stem-changing verb *acordar* changes the internal *o* to *ue*, reflecting the change that is made in the *yo* form of the present indicative. Add the *Uds.* subjunctive ending for *-ar* verbs *(-en)*. The *-se* attached to the infinitive indicates a reflexive verb. Use the reflexive pronoun *se*, which agrees with the subject. Attach the reflexive pronoun to the end of the command form. To find the stressed vowel, count back three vowels and add an accent to the *e*. To negate the second command, form the *Uds.* present subjunctive for regular *-ar* verbs by dropping the final *-o* from the *yo* form of the present tense and adding *-en*. Put the reflexive pronoun before the conjugated verb and put *no* before the reflexive pronoun.

2. **Ponte un abrigo. No te quites el suéter.**   The verb *poner* has an irregular affirmative informal command form: *pon*. The *-se* attached to the infinitive indicates a reflexive verb. Use the reflexive pronoun *te*, which agrees with the subject. Attach the reflexive pronoun to the end of the command form. No accent is needed because the verb portion of the command has only one syllable. To negate the second verb with *tú*, use the present subjunctive *tú* form. To form the present subjunctive for regular *-ar* verbs, drop the *-ar* ending and add the present subjunctive ending for *tú (-es)*. To negate the command, put the reflexive pronoun before the conjugated verb and put *no* before the reflexive pronoun.

3. **Despertaos temprano. No os acostéis tarde.**   To form an affirmative command with *vosotros*, drop the final *-r* from the infinitive and add *-d*. This *-d* is dropped when the reflexive pronoun *os* is added and attached to the end of the command form. No accent is necessary. To form a negative command for the second verb with *vosotros*, use the present subjunctive *vosotros* form. To form the present subjunctive for regular *-ar* verbs, drop the final *-o* from the *yo* form of the present tense and add the *vosotros* subjunctive ending *(áis)*. The *-se* attached to the infinitive indicates a reflexive verb. Use the reflexive pronoun *os*, which agrees with the subject. To negate the command, put the reflexive pronoun before the conjugated verb and put *no* before the reflexive pronoun.

4. **Asegúrese de buscar un portero. No se haga daño.**   To form a command with *Ud.*, use the present subjunctive of the verb. To form the present subjunctive for regular *-ar* verbs, drop the final *-o* from the *yo* form of the present tense and add *-e*. The *-se* attached to the infinitive indicates a reflexive verb. Use the reflexive pronoun *se*, which agrees with the subject. Attach the reflexive pronoun to the end of the command form. To find the stressed vowel, count back three vowels and add an accent to the *u*. To form a negative command for the second verb, use the irregular subjunctive stem for *hacer (hag-)* and add the subjunctive ending for *Ud. (-a)*. To negate the command, put the reflexive pronoun before the conjugated verb and put *no* before the reflexive pronoun.

5. **Atrévete a hablar. No te calles.**   To form an affirmative command with *tú*, drop the final *-s* from the second person singular present indicative form of *tú (atreves)*. Attach the reflexive pronoun to the end of the command form. To find the stressed vowel, count back three vowels and add an accent to the *e*. To form a negative command with *tú*, use the present subjunctive *tú* form. To form the present subjunctive for regular *-ar* verbs,

drop the *-ar* ending and add the present subjunctive ending for *tú (-es)*. The *-se* attached to the infinitive indicates a reflexive verb. Use the reflexive pronoun *te*, which agrees with the subject. To negate the command, put the reflexive pronoun before the conjugated verb and put *no* before the reflexive pronoun.

6. **Alégrense. No se apuren.**   To form a command with *Uds.*, use the present subjunctive of the verb. To form the present subjunctive for regular *-ar* verbs, drop the final *-o* from the *yo* form of the present tense and add *-en*. The *-se* attached to the infinitive indicates a reflexive verb. Use the reflexive pronoun *se*, which agrees with the subject. Attach the reflexive pronoun to the end of the command form. To find the stressed vowel, count back three vowels and add an accent to the e. To form a negative command for the second verb, form the present subjunctive for regular *-ar* verbs by dropping the final *-o* from the *yo* form of the present tense and adding the *Uds.* subjunctive ending *(-en)*. Put the reflexive pronoun before the conjugated verb and put *no* before the reflexive pronoun.

Chapter Problems and Solutions

Problems

In problems 1–10, give one friend directions to your house.

1. (empezar) _____ al cruce de las avenidas Carlos V y Francisco III.

2. (conducir) No _____.

3. (pedir) No _____ información a ninguna otra persona.

4. (ir) _____ al sur.

5. (seguir) _____ caminando derecho.

6. (dar) _____ vuelta a la izquierda en el tercer semáforo.

7. (pararse) No _____ al puente.

8. (atravesar) No _____ el puente.

9. (permanecer) _____ en esta calle hasta el segundo semáforo.

10. (continuar) No _____ porque mi casa esta allá, a la derecha.

In problems 11–20, a person you don't know well tells you about a situation he/she has encountered. Give advice to this person.

11. Tengo la gripe. (no venir a mi casa)

12. Tengo una entrevista muy importante esta tarde. (llegar temprano)

13. No me gusta nadar. (no ir a la playa)

14. Estoy siguiendo un régimen. (no perder demasiado peso)

15. Pasé dos horas en la gimnasia. (bañarse)

16. No puedo encontrar mi libro. (buscarlo)

17. Tengo miedo de decirle a Ud. la verdad. (no decir mentiras)

18. Quiero ir al concierto el sábado por la noche. (pedir permiso a sus padres)

19. Yo no puedo ir al centro con Ud. (no preocuparse)

20. Tengo que hablar en mi clase. (tener confianza)

Solutions

1. **Answer: Empieza.** To form an affirmative command with *tú,* drop the final *-s* from the second person singular present indicative form of *tú (empiezas).* Note that *empezar* is a stem-changing *-zar* verb that has an internal change from *e* to *ie.*

2. **Answer: conduzcas.** To form a negative command with *tú,* use the present subjunctive *tú* form. To form the present subjunctive for the spelling-change verb *conducir,* change the internal *c* to *zc* (the same change made for the present indicative *yo* form). Drop the final *-ir* ending and add the present subjunctive ending for *tú (-as).*

3. **Answer: pidas.** To form a negative command with *tú,* use the present subjunctive *tú* form. To form the present subjunctive for the stem-changing verb *pedir,* change the internal *e* to *i* (the same change made for the present indicative *yo* form). Drop the final *-ir* ending and add the present subjunctive ending for *tú (-as).*

4. **Answer: Ve.** The informal affirmative command form of *ir* is irregular and must be memorized: *ve.*

5. **Answer: Sigue.** To form an affirmative command with *tú,* drop the final *-s* from the second person singular present indicative form of *tú (sigues).*

6. **Answer: Da.** To form an affirmative command with *tú,* drop the final *-s* from the second person singular present indicative form of *tú (das).*

7. **Answer: te pares.** To form a negative command with *tú,* use the present subjunctive *tú* form. To form the present subjunctive for regular *-ar* verbs, drop the *-ar* ending and add the present subjunctive ending for *tú (-es).* To negate the command, put the reflexive pronoun before the conjugated verb and put *no* before the reflexive pronoun.

8. **Answer: atravieses.** To form a negative command with *tú,* use the present subjunctive *tú* form. To form the present subjunctive for regular *-ar* verbs, drop the *-ar* ending and add the present subjunctive ending for *tú (-es).* To negate the command, put the reflexive pronoun before the conjugated verb and put *no* before the reflexive pronoun.

9. **Answer: Permanece.** To form an affirmative command with *tú,* drop the final *-s* from the second person singular present indicative form of *tú (permaneces).*

10. **Answer: continúes.** To form a negative command with *tú,* use the present subjunctive *tú* form. To form the present subjunctive for the spelling-change verb *continuar,* change the *u* before the *-ar* ending to *ú* (the same change made for the present indicative *yo* form). Drop the final *-ir* ending and add the present subjunctive ending for *tú (-as).*

11. **Answer: No venga a mi casa.** To form a command with *Ud.*, use the present subjunctive of the verb. To form the present subjunctive for the irregular verb *venir*, drop the final -*o* from the *yo* form of the present tense *(vengo)* and add -*a*. To negate the command, put *no* before the conjugated verb.

12. **Answer: Llegue temprano.** To form a command with *Ud.*, use the present subjunctive of the verb. To form the present subjunctive for the spelling-change verb *llegar*, drop the final -*é* from the *yo* form of the preterit tense *(llegué)* and add -*e*.

13. **Answer: No vaya a la playa.** To form a command with *Ud.*, use the present subjunctive of the verb. To form the present subjunctive for the irregular verb *ir*, use the irregular subjunctive stem *(vay-)* and add -*a*. To negate the command, put *no* before the conjugated verb.

14. **Answer: No pierda demasiado peso.** To form a command with *Ud.*, use the present subjunctive of the verb. The present tense of the stem-changing verb *perder* changes the internal *e* to *ie*. To form the present subjunctive for *perder*, drop the final -*o* from the *yo* form of the present tense *(pierdo)* and add -*a*. To negate the command, put *no* before the conjugated verb.

15. **Answer: Báñese.** To form a command with *Ud.*, use the present subjunctive of the verb. To form the present subjunctive for regular -*ar* verbs, drop the final -*o* from the *yo* form of the present tense and add -*e*. The -*se* attached to the infinitive indicates a reflexive verb. Use the reflexive pronoun *se*, which agrees with the subject. Attach the reflexive pronoun to the end of the command form. To find the stressed vowel, count back three vowels and add an accent to the *a*.

16. **Answer: Búsquelo.** To form a command with *Ud.*, use the present subjunctive of the verb. To form the present subjunctive for the spelling-change verb *buscar*, drop the final -*é* from the *yo* form of the preterit tense *(busqué)* and add -*e*. Add the direct object pronoun to the affirmative command form. Note that the *ue* diphthong counts as only one vowel. Count back three vowels and put the accent on the first *u*.

17. **Answer: No diga mentiras.** To form a command with *Ud.*, use the present subjunctive of the verb. To form the present subjunctive for the irregular verb *decir*, drop the final -*o* from the *yo* form of the present tense *(digo)* and add -*a*. To negate the command, put *no* before the conjugated verb.

18. **Answer: Pida permiso a sus padres.** To form a command with *Ud.*, use the present subjunctive of the verb. To form the present subjunctive for the stem-changing verb *pedir*, change the internal *e* to *i* (the same change made for the present indicative *yo* form). Drop the final -*ir* ending and add the present subjunctive ending for *Ud.* (-*a*).

19. **Answer: No se preocupe.** To form a command with *Ud.*, use the present subjunctive of the verb. To form the present subjunctive for regular -*ar* verbs, drop the final -*o* from the *yo* form of the present tense and add -*e*. The -*se* attached to the infinitive indicates a reflexive verb. Use the reflexive pronoun *se*, which agrees with the subject. To negate the command, put the reflexive pronoun before the conjugated verb and put *no* before the reflexive pronoun.

20. **Answer: Tenga confianza.** To form a command with *Ud.*, use the present subjunctive of the verb. To form the present subjunctive for the irregular verb *tener*, drop the final -*o* from the *yo* form of the present tense *(tengo)* and add -*a*.

Supplemental Chapter Problems

Problems

In problems 1–10, tell a person what to do in case of emergency.

1. no acercarse a las ventanas

2. telefonear a la policía

3. cerrar la puerta y las ventanas

4. apagar la televisión

5. no salir

6. no ponerse nervioso

7. pedir información a las autoridades

8. no tener miedo

9. evaluar la situación

10. no dar gritos

In problems 11–20, give advice to the friend who is speaking to you.

11. Tengo mi permiso de conducir. (no conducir rápidamente)

12. No comprendo la gramática. (tener paciencia)

13. Está nevando y hace mucho frío. (no salir)

14. Estoy enfermo. (no ir a la escuela)

15. Tengo un examen. (no estar nervioso)

16. Tengo buenas notas. (seguir estudiando)

17. Recibí una invitación a una fiesta pero tengo que trabajar esta noche. (decir la verdad)

18. No puedo acompañarte al cine esta tarde. (no preocuparse)

19. Voy a casa de Diana para celebrar la Navidad. (traer regalos para la familia)

20. Quiero hacer un viaje a Madrid. (ir a España en el verano)

Solutions

1. No se acerque a las ventanas. (negative formal commands of reflexive spelling-change verbs, p. 330)

2. Telefonee a la policía. (formal commands of regular verbs, p. 327)

3. Cierre la puerta y las ventanas. (formal commands of stem-changing verbs, p. 330)

4. Apague la televisión. (formal commands of spelling-change verbs, p. 330)

5. No salga. (formal commands of irregular verbs, p. 329)

6. No se ponga nervioso. (negative formal commands of irregular reflexive verbs, p. 329)

7. Pida información a las autoridades. (formal commands of stem-changing verbs, p. 330)

8. No tenga miedo. (formal commands of irregular verbs, p. 329)

9. Evalúe la situación. (formal commands of spelling-change verbs, p. 330)

10. No dé gritos. (formal commands of spelling-change verbs, p. 330)

11. No conduzcas rápidamente. (negative informal commands of spelling-change verbs, p. 330)

12. Ten paciencia. (informal commands of irregular verbs, p. 334)

13. No salgas. (negative informal commands of irregular verbs, p. 334)

14. No vayas a la escuela. (negative informal commands of irregular verbs, p. 334)

15. No estés nervioso. (negative informal commands of irregular verbs, p. 334)

16. Sigue estudiando. (informal commands of spelling-change verbs, p. 334; informal commands of stem-changing verbs, p. 334)

17. Di la verdad. (informal commands of irregular verbs, p. 334)

18. No te preocupes. (negative informal commands of regular -ar verbs, p. 333)

19. Trae regalos para la familia. (informal commands of regular -er verbs, p. 333)

20. Ve a España en el verano. (informal commands of irregular verbs, p. 334)

Customized Full-Length Exam

This test will give you an idea of what areas you still need to focus on.

Problems 1–5

Your school will be presenting a fashion show on **Thursday** (1), **April 1, 2003** (2), **from noon until 3 p.m.** (3) in room **362** (4) on the **third** (5) floor. Fill in the necessary information on the announcement by changing all the information in bold to Spanish.

Desfile de Modelos

Fecha: _____

Hora: _____

Sala: _____

Piso: _____

Answers 1–5

1. jueves

If you answered problem 1 **correctly,** go to problem 2.
If you answered problem 1 **incorrectly,** go to problem 8.

2. el primero de abril de dos mil tres

If you answered problem 2 **correctly,** go to problem 3.
If you answered problem 2 **incorrectly,** go to problems 7–8.

3. desde el mediodía hasta las tres de la tarde

If you answered problem 3 **correctly,** go to problem 4.
If you answered problem 3 **incorrectly,** go to problem 9.

4. trescientos sesenta y dos

If you answered problem 4 **correctly,** go to problem 5.
If you answered problem 4 **incorrectly,** go to problem 10.

5. tercero *or* tercer piso

If you answered problem 5 **correctly,** go to problem 11.
If you answered problem 5 **incorrectly,** go to problem 6.

Problems 6–10

Your school is having its **10th** (6) class reunion for the Class of **1993** (7) on **Friday, January 21** (8), **from 7 p.m. until midnight** (9) in room **534** (10). Fill in the necessary information on the announcement by changing all the information in bold to Spanish.

Reunión

Para la clase de: _____

Fecha: _____

Hora: _____

Sala: _____

Answers 6–10

6. décima

If you answered problem 6 **correctly,** go to problem 11.
If you answered problem 6 **incorrectly,** review ordinal numbers, p. 20.

7. mil novecientos noventa y tres

If you answered problem 7 **correctly,** go to problem 3.
If you answered problem 7 **incorrectly,** review dates, p. 25.

8. viernes, el veintiuno de enero

If you answered problem 8 **correctly,** go to problem 3.
If you answered problem 8 **incorrectly,** review dates, p. 25.

9. desde las siete hasta la medianoche

If you answered problem 9 **correctly,** go to problem 4.
If you answered problem 9 **incorrectly,** review time, p. 29.

10. quinientos treinta y cuatro

If you answered problem 10 **correctly,** go to problem 5.
If you answered problem 10 **incorrectly,** review cardinal numbers, p. 15.

Problems 11–15

Describe the school items by completing the sentence with the appropriate demonstrative adjective.

11. _____ mapa ahí es muy grande.

12. _____ lecciones aquí son interesantes.

13. _____ clase allá es una clase de español.

14. _____ examen ahí es muy difícil.

15. _____ papeles aquí son importantes.

Answers 11–15

11. Ese

If you answered problem 11 **correctly,** go to problem 12.
If you answered problem 11 **incorrectly,** go to problem 16.

12. Estas

If you answered problem 12 **correctly,** go to problem 13.
If you answered problem 12 **incorrectly,** go to problems 7 and 10.

13. Aquella

If you answered problem 13 **correctly,** go to problem 14.
If you answered problem 13 **incorrectly,** go to problem 16.

14. Ese

If you answered problem 14 **correctly,** go to problem 15.
If you answered problem 14 **incorrectly,** go to problems 8–9.

15. Estos

If you answered problem 15 **correctly,** go to problem 21.
If you answered problem 15 **incorrectly,** go to problems 7 and 10.

Problems 16–20

Describe the food by completing the sentence with the appropriate demonstrative adjective.

16. Me gustaría _____ pastel allá.

17. Voy a beber _____ leche aquí.

18. Quisiera comprar _____ melocotones ahí.

19. _____ porciones ahí son grandes.

20. Deme _____ pan aquí, por favor.

Answers 16–20

16. aquel

If you answered problem 16 **correctly,** go to problem 17.
If you answered problem 16 **incorrectly,** review gender of nouns, p. 55; demonstrative adjectives, p. 51.

17. esta

If you answered problem 17 **correctly,** go to problem 18.
If you answered problem 17 **incorrectly,** review gender of nouns, p. 55, and demonstrative adjectives, p. 51.

18. esos

If you answered problem 18 **correctly,** go to problem 21.
If you answered problem 18 **incorrectly,** review gender of nouns, p. 55, and demonstrative adjectives, p. 51.

19. Esas

If you answered problem 19 **correctly,** go to problem 21.
If you answered problem 19 **incorrectly,** review gender of nouns, p. 55, and demonstrative adjectives, p. 51.

20. este

If you answered problem 20 **correctly,** go to problem 21.
If you answered problem 20 **incorrectly,** review gender of nouns, p. 55, and demonstrative adjectives, p. 51.

Problems 21–25

In each of the following Spanish dialogues, the first person states a fact that the second person doesn't hear very well. Write the first speaker's reply.

> Example: 1: Tengo un libro que le voy a dar a Anita.
>
> 2: ¿Qué le vas a dar a Anita? 1: <u>Mi libro.</u>

21. 1: Julia y yo tenemos una cámara. Marta quiere sacar fotografías.

2: ¿Qué le prestan Uds. a Marta? 1: _____

22. 1: Mi nieto tiene juguetes nuevos. Él le da sus juguetes a un amigo.

2: ¿Qué le da a un amigo? 1: _____

23. 1: Tengo un suéter nuevo. Mi hermano quiere ponérselo.

2: ¿Qué quiere ponerse su hermano? 1: _____

24. 1: Tú tienes una computadora portátil. Yo tengo que escribir un mensaje electrónico.

2: ¿Qué necesitas? 1: _____

25. 1: Vosotros tenéis ideas interesantes.

2: ¿Qué son interesantes? 1: _____

Answers 21–25

21. Nuestra cámara.

If you answered problem 21 **correctly,** go to problem 22.
If you answered problem 21 **incorrectly,** go to problem 26.

22. Sus juguetes.

If you answered problem 22 **correctly,** go to problem 23.
If you answered problem 22 **incorrectly,** go to problem 27.

23. Mi suéter.

If you answered problem 23 **correctly,** go to problem 24.
If you answered problem 23 **incorrectly,** go to problem 28.

24. Tu computadora.

If you answered problem 24 **correctly,** go to problem 25.
If you answered problem 24 **incorrectly,** go to problem 29.

25. Vuestras ideas.

If you answered problem 25 **correctly,** go to problem 31.
If you answered problem 25 **incorrectly,** go to problem 30.

Problems 26–30

In each of the following Spanish dialogues, the first person states a fact that the second person doesn't hear very well. Write the first speaker's reply.

26.   1: Javier y yo tenemos dos refrescos. Queremos beberlos.

  2: ¿Qué quieren Uds. beber? 1: _____

27.   1: La mujer tiene un coche nuevo. Ella lo conduce con mucho cuidado.

  2: ¿Qué conduce con mucho cuidado? 1: _____

28.   1: Yo tengo buenas recetas. Mi hermana siempre quiere copiarlas.

  2. ¿Qué quiere copiar su hermana? 1: _____

29.   1: Tú tienes muchos discos compactos. Yo quiero escucharlos.

  2: ¿Qué quieres escuchar? 1: _____

30.   1: Vosotros tenéis un problema serio.

  2: ¿Qué es serio? 1: _____

Answers 26–30

26. Nuestros refrescos.

If you answered problem 26 **correctly,** go to problem 22.
If you answered problem 26 **incorrectly,** review possessive adjectives, p. 72.

27. Su coche.

If you answered problem 27 **correctly,** go to problem 23.
If you answered problem 27 **incorrectly,** review possessive adjectives, p. 72.

28. Mis recetas.

If you answered problem 28 **correctly,** go to problem 24.
If you answered problem 28 **incorrectly,** review possessive adjectives, p. 72.

29. Tus discos compactos.

If you answered problem 29 **correctly,** go to problem 25.
If you answered problem 29 **incorrectly,** review possessive adjectives, p. 72.

30. Vuestro problema.

If you answered problem 30 **correctly,** go to problem 31.
If you answered problem 30 **incorrectly,** review possessive adjectives, p. 72.

Problems 31–35

Express what housework the following people do by giving the correct form of the verb in parentheses in the present tense.

31. (escribir) Yo _____ cheques.

32. (cocinar) Francisco y yo _____.

33. (correr) Ud. _____ al supermercado.

34. (pasar) Elena _____ la aspiradora.

35. (sacudir) Tú _____ los muebles.

Answers 31–35

31. escribo

If you answered problem 31 **correctly,** go to problem 32.
If you answered problem 31 **incorrectly,** go to problems 37 and 40.

32. cocinamos

If you answered problem 32 **correctly,** go to problem 33.
If you answered problem 32 **incorrectly,** go to problem 39.

33. corre

If you answered problem 33 **correctly,** go to problem 34.
If you answered problem 33 **incorrectly,** go to problems 36 and 38.

34. pasa

If you answered problem 34 **correctly,** go to problem 35.
If you answered problem 34 **incorrectly,** go to problem 39.

35. sacudes

If you answered problem 35 **correctly,** go to problem 41.
If you answered problem 35 **incorrectly,** go to problems 37 and 40.

Problems 36–40

Express what the following people do on a snowy day by giving the correct form of the verb in parentheses in the present tense.

36. (prometer) Tú _____ barrer la nieve.

37. (insistir) Carlos _____ en trabajar.

38. (deber) Sarita y yo _____ ir al centro.

39. (escuchar) Yo _____ el pronóstico.

40. (decidir) Miguel y Ud. _____ quedarse en casa.

Answers 36–40

36. prometes

If you answered problem 36 **correctly,** go to problem 41.
If you answered problem 36 **incorrectly,** review present tense -*er* verb conjugation, p. 92.

37. insiste

If you answered problem 37 **correctly,** go to problem 32.
If you answered problem 37 **incorrectly,** review present tense -*ir* verb conjugation, p. 92.

38. debemos

If you answered problem 38 **correctly,** go to problem 41.
If you answered problem 38 **incorrectly,** review present tense -*er* verb conjugation, p. 92.

39. escucho

If you answered problem 39 **correctly,** go to problem 33.
If you answered problem 39 **incorrectly,** review present tense -*ar* verb conjugation, p. 92.

40. deciden

If you answered problem 40 **correctly,** go to problem 41.
If you answered problem 40 **incorrectly,** review present tense -*ir* verb conjugation, p. 92.

Problems 41–45

Complete each sentence in the present tense with the correct form of the verb that best describes each person.

contar	estar	exigir	ser	tener

41. Roberto _____ con su familia cuando necesita ayuda.

42. Uds. _____ inteligentes.

43. Julio y yo _____ contentos.

44. Tú _____ pelo rubio.

45. Yo _____ mucho de mis amigos.

Answers 41–45

41. cuenta

If you answered problem 41 **correctly,** go to problem 42.
If you answered problem 41 **incorrectly,** go to problems 39 and 50.

42. son

If you answered problem 42 **correctly,** go to problem 43.
If you answered problem 42 **incorrectly,** go to problems 46 and 48.

43. estamos

If you answered problem 43 **correctly,** go to problem 44.
If you answered problem 43 **incorrectly,** go to problems 46 and 48.

44. tienes

If you answered problem 44 **correctly,** go to problem 45.
If you answered problem 44 **incorrectly,** go to problems 46–48.

45. exijo

If you answered problem 45 **correctly,** go to problem 51.
If you answered problem 45 **incorrectly,** go to problems 49–50.

Problems 46–50

Complete each sentence in the present tense with the correct form of the verb that best describes each person.

ir	pensar	preferir	reír	saber

46. Yo _____ lo que yo quiero.

47. Ellos _____ cuando se divierten.

48. Jorge y yo _____ a salir bien en la escuela.

49. Ud. _____ vivir rápidamente.

50. Tú _____ por ti mismo.

Answers 46–50

46. sé

If you answered problem 46 **correctly,** go to problem 41.
If you answered problem 46 **incorrectly,** review present tense irregular verb conjugation, p. 100.

47. ríen

If you answered problem 47 **correctly,** go to problem 32.
If you answered problem 47 **incorrectly,** review present tense irregular verb conjugation, p. 100.

48. vamos

If you answered problem 48 **correctly,** go to problem 41.
If you answered problem 48 **incorrectly,** review present tense irregular verb conjugation, p. 100.

49. prefiere

If you answered problem 49 **correctly,** go to problem 33.
If you answered problem 49 **incorrectly,** review present tense -*ir* stem-changing verb conjugation, p. 97.

50. piensas

If you answered problem 50 **correctly,** go to problem 51.
If you answered problem 50 **incorrectly,** review present tense -*ar* stem-changing verb conjugation, p. 97.

Problems 51–55

Express what the following subjects do to prepare themselves by giving the correct form of the reflexive verb in the present tense, the present progressive, an infinitive, or a command form and by placing the reflexive pronoun in its proper place.

51. (maquillarse) Ella _____.

52. (afeitarse) Nosotros vamos a _____.

53. (prepararse) Estoy _____.

54. (dormirse) ¡No _____ tú!

55. (levantarse) ¡_____ Ud!

Answers 51–55

51. se maquilla

If you answered problem 51 **correctly,** go to problem 52.
If you answered problem 51 **incorrectly,** go to problem 56.

52. afeitarnos

If you answered problem 52 **correctly,** go to problem 53.
If you answered problem 52 **incorrectly,** go to problem 57.

53. preparándome

If you answered problem 53 **correctly,** go to problem 54.
If you answered problem 53 **incorrectly,** go to problem 58.

54.   te duermas

If you answered problem 54 **correctly,** go to problem 55.
If you answered problem 54 **incorrectly,** go to problem 60.

55.   Levántese

If you answered problem 55 **correctly,** go to problem 61.
If you answered problem 55 **incorrectly,** go to problem 59.

Problems 56–60

Express what the following subjects do to prepare themselves by giving the correct form of the reflexive verb in the present tense, the present progressive, an infinitive, or a command form and by placing the reflexive pronoun in its proper place.

56.   (lavarse) Yo _____ .

57.   (desayunarse) Vosotros vais a _____ .

58.   (vestirse) Ellas están _____ .

59.   (sentarse) ¡_____ tú!

60.   (desvestir) ¡No _____ Uds.!

Answers 56–60

56.   me lavo

If you answered problem 56 **correctly,** go to problem 52.
If you answered problem 56 **incorrectly,** review present tense of reflexive verbs, p. 142.

57.   desayunaros

If you answered problem 57 **correctly,** go to problem 53.
If you answered problem 57 **incorrectly,** review present tense of reflexive verbs, p. 142.

58.   vistiéndose

If you answered problem 58 **correctly,** go to problem 54.
If you answered problem 58 **incorrectly,** review present tense of stem-change verbs, p. 97, and the present progressive of reflexive verbs, p. 177.

59.   Siéntate

If you answered problem 59 **correctly,** go to problem 55.
If you answered problem 59 **incorrectly,** review present tense of stem-change verbs, p. 97, and informal commands of reflexive verbs, p. 333.

60.   se desvistan

If you answered problem 60 **correctly,** go to problem 61.
If you answered problem 60 **incorrectly,** review present tense of stem-change verbs, p. 97, and formal commands of reflexive verbs, p. 327.

Problems 61–65

Express what each person does to prepare for a meal by substituting a direct and/or indirect object pronoun for the underlined noun.

61. Yo compro <u>los comestibles</u>.

62. Ella va a llamar <u>a sus invitados</u>.

63. Nosotros estamos pelando <u>las frutas</u>.

64. Pide ayuda <u>a tu amiga</u>.

65. No preparen Uds. <u>el jamón</u> ahora.

Answers 61–65

61. Yo los compro.

If you answered problem 61 **correctly,** go to problem 62.
If you answered problem 61 **incorrectly,** go to problem 66.

62. Ella va a llamarles. Ella les va a llamar.
   or Ella va a llamarlos. Ella los va a llamar.

If you answered problem 62 **correctly,** go to problem 63.
If you answered problem 62 **incorrectly,** go to problem 67.

63. Nosotros estamos pelándolas.
   or Nosotros las estamos pelando.

If you answered problem 63 **correctly,** go to problem 64.
If you answered problem 63 **incorrectly,** go to problem 68.

64. Pídele ayuda.

If you answered problem 64 **correctly,** go to problem 65.
If you answered problem 64 **incorrectly,** go to problem 69.

65. No lo preparen Uds. ahora.

If you answered problem 65 **correctly,** go to problem 71.
If you answered problem 65 **incorrectly,** go to problem 70.

Problems 66–70

Express what each person does to play a game by substituting a direct and/or indirect object pronoun for the underlined noun.

66. Ella busca <u>la pelota</u>.

67. Nosotros vamos a explicar las reglas <u>al grupo</u>.

68. Yo estoy preparando <u>el campo</u>.

69.   Da la pelota <u>a tus amigos</u>.

70.   No lancen Uds. <u>la pelota</u>.

Answers 66–70

66.   Ella la busca.

If you answered problem 66 **correctly,** go to problem 62.
If you answered problem 66 **incorrectly,** review direct object pronouns, p. 155.

67.   Nosotros vamos a explicarle las reglas. Nosotros le vamos a explicar las reglas.

If you answered problem 67 **correctly,** go to problem 63.
If you answered problem 67 **incorrectly,** review indirect object pronouns, p. 158.

68.   Yo estoy preparándolo. (Yo lo estoy preparando.)

If you answered problem 68 **correctly,** go to problem 64.
If you answered problem 68 **incorrectly,** review direct object pronouns, p. 155, and the present progressive, p. 177.

69.   Dales la pelota.

If you answered problem 69 **correctly,** go to problem 65.
If you answered problem 69 **incorrectly,** review indirect object pronouns, p. 158, and informal commands, p 333.

70.   No la lancen Uds.

If you answered problem 70 **correctly,** go to problem 71.
If you answered problem 70 **incorrectly,** review direct object pronouns, p. 155, and formal commands, p. 327.

Problems 71–75

Express what each person is doing at 6 p.m. by using the correct form of *estar* and the present participle to form the present progressive tense.

71.   (corregir) Tú _____ tus tareas.

72.   (morirse) Silvia y yo _____ de hambre.

73.   (seguir) Ellos _____ las noticias en la televisión.

74.   (venir) Ud. _____ a casa.

75.   (ir) Yo _____ al supermercado.

Answers 71–75

71.   estás corrigiendo

If you answered problem 71 **correctly,** go to problem 72.
If you answered problem 71 **incorrectly,** go to problem 76.

72. estamos muriendonos

If you answered problem 72 **correctly,** go to problem 73.
If you answered problem 72 **incorrectly,** go to problem 77.

73. están siguiendo

If you answered problem 73 **correctly,** go to problem 74.
If you answered problem 73 **incorrectly,** go to problem 78.

74. está viniendo

If you answered problem 74 **correctly,** go to problem 75.
If you answered problem 74 **incorrectly,** go to problem 79.

75. estoy yendo

If you answered problem 75 **correctly,** go to problem 81.
If you answered problem 75 **incorrectly,** go to problem 70.

Problems 76–80

Express what each person is doing at 6 p.m. by using the correct form of *estar* and the present participle to form the present progressive tense.

76. (repetir) María y Ana _____ un poema.

77. (dormir) Tú _____.

78. (distribuir) Ellos _____ folletos.

79. (divertirse) Nosotros. _____.

80. (leer) Yo _____ el periódico.

Answers 76–80

76. están repitiendo

If you answered problem 76 **correctly,** go to problem 72.
If you answered problem 76 **incorrectly,** review present participles of *-ir* stem-changing verbs with *e* to *i* change, p. 177.

77. estás durmiendo

If you answered problem 77 **correctly,** go to problem 73.
If you answered problem 77 **incorrectly,** review present participles of *-ir* stem-changing verbs with *o* to *u* change, p. 177.

78. están distribuyendo

If you answered problem 78 **correctly,** go to problem 74.
If you answered problem 78 **incorrectly,** review present participles of *-uir* spelling-change verbs, p. 177.

79.   estamos divirtiéndonos/nos estamos divirtiendo

If you answered problem 79 **correctly,** go to problem 75.
If you answered problem 79 **incorrectly,** review present participles of *-ir* stem-changing verbs with *e* to *i* change, p. 177, and reflexive verbs, p. 141.

80.   estoy leyendo

If you answered problem 80 **correctly,** go to problem 81.
If you answered problem 80 **incorrectly,** review present participles of *-er* verbs with stems ending in a vowel, p. 177.

Problems 81–85

Describe each person by giving the correct form of the adjective in bold.

81.   François es **francés** y François y Albert son _____.

82.   Los hombres son **corteses** y el muchacho es _____.

83.   Los profesores son **sagaces** y el director es _____.

84.   Eva es una **buena** alumna y Miguel es un _____ alumno.

85.   Esa muchacha es **habladora** y ese muchacho es _____.

Answers 81–85

81.   franceses

If you answered problem 81 **correctly,** go to problem 82.
If you answered problem 81 **incorrectly,** go to problem 86.

82.   cortés

If you answered problem 82 **correctly,** go to problem 83.
If you answered problem 82 **incorrectly,** go to problem 86.

83.   sagaz

If you answered problem 83 **correctly,** go to problem 84.
If you answered problem 83 **incorrectly,** go to problem 87.

84.   buen

If you answered problem 84 **correctly,** go to problem 84.
If you answered problem 84 **incorrectly,** go to problems 88–89.

85.   hablador

If you answered problem 85 **correctly,** go to problem 91.
If you answered problem 85 **incorrectly,** go to problem 90.

Problems 86–90

Describe each person by giving the correct form of the adjective in bold.

86. Heidi es **alemana** y Hans es _____.

87. Mi prima es **feliz** y mis primos son _____.

88. Ese hombre es un **gran** artista y esa mujer es una _____ artista también.

89. Ana es una **mala** muchacha y Antonio es un _____ muchacho.

90. Ella es **trabajadora** y ellos son _____.

Answers 86–90

86. alemán

If you answered problem 86 **correctly,** go to problem 83.
If you answered problem 86 **incorrectly,** review agreement of adjectives, p. 185.

87. felices

If you answered problem 87 **correctly,** go to problem 84.
If you answered problem 87 **incorrectly,** review agreement of adjectives, p. 185.

88. gran

If you answered problem 88 **correctly,** go to problem 85.
If you answered problem 88 **incorrectly,** review agreement of adjectives, p. 185.

89. mal

If you answered problem 89 **correctly,** go to problem 85.
If you answered problem 89 **incorrectly,** review agreement of adjectives, p. 185.

90. trabajadores

If you answered problem 90 **correctly,** go to problem 91.
If you answered problem 90 **incorrectly,** review agreement of adjectives, p. 185.

Problems 91–95

Describe how each person does things by changing the preposition + the noun to an adverb.

> Example: Él habla con paciencia.
>
> > Él habla pacientemente.

91. Ella escribe con sagacidad.

92. Yo camino con lentitud.

93. Uds. hablan con claridad.

94. Nosotros dibujamos con alegría.

95. Tú escuchas con seriedad.

Answers 91–95

91.   Ella escribe sagazmente.

If you answered problem 91 **correctly,** go to problem 92.
If you answered problem 91 **incorrectly,** go to problem 96.

92.   Yo camino lentamente.

If you answered problem 92 **correctly,** go to problem 93.
If you answered problem 92 **incorrectly,** go to problem 97.

93.   Uds. hablan claramente.

If you answered problem 93 **correctly,** go to problem 94.
If you answered problem 93 **incorrectly,** go to problem 98.

94.   Nosotros dibujamos alegremente.

If you answered problem 94 **correctly,** go to problem 95.
If you answered problem 94 **incorrectly,** go to problem 99.

95.   Tú escuchas seriamente.

If you answered problem 95 **correctly,** go to problem 101.
If you answered problem 95 **incorrectly,** go to problem 100.

Problems 96–100

Describe how each person does things by changing the preposition + the noun to an adverb.

96.   Yo respondo con felicidad.

97.   Nosotros trabajamos con habilidad.

98.   Él comprende con facilidad.

99.   Tú contestas con sinceridad.

100. Ellas conducen con cortesía.

Answers 96–100

96.   Yo respondo felizmente.

If you answered problem 96 **correctly,** go to problem 92.
If you answered problem 96 **incorrectly,** review formation of adverbs, p. 201.

97.   Nosotros trabajamos hábilmente.

If you answered problem 97 **correctly,** go to problem 93.
If you answered problem 97 **incorrectly,** review formation of adverbs, p. 201.

98.   Él comprende fácilmente.

If you answered problem 98 **correctly,** go to problem 94.
If you answered problem 98 **incorrectly,** review formation of adverbs, p. 201.

99. Tú contestas sinceramente.

If you answered problem 99 **correctly,** go to problem 95.
If you answered problem 99 **incorrectly,** review formation of adverbs, p. 201.

100. Ellas conducen cortésmente.

If you answered problem 100 **correctly,** go to problem 101.
If you answered problem 100 **incorrectly,** review formation of adverbs, p. 201.

Problems 101–105

Compare the follow people using adjectives and adverbs as necessary.

> Example: Margarita es perezosa. (+/Pablo)
>
> Margarita es más perezosa que Pablo.
>
> Margarita estudia con diligencia. (–/su hermana)
>
> Margarita estudia menos diligentemente que su hermana.

101. Juana canta mal. (+/Lupe)

102. Víctor es optimista. (–/Alberto)

103. Yo trabajo duro. (–/tú)

104. Alicia es habladora. (=/su hermana)

105. Este profesor es bueno. (+/el otro)

Answers 101–105

101. Juana canta peor que Lupe.

If you answered problem 101 **correctly,** go to problem 102.
If you answered problem 101 **incorrectly,** go to problem 106.

102. Víctor es menos optimista que Alberto.

If you answered problem 102 **correctly,** go to problem 103.
If you answered problem 102 **incorrectly,** go to problem 107.

103. Yo trabajo menos duro que tú.

If you answered problem 103 **correctly,** go to problem 104.
If you answered problem 103 **incorrectly,** go to problem 108.

104. Alicia es tan habladora como su hermana.

If you answered problem 104 **correctly,** go to problem 105.
If you answered problem 104 **incorrectly,** go to problem 109.

105. Este profesor es mejor que el otro.

If you answered problem 105 **correctly,** go to problem 111.
If you answered problem 105 **incorrectly,** go to problem 110.

Problems 106–110

Compare the follow people and things using adjectives and adverbs as necessary.

106. Esta película es buena. (–/la otra)

107. El español es fácil. (+/el francés)

108. Martín es supersticioso. (–/yo)

109. Yo corro despacio. (=/Uds.)

110. Gloria baila bien. (+/tú)

Answers 106–110

106. Esta película es peor que la otra.

If you answered problem 106 **correctly,** go to problem 102.
If you answered problem 106 **incorrectly,** review comparison of irregular adjectives, p. 217.

107. El español es más fácil que el francés.

If you answered problem 107 **correctly,** go to problem 103.
If you answered problem 107 **incorrectly,** review comparison of adjectives, p. 214.

108. Martín es menos supersticioso que yo.

If you answered problem 108 **correctly,** go to problem 104.
If you answered problem 108 **incorrectly,** review comparison of adjectives, p. 214.

109. Yo corro tan despacio como Uds.

If you answered problem 109 **correctly,** go to problem 105.
If you answered problem 109 **incorrectly,** review comparison of adverbs, p. 220.

110. Gloria baila mejor que tú.

If you answered problem 110 **correctly,** go to problem 111.
If you answered problem 110 **incorrectly,** review comparison of irregular adverbs, p. 217.

Problems 111–115

Complete each sentence with the correct preposition.

a	de	en	para	por

111. Tengo un regalo _____ ti.

112. Ella está _____ la escuela ahora.

113. Quiero beber un vaso _____ agua.

114. Estoy mirando _____ la ventana.

115. Comienza _____ llover.

Answers 111–115

111. para

If you answered problem 111 **correctly,** go to problem 112.
If you answered problem 111 **incorrectly,** go to problem 116.

112. en

If you answered problem 112 **correctly,** go to problem 113.
If you answered problem 112 **incorrectly,** go to problem 117.

113. de

If you answered problem 113 **correctly,** go to problem 114.
If you answered problem 113 **incorrectly,** go to problem 118.

114. por

If you answered problem 114 **correctly,** go to problem 115.
If you answered problem 114 **incorrectly,** go to problem 119.

115. a

If you answered problem 115 **correctly,** go to problem 121.
If you answered problem 115 **incorrectly,** go to problem 120.

Problems 116–120

Complete each sentence with the correct preposition.

a	de	en	para	por

116. Vamos _____ casa de Enrique.

117. Es una loción _____ broncearse.

118. Fui a España _____ un mes.

119. Él insiste _____ venir a las tres de la tarde.

120. Me olvidé _____ nuestra cita.

Answers 116–120

116. a

If you answered problem 116 **correctly,** go to problem 112.
If you answered problem 116 **incorrectly,** review the use of the preposition *a*, p. 233.

117. para

If you answered problem 117 **correctly,** go to problem 113.
If you answered problem 117 **incorrectly,** review prepositional modifiers, p. 242.

118. por

If you answered problem 118 **correctly,** go to problem 114.
If you answered problem 118 **incorrectly,** review the use of *por* and *para,* p. 236.

119. en

If you answered problem 119 **correctly,** go to problem 115.
If you answered problem 119 **incorrectly,** review prepositions that follow verbs, p. 233.

120. de

If you answered problem 120 **correctly,** go to problem 121.
If you answered problem 120 **incorrectly,** review prepositions that follow verbs, p. 233.

Problems 121–125

Rewrite the paragraph changing the words in bold from the present to the preterit.

Yo me **caigo** (121) al suelo y me **doy** (122) un golpe en la cabeza. Yo me **hago** (123) daño. Es claro que yo no **río** (124). Yo **comienzo** (125) a gritar.

Answers 121–125

121. caí

If you answered problem 121 **correctly,** go to problem 122.
If you answered problem 121 **incorrectly,** go to problem 126.

122. di

If you answered problem 122 **correctly,** go to problem 123.
If you answered problem 122 **incorrectly,** go to problem 127.

123. hice

If you answered problem 123 **correctly,** go to problem 124.
If you answered problem 123 **incorrectly,** go to problem 129.

124. reí

If you answered problem 124 **correctly,** go to problem 125.
If you answered problem 124 **incorrectly,** go to problem 130.

125. comencé

If you answered problem 125 **correctly,** go to problem 131.
If you answered problem 125 **incorrectly,** go to problem 128.

Problems 126–130

Continue the story. Rewrite the paragraph changing the words in bold from the present to the preterit.

Al principio, mi hermano no me **oye** (126). Entonces él **viene** (127) a mi ayuda. Yo le **explico** (128) que **tengo** (129) un accidente. Él me **trae** (130) un vaso de agua.

Answers 126–130

126. oyó

If you answered problem 126 **correctly,** go to problem 122.
If you answered problem 126 **incorrectly,** review the preterit of verbs that change *i* to *y* in the preterit, p. 256.

127. vino

If you answered problem 127 **correctly,** go to problem 123.
If you answered problem 127 **incorrectly,** review the preterit of irregular verbs, p. 258.

128. expliqué

If you answered problem 128 **correctly,** go to problem 125.
If you answered problem 128 **incorrectly,** review the preterit of spelling-change verbs, p. 253.

129. tuve

If you answered problem 129 **correctly,** go to problem 124.
If you answered problem 129 **incorrectly,** review the preterit of irregular verbs, p. 258.

130. trajo

If you answered problem 130 **correctly,** go to problem 131.
If you answered problem 130 **incorrectly,** review the preterit of irregular verbs, p. 258.

Problems 131–140

Complete the story with the correct form of the verb in the preterit or the imperfect.

Mi amiga Sara (llegar) _____ a mi casa a las nueve porque nosotros (ir) _____ a la playa.
131 132

Nosotros (estar) _____ a punto de salir cuando de repente el cielo (ponerse) _____ gris.
133 134

En momento, nosotros (tener) _____ que cambiar nuestros planes. Yo le (decir) _____ a
135 136

Sara que en vez de ir a la playa, nosotros (poder) _____ ir al cine. Solución (satisfacer)
137

_____ a mi amiga. Según Sara, esa (ser) _____ una buena idea. Yo (escoger) _____
138 139 140

una película de amor.

Answers 131–140

131. llegó

132. íbamos

133. estábamos

134. se puso

135. tuvimos

136. dije

137. podíamos

138. satisfizo

139. era

140. escogí

If you answered 8 or more of the above 10 problems **correctly,** go to problem 151.
If you answered more than 2 of the above problems **incorrectly,** go to problems 141–150.

Problems 141–150

Complete the story with the correct form of the verb in the preterit or the imperfect.

Anoche, después del trabajo, Alberto (andar) _____ a su casa. Después de la cena, él (hacer)
$\overline{}_{141}$

_____ejercicios y entonces (desvestirse) _____. (mirar) _____ la televisión cuando
$\overline{}_{142}$ _{143} _{144}

(dormirse) _____. Evidentemente, él (estar) _____ muy cansado y no (poder) _____
_{145} _{146} _{147}

mantenerse despierto. Durante el día, Alberto les (servir) _____ a muchos clientes que (ir)
_{148}

_____ a Europa y que (querer) _____ sus consejos.
_{149} _{150}

Answers 141–150

141. anduvo

If you answered problem 141 **correctly,** go to problem 142.
If you answered problem 141 **incorrectly,** review the preterit of irregular verbs, p. 258, and review the uses of the preterit and the imperfect.

142. hizo

If you answered problem 142 **correctly,** go to problem 143.
If you answered problem 142 **incorrectly,** review the preterit of irregular verbs, p. 258, and review the uses of the preterit and the imperfect.

143. se desvistió

If you answered problem 143 **correctly,** go to problem 144.
If you answered problem 143 **incorrectly,** review the preterit of stem-changing *e* to *i* -*ir* verbs, p. 259, and review the uses of the preterit and the imperfect.

144. Miraba

If you answered problem 144 **correctly,** go to problem 145.
If you answered problem 144 **incorrectly,** review the imperfect of regular -*ar* verbs, p. 269, and review the uses of the preterit and the imperfect.

145. se durmió

If you answered problem 145 **correctly,** go to problem 146.
If you answered problem 145 **incorrectly,** review the preterit of stem-changing o to u -ir verbs, p. 259, and review the uses of the preterit and the imperfect.

146. estaba

If you answered problem 146 **correctly,** go to problem 147.
If you answered problem 146 **incorrectly,** review the imperfect of regular -ar verbs, p. 269, and review the uses of the preterit and the imperfect.

147. podía

If you answered problem 147 **correctly,** go to problem 148.
If you answered problem 147 **incorrectly,** review the imperfect of -er verbs, p. 269, and review the uses of the preterit and the imperfect.

148. sirvió

If you answered problem 148 **correctly,** go to problem 149.
If you answered problem 148 **incorrectly,** review the preterit of e to i stem-changing -ir verbs, p. 259, and review the uses of the preterit and the imperfect.

149. iban

If you answered problem 149 **correctly,** go to problem 150.
If you answered problem 149 **incorrectly,** review the imperfect of irregular verbs, p. 269, and review the uses of the preterit and the imperfect.

150. querían

If you answered problem 150 **correctly,** go to problem 151.
If you answered problem 150 **incorrectly,** review the imperfect of -er verbs, p. 269, and review the uses of the preterit and the imperfect.

Problems 151–155

Express what happened at school by using the present perfect.

151. (ver) Tú no _____ la tarea en la pizarra.

152. (decir) La profesora _____ "buenos días."

153. (escribir) Uds. _____ el vocabulario.

154. (poner) Yo _____ mi cuaderno en mi pupitre.

155. (abrir) Manuel y yo _____ nuestros libros.

Answers 151–155

151. has visto

If you answered problem 151 **correctly,** go to problem 152.
If you answered problem 151 **incorrectly,** go to problem 156.

152. ha dicho

If you answered problem 152 **correctly,** go to problem 153.
If you answered problem 152 **incorrectly,** go to problem 157.

153. han escrito

If you answered problem 153 **correctly,** go to problem 154.
If you answered problem 153 **incorrectly,** go to problem 158.

154. he puesto

If you answered problem 154 **correctly,** go to problem 155.
If you answered problem 154 **incorrectly,** go to problem 159.

155. hemos abierto

If you answered problem 155 **correctly,** go to problem 161.
If you answered problem 155 **incorrectly,** go to problem 160.

Problems 156–160

It snowed. Express what the following people have done by using the present perfect.

156. (escuchar) Ellos _____ el pronóstico.

157. (caerse) El señor Cruz _____.

158. (volver) Nosotros _____ a nuestra casa.

159. (ponerse) Yo _____ un abrigo.

160. (cubrirse) Tú _____ la cabeza.

Answers 156–160

156. han escuchado

If you answered problem 156 **correctly,** go to problem 152.
If you answered problem 156 **incorrectly,** review the present perfect of regular verbs, p. 283.

157. se ha caído

If you answered problem 157 **correctly,** go to problem 153.
If you answered problem 157 **incorrectly,** review the present perfect of verbs that add an accent, p. 283.

158. hemos vuelto

If you answered problem 158 **correctly,** go to problem 154.
If you answered problem 158 **incorrectly,** review the present perfect of irregular verbs, p. 286.

159. me he puesto

If you answered problem 159 **correctly,** go to problem 155.
If you answered problem 159 **incorrectly,** review the present perfect of irregular verbs, p. 286.

160. te has cubierto

If you answered problem 160 **correctly,** go to problem 161.
If you answered problem 160 **incorrectly,** review the present perfect of irregular verbs, p. 286.

Problems 161–165

Express what will happen in the future by changing the verbs to the future tense.

161. tú/sonreír todo el tiempo

162. yo/querer ir a la luna

163. las creaturas extraterrestres/venir a la Tierra

164. un dólar/valer menos

165. nosotros/no caber en la planeta

Answers 161–165

161. Tú sonreirás todo el tiempo.

If you answered problem 161 **correctly,** go to problem 162.
If you answered problem 161 **incorrectly,** go to problem 166.

162. Yo querré ir a la luna.

If you answered problem 162 **correctly,** go to problem 163.
If you answered problem 162 **incorrectly,** go to problem 167.

163. Las criaturas extraterrestres vendrán a la Tierra.

If you answered problem 163 **correctly,** go to problem 164.
If you answered problem 163 **incorrectly,** go to problem 168.

164. Un dólar valdrá menos.

If you answered problem 164 **correctly,** go to problem 165.
If you answered problem 164 **incorrectly,** go to problem 169.

165. Nosotros no cabremos en planeta.

If you answered problem 165 **correctly,** go to problem 171.
If you answered problem 165 **incorrectly,** go to problem 170.

Problems 166–170

Express what these people will be able to do in the future.

166. ella/retirarse con una buena pensión

167. nosotros/poder divertirnos mucho

168. tú/tener muchas responsabilidades

169. yo/saber conducir

170. Uds./hacerse ricos

Answers 166–170

166. Ella se retirará con una buena pensión.

If you answered problem 166 **correctly,** go to problem 162.
If you answered problem 166 **incorrectly,** review the future of regular verbs, p. 297.

167. Nosotros podremos divertirnos mucho.

If you answered problem 167 **correctly,** go to problem 163.
If you answered problem 167 **incorrectly,** review the future of irregular verbs, p. 299.

168. Tú tendrás muchas responsabilidades.

If you answered problem 168 **correctly,** go to problem 164.
If you answered problem 168 **incorrectly,** review the future of irregular verbs, p. 299.

169. Yo sabré conducir.

If you answered problem 169 **correctly,** go to problem 165.
If you answered problem 169 **incorrectly,** review the future of irregular verbs, p. 299.

170. Uds. se harán ricos.

If you answered problem 170 **correctly,** go to problem 171.
If you answered problem 170 **incorrectly,** review the future of irregular verbs, p. 299.

Problems 171–175

Express what these people would do if they met someone new. Use the conditional.

171. Nosotros (ser) _____ pacientes.

172. Yo (oír) _____ sus quejas.

173. Tú le (decir) _____ tu nombre.

174. Ella (ponerse) _____ contenta.

175. Uds. (saber) _____ escucharlo.

Answers 171–175

171. seriamos

If you answered problem 171 **correctly,** go to problem 172.
If you answered problem 171 **incorrectly,** go to problem 176.

172. oiría

If you answered problem 172 **correctly,** go to problem 173.
If you answered problem 172 **incorrectly,** go to problem 177.

173. dirías

If you answered problem 173 **correctly,** go to problem 174.
If you answered problem 173 **incorrectly,** go to problem 178.

174. se pondría

If you answered problem 174 **correctly,** go to problem 175.
If you answered problem 174 **incorrectly,** go to problem 179.

175. sabrían

If you answered problem 175 **correctly,** go to problem 181.
If you answered problem 175 **incorrectly,** go to problem 180.

Problems 176–180

Express what these people would do if they had free time. Use the conditional.

176. Yo (descansarme) _____.

177. Ellos (ir) _____ al cine.

178. Tú (ver) _____ muchas obras de teatro.

179. Nosotros (salir) _____ con nuestros amigos.

180. Ud. (hacer) _____ muchos viajes.

Answers 176–180

176. me descansaría

If you answered problem 176 **correctly,** go to problem 172.
If you answered problem 176 **incorrectly,** review the conditional of regular verbs, p. 301.

177. irían

If you answered problem 177 **correctly,** go to problem 173.
If you answered problem 177 **incorrectly,** review the conditional of irregular verbs with regular conditional formation, p. 301.

178. verías

If you answered problem 178 **correctly,** go to problem 174.
If you answered problem 178 **incorrectly,** review the conditional of irregular verbs with regular conditional formation, p. 301.

179. saldríamos

If you answered problem 179 **correctly,** go to problem 175.
If you answered problem 179 **incorrectly,** review the conditional of irregular verbs, p. 301.

180. haría

If you answered problem 180 **correctly,** go to problem 181.
If you answered problem 180 **incorrectly,** review the conditional of irregular verbs, p. 301.

Problems 181–185

Complete the message that a teenager left for his mom on his family's answering machine. Use the subjunctive, if necessary.

Es probable que yo (volver) _____ a casa tarde. Es imperativo que yo (ir) _____ a la
                                     181   182

biblioteca porque tengo que (buscar) _____ un libro para mi clase de historia. Es
                                                          183

improbable que yo (llegar) _____ antes de las seis. Sugiero que tú (empezar) _____ a
                                                  184   185

preparar la cena a eso de las cinco y media.

Answers 181–185

181. vuelva

If you answered problem 181 **correctly,** go to problem 182.
If you answered problem 181 **incorrectly,** go to problem 182.

182. vaya

If you answered problem 182 **correctly,** go to problem 183.
If you answered problem 182 **incorrectly,** go to problem 183.

183. buscar

If you answered problem 183 **correctly,** go to problem 184.
If you answered problem 183 **incorrectly,** go to problem 184.

184. llegue

If you answered problem 184 **correctly,** go to problem 185.
If you answered problem 184 **incorrectly,** go to problem 189.

185. empieces

If you answered problem 185 **correctly,** go to problem 191.
If you answered problem 185 **incorrectly,** go to problem 190.

Problems 186–190

Complete the message that a tutor left on his student's answering machine. Use the subjunctive, if necessary:

Yo sé que tú (contar) _____ conmigo, pero dudo que yo (poder) _____ venir a tu casa esta
                                    186   187

noche. Por ahora, es importante que tú (ponerse) _____ serio. Es urgente que tú (saber)
                                                                              188

_____ todas la reglas de gramática para tu examen mañana. Es necesario que tú (dormir)
   189

_____ bien antes de tomar el examen.
   190

Answers 186–190

186. cuentas

If you answered problem 186 **correctly,** go to problem 187.
If you answered problem 186 **incorrectly,** review the uses of the subjunctive, p. 318, and review the present of *o* to *ue* stem-changing verbs, p. 97.

187. pueda

If you answered problem 187 **correctly,** go to problem 183.
If you answered problem 187 **incorrectly,** review the uses of the subjunctive, p. 318, and; review the formation of the subjunctive, p. 309.

188. te pongas

If you answered problem 188 **correctly,** go to problem 184.
If you answered problem 188 **incorrectly,** review the uses of the subjunctive, p. 318, and review the formation of the subjunctive, p. 309.

189. sepas

If you answered problem 189 **correctly,** go to problem 185.
If you answered problem 189 **incorrectly,** review the uses of the subjunctive, p. 318, and review the formation of the subjunctive of irregular verbs, p. 312.

190. duermas

If you answered problem 190 **correctly,** go to problem 191.
If you answered problem 190 **incorrectly,** review the uses of the subjunctive, p. 318, and review the formation of the subjunctive of *o* to *ue* stem-changing verbs, p. 316.

Problems 191–195

Express how to be a good person by giving a command to the person(s) indicated.

191. (tú) no pedir préstamo a tus amigos

192. (vosotros) pagar vuestras deudas

193. (Uds.) no exigir nada de nadie

194. (tú) saber tus firmezas

195. (vosotros) no ofrecer malos consejos a vuestros amigos

Answers 191–195

191. No pidas préstamos a tus amigos.

If you answered problem 191 **correctly,** go to problem 192.
If you answered problem 191 **incorrectly,** go to problem 197.

192. Pagad vuestras deudas.

If you answered problem 192 **correctly,** go to problem 193.
If you answered problem 192 **incorrectly,** go to problem 196.

193. No exijan nada de nadie.

If you answered problem 193 **correctly,** go to problem 194.
If you answered problem 193 **incorrectly,** go to problem 200.

194. Sabe tus firmezas.

If you answered problem 194 **correctly,** go to problem 195.
If you answered problem 194 **incorrectly,** go to problem 199.

195. No ofrezcáis malos consejos a vuestros amigos.

If you answered problem 195 **correctly,** congratulations! You have successfully completed the test.
If you answered problem 195 **incorrectly,** go to problem 198.

Problems 196–200

Give your advice by issuing commands to the person(s) indicated.

196. (vosotros) ser honrados

197. (tú) no hacerle daño a nadie

198. (vosotros) no tener ninguna expectativa de nadie

199. (tú) siempre decir la verdad

200. (Ud.) devolver todo a sus amigos

Answers 196–200

196. Sed honrados.

If you answered problem 196 **correctly,** go to problem 192.
If you answered problem 196 **incorrectly,** review the affirmative informal plural imperative, p. 337.

197. No le hagas daño a nadie.

If you answered problem 197 **correctly,** go to problem 193.
If you answered problem 197 **incorrectly,** review the negative informal singular imperative, p. 333.

198. No tengáis ninguna expectativa de nadie.

If you answered problem 198 **correctly,** go to problem 194.
If you answered problem 198 **incorrectly,** review the negative informal plural imperative, p. 337.

199. Siempre di la verdad.

If you answered problem 199 **correctly,** go to problem 195.
If you answered problem 199 **incorrectly,** review the affirmative informal singular imperative, p. 333.

200. Devuelva todo a sus amigos.

If you answered problem 200 **correctly,** congratulations! You have successfully completed the test.
If you answered problem 200 **incorrectly,** review the formal singular imperative, p. 327.

Verb Charts

Regular Verbs

-ar Verbs
HABLAR (to speak)

Gerund: hablando

Past Participle: hablado

Commands: ¡Hable Ud.! ¡Hablen Uds.! ¡Hablemos!

¡Habla tú! ¡No hables tú!

¡Hablad vosotros! ¡No habléis vosotros!

Present	Preterite	Imperfect	Future	Conditional	Subjunctive
(do)	(did)	(was)	(will)	(would)	
hablo	hablé	hablaba	hablaré	hablaría	hable
hablas	hablaste	hablabas	hablarás	hablarías	hables
habla	habló	hablaba	hablará	hablaría	hable
hablamos	hablamos	hablábamos	hablaremos	hablaríamos	hablemos
habláis	hablasteis	hablabais	hablaréis	hablaríais	habléis
hablan	hablaron	hablaban	hablarán	hablarían	hablen

-er Verbs
BEBER (to drink)

Gerund: bebiendo

Past Participle: bebido

Commands: ¡Beba Ud.! ¡Beban Uds.! ¡Bebamos!

¡Bebe tú! ¡No bebas tú!

¡Bebed vosotros! ¡No bebáis vosotros!

Present	Preterit	Imperfect	Future	Conditional	Subjunctive
bebo	bebí	bebía	beberé	bebería	beba
bebes	bebiste	bebías	beberás	beberías	bebas
bebe	bebió	bebía	beberá	bebería	beba
bebemos	bebimos	bebíamos	beberemos	beberíamos	bebamos
bebéis	bebisteis	bebíais	beberéis	beberíais	bebáis
beben	bebieron	bebían	beberán	beberían	beban

-ir Verbs

SUBIR (to go up)

Gerund: subiendo

Past Participle: subido

Commands: ¡Suba Ud.! ¡Suban Uds.! ¡Subamos!

¡Sube tú! ¡No subas tú!

¡Subid vosotros! ¡No subáis vosotros!

Present	Preterite	Imperfect	Future	Conditional	Subjunctive
subo	subí	subía	subiré	subiría	suba
subes	subiste	subías	subirás	subirías	subas
sube	subió	subía	subirá	subiría	suba
subimos	subimos	subíamos	subiremos	subiríamos	subamos
subís	subisteis	subíais	subiréis	subiríais	subáis
suben	subieron	subían	subirán	subirían	suban

Stem-Change Verbs

-ar Verbs

CERRAR (e to ie) (to close)

Present: cierro, cierras, cierra, cerramos, cerráis, cierran

Subjunctive: cierre, cierres, cierre, cerremos, cerréis, cierren

Other verbs like *cerrar* include *comenzar* (to begin), *despertarse* (to wake oneself up), *empezar* (to begin), *pensar* (to think), and *sentarse* (to sit oneself down).

CONTAR (*o* to *ue*) (to tell)

Present: cuento, cuentas, cuenta, contamos, contáis, cuentan

Subjunctive: cuente, cuentes, cuente, contemos, contéis, cuenten

Other verbs like *mostrar* include *acordarse de* (to remember), *almorzar* (to eat lunch), *acostarse* (to go to bed), *costar* (to cost), *encontrar* (to find), *mostrar* (to show), *probar* (to prove, to try) and *recordar* (to remember).

JUGAR (to play [a sport or game])

Present: juego, juegas, juega, jugamos, jugáis, juegan

Subjunctive: juegue, juegues, juegue, juguemos, juguéis, jueguen

-*er* Verbs

PERDER (*e* to *ie*) (to lose)

Present: pierdo, pierdes, pierde, perdemos, perdéis, pierden

Subjunctive: pierda, pierdas, pierda, perdamos, perdáis, pierdan

Other verbs like *perder* include *defender* (to defend), *descender* (to descend),

entender (to understand), and *querer* (to want).

MOVER (*o* to *ue*) (to move)

Present: muevo, mueves, mueve, movemos, movéis, mueven

Subjunctive: mueva, muevas, mueva, movamos, mováis, muevan

Other verbs like *mover* include *devolver* (to return), *envolver* (to wrap), *llover* (to rain), *morder* (to bite), *poder* (to be able to, can), and *volver* (to return).

-*ir* Verbs

MEDIR (*e* to *i*) (to measure)

Gerund: midiendo

Present: mido, mides, mide, medimos, medís, miden

Preterite: medí, mediste, midió, medimos, medisteis, midieron

Subjunctive: mida, midas, mida, midamos, midáis, midan

Other verbs like *medir* include *impedir* (to prevent), *pedir* (to ask), *repetir* (to repeat), and *servir* (to serve).

MENTIR (*e* to *ie/i*) (to lie)

Gerund: mintiendo

Present: miento, mientes, miente, mentimos, mentís, mienten

Preterite: mentí, mentiste, mintió, mentimos, mentisteis, mintieron

Subjunctive: mienta, mientas, mienta, mintamos, mintáis, mientan

Other verbs like *mentir* include *advertir* (to warn, to notify), *consentir* (to consent), *preferir* (to prefer), *referir* (to refer), and *sentir* (to feel).

DORMIR (*o* to *ue/u*) (to sleep)

Gerund: durmiendo

Present: duermo, duermes, duerme, dormimos, dormís, duermen

Preterite: dormí, dormiste, durmió, dormimos, dormisteis, durmieron

Subjunctive: duerma, duermas, duerma, durmamos, durmáis, duerman

Another verb like *dormir* is *morir* (to die).

-*uir* Verbs (except -*guir*)
CONCLUIR (*y*) (to conclude)

Gerund: concluyendo

Present: concluyo, concluyes, concluye, concluimos, concluís, concluyen

Preterite: concluí, concluiste, concluyó, concluimos, concluisteis, concluyeron

Subjunctive: concluya, concluyas, concluya, concluyamos, concluyáis, concluyan

Other verbs like *concluir* include *construir* (to construct), *contribuir* (to contribute), *destruir* (to destroy), *incluir* (to include), and *sustituir* (to substitute).

-*eer* Verbs
LEER (*i* to *y*) (to read)

Gerund: leyendo

Preterite: leí, leíste, leyó, leímos, leísteis, leyeron

Other verbs like *leer* include *creer* (to believe), *poseer* (to possess), and *proveer* (to provide).

-*iar* Verbs
ENVIAR (*i* to *í*) (to send)

Present: envío, envías, envía, enviamos, enviáis, envían

Subjunctive: envíe, envíes, envíe, enviemos, enviéis, envíen

Other verbs like *enviar* include *confiar + en* (to confide in), *esquiar* (to ski), *guiar* (to guide), and *variar* (to vary).

-*uar* Verbs (except -*guar*)

ACTUAR (*u* to *ú*) (to act)

Present: actúo, actúas, actúa, actuamos, actuáis, actúan

Subjunctive: actúe, actúes, actúe, actuemos, actuéis, actúen

Another verb like *actuar* is *continuar* (to continue).

Spelling-Change Verbs

-*car* Verbs

SACAR (*c* to *qu*) (to take out)

Preterite: saqué, sacaste, sacó, sacamos, sacasteis, sacaron

Subjunctive: saque, saques, saque, saquemos, saquéis, saquen

Other verbs like *sacar* include *acercar* (to bring near), *aplicar* (to apply), *buscar* (to look for), *criticar* (to criticize), *educar* (to educate), *explicar* (to explain), *identificar* (to identify), *pescar* (to fish), *practicar* (to practice), and *significar* (to mean).

-*gar* Verbs

PAGAR (*g* to *gu*) (to pay)

Preterite: pagué, pagaste, pagó, pagamos, pagasteis, pagaron

Subjunctive: pague, pagues, pague, paguemos, paguéis, paguen

Other verbs like *pagar* include *apagar* (to extinguish), *castigar* (to punish), *llegar* (to arrive), and *pegar* (to glue).

-*zar* Verbs

GOZAR (*z* to *c*) (to enjoy)

Preterite: gocé, gozaste, gozó, gozamos, gozasteis, gozaron

Subjunctive: goce, goces, goce, gocemos, gocéis, gocen

Other verbs like *gozar* include *avanzar* (to advance), *lanzar* (to throw), *memorizar* (to memorize), *organizar* (to organize), and *utilizar* (to use).

consonant + -*cer* or -*cir* Verbs

VENCER (*c* to *z*) (to conquer)

Present: venzo, vences, vence, vencemos, vencéis, vencen

Subjunctive: venza, venzas, venza, venzamos, venzáis, venzan

Other verbs like *vencer* include *convencer* (to convince) and *ejercer* (to exercise a profession).

FRUNCIR (*c* to *z*) (to frown)

Present: frunzo, frunces, frunce, fruncimos, fruncís, fruncen

Subjunctive: frunza, frunzas, frunza, frunzamos, frunzáis, frunzan

Another verb like *fruncir* is *esparcir* (to spread).

vowel + -*cer* or -*cir* Verbs
CONOCER (*c* to *zc*) (to know)

Present: conozco, conoces, conoce, conocemos, conocís, conocen

Subjunctive: conozca, conozcas, conozca, conozcamos, conozcáis, conozcan

Other verbs like *conocer* include *crecer* (to grow), *desobedecer* (to disobey), *desaparacer* (to disappear), *establecer* (to establish), *obedecer* (to obey), *ofrecer* (to offer), and *parecer* (to seem).

CONDUCIR (*c* to *zc*) (to drive)

Present: conduzco, conduces, conduce, conducimos, conducís, conducen

Subjunctive: conduzca, conduzcas, conduzca, conduzcamos, conduzcáis, conduzcan

Other verbs like *conducir* include *deducir* (to deduce), *inducir* (to induce), and *traducir* (to translate).

-*ger* or -*gir* Verbs
COGER (*g* to *j*) (to seize)

Present: cojo, coges, coge, cogemos, cogéis, cogen

Subjunctive: coja, cojas, coja, cojamos, cojáis, cojan

Other verbs like *coger* include *escoger* (to choose), *proteger* (to protect), and *recoger* (to pick up).

EXIGIR (*g* to *j*) (to demand)

Present: exijo, exiges, exige, exigimos, exigís, exigen

Subjunctive: exija, exijas, exija, exijamos, exijáis, exijan

Another verb like *exigir* is *dirigir* (to direct).

-*guir* Verbs
DISTINGUIR (*gu* to *g*) (to distinguish)

Present: distingo, distingues, distingue, distinguimos, distinguís, distinguen

Subjunctive: distinga, distingas, distinga, distingamos, distingáis, distingan

Other verbs like *distinguir* include *perseguir* (to pursue) and *seguir* (to follow).

Irregular Verbs

DAR (to give)

Present: doy, das, da, damos, dáis, dan

Preterite: di, diste, dio, dimos, disteis, dieron

Subjunctive: dé, des, dé, demos, déis, den

DECIR (to say)

Gerund: diciendo

Past Participle: dicho

Affirmative Familiar Singular Command: di

Present: digo, dices, dice, decimos, decís, dicen

Preterite: dije, dijiste, dijo, dijmos, dijisteis, dijeron

Future: diré, dirás, dirá, diremos, diréis, dirán

Conditional: diría, dirías, diría, diríamos, diríais, dirían

Subjunctive: diga, digas, diga, digamos, digáis, digan

ESTAR (to be)

Affirmative Familiar Singular Command: está

Present: estoy, estás, está, estamos, estáis, están

Preterite: estuve, estuviste, estuvo, estuvimos, estuvisteis, estuvieron

Subjunctive: esté, estés, esté, estemos, estéis, estén

HACER (to make, to do)

Past Participle: hecho

Affirmative Familiar Singular Command: Haz

Present: hago, haces, hace, hacemos, hacéis, hacen

Preterite: hice, hiciste, hizo, hicimos, hicisteis, hicieron

Future: haré, harás, hará, haremos, haréis, harán

Conditional: haría, harías, haría, haríamos, haríais, harían

Subjunctive: haga, hagas, haga, hagamos, hagáis, hagan

IR (to go)

Gerund: yendo

Affirmative Familiar Singular Command: vé

Present: voy, vas, va, vamos, vais, van

Preterite: fui, fuiste, fue, fuimos, fuisteis, fueron

Conditional: iba, ibas, iba, íbamos, ibais, iban

Subjunctive: vaya, vayas, vaya, vayamos, vayáis, vayan

OÍR (to hear)

Gerund: oyendo

Affirmative Familiar Singular Command: oye

Affirmative Familiar Plural Command: oíd

Present: oigo, oyes, oye, oímos, oís, oyen

Preterite: oí, oíste, oyó, oímos, oísteis, oyeron

Subjunctive: oiga, oigas, oiga, oigamos, oigáis, oigan

PODER (o to ue) (to be able to, can)

Gerund: pudiendo

Present: puedo, puedes, puede, podemos, podéis, pueden

Preterite: pude, pudiste, pudo, pudimos, pudisteis, pudieron

Future: podré, podrás, podrá, podremos, podréis, podrán

Conditional: podría, podrías, podría, podríamos, podríais, podrían

Subjunctive: pueda, puedas, pueda, podamos, podáis, puedan

PONER (to put)

Past Participle: puesto

Affirmative Familiar Singular Command: pon

Present: pongo, pones, pone, ponemos, ponéis, ponen

Preterite: puse, pusiste, puso, pusimos, pusisteis, pusieron

Future: pondré, pondrás, pondrá, pondremos, pondréis, pondrán

Conditional: pondría, pondrías, pondría, pondríamos, pondríais, pondrían

Subjunctive: ponga, pongas, ponga, pongamos, pongáis, pongan

QUERER (to want)

Affirmative Familiar Singular Command: quiere

Present: quiero, quieres, quiere, queremos, queréis, quieren

Preterite: quise, quisiste, quiso, quisimos, quisisteis, quisieron

Future: querré, querrás, querrá, querremos, querréis, querrán

Conditional: querría, querrías, querría, querríamos, querríais, querrían

Subjunctive: quiera, quieras, quiera, queramos, queráis, quieran

SABER (to know)

Present: sé, sabes, sabe, sabemos, sabéis, saben

Preterite: supe, supiste, supo, supimos, supisteis, supieron

Future: sabré, sabrás, sabrá, sabremos, sabréis, sabrán

Conditional: sabría, sabrías, sabría, sabríamos, sabríais, sabrían

Subjunctive: sepa, sepas, sepa, sepamos, sepáis, sepan

SALIR (to go out, to leave)

Affirmative Familiar Singular Command: sal

Present: salgo, sales, sale, salimos, salís, salen

Future: saldré, saldrás, saldrá, saldremos, saldréis, saldrán

Conditional: saldría, saldrías, saldría, saldríamos, saldríais, saldrían

Subjunctive: salga, salgas, salga, salgamos, salgáis, salgan

SER (to be)

Affirmative Familiar Singular Command: sé

Present: soy, eres, es, somos, sois, son

Preterite: fui, fuiste, fue, fuimos, fuisteis, fueron

Imperfect: era, eras, era, éramos, erais, eran

Subjunctive: sea, seas, sea, seamos, seáis, sean

TENER (to have)

Affirmative Familiar Singular Command: ten

Present: tengo, tienes, tiene, tenemos, tenéis, tienen

Preterite: tuve, tuviste, tuvo, tuvimos, tuvisteis, tuvieron

Future: tendré, tendrás, tendrá, tendremos, tendréis, tendrán

Conditional: tendría, tendrías, tendría, tendríamos, tendríais, tendrían

Subjunctive: tenga, tengas, tenga, tengamos, tengáis, tengan

TRAER (to bring)

Past Participle: traído

Present: traigo, traes, trae, traemos, traéis, traen

Preterite: traje, trajiste, trajo, trajimos, trajisteis, trajeron

Subjunctive: traiga, traigas, traiga, traigamos, traigáis, traigan

---

VENIR (to come)

Gerund: viniendo

Affirmative Familiar Singular Command: ven

Present: vengo, vienes, viene, venimos, venís, vienen

Preterite: vine, viniste, vino, vinimos, vinisteis, vinieron

Future: vendré, vendrás, vendrá, vendremos, vendréis, vendrán

Conditional: vendría, vendrías, vendría, vendríamos, vendríais, vendrían

Subjunctive: venga, vengas, venga, vengamos, vengáis, vengan

VER (to see)

Past Participle: visto

Present: veo, ves, ve, vemos, veis, ven

Preterite: vi, viste, vio, vimos, visteis, vieron

Imperfect: veía, veías, veía, veíamos, veíais, veían

Subjunctive: vea, veas, vea, veamos, veáis, vean

Index